A

Philip E. Lilienthal

B O O K

The Philip E. Lilienthal imprint
honors special books
in commemoration of a man whose work
at University of California Press from 1954 to 1979
was marked by dedication to young authors
and to high standards in the field of Asian Studies.
Friends, family, authors, and foundations have together
endowed the Lilienthal Fund, which enables UC Press
to publish under this imprint selected books
in a way that reflects the taste and judgment
of a great and beloved editor.

The publisher and the University of California Press Foundation gratefully acknowledge the generous support of the Philip E. Lilienthal Imprint in Asian Studies, established by a major gift from Sally Lilienthal.

The publisher and the University of California Press Foundation also gratefully acknowledge the generous support of the Chiang Ching-kuo Foundation for International Scholarly Exchange in making this book possible.

In the Global Vanguard

In the Global Vanguard

Agrarian Development and the Making of Modern Taiwan

James Lin

UNIVERSITY OF CALIFORNIA PRESS

University of California Press
Oakland, California

Parts of this book were previously published as articles. See
James Lin, "Martyrs of Development: Taiwanese Agrarian Development
and the Republic of Vietnam, 1959–1975," *Cross-Currents: East Asian
History and Culture Review* 9, no. 1 (2020): 67–106, https://doi.org/10.1353
/ach.2020.0000, reprinted with permission from University of Hawai'i
Press; and James Lin, "Sowing Seeds and Knowledge: Agricultural
Development in Taiwan and the World, 1925–1975." *East Asian
Science, Technology and Society* 9, no. 2 (June 1, 2015): 127–49, https://
doi.org/10.1215/18752160-2872116, copyright 2015 National Science and
Technology Council, Taiwan, reprinted by permission of Taylor & Francis
Ltd, https://www.tandfonline.com on behalf of 2015 National Science and
Technology Council, Taiwan.

Suggested citation: Lin, J. *In the Global Vanguard: Agrarian Development
and the Making of Modern Taiwan*. Oakland: University of California Press,
2025. DOI: https://doi.org/10.1525/luminos.225

Library of Congress Cataloging-in-Publication Data

Names: Lin, James (James Yushang), author.
Title: In the global vanguard : agrarian development and the making of
    modern Taiwan / James Lin.
Other titles: Asia Pacific modern ; 21.
Description: Oakland, California : University of California Press, [2025] |
    Series: Asia Pacific modern ; 21 | Includes bibliographical references
    and index.
Identifiers: LCCN 2024034304 (print) | LCCN 2024034305 (ebook) | ISBN
    9780520398665 (paperback) | ISBN 9780520398689 (ebook)
Subjects: LCSH: Shen, Zonghan, 1895–1980—Influence. | Zhongguo nong
    cun fu xing lian he wei yuan hui—Influence. | Land
    reform—Taiwan—History—20th century. | Agriculture and
    state—Taiwan—History—20th century. | Agricultural assistance,
    Taiwan—Africa—History—20th century. | Agricultural assistance,
    Taiwan—Vietnam—History—20th century. | Agricultural assistance,
    Taiwan—Developing countries—History—20th century.
Classification: LCC HD1333.T28 L56 2025 (print) | LCC HD1333.T28 (ebook)
    | DDC 333.3/151249—dc23/eng/20241227

LC record available at https://lccn.loc.gov/2024034304
LC ebook record available at https://lccn.loc.gov/2024034305

GPSR Authorized Representative: Easy Access System Europe,
Mustamäe tee 50, 10621 Tallinn, Estonia, gpsr.requests@easproject.com

34 33 32 31 30 29 28 27 26 25
10 9 8 7 6 5 4 3 2 1

To my mother

CONTENTS

LIST OF ILLUSTRATIONS

FIGURES

TABLE

This book is the culmination of a decade of learning through the help of colleagues, mentors, scholars, archivists, librarians, donors, friends, and family. I am indebted to their contributions to this project, without which this would not have been possible.

This began as a PhD dissertation at the University of California, Berkeley. Above all, I thank Daniel Sargent, whose steadfast support, constant reminders to prioritize "first-order" problems, and attention to political economy and the international system brought this project from an idea to a dissertation. Wen-hsin Yeh has likewise been a crucial supporter of my research; her critical questions and dedication to scholarship and archival evidence have honed my argument and framing. Tom Gold knows more about Taiwan than any scholar or individual I have met, and I was fortunate to have learned about states and markets under his guidance. Alexander Cook's teaching and writing on global and international history shaped many of the broad intellectual interests underlying this book. David Hollinger was the first to introduce me to professional historical research, and I am deeply indebted to his belief in my ability to pursue a career in history as a young and naive undergraduate student. I am grateful as well to many years of support and mentorship from Richard Candida-Smith, Michael Nylan, Peggy Anderson, and Brian DeLay.

The University of Washington has been an important intellectual home for the development of this book. The Jackson School of International Studies, the Taiwan Studies Program, the China Studies Program, the History Department, and the College of Arts and Sciences provided funds to support my research. The History Department included one of the chapters in their colloquium series, and

I thank Adam Warren, Madison Heslop, Joel Walker, and the attendees of the colloquium for their engaging feedback and discussion. I am grateful to my colleagues Vanessa Freije, Liora Halperin, Danny Bessner, Nova Robinson, Arbella Bet-Shlimon, and Devin Near for their reading of the introduction to the book in a history writing group. The China Studies Program community discussed another chapter, and I am grateful to Madeleine Dong, Susan Whiting, David Bachman, Phil Neel, and others for their reading. Bill Lavely, Mark Metzler, Matthew Mosca, Anand Yang, Resat Kasaba, Danny Hoffman, Sunila Kale, Christian Novetzke, Robert Pekannen, Saadia Pekkanen, Glennys Young, Jonathan Warren, Yongchool Ha, Clark Sorenson, Christoph Giebel, Hwasook Nam, Gary Hamilton, and Steve Harrell, among others, offered advice and encouraged me as a scholar and colleague. Our wonderful librarians, Zhijia Shen, Lucy Li, and Theresa Mudrock, have assisted me in countless requests over the years. The work of Ian Oates, Paul Carrington, Jennifer Joy, Eryk Waligora, Kristi Roundtree, Annette Bernier, Gail Schmitz, Sara Guthu, and others in the Jackson School made this research possible. The wonderful students throughout the years, especially in my Making Modern Taiwan, History of Global Development, and Global History of Capitalism classes, have expanded my own thinking on the broad topics of Taiwan history, development, and capitalism.

Over the years, countless individuals have read my writing and offered feedback. I especially thank Sigrid Schmalzer, Megan Greene, Hiromi Mizuno, Rebecca Karl, Ken Pomeranz, Fan Fa-ti, and Mark Metzler, who offered extensive, critical, and constructive feedback across the entire manuscript. Others who read parts of this research include Joseph Lawson, Patrick Chung, Eric Gade, John Chung-en Liu, Yi-Tang Lin, Patrick Sharma, Matthew Berry, William Ma, Paulina Hartono, Jonathan Tang, Jeannette Ng, Jerry Zee, Emily Ng, Sujin Eom, Jeffrey Weng, Gustavo Oliveira, Dongmin Park, Kristen Sun, Kira Donnell, Grace Kim, Ti Ngo, Jonathan Tang, Paulina Harpoon, Larissa Pitts, Linh Vu, Peiting Li, Jeffrey Weng, Haijian Zhou, Jaewoong Jeon, Brian DeLay, Rebecca Herman, Brandon K. Williams, Miles Culpepper, Clare Ibarra, Derek O'Leary, Robert Cole, Andy Liu, Soonyi Lee, Jenny Lee, Mirela David, Jeongmin Kim, I-Yi Hsieh, Myung-Ho Hyun, Anatoly Detwyler, and Gal Gvili.

I thank the community at the Center for Global Development at Shanghai University, and especially Iris Borowy, who kindly invited me as a postdoctoral fellow. This research was only possible with support from a number of organizations: the University of Washington Jackson School of International Studies; the University of Washington Royalty Research Fund; the Chiang Ching-Kuo Foundation, which funded this research as a dissertation and later as a book; the Chiu Scholarly Exchange Program for Taiwan Studies at Oregon State University; the Chun and Jane Chiu Family Foundation Fellowship in Taiwan Studies at the Wilson Center; the Fulbright Program; the Society for Historians of American Foreign Relations Dissertation Completion Fellowship; the UC Berkeley Institute for International

Studies, the ROC Ministry of Foreign Affairs Taiwan Fellowship; the Liu Fellowship and ROC Fellowship from the UC Berkeley Center for Chinese Studies; the Association for Asian Studies; the Lyndon B. Johnson Presidential Library; the Oberlin College Archives; the Rockefeller Archive Center; Calum Turvey; and the History Department at UC Berkeley.

I have been honored to have presented different aspects of this book at different university communities. I thank Tom Gold and the Institute of East Asian Studies at University of California, Berkeley; Howard Jinghao Sun and the History Department at Zhejiang University; Irene Pang and the Global China colloquium series at Simon Fraser University; Howard Chiang, Eddy U, and the East Asian Studies Program at the University of California, Davis; Lydia Walker and Center for East Asian Studies at Ohio State University; and Peter Chang at the Center for Chinese Studies at National Central Library in Taiwan. Discussions from these talks have shaped the current manuscript. Furthermore, I thank the many scholars who discussed my research at conferences and workshops: Emily Hill, Tom Rawski, Elisabeth Koll, Janet Hunter, Man-houng Lin, He Bian, Ian Campbell, Ban Wang, Meredith Oyen, Micah Muscolino, Jia-Ching Chen, J. Megan Greene, Bill Kirby, Fred Dickinson, Emily Rosenberg, Shiuh-shen Chien, Chuck Hayford, Charles Armstrong, Yi-tze Lee, Yu-Tsai Huang, Tore Olsson, Dagmar Schäfer, Nicole Sackley, Shirley Syaru Lin, Nicholas Cull, Julia Stephens, as well as the members of the Land/scaping Taiwan workshop in 2020 at University of Washington, the Revisiting the Cold War on Taiwan workshop at the Wilson Center in 2019, the Connected Histories: Decolonization & the 20th Century conference at Yale in 2019, and the Global Island: Taiwan and the World workshop at University of Washington in 2018. I have also been blessed to have friends, colleagues, and mentors who were more than happy to offer advice. I thank Wayne Soon, John DiMoia, Peter Lavelle, Zack Guthrie, Peter Thilly, Albert Wu, Craig Smith, Macabe Keliher, Chuck Kraus, Prakash Kumar, Seiji Shirane, James Gerien-Chen, Eli Friedman, Greg Traxler, Guo-Sian Lin, Chiting Peng, Covell Meyskens, Paul Barclay, Hsiao-wen Cheng, Robert Cole, Stephen Wertheim, Daniel Immerwahr, Gene Zubovich, Margaret Tillman, Stuart Spencer, Aaron S. Moore, Julia Strauss, Victor Seow, Andy Liu, Holly Stephens, Dong Yan, Yanqiu Zheng, Federico Pachetti, Venus Bivar, Evan Dawley, Andrea Horbinski, Jeremy Rappleye, Andrew Elmore, and Philip Thai.

Megan Pugh and Phil Neel read through this manuscript with a fine-tooth comb and were invaluable in offering their editorial expertise. I am deeply indebted to the help of Kevin Li, Simon Toner, and Nu-Anh Tran, who helped me navigate the intricacies of the Vietnamese National Archives. I owe special thanks to Simon Toner and Vinh Nguyen, who translated documents for me from Vietnamese to English, and Jamie Cheng, who helped me with particularly difficult translations from Chinese. Alvin Bui and Hung Nguyen assisted me with research on Vietnam, and John DiMoia with research on South Korea. Macabe Keliher, Yi Jing Lin,

Jie Yu, Gaozhan Zhang, and Samuel Valdes helped me locate several archival and database documents. And thanks to Jason Chang, who transcribed oral history interviews.

Many scholars generously made the connections necessary for me to access oral history interviewees and archival materials for this research. I especially thank Yu-Tsai Huang, Calum Turvey, Bob Sheeks, Wenlung Wang, Hsiao-pong Liu, Shiuh-shen Chien, Jim Riddell, and Elinor Levine for their invaluable assistance; without them, this book would not have been possible. I am also deeply grateful to my oral history interviewees for inviting me to meals, their homes, and their farms to speak to a historian about their lives. I thank the archivists and librarians at the UC Berkeley East Asian Library, Stanford University East Asian Library, the Land Reform Training Institute, the Taiwan Land Reform Museum, Institute of Modern History at Academia Sinica, Academia Historica, the Taiwan National Archives Administration, the Asian Development Bank, Vietnam National Archives II in Ho Chi Minh City, the US National Archives in College Park, the Columbia University Rare Book and Manuscript Library, the Burke Library at Union Theological Seminary, the Presbyterian Historical Society Archives, Oberlin College Archives, Cornell University Library, University of Wisconsin-Madison Library, the University of Hartford Archives, the Hoover Institute Archives, the Rockefeller Archive Center, the Ford Foundation Archives, the United Nations Archives, the Lyndon B. Johnson Presidential Library, the Food and Fertilizer Technology Center, the Asian Vegetable Research and Development Center (World Vegetable Center), the Second Historical Archives of China in Nanjing, the Guangdong Provincial Archives, the Jiangsu Provincial Archives, the Sichuan Provincial Archives, the Shanghai Municipal Library, and Nanjing Agricultural University Archives. A special thanks is owed to Ken Grossi at Oberlin, Monica Blank at the Rockefeller Archives, Idelle Nissila at the Ford Foundation, and Jennifer Cuddeback at the LBJ Presidential Library. There are dozens of archivists and librarians who had facilitated my access to tens of thousands of documents and whose names are not mentioned here, and your work is deeply important for us to understand the past.

From the University of California Press, I was incredibly fortunate to work with Enrique Ochoa-Kaup, who is the epitome of patience and generosity. Sylvie Bower, Richard Feit, and Stacy Eisenstark helped in bringing this book to publication. I am grateful to Tak Fujitani as the series editor. Thanks to the Chiang Ching-kuo Foundation for their subvention for this book, and to the University of California for financially supporting the inclusion of this book in the Luminos Open Access platform. I appreciate the support from Ariana King, Ross Yelsey, and the Weatherhead East Asia Institute at Columbia University for including this in the Studies of the Weatherhead East Asian Institute series.

Finally, I thank my friends and family for their support over the years. This work belongs to you as much as anyone else.

AACFR	American Advisory Committee for Famine Relief
AACB	American Advisory Committee in Beijing
ASPAC	Asia-Pacific Council
AVRDC	Asian Vegetable Research and Development Center (today the World Vegetable Center)
CATM	Chinese (Republic of China) Agricultural Technical Mission
CGIAR	Consultative Group for International Agricultural Research
CNRRA	Chinese National Relief and Rehabilitation Administration
CUSA	Republic of China Council for US Aid
DGWG	Dee-Geo-Woo-Gen (低腳烏尖, Dijiao Wujian)
ECA	United States Economic Cooperation Administration
FAO	United Nations Food and Agriculture Organization
FFTC	Food and Fertilizer Technology Center
GMD	Guomindang (Chinese Nationalist Party, also known as Kuomintang)
ICA	United States International Cooperation Administration
IRRI	International Rice Research Institute
JCRR	(Sino-American) Joint Commission on Rural Reconstruction
LRTI	Land Reform Training Institute (today the International Center for Land Policy Studies and Training)
MEM	Mass Education movement
MOAF	Republic of China Ministry of Agriculture and Forestry
MOFA	Republic of China Ministry of Foreign Affairs
NARB	National Agricultural Research Bureau

NCRR	National Council for Rural Reconstruction
PRC	People's Republic of China
ROC	Republic of China
RVN	Republic of Vietnam
SAATCC	Sino-African Agricultural Technical Cooperation Conference (Séminaire Afro-Chinois pour la Coopération Technique Agricole)
TARI	Taiwan Agricultural Research Institute
UN	United Nations
UNRRA	United Nations Relief and Rehabilitation Administration
USAID	United States Agency for International Development
USIS	United States Information Service
USOM	United States Operations Mission

Introduction

On July 26, 1965, agricultural scientist Shen Zonghan (沈宗瀚, T. H. or Tsung-han Shen) presented in front of a group of developing world peers in the Sino-African Agricultural Technical Cooperation Conference (SAATCC, Séminaire Afro-Chinois pour la Coopération Technique Agricole) in Côte d'Ivoire. Organized by the Republic of China (ROC) Ministry of Foreign Affairs, SAATCC invited agricultural experts and bureaucrats from Taiwan and fourteen African nations: Côte d'Ivoire (Ivory Coast), Liberia, Cameroon, Senegal, Sierra Leone, Congo, Gabon, French Upper Volta (Haute Volta, today Burkina Faso), Congo-Leopoldville (today Zaire), Madagascar, Niger, Rwanda, Chad, and Togo. Numerous Taiwanese agricultural scientists and technicians accompanied Shen to the conference, among them directors of experiment stations, crop improvement stations, and fertilizer associations in Taiwan, as well as senior scientists in charge of ROC agricultural development teams throughout the African continent. Shen's presentation was nominally about agricultural development and how to best achieve it. But his presentation was also part of a longer and much more consequential history of how scientists, technicians, state planners, and other officials imagined the Republic of China on Taiwan as a vanguard nation of the developing world.

Shen was among the most decorated agricultural scientists in Taiwan. With a doctoral degree in agronomy from Cornell, he had worked his entire life in the agricultural sciences, first in China and then after 1949 in Taiwan. In the same year SAATCC was held, Shen was promoted to chairman of the Joint Commission on Rural Reconstruction (JCRR, 中國農村復興聯合委員會, Zhongguo Nongcun Fuxing Lianhe Weiyuanhui), the government body that had been charged with designing and enacting agricultural development in the ROC. The post–

World War II era saw agricultural scientists like Shen make an increasingly public case for the importance of science and technology, which helped lead to rapid agricultural economic growth and rural social uplift. While Shen had worked largely in the confines of China and Taiwan, global decolonization and the intensifying Cold War of the 1960s provided Taiwanese scientists another platform: the developing world.[1]

In his speech to his African counterparts, Shen Zonghan spoke not of his personal experiences as a plant breeder but rather as a representative of what he framed as a Taiwan agrarian miracle. According to Shen, Taiwan could serve as a model for Africa. He showcased graph after graph demonstrating remarkable agricultural growth in Taiwan, as well as its benefits for Taiwanese society and the economy. Most prominent was the growth curve, a visualization of economic growth that went on to become a motif for Taiwanese development presentations given around the world (figure 1).[2]

Shen argued that most tropical and subtropical countries in the world were "confronted with somewhat similar problems," namely that "they have not yet adequately developed their natural resources and their economies are primarily agricultural." As a result, they are "poor and dissatisfied" and "easily taken in by Communist propaganda." His solution: "Only with increased farm production and increased income can their livelihood be bettered and the social and political order be stabilized and democratic institutions strengthened."[3] Shen implied that his African peers should learn from the path laid by Taiwan.

Superficially, Shen's statements were a simple assertion of political economic relationships: as productivity and rural livelihoods improved, the state would benefit as well. But Shen's speech was also part of a broader, state-building project in Taiwan and the rest of the world. State leaders and technocrats were advancing seemingly universal, modernist, and scientific claims in order to consolidate their power. The focus on incomes and production was one example, reflecting the burgeoning influence of economics and social science.[4] Many African members in the audience listening to Shen in 1965 similarly deployed science and economics to support their own state-building projects, some as autocratic as the ROC.[5]

The ROC, led by the single party rule of the Guomindang under Chiang Kaishek, controlled Taiwan through martial law and a regime of terror that violently repressed, imprisoned, or executed dissenters. By the 1960s, the GMD had seized upon the discourse and practice of agrarian development to further its authoritarian control. Thus, while growth and productivity were the short-term goals of SAATCC, the ultimate aims of the development project for Taiwan was to sell an image of itself at the global scientific and economic vanguard in order to justify its authoritarian grip.

Shen's presentation in front of his African peers was typical of the wider zeitgeist, in which development was understood to be of greater and greater importance. This book tracks the history of how development emerged as a project undertaken

1875

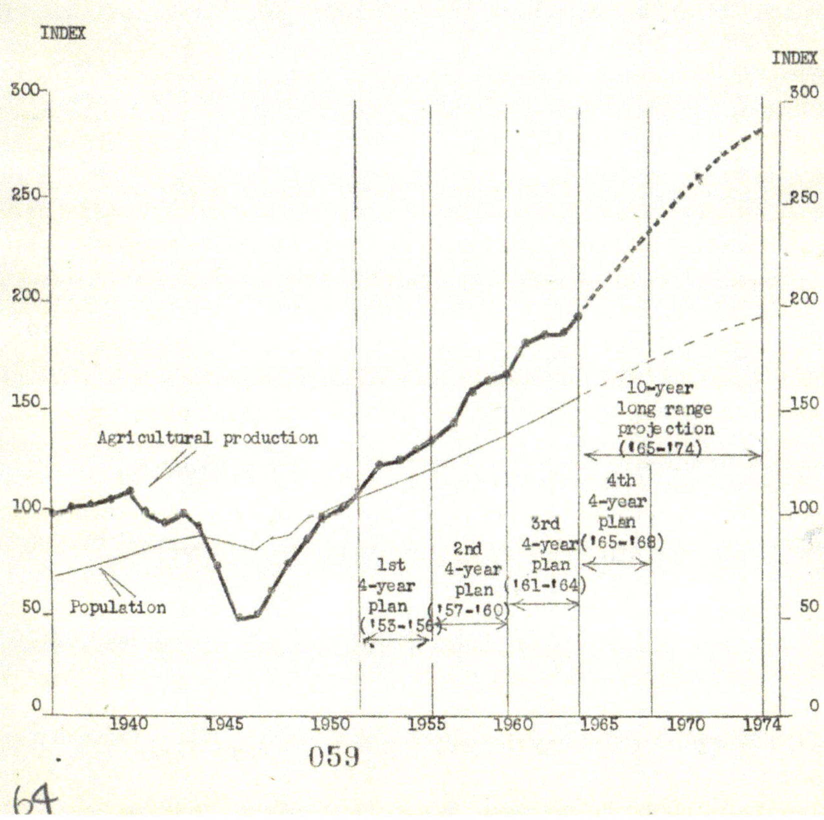

FIGURE 1. This Taiwanese growth curve represents Taiwanese agricultural production from prewar (under Japanese colonialism) to postwar (under the Guomindang) and production figures projected into the future. Given to audience members to accompany Shen Zonghan's speech to the Sino-African Agricultural Technical Cooperation Conference held in Ivory Coast, July 26–30, 1965, it was typical of graphs representing Taiwan's agricultural miracle to audiences throughout the world. 中非農技合作討論會 [Sino-African Agricultural Technical Cooperation Conference], July 16, 1965, page 1875, archive number 0200000039124A, Ministry of Foreign Affairs Collection, Academia Historica.

and co-opted by states seeking to build power in the vacuum left by global decolonization. I focus on Taiwan, a small state that faced a growing existential crisis, in part sparked by decolonization. But the turn to development was seen in nearly all states in the twentieth century. Leaders around in the world, especially those in postcolonial, rural, and poor states, wielded discourses of modernity and science for social and political control. The ROC was merely one of the first to achieve significant success with development, and it utilized that success to its own gain by positioning itself as leading a global vanguard.

Scholars have previously sought to understand and explain how to replicate Taiwan's success from the perspective of institutions, policies, or materiality.[6] However, I am ultimately interested in the consequences of development for society. Development began as a state project to modernize rural communities and achieve higher production yields while also inculcating state power into societal structures. In Taiwan, development also rendered a new social imaginary based on technical and scientific modernity, capitalism with elements of social welfare, and the gravity of economic growth. To illustrate with one powerful visual image, by the 1970s, the growth curve became a recurring motif of the Taiwan miracle (see figure 1). Deployed in conferences like SAATCC and in front of scientists from Africa, Asia, and the Americas, growth, in the developing world, became equated with Taiwan. From there, the GMD regime invoked the growth curve, along with images of the luscious, green Taiwanese vegetables transplanted to the fields of Vietnam and the Taiwanese technicians planting rice side by side with African villagers for Taiwanese in the metropole. Through the farmers' associations that helped make the Taiwan model an attraction for Third World bureaucrats, the Guomindang translated a new visual and documentary narrative of their success abroad. Through state-disseminated propaganda, pro-government media, and color films, Taiwanese farmers in the countryside and urban city dwellers in Taipei understood that Taiwanese rice and technicians were benefitting peoples at all corners of the world, a reflection of the modernity, perseverance, and expertise of their nation as a whole. Agrarian development became an instrument of state power and a hegemonic discourse that state leaders and ROC elites on Taiwan utilized to shape societal behavior and further their own political ends.[7] Anthropologist Arturo Escobar calls development a type of "colonization of reality" where "certain representations become dominant and shape indelibly the ways in which reality is imagined and acted upon."[8] Throughout the decades, the content of development changed, from famine prevention to land reform to vegetable breeding. What remained constant was the deployment of development, for state-building, diplomacy, or to sustain an authoritarian martial law regime.

ROC leaders emphasized Taiwan was actively pioneering development not just for its own society, but also for the benefit of others. Taiwan, they implied, was leading the vanguard. In government circles of the ROC Ministry of Foreign

Affairs and the United States, this was explicit; beginning in the early 1960s, Taiwanese agricultural development missions were collectively referred to as Operation Vanguard (先鋒案, Xianfeng An). It was a clever moniker for a diplomatic initiative, but it also reflects the ROC's broader effort to position itself as a global leader in development. The role of the state in creating a social imaginary for political purposes is a theme common to studies of Taiwan society, in part because the GMD government's authoritarian leverage over politics and education that granted hegemony over discourse.[9] As science, technology, and society (STS) scholars like Sheila Jasanoff, Sang-hyun Kim, and Aaron Moore have argued, technological systems can powerfully shape society and social identities.[10] The sociotechnical imaginary and meaning of agrarian development as leading the world proved powerful for the ROC national project.

Taiwan's imagination of the vanguard cannot be understood without a global frame. From 1959 onward, Taiwan sent agrarian development missions to nearly all corners of the developing world: South and Southeast Asia, the Middle East, Africa, and Latin America. This turn to the global followed the emergence of postcolonial politics, wherein states of the developing world attempted to locate alternatives to Western-dominated discourses of knowledge.[11] Taiwanese state planners, scientists, and social scientists seized an opening in this global moment by assembling aspects of Taiwan's recent agricultural, rural, and economic success into what they suggested was an exportable model. Evoking principles of low capital costs, scientific modernism, and an ethos of perseverance and non-Western solidarity, the Taiwanese model, its practitioners argued, was more applicable to developing states than capitalist (American) or communist models. Newspapers, speeches, and media in the ROC valorized Taiwanese development experts abroad. And the sustained demand for Taiwanese methods and experts helped the ROC claim that it was in a global vanguard of development modernity. "The global" became an expansive metaphor for the imagination of Taiwan in the vanguard. It was precisely because the world implied grand scales of leadership that Taiwan's position in a global vanguard was so compelling as an imaginary.

While understanding the construction of the development project and discourse is important, this book is not just a discursive or intellectual history—it also delves deeply into how development was actually carried out on the ground. The sociotechnical imaginary of agrarian development arose from a history of efforts at improving agricultural sciences and rural livelihoods. So in addition to examining presentations at academic conferences like the SAATCC, I also follow development practitioners in Taiwan and across Southeast Asia, Africa, and Latin America to show how the Taiwan model was translated on the ground in the rest of the world. As is typical of "modernization comes to town" narratives, Taiwanese teams rarely actually realized long-term, structural improvements in livelihoods or economic gains.[12] However, Taiwanese development abroad did eventually transform what it meant to be Taiwanese at home: as imagined pioneers of rural modernity.

MAKING A MIRACLE

Taiwan is an island in the maritime crossroads between Southeast and East Asia and home to Taiwanese Indigenous peoples for millennia. Chinese migrants began to settle the island in small numbers during the Ming Dynasty (1368–1644). The arrival of Dutch colonial rule on Taiwan (1624–62) encouraged larger scale migration from the mainland for what historian Tonio Andrade has called "co-colonization," referring to the colonial rule of the Dutch East India Company and the settlement of Taiwan by migrant Chinese laborers.[13] The ROC was founded in 1912 following the overthrow of the Qing Empire (1636–1911). At the time, Taiwan was not a part of ROC territory, since the Qing court was forced to cede the island to Japan following its defeat in the First Sino-Japanese War (1894–95). For a half century from 1895 to 1945, Japan ruled Taiwan as a prized agricultural export colony producing predominantly rice and sugar. In 1934, Taiwan was the third largest producer of sugar in the world after India and Cuba.[14] The ROC took possession of Taiwan at the end of the Second Sino-Japanese War (1937–45) as part of the peace agreement brokered by the Allied powers. At the time, a protracted, on-and-off civil war was still taking place on the mainland. When the ROC was defeated by the Chinese Communists in 1949, the ROC government fled to the island of Taiwan. So did a million soldiers, government officials, and other refugees.

ROC leader and dictator Chiang Kai-shek (蔣介石, Jiang Jieshi) made Taiwan the ROC's "temporary" home until its military could retake mainland China from the Communists. Under Chiang, the Guomindang (國民黨, Nationalist Party, GMD for short, also spelled Kuomintang) ruled Taiwan as a settler colonial regime, imposing brutal martial law and authoritarian rule. The then one-year-old JCRR moved as well. In the mainland, the JCRR was a novel government bureaucracy, established with US aid and with two US experts appointed to its leadership, a five-person commission. All five of its commissioners represented important intellectual lineages in agrarian reform, from community development and rural education to modernist agricultural science that presaged the Green Revolution. But its work was cut short by civil war, and it was granted a new opportunity when it moved to Taiwan in 1949 with the rest of the ROC government. Given the far smaller area of land it was responsible for on the island of Taiwan, the US$1.5 billion that Taiwan received in economic aid from the US (from 1951–65), and the physical and social infrastructure critical to agricultural productivity left by the Japanese colonial government, the JCRR oversaw significant growth in the agricultural sector.[15]

By the 1960s, the JCRR was well known both in Taiwan and across the rest of the world for its agricultural advances. *Time* magazine reported in 1962 of "Formosa: A Success Story."[16] This eventually snowballed over the following two decades into the narrative of the "Taiwan miracle." Taiwan's emergence from a small island colony to global export power in a span of a quarter-century captured the attention of news media, academics, and government policymakers. Today, Taiwan's gross domestic product (GDP) ranks twenty-second highest in the world, unemployment rate is under 4 percent, and 0 percent of its population lives under the World Bank's global poverty line.[17] Few other states saw the economic markers of success as Taiwan did, from GDP growth to unemployment to daily caloric intake. Even fewer began as Taiwan did at the end of World War II, as an agrarian colony whose main purpose in the Japanese empire was exporting rice and sugar. Agricultural commodities constituted 80 percent of its exports just before the end of World War II. As of 2022, that number is 0.76 percent.[18] Whereas the 1962 *Time* article praised Taiwan for its success in exporting mushrooms (worth $10 million USD per annum in 1962) and canned pineapples ($12 million USD per annum in 1962), today Taiwan is known for manufacturing Apple iPhones and advanced semiconductors.

The development project emerged at a critical juncture in Taiwanese and global history. The end of Japanese imperial rule and the ROC takeover of Taiwan from Japan in 1945 was initially met with enthusiasm by Taiwanese society, but just two years later, in 1947, it turned bloody and violent. Early GMD rule was characterized by poor public administration and ham-fisted economic policies, exacerbated by soaring postwar inflation that drew widespread ire from the Taiwanese, who had been used to better economic conditions under Japanese rule. After a woman selling black market cigarettes was pistol whipped by government authorities in charge of maintaining a state monopoly on tobacco, protesters sprang up island-wide against GMD rule. GMD authorities responded by deploying soldiers from mainland China, killing an estimated thousands to tens of thousands of civilians during the aftermath of the February 28, 1947 Incident.[19] The GMD government declared martial law for several months afterward. Martial law returned again in 1949 when the GMD moved its government to Taiwan, lasting until 1987. During those four decades, in what became known as the White Terror, the state not only curtailed civil liberties but also secretly imprisoned and routinely executed perceived enemies of the state. The reign of terror silenced the masses and disciplined the population into accepting and supporting the new government.

Following the retreat to Taiwan, the GMD government continued to maintain that it was the sole legitimate government for all of China and would imminently seize back its lost territories. Chiang Kai-shek in particular devoted substantial public rhetoric to retaking the mainland from the Communist "bandits," and the ROC incited the Taiwanese people in schools and in public spaces through slogans such as "recover the mainland" (光復大陸, *guangfu dalu*) and "counterattack the mainland" (反攻大陸, *fangong dalu*). GMD propaganda targeted both the *waishengren* (外省人), the "mainland" Chinese who fled to Taiwan mostly during 1948–49 and formed much of the GMD ruling elite, and the *benshengren* (本省人), the

Taiwanese present on the island prior to GMD takeover, mostly consisting of those who migrated to Taiwan during the Qing dynasty from southeastern China. Yet by the 1960s, cracks began to appear. GMD elites recognized that military reconquest of the mainland would be increasingly difficult, especially given the population and manpower discrepancy between the People's Republic of China (PRC) and the much smaller Taiwan. Furthermore, in Taiwan, ethnic tensions between *benshengren* and *waishengren* required strict disciplining and attention from the state. Problems on the island seemed more pressing, and turning to development seemed a way to move past the military stalemate and internal divisions in the ROC.

Moreover, international Cold War politics were posing an existential threat to the ROC. Almost immediately after the Communist victory, the newly established PRC asserted that it, not the defeated and ousted ROC regime, was the rightful representative of China. Although the United States and many Western powers did not recognize the PRC at first, by the late 1960s, pressure from the international community was mounting to correct the PRC's exclusion, especially in the United Nations, where the ROC held a valuable permanent seat on the UN Security Council. When the PRC's communist ally, Albania, introduced measures to replace the ROC with the PRC in the United Nations, the ROC risked losing an important platform of legitimacy and to sustain its long term goal of defeating the Communists.[20]

At this juncture, newly decolonized and independent nation-states, predominantly in Africa, provided the ROC with an opportunity to gain crucial allies and votes in the UN. These nation-states were working to cast off the legacies of colonialism and to consolidate power behind new leaders, many of whom were, like the GMD, essentially elites supported by military rule. GMD leaders saw an opportunity to horse-trade—the ROC sending agricultural experts and development projects in exchange for a vote in the UN. The GMD deployed both its technocratic elite and its rural technicians to state capitals, academic conference rooms, and fields across Africa, Latin America, and Asia. ROC leaders implied that over time, postcolonial countries could gain sufficient economic independence from agriculture to transition into even more profitable industrial growth. This economic independence was the path to a future free from the historical shackles of colonialism and the West. But the GMD's development diplomacy was cut short when the ROC lost its UN seat in 1971 due to UN General Assembly Resolution 2758, eliminating the main driver for Taiwanese development in Africa.

In the language of development, modern agricultural science and technology were a source of strength and power. Development offered a basis for postcolonial nation-building that political leaders in the Global South coveted. However, Taiwan's rhetoric of postcolonial solidarity was at odds with the reality that the Guomindang regime was itself a settler colonial power. So too was the ROC's framing of development as carried out in the name of anti-Communism and "freedom." For while it was true that Taiwan was decolonized from Japanese rule after 1945, the GMD's swift introduction of martial law made for an era, as historian Masuda Hajimu writes, of "decolonization as recolonization."[21] From the lived experience of most Taiwanese, the GMD government's policy of Sinicization and regime of terror constituted a new colonial rule. Nonetheless, the GMD relied on the facade of postcolonialism, including its language of having a strong nation-state that was "free" and represented the will of the Chinese people, to give credence to the ROC's colonial rule at home.[22] It also helped the ROC develop an imperial imaginary abroad, in its relations with Southeast Asia and the rest of the Global South.

Scholars like Chen Kuan-hsing and others have framed Taiwan as a "subempire," a "lower-level empire that is dependent upon" US empire, or as a Cold War client state of the United States.[23] While the ROC indeed benefitted from the United States, including by the infusion of American capital and technical knowledge to Taiwan, US diplomatic pressure on other countries to support the ROC in the United Nations, and clandestine funding of Taiwan's Operation Vanguard missions, it is also important to recognize that US hegemony, capital, and power alone were not the primary agents behind the ROC's own settler colonialism of Taiwan and its constructed imaginary as a global power. The ROC portrayed Taiwan in the global vanguard and for the benefit of ROC authoritarian rule at home on its own accord. Though US capital enabled a greater reach of these missions, ROC planners were unhindered in designing and leading these missions. Taiwanese technicians performed the critical knowledge transfers on the ground. The asymmetry of power relations between the ROC development experts and local recipients in the Global South was a result of the ROC-Global South relationship. Most importantly, GMD elites saw the Republic of China as a great state and felt that this imposed on its people a responsibility to share the technology and knowledge it pioneered. In this regard, the ROC was not merely a subempire or a client state but a settler colonial power at home in Taiwan with aspirations for global power. The GMD utilized the world stage, both through development missions dispatched to corners of the Global South and as imagined through the media representations of Taiwanese development abroad and at home, to bolster its colonial control over Taiwan. It is thus crucial to understand Taiwan both in the project of settler colonialism in the metropole and as the global project of imagined power in the world, in short, as an imperial imaginary.

Even though development was led by the state and its chosen technocrats, the GMD sought to vernacularize the project to garner support from Taiwanese subjects, a keystone of which was state efforts to unite the native Taiwanese *benshengren* and the newly arrived *waishengren*, Chinese mainlanders who by the 1960s were beginning to lose faith in the Guomindang's primary goal of retaking the mainland from the Communists.[24] This rendered a new Taiwan-specific and GMD-dominated vision, disseminated in the developing world abroad, and then re-represented at home as evidence of success and superiority.

The makeup of overseas development missions tended to conform to a colonial hierarchy on the island itself, with "mainlander" *waishengren* in positions of power and "Taiwanese" *benshengren* comprising most of the junior technicians. When I interviewed these former junior technicians, many told me that they saw their mission in technical terms, to assist the less privileged elsewhere in the world. They also saw opportunities for personal financial gain, since these positions paid well. In essence, the colonizing ruling class had co-opted the colonized to serve the ROC's political will.

But the presence of both *benshengren*, who represented local agricultural knowledge from the island, and *waishengren*, also meant that the "Republic of China" in this instance was already "Taiwanized" since the agricultural knowledge they were transmitting was rooted in the ecology, society, and history of Taiwan, not China. Some techniques presented to the Global South by Taiwanese experts had their roots in Japanese colonial policies, such as Taiwan's farmers' associations that the Japanese colonial administration had used in part to control rural Taiwanese. This was glossed over by ROC development scientists in their presentations to African counterparts in Cote d'Ivoire and elsewhere, an act of historical silencing that went hand in hand with the ROC colonial policies of Sinicization and de-Japanification. Despite this, the countless charts, maps, and graphs showcased by Taiwanese scientists in agricultural and economics conferences in front of their developing world peers in the 1960s and 70s in effect undermined the political logic of the "Republic of China" that was even then an ideological imaginary. It was not "China" that had achieved miraculous agricultural productivity. Rather, it was the economic, social, and ecological unit of Taiwan, conjuring a new geo-body in these contexts as a development alternative for the Third World.[25] Rural Taiwanese farmers, urban Taiwanese middle class, and Guomindang elites became aware through state publications and pro-government media of how Taiwanese knowledge and methods were being deployed throughout the world, in turn defining their understanding of what it meant to be Taiwanese.

These interactions reshaped consciousness of Taiwan in the twentieth century so that it was seen not just as an ecological and economic model but eventually as a modern, wealthy society. This reflective identity was a consequence of a twentieth-century state project of development carried out amid the rising allure of economic growth as a means to power. Under the Guomindang regime, development embodied one of the highest state priorities, both to legitimize its repressive, authoritarian rule and also in furthering its assumed identity as a modern, vanguard state. Despite its limited successes in translating a Taiwan model for the rest of the world, the development project was nonetheless a powerful one in transforming Taiwan itself.

WHAT IS DEVELOPMENT?

The concept of development, so central to this study, can seem so capacious and contested as to be amorphous. Literature scholar Andrew Jones sees development as falling into two camps. One is the supposedly "inevitable historical unfolding" in which humankind moves, teleologically, toward progress. (This idea has been popular from Greco-Roman philosophical traditions on up to the Enlightenment and continues to show up in philosophical traditions of G. W. F. Hegel and evolutionary theorists like Jean-Baptiste Lamarck, Charles Darwin, and Herbert Spencer.)[26] Brought to the modern era, this centuries-long development crescendos in what geographer Gillian Hart terms "'big D' Development" to describe what she sees as a singular, global, post-1945 project emerging internationally, characterized largely by intervention of the Global North into the Third World.[27] The second camp involves, as Jones writes, the "transitive and purposeful activity of active historical agents," in which states and individuals actively sought to improve their societies and nations.[28] Many historians of development take this more generic definition of development as their standard frame of reference. For example, historian David Engerman defines development as "state-centered efforts to effect linked social and economic transformation."[29] Daniel Immerwahr sees development as "increasing social capacity," a broader categorization that encompasses community development he studies.[30]

In this book, I am concerned with both forms of development. While most development histories focus on the Global North, I center the Taiwanese and ROC perspectives. For most of the era the book chronicles, Taiwan was a small state and positioned itself more with the Global South than the Global North. Its imminent expulsion from the United Nations limited its reach and influence and moreover triggered an existential crisis among its society. Yet it wielded its scientific and technical prowess from a position of power relative to recipient nations, resulting in an asymmetry similar to that seen in Global North/Global South development histories. In some cases, being seen as a poor rural country benefitted Taiwan, especially in its mission to the Republic of Vietnam, where Vietnamese officials valued Taiwan's similar socioeconomic status. In other cases, being excluded from the UN hamstrung Taiwan's efforts, such as in the case of the Asian Vegetable Research and Development Center where Taiwanese planners' vision to lead in the Green Revolution was thwarted by its status as a non-nation. Depending on the relationship, Taiwan could be both powerful and powerless, a reality that complicates standard understandings of development proceeding from bifurcated North/South models.

I am also interested in deliberate and concerted efforts to improve livelihoods, usually through accelerating economic growth or raising standards of living. This is a "big tent" definition that I have arrived at empirically, based on close reading of tens of thousands of primary documents by policymakers, philanthropists, scientists, technocrats, intellectuals, and others who made it part of their professional and personal goals to improve the well-being of their own societies and their fellow humans. It serves to include the types of development that occurred historically both in Taiwan and by Taiwanese actors abroad after 1949, from agricultural science to rural reform to economic changes to massive infrastructure engineering. It also brings into focus the common principles that eventually characterized Taiwanese development: scientific and technological modernity, capitalism with socialist characteristics, and rural social organizations. These principles, in turn, tell us how the Taiwanese thought of themselves when they represented their experiences to the developing world and how those representations—narrated as evidence of Taiwanese mastery—helped to sprout a newly growing Taiwanese consciousness.

Development practitioners utilized development to instantiate visions of modernity.[31] For example, in Cote d'Ivoire, Shen Zhonghan argued for an agrarian modernity wherein high agricultural productivity would lead to higher incomes and increased rural standards of living. In Taiwan, GMD planners envisioned land reform as providing the financial instruments and legal institutions turning landlords and tenant farmers into modern capitalists, accumulating wealth. Scholars like James Scott have argued that development is a muscle-bound, top-down effort at modernization.[32] But as shown by scholars like Daniel Immerwahr, communitarian development did not reflect Scott's version of "high modernism" and instead was anti-modernist in its rejection of modernizing principles of centralization and standardization.[33] 4-H organizations in Taiwan in the 1950s, for example, pushed central policies on hygiene for public health and Taylorist quantification of production. But at the same time, 4-H in Taiwan emphasized community development of democracy at the grassroots village level as the primary political driver of social change. Widening the scope for what constitutes development also brings into the picture what can be seen as a spectrum of modernities, visions that fall at both poles of high modernism and low modernism as well as the many shades of gray between them that is actually what occurred on the ground.

Taiwanese actors packaged their development ideas into what I sometimes refer to as a "Taiwan model." Historical Taiwanese actors used the word *model* on occasion, and more modest vocabulary such as *experience* (經驗, *jingyan*) was far more common. Nonetheless, I choose to emphasize *model* because Taiwanese science, technology, and knowledge were presented as a paradigm to developing world audiences, and one worth emulating. Taiwanese scientists and bureaucrats genuinely intended for African, Asian, and Latin American scientists and leaders to follow in the path of Taiwan and earnestly believed in both their universal (outside of Taiwan) and particular (tailored for local and even community contexts) applicability.

The particulars of Taiwanese development efforts varied widely, depending on time, geography, context, and recipient. Abroad, Taiwanese often promoted land reform for states with loose control over rural societies; the aim was to consolidate state capacity and increase central revenues by gaining greater legibility and turning rural peasants and landlords into capitalists. Yet these efforts failed to result in any meaningful structural change, because so many states were beholden to the landowning classes that land reform targeted. In other contexts, precisely because of the volatility of land reform, Taiwanese development experts offered a more technical and apolitical package of science and technology. These were likelier to appeal to authoritarian regimes that desired transferrable knowledge and capital without the difficult structural reforms that could have challenged their power. In her interviews of Taiwanese officials in Central America, for example, anthropologist Monica DeHart has argued that "rather than exporting a certain model of economic development, [the Taiwanese] worked with the Central American states to elicit ideas about local needs and to fund projects that reflected those priorities."[34] These reflected Central American interests in the success and experience of Taiwan stemming from its own economic miracle. As historian Simon Toner has shown, Global South interest in Taiwan's economy as a model of development date back to the 1970s.[35] Interestingly, this approach of local collaboration mirrors rhetoric deployed by the People's Republic of China in its missions abroad as well, even into the present.[36] Regardless of the specifics, the Taiwanese portrayed their ideas for development as unique, effective, and tailored for the needs of similar societies across the Global South.

The South-to-South aspect of this history is also consequential for understanding development. Decentering development from the West, as David Engerman and Corinna Unger have argued, allows us to see not just how development affected the lives of those on the ground but also how power brokers within the Global South sought to utilize development for their own purposes.[37] The core chapters of this book thus focus at length on South-to-South development, namely Taiwanese development missions to Africa and Asia. In some cases, this attention on South-to-South development reinforces what critical development anthropologists like James Ferguson have shown, namely that development often claims to be a technical panacea that can transcend politics but almost always fails, because development does not address the complex social, culture, and political structures that underlie human societies.[38] In other cases, examining development through a South-to-South lens reveals new dimensions that may not have been obvious from the predominant examples of North-to-South development in the literature. For example, Taiwanese missions in the 1960s in Vietnam and Africa did not point to the benefits of cutting-edge technology. Rather, they demonstrated that Taiwanese agrarian methods, which involved blue-collar technicians working the fields side by side with farmers, arose from the same tropical and poor conditions as the African and Asian fields to which they were sent. These methods, often emphasizing the well-developed farmers' associations of Taiwan and the efficacy of agricultural extension—that is, extending technologies from center to periphery— were the result of Taiwan's long-standing experiences with farmers' associations rather than large capital investments in science and technology or infrastructure, which would have been impractical for both sides of a South-to-South relationship. This accords with other historical instances of South-to-South development, such as Israel's MASHAV or South Korea's KOICA.[39]

Most consequentially, the implications of studying South-to-South connections are that Taiwan's motivations for doing so can be more clearly explained in the global postcolonial context. Initially driven by Cold War geopolitics to trade development for diplomatic favors, Taiwan's Global South missions grew, in content and in representation, to be something more. International development became a powerful mirror that allowed Taiwan to reflect upon its own process of decolonization and nation-building. In representing itself as having excelled at development, which had become the object of desire for nearly all of the Global South, Taiwan sought to find a new, global identity. And in being able to teach other nations how to achieve the same success, it positioned itself among the vanguard nations of the world. This reimagining of Taiwan's contemporary history as one of miraculous colony-to-vanguard transformation became a powerful governing logic and vision of modernity that was wielded internationally and at home.

Within development, I especially focus on the agricultural sciences, a domain where science, technology, environment, state, and society shaped one another.[40] Scholars of science and environment have explored the social and political construction of science and technology and interactions between human and non-human actors, especially in the "Green Revolution" narrative about the emergence of high-yield crop cultivars that rapidly increased food production across the world in the twentieth century.[41] But most histories of the Green Revolution have overlooked Taiwan and its interactions with the world. Scientific practices of the Green Revolution and development more broadly were contextualized and contested by indigenous local farmers, globally deployed Taiwanese technicians, Cold War geopolitics, and ecological actors such as local/foreign seeds, chemicals, soils, and climate. For example, I interviewed one retired Taiwanese technician deployed to over a half-dozen African nations who described how extreme daytime temperature fluctuations in Chad affected soil moisture that then necessitated the Taiwanese adopting different climatological considerations in Africa. In another instance, transplantation of Asian rice varieties such as IR-8 resulted in higher productivity than indigenous west African rice but sold less well in local markets due to local taste preferences. This led Taiwanese scientists to create three Taiwanese-operated crop experimentation stations in west Africa to select both local and foreign varieties. In Vietnam, success of Taiwanese transplanting American varieties of watermelon was co-opted as visual propaganda, juxtaposing a massive variety that arrived in Vietnam via Cold War geopolitically induced scientific networks and once again deployed in popular magazines for a lay audience in Taiwan and globally. Agriculture was central to the economy and identities of countless Global South nations and offers a critical lens to see how development unfolds across state, society, economy, science, and environment.

Development is essential for understanding both the historical Republic of China regime and modern Taiwan. Dating back to the late Qing and early Republican era, the modern Chinese state proclaimed that producing economic wealth and distributing that wealth to the citizenry was a core goal.[42] During the ROC period on Taiwan, the state ultimately fulfilled that economic promise, a reality that shaped Taiwanese identity itself. Scholars of Taiwanese identity have explored the origins of a separate Taiwanese consciousness as a reaction to Japanese and early Guomindang colonial rule, but the economic livelihood enabled by a global sociotechnical modernity also played an important role.[43] As Taiwanese scientists and bureaucrats successfully promoted their visions of modernity to other parts of the Global South, the GMD pointed not just to local success but to international respect to bind its home audience together.[44] It evoked a more powerful political logic for *waishengren*, who were beginning to question regime legitimacy centered on Chinese nationalism given the increasing unlikelihood of returning to China by the 1960s, and *benshengren*, to whom the GMD were, in effect, foreign colonizers and who saw little benefit under its repressive authoritarianism. Even after martial law ended and democratization advanced in the 1980s and 90s, development persisted as a predominant subject of Taiwanese party politics and legitimacy.

CHAPTER OUTLINE

Many of the dominant developmental ideas during the post-1949 period on Taiwan can be traced back to the scientific and intellectual centers of both the Japanese colonial era and this Republican period in China. Chapter 1 explores those origins, with a focus on how missionaries, scientists, engineers, and foreign experts engaged in famine relief efforts in Republican-era China (1912–49). What began as reactive relief changed over time into famine prevention. Practices such as hydraulic engineering, high-yield crops, and rural reform, designed to bolster the well-being and security of both rural villages and the country as a whole, became precursors to a developmentalist approach to national rural development.

After a traumatic defeat by Communists, GMD planners on Taiwan politicized a capitalist land reform and redistribution, explored in chapter 2. Specifically, land reform in Taiwan became represented as a social revolution accomplished not through executing landlords, as was the case in Communist China, but through modern legal and financial instruments. Forced sales of land recompensed through the financialization of land bonds provided the capital transfers that funded urbanization and industrialization.

In Taiwan during the 1950s, 60s, and 70s, as chapter 3 recounts, JCRR planners focused on rural society and agricultural science. The JCRR created new or co-opted existing social organizations in Taiwan to instill capitalist modes of production through credit and marketing cooperatives and discipline society through public health and youth 4-H campaigns. Simultaneously, the JCRR used science and technology—namely rice breeding, seed multiplication, chemical fertilizers, and agricultural extension—and focused on the translation of scientific knowledge to the countryside.

Beginning in 1959, the ROC sent agricultural development missions to Vietnam, marking the turn of Taiwanese development to a global audience. Chapter 4 shows that within these missions, Taiwanese experts first began to realize the potential value of a Taiwanese approach to development that emphasized modern science and Taiwan's successful farmers' associations. Farmers' associations not only generated economic self-sufficiency for farmers but also theoretically extended state authoritarianism into the countryside. This, Taiwanese technocrats suggested, could help counter the Communist insurgency that beset the Republic of Vietnam.

The success of the Vietnam missions encouraged the GMD to send agricultural development missions to Africa as well. Chapter 5 explores the apogee of Taiwanese development in Operation Vanguard, conducted by the Ministry of Foreign Affairs across two dozen African nations. Entrenched in a global Cold War, Taiwanese technicians demonstrated superior Taiwanese high-yielding crop varieties and handmade farm implements, while Taiwanese scientists extolled the values of modern agricultural science for strength and self-sufficiency. At home, these demonstrations were marshaled as evidence of the Guomindang regime's modernity and largesse in the Global South. And in the context of the global Cold War, they helped the ROC build diplomatic support for their threatened existence as a nation.

Along with agricultural development, GMD technocrats also taught land reform to representatives from the Global South. Chapter 6 explores the Land Reform Training Institute, established to train bureaucrats from over three dozen Third World nations, primarily from the South Pacific Rim and Latin America, in Taiwanese land reform. The institute showcased a technocratic vision of how policy and capitalism could engender the social equality envisioned by ROC founding father Sun Yat-sen. Yet Taiwanese-style land reform did not take hold abroad. This failure reveal a Janus-faced reality of land reform: land reform as carried out on Taiwan was a form of state consolidation by the GMD regime, while land reform pedagogy was performative, carried out for the purpose of the GMD's development diplomacy efforts.

With the rise of the Green Revolution globally, Taiwan sought to utilize agricultural science to bolster its own international position. Taiwanese rice had contributed the *sd1* allele responsible for the semi-dwarfing characteristic that made IR-8, the "miracle rice" of the Green Revolution, highly productive. The Asian Vegetable Research and Development Center (AVRDC) was designed to be Taiwan's entry into the global Green Revolution, and Taiwanese scientists bet that vegetables and the nutritional value of minerals and vitamins would be the next Green Revolution wave to follow caloric intake and cereal grains. As chapter 7 discusses, the AVRDC was intended to bring Taiwan's agricultural science expertise into the vanguard of global agricultural science. However, the AVRDC languished, signaling the late 1970s decline of state-led development, which gradually became surpassed by private corporations and neoliberalization, and Taiwan's increasing post-UN isolation on the global stage. The AVRDC punctuated a rise and fall narrative of development for Taiwan. Yet even though the AVRDC represented a demoralizing setback for agricultural development, the development project had already transformed what it meant to be Taiwanese at home.

1

Famine Relief to Prevention

Science, Missionaries, and the Origins
of Development, 1920–1948

We Chinese are a nation of farmers. . . . Under the cultural conditions in China, men of intellect and learning have not thought it worthwhile to pay any attention to practical matters. It was beneath the dignity of an educated person to soil his hands in labor . . . Confucian culture is rich in the understanding of human nature and social relationships, but it is at the same time woefully deficient in understanding and mastery of material and animal nature.

—JIANG TINGFU

INTRODUCTION

In popular and literary portrayals at the turn of the twentieth century, famine was a topic of global discussion. From Pearl Buck's novel *The Good Earth* to newspaper reports on the north China famine of the early 1920s, hunger and death became associated with agrarian societies like China.[1] The Qing government (1644–1911) had developed extensive economic management systems, utilizing state-managed grain storage that would flood the market with state-owned surplus during times of shortage.[2] The Qing state also practiced modern agricultural sciences and engineering that sought to transform the environment to the will of the state.[3] The Guomindang regime (1912–49 on the mainland, thereafter on Taiwan) continued and intensified these practices. By the early twentieth century, increasing numbers of policymakers and scientists viewed famine as a preventable, technical phenomenon as opposed to just an act of nature. This transformation, from famine relief to famine prevention, marked the emergence of rural and agrarian developmentalist thought in China. This intellectual origin story bears consequences for Taiwan's later agrarian development model.

18

Agrarian development became a deliberate project, often led by the state but also engaging non-state actors, to improve rural social conditions. Historians have usually portrayed international development as a predominantly American state project, one prompted by the belief that the rural and agrarian populations of the world needed help in order not to fall to the rising forces of Communism in the postwar era.[4] These histories are narrowly focused on postwar institutions and extend their teleologies backward in time. This chapter, instead, examines conditions on the ground in China. There, social and state actors and intellectual movements were already thinking developmentally, seeking to improve economic and social conditions, well before the Cold War and World War II. Ideas that later became prominent in postwar development, such as community development and increased agricultural yields through plant breeding science, had already been deployed battling famine during the Republican period (1912–49) and earlier.

In China, religious missionaries, universities, and philanthropic organizations carried out this work. In contrast to narratives of development that began their arcs with high-yielding wheat in Mexico or eastern Washington in the 1940s, the visions for a postwar order among Bretton Woods planners, or with the Tennessee Valley Authority and the New Deal in the United States, development in the case of China began with religious, scientific, and philanthropic efforts to battle hunger and famine.[5] Protestant missionaries, Cornell-trained Chinese scientists, the Rockefeller Foundation, and the Guomindang state worked in mitigating the effects of droughts, floods, and other sources of famine.[6] By the 1930s, these efforts had begun to shift their focus from reactive famine *relief* to proactive famine *prevention*. Through preemptive investment in hydraulic infrastructure, basic and applied research in crops, insects, and soils, and dissemination of practices and social reform through village education, famine prevention formed the basis of development.

The Republican period in China witnessed substantial diversity in social movements and intellectuals writing on societal improvement.[7] This chapter focuses on a few select development practitioners and their intellectual and institutional milieu. These practitioners were natural scientists, social scientists, and engineers, both Chinese trained in pioneering centers of agricultural and social sciences in the United States and Americans who resided in China. This is not to overemphasize the role of Americans or foreigners in general in famine relief in China, nor, for that matter, the role of missionaries and scientists. Foreigners represented a small fraction of famine relief efforts in manpower and in intellectual production. However, all three groups made important contributions to development practices, not just in Republican period China but also in Taiwan after 1949. Their shared experiences, beginning with the formative years at American research universities such as Cornell and Columbia, through Chinese institutions such as Yenching University (Yanjing Daxue 燕京大學), Nanking University (Jinling Daxue 金陵大學), and social and rural reform movements such as the Mass Education movement and the North China Council for Rural Reconstruction demonstrated remarkable exchange and debate over how to fight famine and improve rural livelihood.

From these debates emerged different approaches to development. One approach emphasized the importance of social change, and this was taken up by missionaries and Chinese intellectuals and reformists who focused on rural China and believed in dissemination of knowledge for the good of the average village and villager. Out of these beliefs came an emphasis on public health, mass literacy, and agricultural extension—the dissemination, through demonstrations in farms and villages, of agricultural technology and applied science ranging from selected seeds and newly designed agricultural implements to pesticide application practices. Another approach emerged from scientists and engineers, who believed in the transformative power of science, engineering, and technology, and the need to follow their modern logics.[8] These ranged from plant breeders to entomologists to civil engineers. There was significant overlap in the two approaches. They often were implemented side by side, and both approaches converged into a later model of agrarian development.

MISSIONARIES AND FAMINE

By the turn of the century, American missionaries were dispersed throughout the world. In China, over a dozen Western missionary groups had been operating in China by the Republican period, both in the port treaties of China's eastern coast as well as inland provinces like Shaanxi and Sichuan.[9] Historian David Hollinger has estimated four thousand American missionaries were present in China in 1925.[10] Evangelism, converting the Chinese to Christianity, was naturally the primary goal of the missions, but like North American Protestant missionaries elsewhere in the world, they were also contributing to education, public health, and social improvement. A growing number became concerned with famine relief. In the early twentieth century, movements like the Social Gospel in the United States had begun thinking of social uplift as a basic moral imperative of Christianity, and alleviating hunger also was considered another means of saving souls. In India, as historian Prakash Kumar has shown, American Presbyterian missionaries established agricultural research institutes and influenced agricultural modernization projects in furtherance of religious ideals.[11] As historian Ian Tyrrell has argued, the force of American missionaries abroad constituted a "moral empire."[12] At times, bringing Christianity also implied bringing Western values, Western culture, and in the case of agricultural missionaries, Western science. By 1921, according to a report by the United International Famine Relief Committee (國際統一救災總會,

guoji tongyi jiuzai zonghui), the number of foreign workers engaging in famine relief numbered at 385, with missionaries from Presbyterian, Anglican, Roman Catholic, Methodist, Lutheran, and Baptist denominations representing the United States, Canada, Britain, Ireland, Denmark, Sweden, and Norway.[13]

As Christian missions sought to help local peoples, philanthropic organizations in the United States also began to look outward. The Rockefeller Foundation, then run by Rockefeller family scion John D. Rockefeller Jr. and endowed with family wealth, began to fund projects abroad with American expertise. Early foundation work in China began with medicine. For example, the Peking Union Medical College (PUMC) was a foundation-funded medical college that sought to improve public health in China by training Chinese doctors under the supervision of American faculty. Along with nearly a dozen medical colleges, mostly associated with the missionary universities such as St. John's, Nanking, Lingnan, and others, these cooperative training projects in medicine sought to bring Western medical practices to China.[14]

By 1920, the Rockefeller Foundation began to look beyond PUMC, which by then had become a fairly successful organization at demonstrating tangible results through the number of Chinese doctors trained and graduated from PUMC. Part of the Rockefeller Foundation's modus operandi included working with and funding new and existing organizations, like the China Medical Board, that would fundraise from specific donors interested in specific causes, such as medical relief in China, and appoint capable experts to carry out those missions. The year 1920 provided a new window of opportunity for the foundation to expand in China, albeit in response to a national tragedy.

FROM RELIEF TO PREVENTION

In 1920, a severe drought in north China led to a subsequent famine that received considerable attention in the United States. Historian Lillian Li estimated 30.3 million affected by the drought across five provinces, with around half a million dead as a result of the subsequent famine.[15] Newspapers in the United States covered the consequences of the famine with headlines such as "Starving Children Eat Baked Weeds," placing the death count at thousands a day and relaying a figure of $100 million needed for relief efforts.[16] Reports appeared so dire that American presidents Woodrow Wilson and Warren Harding appointed an American Advisory Committee for Famine Relief (AACFR), headed by prominent Americans, in an effort to organize relief in north China.

AACFR, with a goal of raising $5 million in gold, effectively organized both religious and non-religious fundraising pathways, and by 1922, it considered its efforts a success. Starting in 1921, as rainfall began to increase, conditions in north China improved and no longer necessitated the continuation of food distribution. But with significant funds still remaining after relief efforts, AACFR came to a crossroads. A memorandum, drafted by a specially convened subcommittee of AACFR, was circulated by AACFR to the counterpart board in China, the American Advisory Committee in Beijing (AACB), and the major donors, including John Rockefeller Jr. and leading officials within the Rockefeller Foundation. The contents of the memo outlined an emerging debate over the future of humanitarian aid.

The obvious option that presented itself would have been a continuation of the AACFR mission. 1921 had seen flooding along the banks of the Yellow River, and leftover funds could easily have been applied to help mitigate that natural disaster. However, a rising opinion was expressed against such a course of action. Instead, the memo pointed to the existence of discouraging factors. For one, AACFR believed that the Chinese government possessed the funds and capability to attend to the affected flooded population but chose to reserve that funding for "other uses" knowing that foreign aid would flow in. Second, continual foreign aid could potentially "pauperize" the Chinese by making them dependent on foreign aid for future relief (as historian Pierre Fuller argues, an argument with little basis in reality). Third, natural disasters occurred with such certainty that continual fundraising of American sources would see no end and funds should be spent immediately in order to ask for less in the future.[17] In concluding the memo, the AACFR suggested three possible courses of action: continue business as usual; as a middle course, use the experience of the 1920 drought relief efforts as a lesson for future events by continually keeping track of crop conditions so that surplus reallocation could be done in a more timely manner; and at the opposite end, use funds for "specific preventative lines."[18]

The memo triggered an extended and lengthy debate among the policymakers within the Rockefeller and in the humanitarian aid community regarding what "preventative lines" could entail. George Vincent, a doctor serving on the China Medical Board and adviser to the Rockefeller Foundation, remarked that AACFR should follow the precedents set by missionary organizations and Rockefeller and establish an "American Anti-Famine Foundation." Missionary organizations did not attempt to "make a large number of converts," it argued, but rather "to train its converts to the task of spreading the gospel to the masses of their countrymen." Likewise the Rockefeller accomplished the same in setting "standards of medical education so that hundreds and eventually thousands of Chinese physicians shall heal millions of sick." Thus, "no better purpose could be served" than to "put these famine funds to the education of the Chinese people in the prevention of future famine." Vincent's letter closed with a prediction that "there will come a time when the friendship of the common people of China will be worth more to America than the favor of the Mandarins," one that foreshadowed events to follow.[19]

The AACB, the counterpart board based in China, likewise weighed in with their thoughts. Consisting largely of American missionaries in Beijing, AACB leaned heavily toward the latter options. In fact, AACB recommended that no funds be allocated for the alleviation of the 1921 Yellow River floods, firmly believing that local "Chinese officials were in possession of necessary funds, derived from special super-taxes, ample to accomplish the necessary relief" but were withholding the funds "for other purposes and [to] seek American relief."[20] Like Vincent, it believed the most important goal would be to "*prevent* future famine" (emphasis original).

In the full six page letter, AACB laid out a plan of action. AACFR, it asserted, should endow the remaining funds such that the interest from the principal could be administered by a new organization dedicated to finding worthy causes of investment. Next, ventures in two areas should be funded: reforestation and agricultural education. In the former, AACB specifically mentioned the University of Nanking, "an institution of fine character," notable because it was "largely conducted by Americans," and Peking University (Yenching University) in the latter, also notable for the presence of Americans and its already extant extension system on two hundred acres in north China. Most importantly, however, was that Nanking University had the only established and dedicated College of Agriculture and Forestry among universities surveyed, coincidentally at the time also being temporarily administered by agricultural economist, Cornell graduate, and husband of Pearl Buck, John Lossing Buck. That is not to diminish the strength of agricultural sciences in other Chinese universities outside of these two, which dated well prior to the arrival of the Bucks in China, but the presence of Americans undoubtedly swayed AACB in favor of these two.

AACB saw value in reforestation and agricultural education, and in explaining the latter, the board specifically referenced American agricultural experiences: "In America the vast improvements in agriculture in recent years have come as a result of careful experimentation and demonstration and that such work, though not expensive, would constitute a most suitable and certain of famine prevention and that it could easily be made to affect a large part of China's population."[21] The authors saw parallels between American success in agricultural education and its potential applicability to this new shift in discourse from relief to prevention. For a foreign aid situation where resources were limited, population scaled nearly infinitely, and success was rarely guaranteed, agricultural education appeared to be the best investment.

AACB's recommendation was not without its critics, however. Roger S. Greene, director of the China Medical Board and member of the AACB, elaborated his own experience in dealing with other missionary groups. He noted that various missions have been communicating a serious need for relief funds, including from the Presbyterian Board of Foreign Missions, and that diverting surplus from "actual relief" could be "rather embarrassing" given the public facing nature of mission work. Nonetheless, he believed that the plan of the AACB was still the right path in terms of a long term resolution. In his additional comments, he also suggested that one or two Chinese individuals "of high standing" be asked to join in creating an organization in charge of the surplus endowment, in order to give the organization some legitimacy with the Chinese without necessarily displacing the role of the Chinese government.[22]

The greatest concern came not from those who believed that famine relief should remain dedicated to relief but rather from those who thought that prevention was a problem that required alternate technical approaches—namely, infrastructure development instead of agricultural science or forestry. John K. Davis, the American consul in Nanjing in 1922, sent a letter to Roger Greene, throwing his support behind a plan drafted by American Society of Civil Engineers president John Freeman to drain the Huai River basin and thus remove a cause of perennial flooding in northern Jiangsu and Anhui provinces.[23] This was a version of man-versus-nature engineering that sought to remake the natural environment.

Debates over technical strategies would recur throughout foreign assistance efforts in China and later in Taiwan, as each technical group, whether soil scientists, entomologists, educators, or civil engineers, espoused their own profession as the panacea for famine prevention and agrarian modernization. Hydrological engineering especially became a prominent modernizing agenda, particularly given the symbolic nature of massive, man-made concrete structures in the "conquest" of nature.[24] In this instance, however, the agricultural missionaries had sufficient support among AACFR and its supporting missionary boards and philanthropic organizations. Civil engineering and infrastructure development were sidelined in favor of reforestation and agricultural education.

By the end of 1922, the debate had been settled. AACFR, in agreement with AACB, decided to endow US$1 million in surplus funding and provide three-quarters of the funds to Nanking University and one-quarter to Peking University. The funds would be managed by the newly formed China International Famine Relief Commission, consisting of representatives from eight famine relief organizations operating in China at the time.[25] Significant leeway in the terms of the funding allowed the universities to exercise their best judgement to accomplish the stated goals: "the study and investigation of famine causes, prevention or relief, and as a means thereto for the education of the Chinese in agriculture, forestry, and other such activities as may relate to famine."[26]

John Reisner, a missionary, former Cornell professor of agricultural science, and at the time dean of the College of Agriculture and Forestry at University of Nanking, drafted a proposal for utilizing the funds in conjunction with Peking University. The resulting proposal laid out two goals: "development of agricultural education by training teachers of improved agriculture for mission middle school and teacher training centers" and "preparation of courses in general agriculture for higher primary schools, and aid in training of teachers to give such courses."[27] This emphasis on agricultural education, and specifically on training teachers who would be able to teach farmers, would later become crucial in the dissemination of agricultural practice and knowledge that undergirded the Nanking development model.

INSTITUTIONS

Two years after the agreement by AACFR to fund the College of Agriculture and Forestry at Nanking, a subsequent plan was underway from familiar names but under a different social impetus. In the United States, increased institutional support and discussion of missionary activities prompted new discussions over the best ways for missionaries to accomplish their goal of helping the Chinese populace. The discussion in missionary circles began to shift away from a focus on pure education to the environmental and social conditions—flooding, drought, and poverty—that caused recurring famine in China. The reported success of agricultural education in helping agrarian villages from Christian periodicals began to spur the interest of academically trained scientists. Many professors of agricultural science during this time were also religious, often coming from Protestant backgrounds, and deeply believed in the work of missionaries abroad. Some were even returned agricultural missionaries like John Reisner. From the agricultural science centers of the United States, these scientists believed that the panacea for the social obstacles that missionaries faced could best be addressed through agricultural expertise.

Former colleagues John Reisner and Cornell professor of plant breeding Harry Love began to discuss their ideas for institutionalizing agricultural knowledge and bringing the benefits of university research to missionaries working abroad. They started with their home institutions and founded the Nanking-Cornell Crop Improvement Program, which Love would later claim to be the earliest instance of international technical cooperation between two universities in agricultural development. Supported by the International Education Board, which was also funded by the Rockefeller Foundation, the Nanking-Cornell venture aspired to two goals: to select and breed varieties of staple food crops of the famine-prone areas in China that would produce increased yields, demonstrate higher resistance to disease, and be more easily planted and farmed; and to train men in the "principles, methods, application and organization of crop improvement."[28] The cooperative program sent Cornell faculty to Nanking University over a course of seven years, with three Cornell professors making trips to China.

The Nanking-Cornell program set its sights high. It implicitly addressed a social goal in outlining their scientific undertaking. In writing to Love requesting that Cornell dispatch one of its plant breeding scientists, Reisner was clear in the type of personnel he needed: "a man not only of ability, but of experience and one who is able to see the larger implications."[29] In other words, Reisner hoped Cornell would send someone who was not just interested in breeding a better plant, but also the mission of helping others.

The Nanking-Cornell program began field tests of popular local crops—wheat, rice, soybean, millet, barley—that formed the staple of Chinese diets. Reisner realized quickly, however, that plant breeding alone did little to ameliorate the social conditions in China. Brayton C. Case, an agricultural missionary in Burma who visited Reisner in China, relayed Reisner's observations in 1929 after five years of helping to train and direct the Nanking University plant breeding department. One was an anecdote of a village pastor who had come to the College of Agriculture at Nanking University seeking help for his rice-growing village that suffered from regular famine. After one of the College of Agriculture instructors examined the pastor's home village, the instructor advised the pastor to switch his village to sericulture production. Though new to sericulture, the villagers, after training at Nanking, were able to properly grow mulberry, rear silkworms, and most impressively, form credit cooperatives to fund their enterprise.

It is unclear whether this anecdote was apocryphal. Neither a village name nor other details were provided. The anecdote is relayed by Case, who heard it from Reisner, who in turn heard it from an extension instructor.[30] The story oversimplified the circumstances and complexities of village level production; switching a village from one economic commodity to another likely entailed significant risk and encountered problems and very possibly produced negative unforeseen consequences (environmental, social, economic). Credit cooperatives are even more complicated, involving financial commitments and trust. Still, it was nonetheless illustrative of how experts and scientists like Reisner perceived of change in a social context stemming from a matter of the technical, in this case, knowledge dissemination. Reisner believed firmly in the power of agricultural extension. "In China," Case paraphrases Reisner, "there is great need of further research to gain knowledge for solving her agricultural difficulties, as well as the need of developing extension work to have this knowledge applied by the people to their agricultural practices."[31] Dissemination of knowledge was placed on the same level of importance as research.

The final Cornell faculty member left Nanking in 1931. After that, the Nanking-Cornell story was co-opted by the Cornellians in Ithaca and celebrated as a success for agricultural development. Decades later, agricultural economist and the dean of Cornell's College of Agriculture, William I. Meyers, stated he had been told by a State Department official that President Truman's Point Four Program, the first US-led international development program, was influenced by the success of the Nanking-Cornell program. No evidence was provided to back this statement, though it is possible. Regardless, the crop varieties out of the Nanking-Cornell program did not lift China out of famine, in an unsurprising foreshadowing of development to come, given the looming Second Sino-Japanese War.

In the United States, the Nanking-Cornell program also led to changes at Cornell. Seeing the success of the joint venture at increasing international intellectual dialogue and at attracting bright Chinese students and faculty, the faculty of the plant breeding department saw that agricultural science had great potential in the world beyond the United States and began to expand their horizons beyond China. Ralph Felton, another professor of agricultural science at Cornell University, started a foundation dedicated to training missionaries going abroad in agricultural methods—the Agriculture Education Foundation. In 1929, after discussion with "agricultural missionaries" with formal training in agricultural sciences and returning from places like Burma, Brazil, and Africa, Felton and a group of likeminded colleagues from well-established missionary organizations—the International YMCA and the Stokes Fund—began "a united effort to strengthen the work of Agricultural Missions." The theory behind the foundation reflected a belief, expressed by the former commissioner of education for Alabama and later director of the Stokes Fund, that "mission work needed more than anything else an increased emphasis on Agricultural Education."[32] Felton took this belief to heart and recruited fellow colleagues at Cornell, including fellow faculty member and Nanking-Cornell founder, Harry Love.

Love, Felton, and two other colleagues started the Agriculture Education Foundation. Harry Love was chosen by the group as its president; Felton became its first secretary. They set a goal to endow one million dollars, of which interest would be spent annually to support missionary activities in agricultural teaching. More importantly, the goals of their enterprise had to be specific—the institution had to help the farmer out "in a practical way," which meant demonstration farming and tailoring the methods in each country to their specific needs, whether that entailed an emphasis on research, resident teaching, or agricultural extension.[33] Practically speaking, the organization sought to work within the confines of existing missionary groups. It would seek to extend its help where it was wanted by local agricultural missionaries, cooperate with missions abroad, and rely on the expertise of Felton's friend Warren Bristol at the International YMCA to begin fundraising.

As part of its efforts at practical dissemination, the foundation, which later became the Agricultural Missions Foundation and Agricultural Missions Incorporated, organized annual workshops for missionaries going abroad. For over two decades until the late 1940s, Cornell became the host to the Cornell Annual School for Missionaries. As the introductory paragraph of the brochure for the twelfth iteration of the school explained, "Now more than ever before, the problems of missionaries during the next few years are likely to be bound up with the everyday living of the men, women, and children of the communities where they work. Problems of nutrition, food supply and sanitation, and of family life and community-social relationships will be paramount in most parts of the world."[34] As the paragraph hinted, course curricula and faculty specialties included a spectrum of academic disciplines that would later inform the various "schools" of development, from the high sciences of plant pathology and soil conservation to the sociologically oriented family life, rural community organization, and rural education that would form the backbone of community development. Among the list of participants included Presbyterian, Congregationalist, Lutheran, Episcopal, and Methodist denominations, and its missions from Tianjin to Santiago to Uttar Pradesh.[35] As the academic ground for such missionary training, Cornell became an important center of knowledge dissemination abroad. The practices carried on by the earliest agricultural missionaries were crucial in creating a model of agricultural development based on education, extension, and research. These models set important precedents, which in the case of China persisted by means of institutionalization and the seniority of practitioners who later became the technocrats in charge of American and Chinese led efforts.

RURAL SOCIAL MOVEMENTS

Although American missionary and philanthropic organizations were key predecessors for development in China, there were more projects aimed at development initiated and led by Chinese intellectuals and reformers. Chinese groups independent of the state had worked in famine relief during the Qing and earlier.[36] Intellectuals at Chinese universities had also written on and worked within the Nationalist government to enact social reform aimed at rural improvement. Two organizations would later prove particularly important in their roles as models and intellectual schools for later development—the Chinese National Association of the Mass Education movement (中華平民教育促進會, Zhonghua Pingmin Jiaoyu Cujinhui) (MEM) and the National Agricultural Research Bureau (中央農業實驗所, Zhongyang Nongye Shiyansuo) (NARB). Both institutions represented a continuity in religion and science, the former out of Christian education missions, including the YMCA, and the latter out of the Nanking University College of Agriculture and Forestry and its cooperative program with Cornell.

The Mass Education movement began under the leadership of Yan Yangchu (晏陽初, James Y. C. Yen), a social reformer who believed that literacy should be the basis for rural development. Yan hailed from rural Sichuan, and as a young man, he learned English at a Christian missionary school in Sichuan.[37] He went abroad for his university education, studying history and politics first at Yale and then at Princeton. After graduation, he served as a volunteer with the YMCA in France, serving the Chinese laborers who were dispatched to the front to help support the war effort. There, helping the illiterate Chinese laborers pen letters home, Yan became convinced that literacy would lift the rural masses of China out of poverty, and, as the MEM would later adopt as its slogan, "eliminate illiteracy and make new citizens for China" (除文盲作新民 chu wenmang zuo xinmin).[38] After WWI, Yan returned to China and started the Mass Education movement, creating first a "model" village to demonstrate the practices of literacy, public health, and farming education at Ding County (定縣) in north China and later, after the outbreak of the Sino-Japanese War, in Hunan and Sichuan. MEM included among its board some of the most well-known Chinese intellectuals and government officials, including minister of education and Peking University president Jiang Menglin (蔣夢麟, Chiang Mon-lin), later crucial in development on Taiwan, as well as the minister of labor and commerce and the minister of health, who all three had corresponded with Yan regarding the possible contribution of a MEM model to improving national education, public health, and labor value.

The MEM model relied upon villages as units of cohesion and instruction. Ding County the first experimental village of MEM, had around two hundred inhabitants in 1930. MEM workers would teach the principles that Yan had prioritized, which in 1930 began with literacy and education, then agriculture and economic reconstruction, and finally village self-government and "citizenship training."[39] In many reports and published materials, these would be boiled down to four principles that were used to sell the idea of the MEM to donors and potential donors: "Cultural Education, Economic Improvement, Public Health and Citizenship Training."[40] In literacy education, Yan relied on what was called the "1,000 Character Primer," a set of four books consisting of one thousand Chinese characters each, starting with the most commonly used. Unlike other literacy textbooks at the time, which were geared to a classical or literary usage of Chinese, Yan specifically designed his textbooks to provide practical literacy, meaning beginning with vernacular vocabulary that would be common in a rural population.

Yan also believed in the importance of public health, and the MEM had recruited figures like PUMC graduate Chen Zhiqian (陳志潛, C. C. Chen) to help draw up the public health program. As concepts of hygiene and preventative medical practices to halt the spread of sanitation-triggered contagions began to circulate among health officials in China, including those trained from PUMC, MEM incorporated these concepts into its village education. In one example of how public health was taught, Yan outlines in a letter to funders that Ding County seized on "market days" when villagers from ten or twenty *li* away would come to a MEM demonstration village. On market day, MEM organizers would seek help from the local army, students and teachers, the district magistrate, and village elders in order to prepare "the usual campaign posters, very pointed illustrations of common sources of infection; there were parades headed by the military band, there were speeches and little dramas, lantern slides, health motion pictures, and even radio!"[41] In explaining the reason for choosing a community-based path of public health, Chen Zhiqian incorporated a critique of Western methods. In a 1933 report, he quoted a National Health Administration report that outlined the lack of medical professionals outside of large urban centers and the predominance of private or missionary hospitals. Chen lamented the "imposition of the Western practice of private practice" in China, using almost socialist tones to describe the "wasteful line of individual competition" that system had engendered. Instead, Chen pushed for the MEM system as an alternative that still utilized "scientific medicine" but brought it to what he estimated to be 85 percent of the Chinese population, which were farmers in the rural hinterland.[42]

MEM joined forces with five local universities in north China to form the North China Council of Rural Reconstruction (華北鄉村建設協進會, Huabei Xiangcun Jianshe Xiejinhui), which would eventually be renamed the National Council for Rural Reconstruction (全國鄉村建設委員會, Quanguo Xiangcun Jianshe Weiyuanhui) (NCRR).[43] By 1936, the operation at Ding County had attracted the displeasure of local officials who clashed with Yan. Yan departed Ding County to set up in Sichuan and Hunan, but he left some operations to NCRR, which continued to operate in north China even after the outbreak of the Sino-Japanese War and under occupation by the Japanese administration. NCRR operated model villages like Ding County in other areas throughout north China. Eventually, the idea of "rural reconstruction" would become commonplace. As historian Kate Merkel-Hess has demonstrated, rural reconstruction became adopted during the Republican era by nearly every provincial governor (or "warlord," as they were more commonly known), in addition to the Nationalist government. Yan's MEM operations in Sichuan would also grow throughout the 1930s, though after war broke out with Japan, Yan spent most of his time in the United States to lobby the US government. Out of those efforts arose the US-China Aid Act of 1948, to be discussed below.

NATIONAL AGRICULTURAL RESEARCH BUREAU

Though the Nanking-Cornell program was able to send only three Cornell faculty members to Nanking, its impact on development outlasted the tenure of its exchange program, in both intended and unseen ways. As Rockefeller Foundation official George Vincent earlier pointed out with the PUMC model and as Reisner and Love had hoped to establish a similar institution, the men who emerged from the Nanking-Cornell program would later prove to be crucial to directing development in late Republican China and Taiwan. Chinese students had boarded ships for Europe, Japan, and the United States in search of higher education abroad since the late Qing and earlier, but those students were largely the products of upper-class, elite, and literati families who had the financial means to support studies abroad. Many of the students already had spent years in missionary run schools in the United States, giving them an advantage through familiarity with Western languages and cultural exposure through religious study. Contrary to these existing pathways, the Nanking-Cornell program institutionalized a level of exchange that helped attract donor funding for graduate studies in the United States, especially from organizations like the Rockefeller Foundation, and made short-term and longer term studies at Cornell a recurring and even expected pathway for promising Nanking graduate students. Though also often hailing from wealthier families, few Nanking students had the luxury of missionary school training, and even fewer had the financial means to study at an institution like Cornell.

One prominent exception to this pathway was nonetheless still a product of the Nanking-Cornell program and later would become a fervent supporter of this pipeline. Shen Zonghan (沈宗瀚, Shen Tsung-han or T. H. Shen), a Zhejiang native born in 1895, had, as a fresh college graduate, borrowed money from a friend to pursue graduate studies in agriculture in the United States, first at the University of Georgia and then for his PhD at Cornell University. After obtaining his PhD, for which he studied wheat breeding, he decided to return as a faculty member at Nanking University, working with his former teachers in the Nanking-Cornell program. By 1930, Shen had become the head of the Agronomy Department in the College of Agriculture and Forestry at Nanking University.[44]

In the mid 1930s, many of the faculty members at Nanking, including Shen, continued on to work in the National Agricultural Research Bureau that proved a spiritual successor to the Nanking-Cornell program. The NARB was a central Nationalist government–funded bureau founded in 1933 in Nanjing.[45] By 1938, ten agricultural institutions throughout China had become subsumed under the NARB umbrella, with Nanjing serving as the central office overseeing provincial agricultural institutes and stations.[46] Its directors included Xie Jiasheng (謝家聲, K. S. Sie), like Shen a Cornell graduate and a former Nanking faculty member, and eventually Shen himself, who would take over for Xie as director in the last years of NARB. Like Nanking University, the NARB included divisions that specialized in field surveys to collect crop species and experiment stations throughout the provinces of China to select and breed crops best suited for local conditions. But while Nanking University placed great emphasis on training future agricultural scientists and extension workers in addition to its basic and applied research, the NARB focused less on the educational mission and more on basic and applied research, as well as the social mission of a government bureau tasked with agricultural development. For Shen and others who had left Nanking to join the NARB, they felt "a certain responsibility toward the bureau," in part because they were involved with its creation and because they believed in the value of science toward helping society improve as a whole.[47]

The NARB reflected a social mission from its roots with Nanking-Cornell through its increased emphasis on extension work. In one proposal seeking funding from the Rockefeller Foundation for insect control work at NARB, basic and applied research was combined with extension in pursuit of the goal of increasing industrial and food crop production in inland provinces.[48] The proposal outlined typical basic science goals; item five, for example, was for "continued research on the cottonseed-oil emulsion and the testing of other plant oils for the preparation of emulsions." But applied research—"continued research on the construction of other types of sprayer" used to apply pesticides—took equal footing. This was in conjunction with an increase in the size of the machine shop currently producing two types of sprayers. And at the extension end, it was complemented with control campaigns across five provinces to demonstrate use of sprayers, pesticides, and dusters, all under the umbrella of insect control methods.[49]

The pesticide extension system became a point of pride later for the NARB. In a report describing the network of research institutions affiliated with the NARB in 1946, Shen, who by then was NARB director, took special care to highlight the achievements of extension in rural China. The National Pesticides and Experimental Equipment Plant in Sichuan, for example, whose founding Shen attributed to work on pesticide and extension research conducted at NARB as early as 1935, was a crucial apparatus, Shen explained, at the head of the system for distributing pesticides and sprayers. Below the plant was one major provincial station with substations serving important counties. At the local level, "the rural agencies which are the distributing centers for the pesticides and sprayers are taken over by the farmers themselves, primary school teachers, drug-store keepers, or post office men" paid on a commission basis and under supervision from extension workers, a system Shen pointed out is similar to the "key farmers" (farmers who served as contacts for extension workers) in the US agricultural extension system.[50]

Equally important to the NARB mission was the legacy of Nanking in applied and basic research. One report from the Rockefeller officers in Shanghai called the NARB "without doubt one of the outstanding technical bureaus of the Chinese Government" with "well trained, competent, and industrious" personnel and in addition noted its progress in insect control research over a relatively short period.[51] In later years, Shen reminisced upon the ability of the NARB to both innovate new technologies and push those new technologies out. In a 1952 letter to UN Food and Agriculture Organization official H. L. Richardson four years after his departure from NARB, Shen lamented the lack of "college training and fundamental research" done by NARB successor organization, the Joint Commission on Rural Reconstruction (JCRR), which as a result made the JCRR "not so creative" in comparison to the NARB.[52]

POSTWAR REIMAGININGS: THE CHINESE NATIONAL RELIEF AND REHABILITATION ADMINISTRATION

The outbreak of the Second Sino-Japanese War and later World War II hindered the work of famine relief. It also prompted new models and approaches to agrarian development. As World War II reached a high point, both China and the United States began to consider the issue of postwar recovery. By 1943, intellectuals and bureaucrats throughout China had begun to discuss the need to begin tackling postwar issues. The American embassy in Chongqing followed these discussions, forwarding conversation summaries, editorial translations, and relevant commentary to the State Department. Food and relief was a common subject though varied in terms of its relative importance depending on the background of the commentator. International relations scholar Zhang Zhongfu (張忠紱, Chang Chung-fu) penned an editorial in the *China Times* in 1943 that was then translated and forwarded to Secretary of State Cordell Hull. The editorial discussed the importance of tackling potential postwar issues through the establishment of the United Nations. While issues such as international economics and territorial adjustments were complicated matters, he argued issues like food and relief could "easily be agreed upon in separate conferences" since they were "simpler."[53] Zhang's envisioning of food and relief indeed came to fruition in the short lived United Nations Relief and Rehabilitation Administration (UNRRA) and later the UN Food Agriculture Organization (FAO), which for its first few years of existence largely consisted of the "separate conferences" that Zhang had described. But the lessons of UNRRA would provide an impetus not only for the growth of FAO but more importantly for US planners as they realized the importance of food and relief to international relations.

Of greater relevance were the commentators of China's economic development. With China being predominantly an agrarian society, food and agriculture could not be ignored. Some academics and technocrats focused on larger-picture, regional solutions, though they were vague on specific technical recommendations. One, Zhang Qiyun (張其昀, Chang G. Yun), the head of the History and Geography department at Zhejiang University, perceived of China as regions—the northwest, southwest, northeast, and so on—that would specialize in its relative advantage, whether soybean production in the northeast or oil drilling in Gansu. Another, Dong Shijin (董時進, Tung Shih-tsin), an agronomist at Peking University, argued for the importance of the agricultural sector for the overall industrialization and welfare of the Chinese economy. In an article published in *Dagong Bao* (大公報, *Ta Kung Pao*), Dong pointed out that if anything, the Sino-Japanese War has shown the importance of having a "modern country." To shed its label as "a land of famine," China needed to raise the living standard of all Chinese, meaning providing enough food and clothing, and that necessitated an emphasis in improved agriculture. Despite all the discussion among intellectuals for industrialization, Dong reminded readers that in China, "industrialization should be built on the foundation of agriculture. It means better industrial development in addition to better agriculture. Industry cannot replace agriculture." He illustrated his point through the example of cotton, a raw product produced by China's agriculture that was utilized as an input into China's industries and complete as a finished product ready for export.[54]

The head of the National Resources Commission (國家資源委員會, Guojia Ziyuan Weiyuanhui) and the minister of economic affairs at the time, Weng Wenhao (翁文灝, Wong Wen-hao), had a more concrete plan for agriculture. Weng was concerned from an industrial point of view, and specifically with regards to resource inputs and production outputs. With regard to agriculture, Weng was a pragmatist—he believed that improvements in farm implements would be slow to take up in the Chinese context "not only because of the small size of farms but also because of the conservatism of farmers."[55] Weng was correct to an extent. High peasant population density and, in many parts of China, the inelastic supply of arable land meant that economies of scale would not benefit as greatly from the use of labor-saving technologies as other types of agricultural economies. But his doubts over the willingness of Chinese farmers to adopt new technologies was one of the major driving factors behind the shift to agricultural education and extension among projects like Nanking-Cornell and others to follow. At that point, however, the editorials proved to shape the discussions of American post-war reconstruction efforts in China.

In the United States, with the end of the war on the horizon, an internationalist consensus began to reemerge among policy planners. Roosevelt and Secretary of State Hull envisioned an international system with the United States taking an active role. As part of this vision, the United States would have needed to take a role in helping rebuild the war torn regions of the world.[56] One of the earliest manifestations of this idea was UNRRA, to which the United States contributed significant personnel, funding, and administrative direction. Historian Micah Muscolino has explored the role of UNRRA in reconstructing China's war-devastated landscape, in particular formerly productive arable land rendered uninhabitable when flooded by unintentional and intentional damage to China's hydraulic infrastructure, triggering a refugee crisis and lost harvests.[57] Food shortages were further exacerbated due to a shortfall in domestic fertilizer production and damaged logistical infrastructure (roads, railroads, and ports) resulting from the Sino-Japanese War that prevented imported food and agricultural supplies from reaching areas of greatest need.[58] Reflecting the ideas of both Dong and Weng, as well as requests from the Chinese government, which specifically sought American expertise, UNRRA placed a heavy emphasis on agricultural rehabilitation to repair the damage caused by the Sino-Japanese War.[59] It stepped in by sending personnel to distribute to farmers in need of fertilizer supplies and basic agricultural goods such as flour . In contrast with the religious missions and philanthropic organizations of the past, UNRRA was a direct state-to-state reconstruction project on a national scale. Its ambitions and arguably its shortcomings stem from the reconstruction approach that called for short-term relief on a national scale performed by a neutral third party that would have little ability to enact genuine structural change.

As part of its efforts, UNRRA recruited American agricultural scientists who had previously spent their careers in the United States. One such was William J. Green, representative of the American agricultural scientist of the New Deal era. Green was born and raised in the American Midwest and trained in agronomy and agricultural economics at the rising land-grant colleges throughout the Midwest: Oklahoma State University, Texas A&M, and the US Department of Agriculture Graduate School. He began his career in the Agricultural Adjustment Administration and Farm Security Administration, working in Washington, DC, and in the farming heartland of America in the Midwest.[60] With the success of New Deal programs and agricultural advances in the United States, the US Department of Agriculture had difficulty justifying the cost of its programs. In other words, American agricultural scientists were victims of their own success. Thus, when UNRRA came calling with an opportunity for agricultural experts to work abroad, scientists like Green jumped at the chance. Green would serve as the chief of the Agricultural Rehabilitation section in UNRRA China office and dictated how UNRRA funding should be spent to help China recover its agricultural regions to prewar levels.

While agricultural advisers like Green came to China full of ideas of the potential of reconstruction for China's future, the reality was that China had problems that ran far deeper than the United States had experienced since the Civil War. China had emerged from one war, lasting over eight years in some regions, and was immediately engaged in a new one as the Nationalist state attempted to eliminate the Communist forces that were spreading from northwest China. With basic agricultural necessities such as fertilizer in short supply and infrastructure over the vast hinterland making distribution difficult even in times of peace, UNRRA struggled to meet even its first stated goal of relief, much less to speak of reconstruction during civil war and revolution. Furthermore, UNRRA's budget was meager compared to the vast needs of rehabilitation across the world.[61] UNRRA's scope was global, and China, despite having suffered massive human displacement in the Second Sino-Japanese War, was deprioritized in favor of Europe.[62] UNRRA's ostensibly nonpolitical operating mission meant that it was obliged to service both Nationalist-controlled and Communist-controlled areas equally, distributing aid only in accordance with the need of the populace.[63] In one instance serving on an official UNRRA mission, Green's jeep convoy was mistaken as having been a Nationalist government convoy, surrounded by the Communist Second Army, and taken into custody. When the commanding general was called to camp and realized his fortune upon having captured highly ranked American UNRRA officials, he immediately set them free, sent for Zhou Enlai, and threw an impromptu celebration complete with banners wishing President Truman well, all in the hopes of currying favor among the Americans to provide greater support for Communist-controlled areas. Though this case ended in a somewhat jovial situation, it exemplified the challenging political situation facing the UNRRA mission.[64]

From the outset, the UNRRA mission appeared destined to be a classic case of development—an idealistic mission that promised miracles through Western manpower, knowledge, and funds to deliver the masses of famished and fatigued from the weariness of war, yet its one-size-fits-all solution did not fit the specific circumstances under which it would operate and, most critically, was unable to address the political realities that underlay the problems it was attempting to ameliorate. The Nationalist government, realizing the difficulty that UNRRA would face, established a sister organization, the Chinese National Relief and Rehabilitation Administration (CNRRA), designed to serve as the local agents of development. CNRRA would oversee distribution and report circumstances on the ground. Appointed to the head of CNRRA was Jiang Tingfu (蔣廷黻, Tsiang Ting-fu), a Columbia PhD graduate who had joined the history faculty of Tsinghua University and later was appointed as Chinese ambassador to the United Nations. Upon the inauguration of Herbert Lehman as the director-general of UNRRA in

1943, Jiang included in his remarks a brief but apt prescription for China's woes: "Of the relief and rehabilitation needs in China, transport comes first. Without transportation facilities, whatever supplies and services UNRRA might send to China, they will be piled up at the ports and will be of no use to the Chinese people."[65] Jiang's words were quite prescient.

The obstacles facing UNRRA were not just due to the consequences of war. The Americans who manned UNRRA were often not able to overcome the problem of distributing reconstruction efforts to where they were needed in China in the short window of opportunity they had. In a report from the China UNRRA office headquartered in Shanghai in 1946, it was noted that "although agricultural rehabilitation had been given No. 1 priority during the spring months, lack of [agricultural rehabilitation] personnel and supplies made it impossible to meet all the requests from regional offices. Very few [agricultural rehabilitation] supplies other than those for the Yellow River project had arrived, and UNRRA was being criticized for not having fertilizer, vegetable seeds and hand tools for distribution."[66] The Second Sino-Japanese War had devastated the infrastructure across vast swaths of China. As Micah Muscolino has shown in his study of Henan Province during the Second Sino-Japanese War, infrastructure was not only purposely targeted to inflict military losses on the enemy by both the Japanese and the Chinese, but infrastructure maintenance and repair were entirely neglected as the Chinese state conscripted able bodied men otherwise tasked with infrastructure duties to fill the ranks of its military and directed tax revenues away from maintenance and toward military expenditures.[67] The result was disastrous for China's villages and farms, hampering their ability to move food and goods, both during war and after. To make matters worse, agricultural rehabilitation had to compete with industrial rehabilitation, which the Nationalist government prioritized after the war to replenish its finances. At Shanghai, the main port of entry for UNRRA food and fertilizers, shipping traffic was so heavy as to cause delays in just offloading and preparing foods for inland transportation. For a country the size of China, basic issues such as distribution were simply too large to overcome with the manpower assigned to UNRRA.

Jiang Tingfu had even harsher words for UNRRA. In 1947, Jiang spoke bitterly to Rockefeller Foundation's officer Roger F. Evans of the CNRRA's experiences dealing with UNRRA, with Evans relaying that "of 1,000 UNRRA technicians and administrators, [Jiang] asserts that 950 Americans were generally far below the standard we could and should have supplied—romanticists, tourists, puffed-up little pencil pushers, calory-counters [sic], and chart-drawers."[68] Jiang's frustrations with UNRRA were documented by historian Rana Mitter, who pointed to the fundamental discrepancy that while UNRRA treated China as an important recipient of aid, funds were simply insufficient to meet its needs.[69] This, combined with China's postwar inflation crisis, proved another obstacle impossible to overcome and eventually prompted Jiang's resignation in 1947. Having spent less than five years in China, Green was officially recalled when UNRRA ended its mission in China in 1948 in accordance with UNRRA policy.[70] Though long-term projects at rehabilitating agricultural and rural industries and domestic production of fertilizer were handed off to the newly formed UN Food and Agriculture Organization, UNRRA nonetheless failed at its stated goals of relieving the war torn regions of China, setting up the discussion in the United States of "Who Lost China?" Though UNRRA would provide a lesson in the difficulties of the relief-importation-distribution model of development, its agricultural experts would carry these lessons to their next destinations. For many of the scientists, Green included, their transnational careers would bring them back to Asia in a number of years, the next time to Taiwan.

THE JOINT COMMISSION ON RURAL RECONSTRUCTION

Meanwhile, in 1948, the United States passed the China Aid Act. Three years after the end of World War II, the Economic Cooperation Act, more popularly known as the Marshall Plan, initiated American reconstruction aid to Europe and established the Economic Cooperation Administration, the predecessor to the current day US Agency for International Development. The China Aid Act of 1948 provided equivalent assistance, albeit a significantly smaller sum, for China, lobbied heavily by Yan Yangchu who had been living in Washington, DC, for much of the Chinese Civil War. The result of the China Aid Act was the Sino-American Agricultural Mission of 1948, which aimed to establish a long-term joint cooperation committee that would provide not just the short term famine relief that UNRRA attempted, but also a long-term development project.[71] The Americans and Chinese who advised the mission, Shen Zonghan, Jiang Menglin, Yan Yangchu, Raymond T. Moyer, an Oberlin and Cornell agronomy graduate and Christian missionary who had spent significant time in Shanxi Province, and Owen L. Dawson, the agricultural attaché at the US Embassy in China, chose to follow the Rural Reconstruction movement and adopt the same name to encapsulate its purpose. In late 1948, the Sino-American Joint Commission on Rural Reconstruction (中國聯合農村復興委員會, Zhongguo Lianhe Nongcun Fuxing Weiyuanhui) (JCRR) was established. Its mission was to further development in China, focusing on rural development, and it was through this institution that China Aid Act was to disburse its significant funding.

From its onset, the JCRR was the subject of an ideological divide over how "rural reconstruction" could best be accomplished. At the heart of the debate were the goals of development—what were the best means to benefit the rural population? For Yan Yangchu, the founder of the Mass Education Movement in China, the priority should lay in four areas, a familiar four for those familiar with his MEM ideology: "(1) education, (2) livelihood, (3) health, and (4) self-government."[72] The goals he thus outlined for the JCRR were the same ones of his Mass Education movement, which was focused on improving rural life through literacy, social education, hygienic practices, and his notions of participatory citizenship in community governance.

In the middle of the spectrum was Jiang Menglin, a graduate of University of California, Berkeley, in botany and later a PhD graduate in education from Columbia, studying under John Dewey. Jiang began his education in the United States as an agricultural scientist, continuing his studies in primary education in China on botany and zoology, stemming from an interest in "observing nature." But his switch to pedagogy and education Jiang attributed to a classmate at Berkeley, who remarked that "though agriculture was very important, there were other studies more vital for China . . . without being able to solve our political and social problems in the light of modern developments in the West we could not very well solve the agricultural ones."[73] Later, the realization came as he sought to apply what he had learned in agriculture—"how to raise animals and plants"— to the social world—"how to raise men."[74] Studying alongside Hu Shi at Columbia under John Dewey, Jiang came to internalize a pragmatist view toward education, and that learned experience was crucial and practical goals were to be lauded. Jiang returned to China and became the president of the prominent Peking University, and just before being appointed to the JCRR, he served as the minister of education for the Nationalist government. Like Yan, Jiang thus believed in the importance of education for the rural population, but Jiang was less interested in literacy as the sole means of its delivery. Jiang placed more trust, as did some of the other agricultural scientists, in the dissemination of practical knowledge through agricultural extension and farmers' cooperatives.

Finally, there was Shen Zonghan. Shen believed that improving crops and methods via applied agricultural research and disseminating these better practices and crops through agricultural extension would lead to rural uplift. Shen Zonghan would eventually become one of the most important commissioners in JCRR in Taiwan, which later chapters explore. Shen's faith in science, and specifically in plant breeding, underlay most of his decision making. Shen was the high modernist of the three, the most likely to place his trust in the transformative social power of crop selection to solve the ills of famine.

Much of the intellectual forces driving the Taiwan model derived from the thoughts and experiences of JCRR commissioners and high level technocrats. Chinese commissioners Jiang Menglin, Shen Zonghan, Yan Yangchu, and their American counterparts all hailed from similar backgrounds as trained scientists and rural reformers. Ideas of reform, education, and pragmatism defined the values of the JCRR and other agricultural and rural technocrats dating back to the turn of the twentieth century. Shen Zonghan wrote in his autobiography of the influence of John Dewey's lectures in Peking University in the 1910s, which Shen attended. In his journal entry from February 7, 1919, Shen remarked on Dewey's argument that "the means by which scientific research discovers truth was nothing other than having a basis in reality, reaching truth through experimentation."[75] For Shen, Jiang Menglin, and others, the pragmatism endorsed by Dewey was realized through working with those that agricultural development was meant to aid. As Shen wrote to his wife upon taking directorship of the NARB, "I am currently dedicating myself to Chinese agricultural improvement policies, and that is how to disseminate the benefits of scientific improvement to farmers."[76]

Other ideas were discussed by prominent agricultural and rural development figures who penned editorials in prominent newspapers or sent letters to the Sino-American Agricultural Mission. Some of these advocated "national self-defense" or "political uplifting." One editorial from *Dagong Bao* feared that the diplomatic privileges offered to the American commissioners was "sacrificing Chinese sovereignty [損中國主權]" and "expanding the scope of extraterritoriality [擴大治外法權的範圍]," in effect raising the specter of continued colonialism in China.[77] The American embassy noted that almost all editorials referenced the need to "avoid the mistakes made by UNRRA and other organizations."[78]

The American-operated *Shanghai Evening Post & Mercury* titled its editorial about the impending creation of the JCRR "New Deal for Farmers," a reference to President Franklin Roosevelt's ambitious social work program in the aftermath of the Great Depression. The editorial hailed the JCRR as "the most important and magnificent event which happened to Chinese farmers during the past several hundred years." The hyperbolic praise was from a larger perspective based on the expectation that China's economic welfare, which according to the editorial derived approximately 70 percent of its exports from the agricultural sector, would improve as a whole so long as its agricultural economy prospered. It was also cautious in recognizing that the "Chinese agricultural problem is not only physically immense but it is complicated and confusing." Thus, the relatively large amount of $3.8 million USD could have been easily misspent. The editorial board thus praised the findings of the Sino-American Agricultural Mission because "instead of placing an unwarranted emphasis on any one aspect of the rural development, they sought to correlate a number of factors." In this regard, it urged against acting on an "erroneous belief that any one program or any one man could be China's rural saviour," interpreted by the American embassy as an "oblique reference" to the commissioner who was the face of the Mass Education movement, Yan Yangchu.[79]

The debates were resolved by the Chinese government through simple appointment. Despite Yan Yangchu's publicly stating his belief that he would be named director-general of the commission, Jiang Menglin was named the chairman of the five-member commission. Yan Yangchu and Shen Zonghan rounded out the three initial Chinese commissioners. Later, Raymond Moyer, Shaanxi missionary and former AACFR member, and John Earl Baker, director of famine relief in China for the Red Cross, joined as the two American commissioners.[80] Yan left the JCRR shortly thereafter for the United States, where he relocated the Mass Education

Movement and founded the International Institute of Rural Reconstruction. Just a few years later, he would turn his attention to the Philippines, organizing community development projects that emphasized improving literacy through education.[81] Yan found public admiration in the United States for his work in the Philippines after leaving China, and communication, to say nothing of intellectual exchange, with the JCRR after his departure was rare.[82]

Unfortunately, despite the potential that the JCRR had with American funding and Chinese government priority, like the UNRRA, the JCRR made little inroad into China before it was forced to leave. With the Nationalist government losing control of the mainland, it moved the government administration to Taiwan. And as American support followed Chiang's Nationalist government, so too did the JCRR follow Chiang as he fled to the island of Taiwan, a "temporary" relocation until, according to the GMD, the mainland could be won back from the Communists. For the scientists of the JCRR, Taiwan became their new home and mission.

CONCLUSION

The Republican era was characterized not only by major political events such as the consolidation of the Guomindang regime, the Second Sino-Japanese War, and the Communist civil war but also by intellectual and on-the-ground debates over how to battle famine and improve the livelihoods of China's predominantly rural farmers. Foreign missionaries and philanthropic organizations like the American Advisory Committee for Famine Relief and the Rockefeller Foundation contributed funding and expertise to Chinese rural reform movements and centers of agricultural science. Nanking University and the National Agricultural Research Bureau utilized global networks of agricultural science to locate new crop cultivars, select and experiment for higher yield and disease resistance, and extend them into rural areas for planting by farmers. Rural reform movements, such as the Mass Education movement and the North China Council of Rural Reconstruction, emphasized literacy, education, public health, and other forms of social improvement at the village level. These disparate groups of intellectuals, scientists, and ideas converged over the need to not just relieve famine but to prevent it, leading to the emergence of a developmentalist approach to rural China.

The intervention of war and the establishment of UNRRA and CNRRA pushed agricultural rehabilitation to a higher profile on the national level. Funding from the United States provided an opportunity in the aftermath of war, but infrastructural damage and economic and political circumstances such as the ongoing civil war and postwar inflation hindered UNRRA-CNRRA cooperation and efforts on the ground. The Sino-American Agricultural Mission provided a new opportunity with the creation of the JCRR for long-term development. The JCRR integrated the emerging paradigms among missionary, rural reform, and scientific communities in China that had been working on famine prevention.

Ultimately, the ideas articulated by these institutions resulted in a spectrum of answers to the fundamental questions of development. How can famine and hunger be eliminated? How can farmers' livelihoods be improved? And how does one bring modernity to a rural and agricultural society? Community-based, grassroots education and social reform, dissemination of knowledge through agricultural education, and modernization through agricultural sciences, represented the gamut of options that would eventually become paradigms in the Cold War period. Community development efforts by the Ford and Rockefeller Foundations in India, infrastructure construction by USAID in Afghanistan, and agricultural research by the International Rice Research Institute in the Philippines, just to name a few, would revisit the same discussions that had occurred decades earlier in China by actors who were faced with the very same dilemmas.[83]

In Taiwan, the JCRR would eventually make astounding strides in agricultural productivity, led by the increase of chemical fertilizers, the breeding of high-yield crop varietals, and the ability to disseminate those varietals and fertilizer practices through agricultural extension. The success under the JCRR proved to be one of the most consequential factors for Taiwan's emergence as a global economic power in the twentieth century, as agricultural success proved to be the spur for Taiwan's industrial miracle. As the next two chapters will discuss in detail, much of the successes and failures of the JCRR resulted from the earlier experimentation in development efforts on the mainland, taking lessons learned and not learned from missionary famine relief, MEM, Nanking University, the NARB, and the UNRRA.

2

____

Executing Contracts, Not Landlords

Capitalism through Land Reform, 1949–1968

The first step in developing agriculture in [Taiwan] was to institute land reform . . . landowners received reasonable compensation for their losses. Resistance to the policy was therefore reduced to a minimum, and land was smoothly transferred into the hands of those who tilled it.

—LEE TENG-HUI

INTRODUCTION

In 1965, future Taiwanese president Lee Teng-hui (李登輝, Li Denghui), then an agricultural economist working for the Republic of China's primary agricultural policymaking body, the Joint Commission on Rural Reconstruction (JCRR, 中國農村復興委員會, Zhongguo Nongcun Fuxing Weiyuanhui), began his graduate studies in agricultural economics at Cornell University. Three years later, Lee finished his doctoral dissertation, titled "Intersectoral Capital Flows in the Economic Development of Taiwan, 1895–1960." The dissertation examined resources flowing out of and into the rural and agricultural sector, arguing that these contributed to growth in other sectors of the economy and thus overall development.[1] It won the American Agricultural Economics Association award for outstanding doctoral dissertation.[2] Economists at the time lauded Lee's work for demonstrating how a predominantly agricultural economy could quickly transform into a successful case of industrial development, based on the example of Taiwan. Capital, specifically how the agricultural sector could provide the necessary capital for economic development, was the central guiding theme of both Lee's doctoral research as well as a prevailing question in agricultural economics.

Two decades before Lee began his graduate studies, the Nationalist government seized control of Taiwan at the end of World War II, occupying an island that had served for centuries as an agricultural colony, exporting sugar, camphor, and rice for the Dutch East India Company, then the Qing Empire, and finally the Japanese

42

Empire. By the end of a half-century of Japanese rule, Taiwan had become a bread-basket for Japanese territories, exporting rice to feed an empire. In 1949, at the end of the Chinese Civil War, the defeat of the Nationalists by the Chinese Communist Party not only led to the exodus of the Nationalist government and over a million refugees to Taiwan but also sparked a political transformation within the Guomindang party-state and in Taiwanese society. Taiwan became a laboratory for a new form of capitalist development, focused on transforming the most ardent symbols of traditional rural society: land and the landlord-peasant relationship. The Nationalist government's land reform program in the 1950s attempted to turn landlords into industrial capitalists, tenant farmers into petty capitalists, and land into financial capital. This all happened in the backdrop of the Guomindang's bitter defeat to Communism and the beginnings of authoritarian settler colonialism on Taiwan.

Lee attributes much of the success in capital formation for Taiwan's miraculous industrial growth in the late 1960s and early 1970s to agricultural development, including land reform. From 1948 to 1953, the authoritarian Guomindang regime on Taiwan carried out land reform in three stages: setting a ceiling on land rent, selling public lands to private owners, and forcing sales of land from large landowners to tenant farmers, better known as "land-to-the-tiller"

This series of land reforms was historically significant. Economists attributed land reform to not only freeing up capital and labor but also encouraging new smallholders to invest in their lands with fertilizer usage and capital investments, which previously they were disincentivized from doing as tenants.[3] This narrative of land reform has become orthodoxy, reinforced by economists and enshrined in the popular imagination, perhaps best exemplified by Joe Studwell in *How Asia Works*.[4] Yet Studwell and the orthodox narrative of land reform offer an uncritical and incomplete narrative. Studwell ignores land reform's disciplining of Taiwan's rural society backed by martial law and overemphasizes the gains from land ownership over the gains from factors, thus mistaking correlation for causation. A recent quantitative study by Oliver Kim and Jen-Kuan Wang has shown that postwar agricultural productivity in Taiwan was the result of factors aside from giving farmers ownership of the land they tilled, such as chemical inputs.[5] Yet Lee and others in the GMD valorized land reform because of the political value it provided for the tenuous, new settler-colonial power GMD on Taiwan—securing the regime's legitimacy.

A major work espousing the miracle narrative of land reform was published in 1961, when Chen Cheng (陳誠) authored the English-language *Land Reform in Taiwan*.[6] Chen served as governor of Taiwan's provincial government under the Guomindang regime on Taiwan and later was promoted to premier of the Republic of China in 1950 and finally vice president in 1954. Chen had risen through the ranks primarily as a military official, a graduate of the prestigious Baoding (保定)

and Whampoa (黃埔, Huangpu) academies and a longtime general under Chiang Kai-shek serving through the Northern Expedition, the Civil War with the Chinese Communist Party, and the Second Sino-Japanese War.[7] Chen Cheng's tenure in Taiwan was defined by overseeing this three-stage land reform program. In the book, Chen focused on land reform's twofold importance: for the social welfare of the rural farmers and for overall economic growth. By the second paragraph of the book, Chen characterized the "vicious cycle" of two thousand years of Chinese history as essentially a Malthusian problem: "Whenever population increased to a point where land was insufficient, violent uprisings broke out and civil wars ensued. But with resulting reduction of population and restoration of the land-population equilibrium, another period of social and political stability would begin." Thomas Robert Malthus, the classical economist who focused on the relationship between population and land, became influential throughout the history of development. Malthusian theories pushed economists and policymakers to fear that population would outstrip food supply over time, leading to inevitable poverty and famine. In addition to discussing land-population equilibrium, Chen argued that "in a country where the economy is predominantly agricultural, capital investment in land and the exploitation of human labor constitute great impediments to such development. We must begin by setting capital and labour free through land reform."[8] *Land Reform in Taiwan* was replete with economic examples that showcase the technocratic principles behind land reform on Taiwan. Land reform, however, was not just an economic issue.

Land reform became a political symbol for the GMD. As historian Brian DeMare and political scientist Julia Strauss have argued, land reform was a primary means through which both the PRC and ROC states performed their regime values to the masses, sometimes backed by violence.[9] In GMD-produced propaganda and state-imposed discourse, land reform represented both the social welfarist principles of GMD political ideology and GMD expertise at development. As Lawrence Zi-Qiao Yang has argued, the GMD elite were haunted by their inability to secure rural China against Communist uprising, a failure that animated GMD land reform policies.[10] Yet as this chapter will show, this narrative of land reform was a constructed discourse, designed to further GMD political objectives to portray itself as a modern, technocratic yet welfarist state.[11] And it conveniently omits that GMD land reform dismantled a potential obstacle to GMD rule: the large Taiwanese landowners whose social and economic capital posed a risk to GMD colonial rule.

The Guomindang's land reform espoused in particular an ideology of capitalism, which I define as a system that reorders society and nature toward the ceaseless pursuit of capital expansion and profit maximization. For the GMD, land reform was intended to enact a new system of capitalism in which land could be unlocked to produce ever greater returns through its commodification and transformation into capital. Emerging scholarship from "new histories of capitalism" in the past several decades have also shifted our gaze toward the social histories of economic lives. Indeed, GMD-enacted land reform did not just seek to commoditize land but also to reengineer rural society by disciplining landlords and peasants and transforming them into capitalists.[12] From new histories of capitalism, we see how capitalism often enabled oppressive state regimes, introducing "technical" concepts like risk, growth, and accounting that in fact reflected growing anxieties over the uncertainty of modern capitalism, entrenched structural racism and institutions such as slavery, and privileged the discourse of (unsustainable) growth and investmentality.[13] GMD land reform was likewise expressed in the technocratic language of standardization, productivity, incentives, contracts, and financial instruments. It also generated social inequalities in its implementation, which GMD state narratives suppressed in favor of a utopian narrative of capitalist modernity and technocracy.[14]

Taiwanese land reform was intended to demonstrate that capitalism was fundamentally a vehicle for social well-being and advancing class interests, not counter to the needs of landless peasant. In this conception, land could be redistributed in a win-win manner, allowing landlords to transition to industrial capital and giving peasants an opportunity to become agricultural capitalists. The state ostensibly won too, because land that was transformed to capital could then be transferred into the industrial sector, where former landlords would become financiers of the future industrialized Taiwan, that would in turn enrich state coffers and strengthen the GMD regime. GMD planners positioned their actions in distinction to land reform across the strait, where Chinese Communists practiced a more violent reform based on class struggle. As Shih-Jung Hsu and Michael Hsin-Huang Hsiao have argued, the GMD's incitement of fear of violent Communist revolution intimidated landlords in Taiwan and made them more compliant to GMD land reform.[15] In contrast to Communist land reform wherein landlords were publicly executed, the GMD portrayal of its government focused on the execution of carefully state-vetted land and bond contracts that ostensibly benefitted both former tenants (the buyers) and dispossessed landlords (the sellers). In effect, the GMD was both battling Communism and demonstrating the superiority of its capitalist alternative.

Land reform was integral to GMD efforts to reterritorialize Taiwan. Capitalism was a crucial foundation for the developmentalist identity of the GMD on Taiwan, going hand in hand with its modernist vision founded on technology, science, and wealth. Land reform transformed the physical landscape of Taiwan, turning its mishmash of usufructuary land rights and natural topologies that were hitherto relatively illegible to the state into a rational system consisting of valuations and transferrable contracts. This was the realization of the GMD vision for a capitalist system whose growth could be taxed for the military and economic needs of the state. This new landscape may be conceptualized as a "capitalscape," a spatial reterritorialization occurring in what Jason Moore has termed the "Capitalocene" to describe the emergence of capitalism as the central system mediating humanity in nature.[16]

LAND REFORM AS POLITICAL DISCOURSE

The Guomindang traces its own history on land reform to the early twentieth century through speeches and writings by Sun Yat-sen (孫中山, Sun Zhongshan). Sun, the founding president of the Republic of China, perhaps the most famous Chinese revolutionary after Mao Zedong and the "Father of China," outlined at various points through his early career the so-called Three Principles of the People (三民主義, Sanmin zhuyi). Historian Marie-Claire Bergère has argued that the Three Principles was more of a malleable political ideology than a rigorous political theory, expediently subservient to the political needs of Sun and later to Chiang and other GMD leaders. One of the Three Principles, Minsheng zhuyi (民生主義), usually translated as the people's livelihood, articulated a basic idea of land reform. Sun described this as land equalization accomplished through "taxing unearned increments from the sale of urban or suburban land, with a view to slowing down building speculation."[17] Bergère has astutely raised this was not the land redistribution that would become the predominant understanding of land reform in the 1960s, but rather a moderate form of an economic school of thought that emerged in the United States in the late nineteenth century, Georgism.

Georgism is the economic thought of Henry George, an American economist who argued for the implementation of a single tax on land. George argued that his single tax would help rein in land speculation and land monopolies by powerful business interests and equalize wealth among landless or smallholder farmers. In Sun's version of land reform via single taxation, landowners were to provide estimates of the value of their land, on which they would be taxed 1 percent by the state, with the understanding that the state would be able to purchase the land at its declared value. This mechanism was designed to allow fair taxation on land values such that underreporting would be disincentivized with the risk of state acquisition. Other Chinese intellectuals in Sun's circle (and later prominent GMD figures), including Zhu Zhixin (朱之鑫) and Feng Ziyou (馮自由), ardently defended this moderate Georgism from what they perceived as the more radical form of land reform espoused by socialists.[18]

In contrast with Sun Yat-sen's Georgist influenced views on land reform, Chiang Kai-shek, de facto ruler of China after the Northern Expedition (1926–28) until the Communist takeover in 1949, understood the political expediency of land redistribution. In a speech in 1932, Chiang argued for the importance of land reform as a "fundamental problem of China" in light of the early battles against the entrenched Jiangxi Soviet led by the fledgling Chinese Communist Party and later attempted to rival some of the Jiangxi Soviet reforms by attempting land redistribution in reclaimed Jiangxi territories.[19] However, as biographer Jay Taylor has argued, land reform during the Republican era under Chiang was markedly conservative. Land reform entailed purchasing of lands as they went on sale and organizing cooperatives that would allow renting land to the landless but not the forced seizure of land from landowners and redistribution to the landless as the Communists had enacted in the Jiangxi Soviets.[20] In Taylor's formulation, this was not merely Chiang and the GMD paying lip service to land reform but rather the desire to moderate their actions so as to not upset existing social order. Other historians, like Stephen Averill, have also posited revisionist accounts of the GMD, arguing that GMD desires for land reform were genuine but that they failed to take hold.[21] In reality, land tenure and ownership during Republican-era China involved multiple layers of local and regional power and politics. In a state as large and disparate as China, the Guomindang lacked strong central authority for forced land seizure and redistribution without risking possible alienation of key supporters, including local elites and capitalists.[22]

There was another school of land reform within the GMD outside of Chiang and Sun, and this was primarily associated with economists Xiao Zheng (蕭錚, Hsiao Tseng) and Chen Guofu (陳果夫). Xiao was a GMD technocrat trained at Peking University and later influential in the Republican-era school of *dizheng* (地政), or land economics. As an early member of the GMD, Xiao held close personal connections with the conservative right of the GMD, especially with the so-called central club clique (中央俱樂部組織, *zhongyang julebu zuzhi*) led by brothers Chen Guofu and Chen Lifu (陳立夫). Though not a prominent figure in the early GMD, Xiao after 1949 became one of the key proponents associated with land reform in Taiwan alongside Chen Cheng. Historian Larissa Pitts has argued that the "land problem" in Republican China was a constructed phenomenon. China's rate of tenancy in 1939 at 19 percent was significantly lower than Mexico's at 79 percent and England's at 85 percent.[23] Pitts also argues that compounding the problem, the GMD Right began to champion land redistribution in spite of its identity and politics as an urban (as opposed to rural), industrial (as opposed to agrarian), and landowner/capitalist (as opposed to landless farmer) supporting entity. What would explain such a contradiction?

Land reform became the means by which competing regimes—whether the GMD, CCP, or any decolonizing regime in the world that turned to technocratic and modernizing development as a means of political legitimacy—could demonstrate their commitment to the downtrodden masses that had suddenly realized their political strength especially in the early Cold War period. Part of the construction of land reform as a political discourse included a mythologizing of Guomindang land reform commitment and ideology. This myth traced land reform to Chiang Kai-shek, Sun Yat-sen and the Three Principles, and in some sources, even as far back in history as the populist and reformist Taiping Rebellion set against the imperial Qing court. When taken in context with the politics, a far more conservative history emerges. The problem of land tenancy rates, for example, was amplified ex post facto for political purposes, to set the ground for a technical solution.

LAND REFORM IN TAIWAN

In the Taiwanese land reform narrative, the watershed moment arrived in the 1949–53 period when a series of reforms eventually culminated in a land-to-the-tiller policy where the state forced sales of large landholdings to tenant farmers. As part of the peace agreement ending the Second Sino-Japanese War, Japan transferred control of Taiwan to the Republic of China. The GMD governed Taiwan beginning in 1945, rather poorly under governor Chen Yi (陳儀), as a province of the ROC. The February 28 Incident of 1947 and the subsequent bloody quashing of island-wide unrest resulted in an oppressive forty-year period of martial law. In 1949, when the GMD retreated to the island, they in effect established rule as a settler colonial regime.

In 1948, the GMD attempted land reform in several counties on mainland China. Though the GMD lost these areas to the Communist Chinese regime just one year later, historian Wankun Li argues that GMD-led land reform in Sichuan Province achieved success in reducing rent burdens on tenant farmers. Contrary to scholarship that portrays the GMD as resistant to land reform, GMD officials in Sichuan, along with American advisers, saw land reform as important for improving rural livelihood, consolidating state control over rural areas, and strengthening local financial markets.[24] The model pioneered in Sichuan provided guiding principles for the period after the GMD fled to Taiwan. After 1949, the Nationalists faced a different set of political challenges in Taiwan. Unlike on the mainland, where the GMD was dependent on local landed gentry and elites for governing rural areas, Taiwan had operated under a half-century of Japanese imperialism. The Japanese Government-General imposed relatively effective structures of social control, such as farmers' associations with appointed officials that directed rural policies.[25] With the small size of the island, the relative ease through which the island could be administered using existing Japanese imperial structures of state control, and the million soldiers that the GMD relocated to Taiwan to maintain its authoritarian grip, the Guomindang did not derive its political legitimacy in cooperation with the Taiwanese rural landed class. In effect, this freed up the Nationalists to enact land reform without drawing the ire of political constituents.

Some histories have pointed to the agency of American advisers such as land reform expert Wolf Ladejinsky, who advised Japanese land reform with General MacArthur's SCAP (Supreme Command Allied Power) and later land reform projects in South Korea, Taiwan, and Vietnam.[26] Yet as other American-involved land reform projects have demonstrated, the largest obstacle to carrying out meaningful land reform, particularly the difficult seizure and redistribution of land from landowners, is structural.[27] In the Philippines, Vietnam, and Latin America, state willingness to address structural social issues were often lacking. Historian Al McCoy wrote in 1971 in the left-leaning academic periodical *Bulletin of Concerned Asian Scholars* that American-led land reform in Asia, contrary to publicized successes in Japan, Taiwan, and South Korea, "has been an unqualified failure." For McCoy, American interest in counter-revolutionary strategy ultimately chose to side with the landowning elites on which they depended for political support rather than the policies and processes of "genuine land reform" that breaks the power of landlords and tackles the "central problems of tenancy." This critique of "the myth of land reform as panacea" would resonate throughout the discussion of land reform in the Cold War, including in GMD rhetoric.[28] Ultimately, in many states, governments and elite interests were often intertwined and inseparable, or key government policymakers benefitted from relationships with the landowning class, so that there was little state interest in enacting meaningful land reform.

In the Taiwanese context, the GMD officials, backed by martial law and military force, were willing to challenge rural landowners. Oral histories, such as those of American JCRR commissioner Raymond Davis, who had formerly advised the SCAP in Japan, and JCRR commissioner Raymond Moyer (see chapter 1) confirm that the Guomindang and Americans both agreed on land reform, and arm-twisting like in SCAP was unnecessary.[29] However, even with a greater willingness to be at odds with the landowning class, GMD officials nonetheless attempted to co-opt landlords whenever possible. Political scientist Kevin Luo has shown that when Taiwanese landlords resisted GMD efforts to reform farmers' associations and eliminate the powerful positions that landlords held in them, the GMD did not take coercive measures to force landlords out.[30] As a later section of this chapter will show, transforming landlords into industrial capitalists would prove far more beneficial for the GMD, both in economic and political terms.

Then-governor Chen Cheng served a crucial role in land reform history. According to an oral history of then JCRR secretary Jiang Yanshi (蔣彥士, Y. S. Tsiang), the decision to enact land reform in Taiwan originated from a conversation between JCRR chairman Jiang Menglin, JCRR commissioner Robert Moyer, and Chen Cheng. The content of this conversation was simple, according to Jiang Yanshi: Were they willing to undertake land reform? According to Jiang, Chen's answer was, "I want to do it. [I] must do it" (我要做, 必須要做).[31] Jiang Yanshi later became secretary-general of the GMD and an important political figure in the party, which might call into question the veracity of this account.[32] Even if apocryphal, the story still asserts Chen's centrality in land reform, which is supported by much of the historiography. Chen was the key figure associated with the enforcement and innovation in land reform in the 1950s that became heavily mythologized in his own book and by the GMD in the 1960s and 70s as a success narrative. Chen's *Land Reform in Taiwan* became the standard narrative that shaped understandings by both Taiwanese and developing world audiences of what Taiwanese land reform was.

Land Reform in Taiwan is a product of both the Cold War and the desire of the ROC regime to portray its system as superior to the Communist system across the strait. Its final chapter makes this quite clear; it is titled "Comparison of Taiwan Land Reform with the Communist 'Land Reform,'" the use of ironic quotation marks being original. Yet a closer reading of the text reveals that the capitalist system Chen was marketing in 1961 was unique for its time, wielding not only a welfare agenda but also financial concepts, economic graphs and charts, legalistic language, and replete with the imagery and language of sociotechnical modernity.

FROM LANDSCAPE TO CAPITALSCAPE: RATIONALIZATION AND LEGIBILITY

As governor in 1949, Chen helped oversee the island-wide implementation of 375 Rent Reduction (三七五減租, Sanqiwu Jianzu). Originally promulgated as a law in 1930 in the mainland, it set a ceiling of 37.5 percent of annual crop yield as the maximum rent for land tenants. This was the first of three stages of land reforms enacted from 1949 to 1953. Chen, who for a short time served as governor of Hubei on the mainland prior to 1949, later argued in *Land Reform on Taiwan* that he and the GMD government had always wanted to implement the 375 Rent Reduction throughout the mainland and did so first in Guangdong, Hunan, Hubei, and Zhejiang.[33] The inability to successfully maintain the rent ceiling across China, he argued, was the fault of "a variety of obstacles," which, he hinted, was the outbreak of war with Japan. He further asserted that by 1940, all of Hubei was theoretically operating under the rent ceiling. For the brief period after the JCRR was established in 1948 and before it evacuated to Taiwan, the JCRR was able to successfully place limits on land rent in several counties in Sichuan.[34]

On Taiwan, as sociologists have examined, land rent was fairly onerous prior to 1949. According to statistics from Japanese colonial surveys analyzed by sociologist Chih-Ming Ka, in 1937, average rent as a percentage of annual income island-wide was 52.43 percent for prime agricultural land and 45.29 percent for lower-grade land.[35] Rent prices were not held in check by contracts and could increase by the landlord's decree on a year-to-year basis, which could create uncertainty and lead to even more difficult conditions, though Ka cites historical surveys from 1924 and 1927 that demonstrate that rent prices generally did not deviate more than a few percentage points from these numbers.[36]

In September 1949, as a special adviser to the JCRR, Wolf Ladejinsky confirmed the tenancy problem with a firsthand report. Tenancy rates were too high, land too sparse, rent too onerous, and as a result, the Taiwanese farmer suffered. "Tenancy as an agrarian institution is not an evil, but it becomes one when tenancy conditions are heavily weighted in favor of landlord against tenant. Taiwan is a case in point," Ladejinsky wrote in a memorandum to JCRR chairman Jiang Menglin. Ladejinsky condemned the exploitation of the farmer in Taiwan in no uncertain terms. In Taiwan, he perceived the potential for another Communist uprising. "One does not have to be a believer in the theory that a man's economic position determines his social and political status, but this is certainly true in tradition-bound rural Taiwan." The result of this, Ladejinsky argued, is a permanent social divide (though Ladejinsky is clear to avoid "class" as a descriptor): "The attitude of the officials of every level toward the various types of farmers is also symptomatic of the fact that as long as the tenant continues to remain in the lowly economic position, the social barriers within the community will persist." Unchecked, it would become a "fertile ground for political extremism and civil dissension."[37]

Decades prior, Japanese colonial officials had enacted a massive, island-wide land tenure reform project under the direction of Gotō Shinpei, minister of civil affairs. Japanese interests align with what James Scott would have considered making Taiwan "legible," namely, clarifying land ownership through cadastral surveys and issuing land deeds.[38] Whereas under Qing administration, land rights were divided and subdivided into multiple layers (usufruct and subsoil rights) involving different types of ownership and tenancy, the Japanese land survey simplified ownership with newly issued deeds. The legibility of space was important for Japanese colonial considerations for the purposes of collecting tax revenue, an argument mirrored by Chih-Ming Ka. Historian Paul Barclay takes this analysis further, arguing that Japanese land surveys, taxation, and deeding embodied a form of governmental rationality, borrowing from Max Weber's conception of rationality: "Weber's foregrounding of capitalism's continuously renewed commitment to positive balances captures the spirit of capitalism as an ethos but also isolates a distinctive feature of statecraft in the post dynastic era."[39] Barclay points to the Japanese desire for the island of Taiwan to be economically self-sufficient, evidenced by the black-ink balances in regular government budgets as well as the emergence of budget projections that depended on predictable, quantified revenues from land.

This capitalist drive to rationalize, quantify, and project applied to GMD policies too. The 375 Rent Reduction, in addition to capping rent at 37.5 percent of crop yield, also required landlords to lodge written contracts with township governments and established committees that would calculate annual yields from which rent prices were derived.[40] Chen Renlong (陳人龍), an official within the Land Economics Unit (地政組, Dizheng Zu) of the JCRR, stated in an oral history that one of the major contributions to land reform was in fact government expenditures to pay for salaries of the significant manpower required. Taiwan's early 1950s land reform relied heavily on the "design of the technical and the rigor of execution" (技術的設計和執行的嚴密) in conducting land surveys for "tens of millions of landlords and tenants and hundreds of thousands of hectares of arable land."[41] Chen explained that all the information amassed in surveys were then recorded on simple index cards that contained information on land and people, such that "all of the land rights holders and land usage information could be found on every land registration card" and "all of the land size and land usage information and land usage information for every landowner could be found on every land rights holder card."[42] The index cards provided a logical and simple rationalization of complicated legal relationships between peoples and land.

For Chen, the greatest challenge of 375 Rent Reduction was the usage of written contracts. Chen described pre-reform leases as being mostly constituted of verbal contracts, which were problematic because later disputes became difficult to settle. The transition to written contracts entailed rationalization and bureaucratization. Contracts were made uniform, such that details in all contracts were the same—they contained all information relating to rights and obligations and would carry over for new contracts by default. Three copies were produced for every executed contract, one for each party and a third copy lodged with the local district or township government office. These triplicates were inspected by local officials for "irregularities," and officials would sometimes conduct interviews of parties to determine if "black-market" or other forms of illegal transactions occurred.[43] Chen proudly showcased a sample of the new standardized contracts in the appendix of *Land Reform in Taiwan*, producing a tidy visual image with clearly numbered clauses and information grids for completing specifics of land being transacted.[44]

In another layer of technicality, Chen addressed the issue of land grading. Arable land had been graded on the basis of productivity for purposes of evaluating taxation well before GMD land reform. However, like most property valuations, the method of grading could be controversial. In some cases, ecological change, such as the gradual draining of a paddy perhaps due to long-term climate change or weather patterns, could transform it to become less productive dry land. This could significantly affect agricultural output and thus valuation. GMD policy planners addressed these possibilities through observation and correction. Land that had changed, for example, to possess multiple subregions with different productivity potentials would be subdivided into plots and assessed separately by local officials in a process called "readjustment." Readjustment would be accompanied by meetings with both tenants and landlords and would be subject to oversight by county-level officials.[45] The implementation of legal processes with continual reevaluation involving government expertise signaled the increased bureaucratization and rationalization of interactions involving humans and land, reinforcing for Chen and the GMD the technical image they wanted to portray.

Negative consequences from the 375 Rent Reduction produced a lengthy discussion in Chen's manuscript. Problems ranged from inaccurate land categorization and grading to refunding excessive security deposits to reduced water services provided by landlords post-reform.[46] For Chen, these matters were of a technical nature. In each scenario, he outlined a rational state response that would include state intervention, oversight and inspection committees, reevaluation, and further changes to legislation. In the section discussing the results of the 375 Rent Reduction, Chen cited government surveys of villages post-reform in 1951 performed by inspection teams, using markers such as "seven families have built new houses . . . 40 families have bought draft cattle . . . 25 families have had marriage celebrations" to demonstrate the "betterment of the tenant farmers' livelihood."[47] The social results were largely superficial, shown to demonstrate anecdotal results, whereas the larger emphasis was on the technical language of land economics, the before and after measurements and multiple variables to consider land value and tenancy rates.

The second series of land reforms—the sales of public (state-owned) lands—ran from 1948 to 1958, with a peak of 1951 after the passing of the Regulations Governing the Sale of Public Farm Lands to Establish Owner-Farmers in Taiwan Province. After the retrocession of Taiwan to China in 1945, the Nationalist government seized control of Japanese government owned lands in Taiwan. These included county and municipal lands and Japanese state-owned enterprise lands, as well as private lands owned by Japanese individuals. These lands, according to Chen, accounted for about 21 percent of total farmland on Taiwan, a total of 434,981 acres.[48] Under Japanese colonial rule, most of these lands were subleased to tenant farmers by the landowners, which ranged from Japanese veteran soldiers to Japanese state-owned corporations.

Chen describes the primary motive of public land sales was to turn former tenant farmers of Japanese imperial lands into owner farmers. The key differentiating factor in the widescale sales under the GMD were the numerous legal conditions to ensure that tenant farmers were qualified for purchase and that transactions were not financially onerous. Sales price was set at 2.5 times the total annual yield of the main crop, paid in ten annual installments without interest. To eliminate the uncertainty of currency valuation and to discourage taking high-interest loans, payment was taken in farm products, which were supposed to be calculated at market value.[49] Legal conditions prevented the resale of this land to potential speculators. Overall, GMD legal protections represented a foundation for modern property rights, enshrined through rule of law and enabling state intervention into private property transactions. These were in line with various types of market regulations by states for capitalist development.

Chen stated that the goal of selling public lands was to take a first step toward private land redistribution. Leading through example, he argued, would demonstrate the resolve of the state striving for ideals of state-led welfare. "How could it be possible to make private landlords content if the Government continued to own a large amount of cultivated lands without offering them for sale and remained [*sic*] a landlord itself?" Chen continued to attribute this ideology to Sun Yat-sen again, quoting a number of articles from the ROC Constitution that emphasized Minsheng zhuyi. Even these references were wrapped within a language of capitalism with ideas of socialism, such as "equalization of landownership and restriction of private capital in order to attain a well-balanced sufficiency" and "the State shall, in principle, assist owner-farmers and persons who make use of the lands by themselves."[50] Though it is doubtful that GMD planners were driven purely by selflessness and Sun's Three Principles as opposed to the political expediency of garnering popular support, the sale of public lands was nonetheless successful in placing land into the hands of formerly landless tenants, effectively increasing the number of farming families tilling land they owned.

TURNING PEASANTS AND LANDLORDS INTO CAPITALISTS

The third and final reform was arguably the most crucial for the overall land reform narrative. This was compulsory land redistribution, or the land-to-the-tiller (耕者有其田, *gengzhe you qitian*) program. Land-to-the-tiller began as draft legislation in 1952 and passed the Legislative Yuan in 1953. The legislation involved two steps: the compulsory purchasing of all tenanted land in excess of a prescribed amount by the GMD government, and the sale of that land to farmers. A total of 344,092 acres were purchased by the ROC state and resold to 194,823 farm families. Land-to-the-tiller also provided legal oversight to ensure that newly sold lands remained in the hands of tillers and not resold, implementing annual inspections of resold land as well as generous loans to disincentivize quick sale in times of financial hardship.[51]

Benefits of land-to-the-tiller reform were multifold. One emphasized basic economic incentives; by granting ownership of land to those who cultivate it, GMD state planners provided the proper economic incentive for full development of land. Prior to land reform, farmers would be reluctant to make capital-intensive improvements to their land, due to the uncertainty of tenancy. At any point, they could be forced off the land, disincentivizing long term improvements. Furthermore, with excessive rent, farmers were unable to accumulate savings or finance capital-intensive purchases and thus make long-term improvements to their land. Chen called this the "psychological factor" and argued that this was responsible for the rise in purchasing and financing of agricultural equipment and farm implements after the land-to-the-tiller reform was implemented.[52] Though this may indeed be the case, as historian Emily Hill has argued, if one considers all the factors increasing overall annual yield in agricultural growth, the influence of land ownership incentives for capital improvement is still less than what she argues is the single most important factor in Taiwan's Green Revolution, which is chemical fertilizer.[53]

Chen also dedicated significant space in *Land Reform in Taiwan* to explaining the financial mechanisms behind land-to-the-tiller. The entire process was financed through credit mechanisms issued by the Land Bank of Taiwan, providing landlords with bonds whose interest would be paid through the income stream of annual payments by tillers over ten years. The Land Bank of Taiwan provided crucial financial services that made land reform possible. The Land Bank was formed in 1946 through the seizure of the five Taiwanese branches of the Japanese colonial bank, Nippon Kangyō, and was infused with cash from the ROC government.

Under the GMD land-to-the-tiller program, land was compensated over-all with 70 percent land bonds and 30 percent stock in recently privatized state owned enterprises (SOEs). The land bonds provide an ideal example of the capitalist-making practices that the GMD wanted to portray. Two types of land bonds were offered: rice bonds to compensate for paddy lands that were purchased, and sweet potato bonds for dry land. Both types of bonds offered future payment in both cash and the corresponding crop type, with the former being the result of sales of the crop at market prices. Bonds provided for payment over ten years at 4 percent interest per year.[54] The floating of bonds, which were guaranteed by the state, offered an introduction to modern finance. Bonds allowed the GMD state to not offer up its own capital for the purchase of the lands, instead using future rent payouts from the former tenant farmers. These inculcated the former landlords and former tenants into capitalist practices, demonstrating, for example, the guarantees of the state-backed bonds as a middleman, as well as the possibility of income for future payout with interest (for the landlord) and the future of current capital investment with future payment (for the farmer).

For Chen, the point of pride of land-to-the-tiller was not that it had broken the power of the landlords but rather that the process was ostensibly fair to land-lords and gave them potential to accumulate even further wealth through capital reinvestment. Chen wrote that "while shaking off the shackles of the tenancy system for the farmers in order to improve their living conditions, the enforcement of the land-to-the-tiller program should also take into account the interests of landlords so as not to cause them to suffer too great a loss."[55] The obvious foil was the confiscation of land across the strait under the CCP, and indeed, Chen dedicates the final chapter of the book to an explicit comparison of "Red 'land reform'" (quotes original) to GMD land reform. As a form of substitution for income from land rents, Chen and GMD planners thought that they could encourage landlords to take an interest in industrial development. Thus, they privatized the formerly state-owned Cement Corporation, Pulp and Paper Corporation, Industrial and Mining Corporation, and Agricultural and Forestry Development Corporation through public offering of shares.[56] For Chen, this was in stark contrast with the Communists, who "have acted contrary to every principle of human nature" in confiscating land "without compensation."[57] In reality, landlord positions were far more precarious living under GMD martial law and violent repression. After the February 28 Incident of 1947 and the following White Terror in which the GMD regime cracked down on supposed local agitators, landlords feared opposing the government, rightly concerned that opposition could result in physical violence, jailing, or even execution.[58]

From the GMD perspective, land-to-the-tiller was not just evidence of the GMD's state's technocratic capabilities, modernity, or even largesse. It was also evidence of the sociotechnical transformations of GMD policies. Whereas rent ceilings and sales of public lands made rural lives easier and more humane, land-to-the-tiller was transformative by making capitalists out of peasants. Through the privatization of land and the inculcation of new legal and financial practices that farmers were subjected to during this process, modern capitalist practices such as deeds, certificates, contracts, and bonds became basic knowledge. All former tenant farmers who had become owner cultivators were introduced to capitalist practices. In a sense, this reflected a financial complement to agricultural science. Whereas agricultural extension agents spread modern practices of fertilizer spraying, pesticide application, seedling spacing, and so on, so too did the provincial land bureau and local officials spread modern practices of triplicate contracts, interest rates, commodity markets, etc.

Perhaps more important for the GMD was their representation of the former landlords. Whereas land was previously the sign of wealth, the GMD wanted capital that had previously been locked up in land instead to be directed to industry, such as manufacturing and chemicals. With the conversion of land to state-owned enterprise equity and bonds, former large landowners, too, were immediately transformed overnight into capitalists. A majority were tragically deprived of much of their capital. Many did not understand the value of their certificates and sold them immediately below market value, not knowing that SOEs would later become highly profitable enterprises, making those stock certificates highly valuable.[59] One National Taiwan University study from 1965 estimates that over 90 percent of landlords who sold their stock did so at a loss.[60] In spite of this exploitation, scholars Ping-Chun Hsiung, Cheng-shu Kao, and Gary Hamilton have argued that land reform offered low-cost rural lands and the impetus (sometimes not by choice) for many "living room factories" to emerge and lead Taiwan's later 1970s and 80s industrial miracle.[61]

VISUALIZING LAND REFORM

Visuality accompanies the narrative form and the technical language of contracts and financial instruments in *Land Reform in Taiwan*. This visuality focused on three key themes: the rational modernity of technocratic land reform, welfarist principles, and human encounters. Whether through posed photographs or through "sample documents" that presented copies of bonds, contracts, and other bureaucratic forms, Chen impressed upon readers that land reform was not just a paradigm of technical mastery but also one that had direct social effects upon Taiwan.

Among the human-centered photographs, several illustrated the socialization of capitalism. Figure 2 depicts a stockholder meeting, which included newly minted capitalists from former landlords and demonstrated the transition from a

FIGURE 2. This photograph was included in Chen Cheng's book on land reform. The caption reads, "Former stockholders landlords attend stockholders' meeting. They received corporate shares instead of cash." The compensation for their landholdings was stock in state-owned enterprises, which turned some (those who did not sell their stocks immediately) into capitalists. Chen, *Land Reform in Taiwan*, 34.

traditional economy to a modern one. In the bottom left a landlord-turned-capitalist garbed in traditional Qing-styled clothing sits next to another shareholder but dressed in a dark Western-style suit. In the back row are a full row of men, all in business suits, perhaps visually comprising the class of industrial capitalists that the GMD hoped to make of erstwhile rural landowners.

In figure 3, tenant farmers are shown smiling as they received certificates demonstrating proof that they were new landowners. The bicycle and farming hats signify their class backgrounds, but the pieces of paper symbolized their newfound transition into a new class designation under GMD land reform. Like the landlords, with bonds or certificates they also entered a new age of finance capitalism.

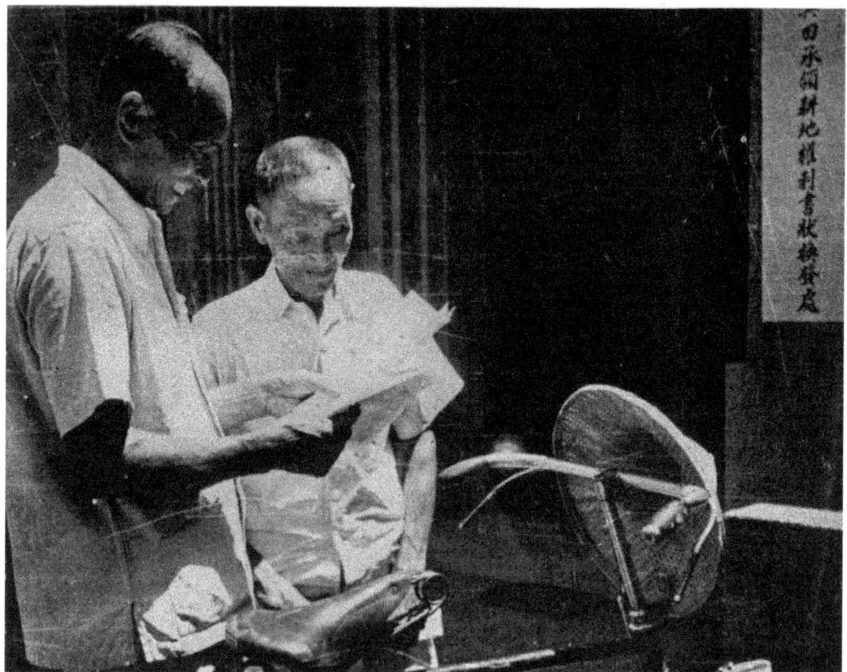

FIGURE 3. The caption to this photograph reads, "New owner-farmers receive their land certificates." The photo captures the elated former tenant farmers becoming landowners. As in the case of landlords receiving equity in state-owned enterprises, these interactions with the state and state agents introduced Taiwanese farmers into modern capitalist practices. Chen, *Land Reform in Taiwan*, 34.

Highlighted in Chen's legalistic processes were also procedures meant to showcase that technocratic land reform kept fairness and principles of people's welfare in mind. This was underscored by the utilization of committees, such as the one in figure 4. Committees allowed for multiple eyes to make decisions on matters subject to interpretation or needing oversight. And committees were legalistic as well; they were built into the required legal procedures for calculating annual yields and other matters that affected tax levies and sale prices.

Human manpower behind GMD land reform was not meant to be conducted only behind closed doors. Much like the agricultural extension networks of industrialized agriculture, so too did bureaucratic land reform have agents in the fields who assisted its efforts, as shown in figure 5. Similar to committee work, the surveys were designed to inspect actual field conditions and to determine fair grading of land values and production capability. Chen placed emphasis on the importance of accurate data, made possible by teams such as this. Like the landlords, too, this juxtaposed the technical officials, in both Zhongshan suits popular in the Republican period and in more modern Western garb. To the left is the barefoot rural farmer, holding onto an ox, who witnesses this technical endeavor firsthand.

FIGURE 4. The caption to this photograph reads, "Committee settles disputes arising from tenancy reform." Committees were central to how Chen envisioned land reform having human oversight to ensure land grades and contracts were determined fairly. Chen, *Land Reform in Taiwan*, 34.

FIGURE 5. The caption to this photograph reads, "Officials check actual conditions of farm tenancy." Survey teams were sent to the field much like agricultural extension teams in order to confirm that land and rent data were accurate. Chen, *Land Reform in Taiwan*, 34.

FIGURE 6. The caption on this photograph reads, "Cooperative credit ends high-interest evil of moneylenders." State-implemented credit cooperatives were meant to give farmers access to loans with reasonable interest rates. Chen, *Land Reform in Taiwan*, 108.

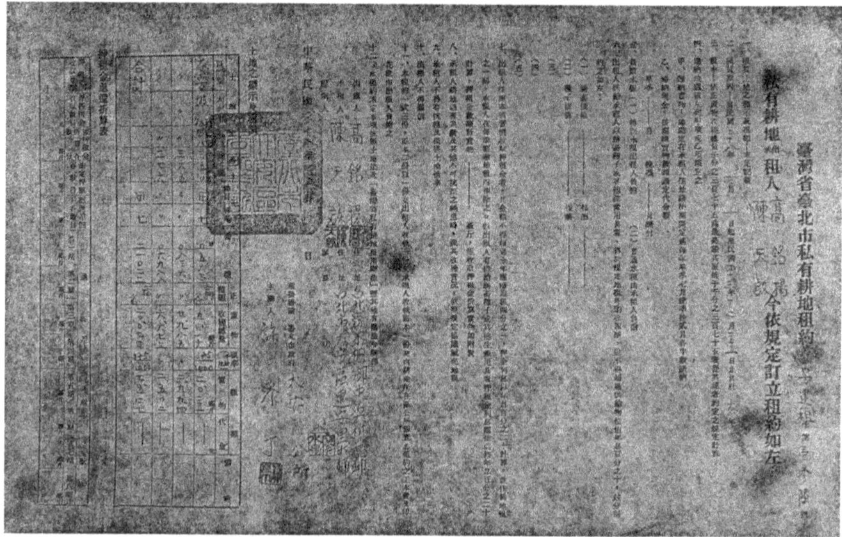

FIGURE 7. The appendix of Chen's book included sample contracts and other legal documents utilized in land reform transactions, grading, and financing. These instances demonstrated the standardization and legalization of land-related finance. Chen, *Land Reform in Taiwan*, 315.

(Form 9)

APPLICATION FORM FOR THE PURCHASE OF PUBLIC LAND

(SERIAL NUMBER... .....)

Applicant: Residence:

This is to request the Taiwan Provincial Government that the applicant be permitted to purchase the public lands specified hereinafter:

Land particulars				Comments	Items to be guaranteed
State or province-owned				Checked by: / Comments by: / Approved by:	1. The purchaser will cultivate the land himself after he has purchased it.
Village, township, or district					2. The purchaser will observe all the laws and regulations governing the sale of public land and pay the installment payments when due.
Land section			Total	Date of application:	3. The guarantors hold themselves responsible for all financial and legal consequences, if the purchaser violates either or both of the above-mentioned points.
Sub-section				Remarks	
Plot number				Enclosures	
Land category			Paddy field / Dry land		
Land grade			Area		
Area				One copy of applicant's household record;........ copies of farm lease contract; and........ copies of other documents.	
Irrigation condition					
Sales value in kind	Farm crop		Land value		
	Amount per chia			Applicant's personal seal:	
	Amount for this plot in kilograms				
Number of installment payments	Year				
	From:		Amounts to be paid		
	To:				
Amount of installment payments	Annual payment in kilograms				
	Semi-annual payment in kilograms				
Action approved					
Remarks					

	Purchaser	Guarantors	Notes
Status			1. The guarantors must be neighbors of the purchaser or responsible businessmen.
Name			2. A new guarantor is necessary if either of the original guarantors migrates to another locality.
Occupation			
Residence			
Relationship with purchaser			
Seal			

FIGURE 8. Another sample government-introduced form to standardize land lease contracts included in Tang Huisun's *Land Reform in Free China* published by the JCRR in 1954. Tang, *Land Reform in Free China*, 301.

Chen emphasized that capitalism in the ROC was benevolent. In extolling the virtues of cooperative credit, *Land Reform in Taiwan* explicitly denounced the prior "evil" system of moneylending that allowed for high-interest loans, which took advantage of farmers.

The appendix of sample documents in *Land Reform in Taiwan* presented a collection of legal and financial documents that occupied a central position within the narrative. These included stock certificates and bonds that were given to landlords in compensation for seized lands, as well as purchase and lease contracts for land transactions. Another publication, *Land Reform in Free China*, authored in 1954 by Tang Huisun (湯惠孫, Hui-Sun Tang), chief of the Land Reform Division of the JCRR, also included sample documents translated to English. In one such sample document, land is rationalized and made legible through new spatial categorizations ("Village, Township, or District; Land section; Sub-section; Plot number") and land characteristics utilized for financial legibility ("Land category; Land grade; Value of farm implements supplied to lessee by lessor").[62]

Forms, contracts, and other documents were how farmers and landlords encountered the modern rationality of GMD-led land reform. Though contracts were certainly not new to farmers and landlords who had utilized contracts for rent and tenancy on Taiwan for centuries, the inclusion of these documents within the land reform narrative was significantly more prominent. And furthermore, through quantification, tables, and forms, the technical disciplining of land reform became represented in visual form, presented as both primary documents and as secondary documents through technical appendices for readers.

CONCLUSION

Land reform, like other facets of agrarian development, served as a vehicle for GMD construction of societal policies. Whereas land reform policy was a series of laws and policy implementations moderately successful at consolidating state control, in the discursive sphere it acquired new meanings and values. Through publicly presented writings, such as Chen Cheng's *Land Reform on Taiwan*, land reform symbolized the highly technical and modern project of GMD development. Through the use of quantification, rationalization, and financialization, GMD leaders showcased how its capitalist system produced superior results.

The specifics of capitalism fleshed out in Taiwanese land reform represented a prescient version of Taiwanese society. Much as the commodification of financial instruments such as derivatives allowed for new levels of leveraging and capitalist finance; so too did the technical implementation of surveys, contracts, and bonds issued for Taiwan land reform. Lee Teng-hui argued for the importance of intersectoral capital flows, and the previously illegible land divided and subdivided in "premodern" systems became the target of GMD reform.

Looming over all this was the foil to GMD land reform: Communism. In indirect or direct contrast with Communist land reform, Guomindang represented their land reform as producing better economic and social results. Guomindang land reform was thus not just technical for the sake of being modern, but also modern in the sense that the technical could also be better for the tenant farmer. This was modern capitalism, with socialist characteristics.

Eventually, the GMD narrative of capitalist-welfarist land reform would become marketed in the 1970s and 80s to the Third World, especially in Southeast Asia, Latin America, and the South Pacific, as a specifically Taiwanese "model" of land reform. As chapter 6 will explore in detail, Taiwanese land economists established a Land Reform Training Institute to teach Taiwanese principles and experiences in land reform so that officials from other developing nations could avoid the fate of Communist China. The Taiwan model possessed socialist characteristics but was sufficiently capitalist. It distracted from popular attention to Communism with technical and arguably magical language of bonds and interest rates and was safe for officials of "free world" nations (despite many being ruled by dictators and autocrats) to implement without fear of their own property being violently seized.

3

The Taiwan Model

Agricultural Science, Farmers' Associations, and Capitalism in Taiwan, 1949–1970

For two decades the growth of the economy has been fueled by the rural sector. Industry took root rapidly because of the foreign exchange, domestic food supplies, and manpower resources that could be drawn from what was fundamentally a farming economy. These contributions of the rural sector were absolutely indispensable to economic modernization in the cities and in industry. . . . The international significance of such a review should be apparent. Other countries, further down the path of development, have tested some of the economic policy routes that Taiwan might follow. Some of what Taiwan has already learned will be useful to others passing through similar stages of development. Some new initiatives which Taiwan is undertaking deserve to be followed closely by any serious student of development.

—SHEN ZONGHAN

If the Chinese and the Americans could have applied the lessons of the fifties to China in the thirties and forties, a different history might well have been written.

—JOHN D. MONTGOMERY, RUFUS B. HUGHES JR., AND RAYMOND DAVIS

INTRODUCTION

On October 15, 1961, Taiwanese (ROC) minister of economic affairs Li Guoding (李國鼎, K. T. Li) and Taiwanese ambassador to the United States Wang Peng (王蓬, Martin Wong) visited the offices of Walt W. Rostow, then serving as deputy national security adviser to President John F. Kennedy. Rostow had risen to fame as an economics professor affiliated with the Center for International Studies at the Massachusetts Institute of Technology (MIT), where he and fellow economist Max Millikan became proponents of modernization theory.[1] Just a year prior, in 1960, Rostow had published his most well-known work, *The Stages of Economic*

64

Growth, which argued that nations progressed along a linear path toward modernity, climbing stages from "traditional society" to "take-off" and finally to "high mass consumption."[2]

Stages of Economic Growth became not only a paradigmatic text for economists, sociologists, and political scientists observing how economies, societies, and states developed, historically and at the present but also a guide for policy planners and technocrats hoping to achieve the elusive goal of "take-off." Though modernization theory fell out of favor in the social sciences by the late 1970s, its effect on national and international economic, political, and military policies reverberated for decades after its apogee. At the height of modernization theory's influence in the 1950s and 60s, US foreign assistance and development expanded drastically, and politicians throughout the First and Third Worlds paid obeisance to economic growth.[3] Many still do today. Taiwan was no exception.

On that day, Li presented Rostow with photos from a "Staging Growth Exhibition," hosted in Taiwan and dedicated to Rostow's formula for economic development. One depicted Taiwan in the middle of the "take-off" stage, meaning that Taiwan was in the midst of transforming from traditional to modern, a point that Rostow agreed with. Another photo emphasized a different matter that was a topic of far greater consternation at home. A man's head was depicted twice. Its first instance illustrated thoughts inside his head, giving "a picture of agricultural activities." The second showed the same head, but instead of agriculture, it depicted "industrial activities."[4] The point here was clear: modernization required a transition from agrarian economy to industrial.

By the time Li Guoding visited Rostow in 1961, the Joint Commission on Rural Reconstruction (JCRR, 中國農村復興聯合委員會, Zhongguo Nongcun Fuxing Lianhe Weiyuanhui) had been driving agrarian and rural development policy in Taiwan for over a decade, with impressive results. From 1949 to 1961, rice yields increased by 50 percent, from 1,663 kilograms of brown rice per hectare to 2,588. Agricultural output nearly doubled over the same period. Overall GDP growth was similar, also increasing by 50 percent from 1949 to 1961, driven by production in the agricultural sector.

This correlation between agricultural success and overall economic growth should not be underestimated—agriculture made modern Taiwan possible. This linkage was understood historically, from the highest echelons of political leadership of the Guomindang, to the mid-level technocrats in charge of implementing economic and agricultural policy, down to ordinary farmers, laborers, and citizens whose understandings of their own national histories were shaped by state media, political rhetoric, and the historical legacy of agricultural strength that Taiwan carried forth internationally in decades to follow.

This chapter examines the rise of agrarian development in Taiwan. Agrarian development portended and was integral to the Republic of China's reimagining of post-1949 Taiwan as a (de facto) nation-state.[5] Taiwan became a sandbox for

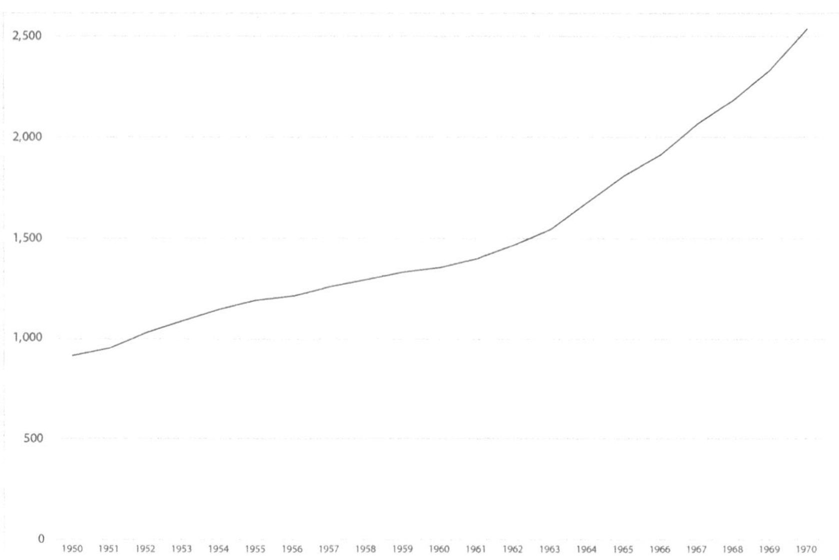

FIGURE 9. Taiwan's GDP per capita (in 1990 US dollars), 1950 to 1970. The Maddison-Project, http://www.ggdc.net/maddison/maddison-project/home.htm, 2013 version.

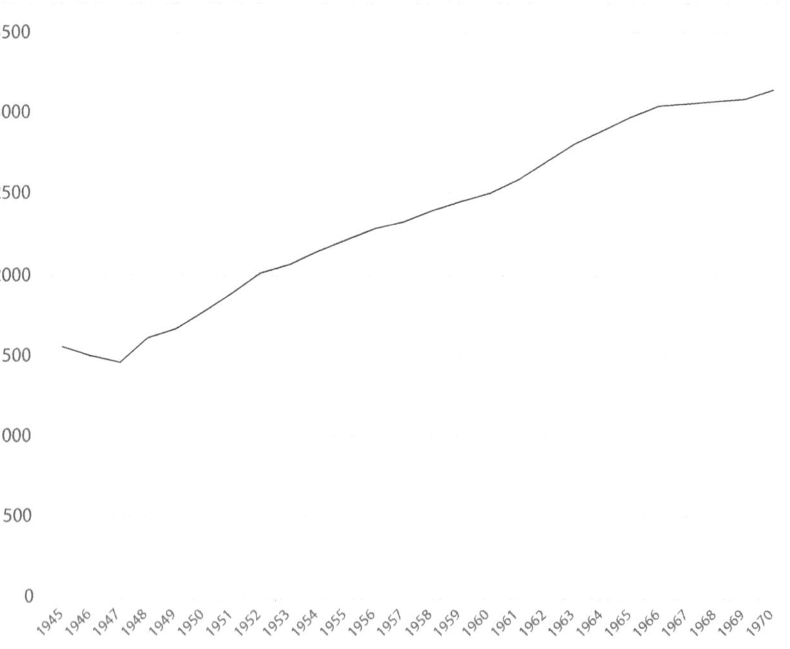

FIGURE 10. Taiwan's rice yield per hectare planted (measured in kilograms of brown rice), 1945 to 1970. Lee Teng-hui and Chen Yueh-eh, *Growth Rates of Taiwan Agriculture, 1911–1972* (Joint Commission on Rural Reconstruction, 1975).

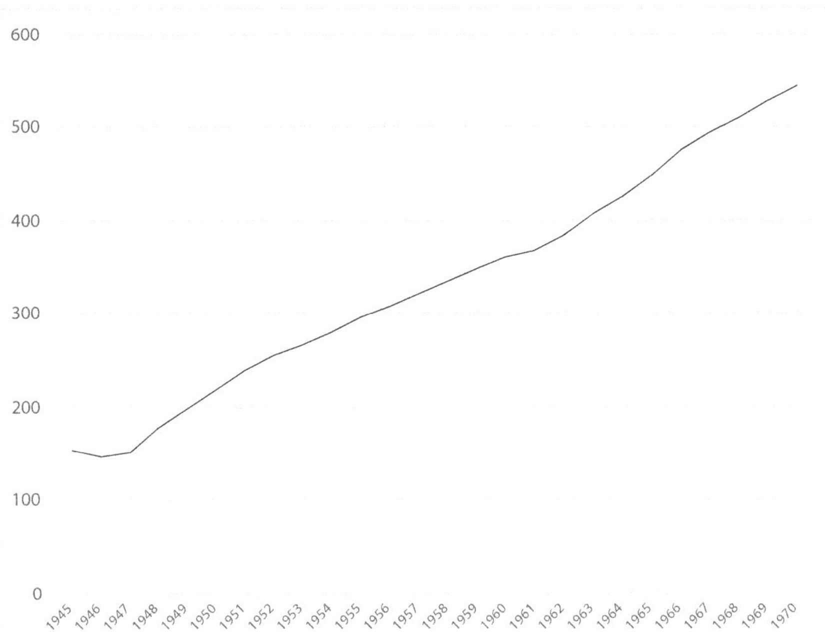

FIGURE 11. Taiwan's total agricultural output, 1945 to 1970. 100.0 is the baseline index for total agricultural output over a five-year moving average starting in 1913, the earliest year of the study compiled by Lee and Chen. Lee Teng-hui and Chen Yueh-eh, *Growth Rates of Taiwan Agriculture, 1911–1972* (Joint Commission on Rural Reconstruction, 1975), 53–54.

agrarian practices, integrating Chinese experts, Japanese colonial infrastructure and social organizations, and American capital. The results impressed. Taiwan by the 1960s had achieved sustained success in crop productivity, agricultural exports, caloric intake, and GDP growth. In two decades, Taiwan transformed from an agrarian export colony providing rice and sugar to the Japanese empire to one of the renowned Asian Dragons (or Tigers) in the 1970s.[6]

As this success unfolded, Taiwan also became a subject of political and academic attention. In some international development circles, particularly networks centered on or involving the United States and its Cold War allies, Taiwan became known as home to the "JCRR Model," referring to the success of agricultural policies under the JCRR. As later chapters will delve into, key aspects of agrarian development on Taiwan were marketed abroad as inherent to Taiwan's approach to agricultural development.

The core of this "Taiwan model" included a focus on rural social organizations (e.g., farmers' associations, irrigation associations), agricultural science (e.g., plant breeding, entomology, soil science), and agricultural extension (the process of disseminating agricultural practices, seeds, and implements from centers of research and production to rural villages and farms). Other aspects were also touted, depending on the circumstances, including land reform (discussed in chapter 2), education, and international exchanges (especially among technocrats and scientists). However, for the most part, the aforementioned three aspects of social organizations, science, and extension were emphasized, mostly due to Taiwanese practitioners arguing that these aspects were most applicable to relatively poorer, decolonizing states like Taiwan and were the most easily transplantable to other nations in terms of ease of implementation.

The chapter will offer a detailed account of the specific institutional and intellectual origins of constitutive elements of the Taiwan model, tracing back to roots in mainland China (bridging the experiences in chapter 1), as well as other actors, including Taiwanese farmers, Japanese imperialism, and American Cold War capital. From this aspect, this chapter is as much a history of an idea—the Taiwan model—as a history of agricultural science, rural Taiwan, Guomindang technocrats, and human interactions with the natural world.

Understanding this history of the Taiwan model accomplishes a number of goals. First and foremost, it helps explain why Taiwan was successful in agricultural development. The historicization of the Taiwan model also elucidates its political origins, namely how these disparate practices became packaged together and then marketed to showcase Taiwan's modernization and expertise.

Though American development practitioners and later social scientists utilized the term *model* to refer to Taiwan's agrarian policies under the JCRR, Taiwanese practitioners themselves rarely used the term to refer to their own experiences, instead preferring less rigid terms such as *strategy, experience*, and *approach*.[7] The word *Taiwan* was typically used in its strictest sense, as describing the place from which this model was refined and not to imply that practices were Taiwanese and not Chinese, as might be interpreted today.[8] However, the construction and discourse stemming from the context of its usage, in particular for literature geared toward public and international audiences, is in line with how we would imagine a model in sociotechnical terms. Taiwanese practitioners argued in favor of selected practices over others for the purpose of its reproducibility and utility in contexts outside of Taiwan.[9] They also emphasized that the Taiwan model was unique, not because its individual constitutive elements were innovated or pioneered by Taiwan but because Taiwan had selected and invested in certain aspects that it deemed most efficient and proved it through its development experience in the 1950s and 60s. This final element was critical in bringing together this package as a model; Taiwan's success in and of itself rendered its strategy of development as worthy of study and dissemination.

The origins of Taiwan's development experience is important in illuminating its later marketing abroad in international development missions to Africa, Asia, and Latin America, as explored in the following chapters. To understand the political exigencies of that enterprise also necessitates looking at the underlying experiences and practices that Taiwanese international development advertised. Though much of what is represented abroad is indeed grounded in reality, a fine-tooth examination of this history yields that the success of the Taiwan model was a convergence of a number of historically contingent factors that, ironically, made the model difficult to reproduce elsewhere.

Perhaps most importantly, this is also an on-the-ground perspective of a salient aspect of Taiwanese history—its evolution from a predominantly agrarian and rural society into a modern one. Outside of the realm of gross domestic product is also a story of how agrarian practices transformed the cultural, social, political, and environmental landscape of Taiwan. Efforts at village level reform led to campaigns inculcating modern practices of hygiene, capitalism, and democracy. The mandate for efficient distribution of seeds and knowledge led to highly organized and integrated social units of farmers' associations. A faith in the infallibility of science led to the rise of the Guomindang technocracy and generations of families hoping for their children to become agricultural technicians and engineers. And increased reliance on Green Revolution methods produced a reliance on fertilizers and pesticides.

THE TAIWAN MODEL

What is the Taiwan model? The term was not invoked among Taiwanese practitioners themselves; instead, it was often used in front of international audiences. Xie Senzhong (謝森中, Sam C. Hsieh), a JCRR agricultural economist who later published prolifically with the Asian Development Bank in the Philippines, gave a lecture at the Philippine Academy of Sciences and Humanities as part of the President F. E. Marcos Series on Chinese and Civilization on August 29, 1969. Titled "Taiwan's Model of Agricultural Progress," it underscored the importance of figuring out how to improve food production in the predominantly agrarian states of Asia. Like other presentations of Taiwan's development history, it laid out quantitative facts: national income (gross domestic product), adjusted for inflation, grew at an average rate of 7.7 percent annually from 1952 to 1969. The average Taiwanese diet intake was 2,400 calories. Ninety-seven percent of school-aged children attended school. Life expectancy reached sixty-six years of age (compared to seventy years in the United States). Two factors explained this success, in his perspective: "Technological: the increasingly productive technologies, the hardware, knowledge, and skills that increase people's capacity for manipulating physical forces and transforming resources into outputs"; and "Organizational: the re-grouping under new rules end of mutually helpful behaviour that enable them to generate and put to widespread use the increasingly productive technologies."[10]

Xie was examining this distinction through the lens of an economist. Technological change would push the production-possibilities frontier, allowing for the increased production of guns and butter (or in the case of Taiwan under the GMD, guns and rice). In economic terms, this was intensive growth, meaning growth achieved as a result of improving productivity without increasing factor inputs. This was preferable to extensive growth, which is achieved only by increasing inputs to the productive process, such as labor or natural resources. Extensive growth came with negative consequences. Population growth strained the resources of the state, requiring additional food, education, and health infrastructure. Developing economies often lacked access to natural resources. Intensive growth was the type that would allow the "take-off" that Rostow and other economists envied.

As an economist, Xie defined technology broadly. In the agricultural realm, it included basic sciences, such as the plant and soil sciences, as well as the improved seeds and chemical fertilizers that basic sciences produced that served as intermediary inputs for a final product (such as canned mushrooms). It also implied more practical and applied knowledge, such as knowing what crops responded best to what types of chemical fertilizers, or how far apart sweet potatoes should be planted, or how many growing seasons of rice one would expect from a certain region. This type of know-how was emphasized by the JCRR as much as scientific research was.

As chapter 1 described, the key pathway for the cultivation and distribution of practical knowledge was agricultural extension. Extension focused on the dissemination of knowledge and practices, as increased production of pesticide sprayers and improved seeds could not produce increased yields without knowing what to do with them. Because technologies were often tested and perfected within the centers of agricultural knowledge such as universities or experiment stations, where new crop cultivars were planted and compared, efficient and thorough dissemination of new ideas and technologies from research station to farms became as significant a problem as the research and development efforts themselves.

From a practical perspective, knowing which villages and farmers should be shown what sorts of farming demonstrations already posed significant obstacles. Crucial to the success of extension efforts in Taiwan were farmers' associations and other rural social organizations that allowed for easier dissemination of agrarian knowledge. These organizations served on multiple fronts, providing a crucial intermediary role between center and periphery for the purposes of demonstration and training, organizing rural peoples into distinct and manageable units, and providing local self-governance to allow for managing distribution of seeds, fertilizer, and water.

Farmers' associations, irrigation associations, agricultural credit banks, the Provincial Land Bureau, extension training centers, experiment stations, and even the JCRR itself were the organizations that Xie referred to as creating the "conditions for a mutually helpful behavior necessary to achieving [productive] technology."[11] Xie was careful to contextualize these factors within the specific circumstances of Taiwan's developmentalist state ("a stable government guided by a strong commitment to use its power to achieve technical advancement") and a Taiwanese culture of productivity ("a people guided by a traditional obligation to be as productive as possible for the sake of improving the income and status of their families"). Nonetheless, he encouraged his Filipino audience to take what factors they could learn from Taiwan and apply them to their own culture.

Land reform was also sometimes included in the Taiwan model but was dependent on political context. For example, missions to autocratic regimes in Africa often did not include any mention of land reform, which would have been politically difficult to carry out since political rule in many African postcolonial states depended on elites who tended to own large plots of land. In other places, like South Vietnam, where land reform was seen as politically expeditious, Taiwanese teams calibrated their showcasing of land reform, offering enough to draw attention to Vietnamese efforts at implementing it but not so much that to provoke questions about why land reform was not being implemented more thoroughly.

FARMERS' ASSOCIATIONS

The ability to develop new technologies for increased production was merely half of the equation. The other half involved making sure that these new technologies and knowledge reached rural areas of need. Agricultural extension, including the use of extension agents, demonstration fields, and training centers, was designed to accomplish precisely this. Yet even states and policymakers who recognized the importance of extending knowledge to rural areas faced numerous barriers, such as understanding the nuances and complexities of local environments. Farmers' associations partially filled this role by providing an infrastructure for a bidirectional knowledge transfer with central government institutions like the JCRR. They served as distribution endpoints for the critical chemical inputs, especially fertilizer, needed to achieve Green Revolution yields. Farmers' associations became a pathway for state-imposed discipline, such as land reform and water control. They also conveyed information in the opposite direction, giving the center knowledge about conditions in the periphery, what James Scott would consider making rural society "legible" to the state.[12]

The crucial role of farmers' associations as an instrument of increasing state and economic capacity began under Japanese colonial rule. Taiwan was ceded from China to Japan in 1895 after the first Sino-Japanese War under the terms of the Treaty of Shimonoseki. Taiwan served as an agricultural colony primarily exporting sugar and rice to the rest of the Japanese empire. Agricultural commodities constituted 80 percent of the value of Taiwan's exports, and nearly 60 percent of Taiwan's population was involved in the agricultural sector.[13] Japanese officials, in cooperation with landlords and wealthy farmers, began to establish farmers' associations and cooperatives as early as 1900 and expanded them starting in 1908 across the island. Associations established small demonstration gardens, cooperated closely with the government agricultural experiment station, and encouraged members to share new techniques or knowledge.[14] Officials saw the benefit in utilizing associations for their economic and political objectives. Japanese administrators established regulations, member hierarchies, and fee collections across the island's associations and organized them by function between cooperatives (for financial economy of scale) and farmers' associations (for agricultural extension and education).[15]

Just five years after the end of Japanese rule in Taiwan, from 1950 to 1951, Cornell professor of rural sociology W. A. Anderson wrote a report on Taiwan's farmers' associations as a consultant for the JCRR. Over a period of five months, he investigated the state of farmers' associations in Taiwan and for two and a half weeks studied farmers' association reorganization under General MacArthur's Supreme Command Allied Power (SCAP) in Japan. Anderson observed that under Japanese administration, farmers' associations had formed a culture among the farming population "that understands and appreciates technical advances" in agricultural science "and seeks their benefits."[16] In colonial Taiwan, farmers' associations were also the only form of organization, thus ensuring that rival rural organizations did not compete for local power or interfere with administrative efforts. The ROC inherited these advantages after it took control of Taiwan in 1945.

Under the JCRR, farmers' organizations underwent further reform. During Japanese colonial rule, and especially in the final years during wartime, farmers' associations were a part of centralized governance.[17] Top-level administrative posts in farmers' associations were appointed by the colonial government and were usually held by Japanese as opposed to Taiwanese individuals. In provincial level farmers' associations, for example, the Japanese governor-general served as the chairman, and Japanese district magistrates likewise served as chairmen of local associations.[18] JCRR commissioner Shen Zonghan wrote that during the colonial period, "farmers' associations were dominated by landlords and the local gentry who knew nothing about agriculture and farming and cared still less."[19] Though Shen was writing to highlight the accomplishments of the JCRR in contrast with earlier colonial rule, Japanese administration was indeed modernist in the sense that it sought centralization of rural governance in order to maximize production from Taiwan's agricultural sector for its imperial needs.

The ROC similarly sought maximization of the agricultural sector since it in effect taxed the agricultural sector through the fertilizer barter system. This tax-in-kind was collected through a system by which farmers were required to pay with rice for state-supplied fertilizer at an exchange ratio far below market value. But it also sought non-economic goals through farmers' organizations.

One study, conducted under the direction of Zhang Zhiwen (章之汶, C. W. Chang), a specialist in agricultural extension and the Dean of the College of Agriculture and Forestry at Nanking University (following the footsteps of

Shen Zonghan), was completed in 1949, while the JCRR was still operating in the mainland. Zhang's first recommendation underscored the important role that farmers' associations had as the on-the-ground partners for agricultural extension. He extended this recommendation from a technical perspective to a sociopolitical one, that "Agricultural Associations shall become a democratic organization of the people, for the people, and by the people," echoing the language of Abraham Lincoln.[20]

Zhang's initial recommendations resulted in the first set of reforms to farmers' associations in Taiwan after 1945, with the merging of existing farmers' associations and cooperatives, thus providing both extension and credit services. JCRR chairman Jiang Menglin invited W. A. Anderson the following year to recommend steps for the further development of farmers' associations at that "critical juncture."[21]

Anderson's study further built on Zhang's suggestions of democratization by recommending the ROC government enact legislation dictating that voting membership and electable candidates be limited to families engaged primarily in farming work. Anderson wanted to realize a vision of local, democratic self-governance. Like most rural sociologists during the mid-twentieth century, Anderson embraced the inherent ideal of a community as an organizing unit of society. As historian Daniel Immerwahr has argued, rural sociologists represented "development without modernization" that sought development via decentralization as opposed to the centralization espoused in James Scott's version of high modernism. Unlike modernization theory's objective to industrialize societies through economic growth, rural sociologists worked for "the preservation of rural society" and a "cultural approach."[22] Cornell, as was the case with agricultural science, was a global center for rural sociology and communitarianism.

Anderson praised the potential of Taiwan to become "the most efficient and productive agricultural and rural life program powered by democratic principles in the Orient," calling for the ROC to take Taiwan's "heritage of organization, knowledge, and ambition and make it work along democratic lines to build the whole life of rural people."[23] In other words, democratic principles were as important as economic productivity, and farmers' associations were key to fostering local democracy. As such, Anderson believed that farmers' association reform would accomplish personal and communitarian goals such as "the development of beauty in the person and his surroundings to enhance harmony and symmetry and promote spiritual well-being" and "right social relations to achieve, within the home, the community, the nation, and internationally, social-civic cooperation" in addition to the traditional development goals of economic welfare and sanitary and healthy living.[24] Shen Zonghan argued that these changes allowed farmers to "practice democracy by choosing the best men among themselves to direct and supervise . . . and by taking an active part in discussions."[25]

After merging farmers' associations and cooperatives, the associations provided a number of services for farmers. Anderson performed surveys of what farmers perceived as the most important roles associations served; from most important to least important, these included furnishing rural credit, distribution or sale of fertilizer and other such goods required for production, giving technical advice to farmers, handling of daily administrative necessities, marketing services, rice milling, warehousing, transportation, and public health. In essence, these associations functionally served as middlemen for transactional services such as obtaining necessary farming supplies and knowledge and for wholesaling agricultural products.[26]

From a finance perspective, farmers' associations had combined the functions of credit cooperatives that allowed farmers to pool their capital and benefit from distributing risk in order to allow steady access to loans for purchasing seeds and fertilizers. Historically, as economic historians like Philip Hoffmann have argued, the development of capital markets has been correlated with the rise of modern and robust economies as well as economic growth.[27] In France, Germany, the United States, and other large agricultural societies, cooperatives were crucial to providing credit where they were hitherto unavailable to farmers in the nineteenth and early twentieth centuries.[28]

That credit became a top priority of the JCRR was one of the key factors to the success of farmers organizations. Shen Zonghan, during his PhD training at Cornell, found mentorship under William I. Myers, then a professor of agricultural economics at Cornell specializing in farm finance. Myers had a long career as an expert in agricultural credit, serving as deputy governor of the Farm Credit Administration in the United States facilitating mortgages for farmers. Shen and Jiang Menglin corresponded frequently with Myers, discussing agricultural credit and also administrative matters of furthering institutional ties between Cornell and Taiwan.

Early in 1951, along with Zhang Zhiwen and W. A. Anderson's reforms, and with oversight from the JCRR and the Provincial Department of Agriculture and Forestry, farmers' associations began modernizing their credit services. Showing that modernization could exist alongside communitarian goals of democratization, Taiwanese farmers' associations streamlined bookkeeping and financial record keeping in order to help facilitate loans.[29] When Shen Zonghan was informed by American JCRR commissioner Raymond Davis years later in 1959 that Myers was retiring and looking to travel, Shen seized the opportunity to invite Myers to Taiwan as a JCRR agricultural economics consultant.[30]

In the resulting report, written in 1960, Myers raised a series of issues regarding agricultural credit. Creditors, Myers described, were generally more eager to lend to large industrial enterprises rather than the small family farms that predominated in the Taiwanese economy. As a result, the agricultural sector represented roughly one-sixth of all capital invested in Taiwan but produced one-third of Taiwan's gross domestic product. This discrepancy in the quantity of credit lending meant Taiwanese farmers were underserved by existing credit markets.

Second, Myers recorded that average annual interest rates charged to farmers were exorbitant, ranging from 18 percent for a secured loan under a one-year period to 22 percent for a six-month unsecured loan, compounded monthly. In comparison to interest rates on deposits at banks, lending to farmers was higher by at least 50 percent, with the average interest on a six-month deposit at 12.6 percent.[31] Furthermore, credit was typically offered in the short term, often with repayment windows too short for farmers who depended on the sales of seasonal produce to repay debts.

Finally, the report found that eight different types of institutions, ranging from government to state-owned enterprises to private banks, provided credit to farmers: Land Bank, Cooperative Bank, farmers' associations, Taiwan Sugar Company, the Provincial Food Bureau, Tobacco and Wine Monopoly Bureau, the JCRR, commercial banks, and mutual savings and loan companies. They offered multitudes of loan types, for everything from purchasing land to marketing agricultural products, that often overlapped between the various lenders. Myers noted that the multitude of options "tend[ed] to perplex the borrowers, and impair the efficiency due to lack of coordination."

Myers lauded that credit reform began in 1955, which involved the use of US International Cooperation Administration (ICA) funding to farmers' associations for the purpose of making loans more accessible, resulting in lower interest rates and extended repayment windows. He proposed additional reforms. Myers suggested the establishment of a long-term credit fund that would help supply stable credit to farmers' associations directly from the government. Myers also called for restrictions on farmers' associations from redepositing their capital into non-agricultural banks. His goal was to prevent a further pull of agricultural capital toward the industrial sector, where investors experienced better returns and less risk.[32] Ironically, this was precisely what later economists explained was a principal driver for Taiwan's economic miracle. Minister of economic affairs Li Guoding wrote that one of the achievements of land reform was to reallocate capital from the agrarian sector to the industrial sector, where it was needed to fuel economic growth.[33] JCRR agricultural economist Lee Teng-hui wrote his PhD dissertation in agricultural economics on this exact mechanism of intersectoral (from agriculture to industry) capital flows, as discussed in the previous chapter.

Within the year, Shen Zonghan had worked to help convince the government to implement Myers's suggestions. The Council for US Aid (CUSA), which managed ICA funding to Taiwan, had previously opposed JCRR's directly providing credit services ("considerable pressure from CUSA to get JCRR out of the loaning business"). CUSA eventually relented, permitting US counterpart funds from ICA to provide direct grants to JCRR's Agricultural Credit Division, a ten-man division that brought on American credit specialist Kenneth Boyden as its division head from 1961 to 1964.[34] The Agricultural Credit Division then designed a long-term credit program to discourage the reinvestment of capital away to non-agricultural investments.[35]

Under Boyden, these plans solidified as the Unified Agricultural Credit Program, which sought to streamline and standardize credit lending practices and regulations across farmers' associations in Taiwan. The program eliminated the confusion between the various types of lending organizations and provided farmers' associations with the ability to provide most types of agricultural credit for their members.[36] By 1964, Boyden's end-of-tour eport analyzed results of the program, indicating that 194 of the roughly 300 farmers' associations in Taiwan were enrolled in the program, with about one-quarter of all farmers' associations members being educated about the new program services. Since the start of the program in 1961, 130,000 loans were issued, totaling US$16,250,000 by 1964.[37]

In agricultural credit, Taiwan integrated a key aspect of capitalist modernization: financialization through capital markets and debt raising to encourage individual intensive agriculture. Xie Senzhong, in corresponding with American JCRR commissioner Gerald Huffman in 1965, also underscored the importance of financialization for the purposes of economic growth. Referring to a recent publication by the renowned University of Chicago agricultural economist Theodore W. Schultz on the transformation of "traditional" to "modern" economies, Xie wrote, "In view of the limited land resources in agriculture in Taiwan, I still think there is a must to inject more capital inputs in agriculture . . . capital requirements [for agricultural resources development or agricultural base expansion and increasing short-run output increase on farms] may come from financing organizations, JCRR or grants, and farmers own income and savings."[38] In other words, capital was crucial for intensive agricultural productivity growth for the Taiwan model. This type of capitalist modernity went hand in hand with technological modernity of fertilizers and pesticides that were critical for Taiwan's agricultural productivity increases. But they also complemented other types of modernization, including social organization, and to be discussed later, rural reform.

The island of Taiwan also posed ecological dilemmas. Taiwan lacked significant natural resources with the exception of its arable land and inland forests. Heavy rainfall and rapid decomposition from high temperatures resulted in little organic matter accumulation and thus relatively low soil fertility. Furthermore, only coastal regions possessed easily tilled, flat, arable land. Arable land accounted for 30 percent of Taiwan's overall landmass, with the remaining mostly inland regions too mountainous to farm easily.[39] Forests provided resources in timber and cinchona (used to produce the antimalarial drug quinine), which Japanese colonial administrators also exported.[40] And Taiwan's expansive coastline gave it easy access to fishing. But timber and fishing were still relatively small compared to the agricultural sector. In agriculture, due to Taiwan's tropical to subtropical climate, water-intensive crops like rice tended to flourish, and these required control of water resources to prevent both drought and flooding. (This climate also had its downsides, as typhoons destroyed crops with regularity.) Japanese administrators engaged in large water infrastructure projects, like the Chianan (嘉南, Jianan) irrigation canal built through Chia-yi and Tainan.[41] Similarly, the JCRR under the Guomindang built with US funding the Shimen reservoir (石門水庫, Shimen

Shuiku) and dam serving Taoyuan and Taipei. Irrigation at the rural level introduced social dynamics and tensions on top of ecological ones.

Though most JCRR reforms involved applied research and dissemination of practices, some mandated reforms were not well received by farmers. Social dissatisfaction with policy directives and reforms rarely reached the upper echelons of the JCRR; the bureaucratic system of the postwar GMD state on Taiwan left policy and research decisions to the relatively small-scale JCRR and left local administrative issues to farmers' associations and especially association leaders, who were usually farmers. Reports of farmer resistance to JCRR policies had to be filtered through multiple levels up the bureaucratic chain before it reached the commission policy makers. Thus, discussion of resistance was relatively rare within JCRR documents. In many cases, policies enacted top-down forced redistributions of privileges.

In one instance related by a JCRR consultant working on irrigation economics, Taiwanese farmers objected to reforms of irrigation management under "irrigation squads" or "irrigation groups." In Taiwan, farm parcels were organized into "rotational units" or "rotational areas" for the purposes of simplifying irrigation management.[42] On occasion, rotational units would have irrigation rerouted or otherwise managed differently. Farmers whose lands were located near the head of the system had first access to incoming irrigation water, and those farmers whose land happened to be located at the end of the irrigation system would theoretically be more prone to receiving insufficient water should the system fail at any point. Whenever changes to irrigation management resulted in certain farmers' being moved to the end of an irrigation system, sometimes they protested these changes, leading to their arrests and being incarcerated for brief periods before they were released.[43] These instances demonstrated that though the ROC government reformed farmers' organizations for self-representation, policies nonetheless created winners and losers, with little social recourse for those who felt aggrieved under Guomindang authoritarianism.

HARVEST MAGAZINE

Though farmers' associations provided crucial human capital for centralized agricultural planning, they were not the only pathway for knowledge dissemination. As chapter one demonstrated, efforts like the Mass Education movement had utilized a variety of written and visual media to complement education in rural villages in northern and southwest China. In 1951, the JCRR worked with the United States Information Service (USIS)—the overseas arm of United States Information Agency responsible for Cold War propaganda projects like Voice of America—the Provincial Department of Agriculture and Forestry, the Provincial Government Information Office, and the Provincial Farmers' Associations, to develop a new avenue of disseminating knowledge: *Harvest* (豐年, *Fengnian*) magazine.

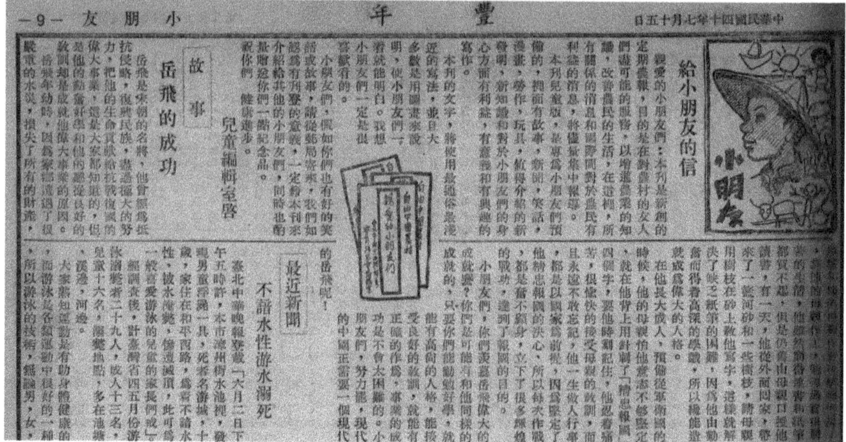

FIGURE 12. One story from *Harvest*, titled "Yue Fei's Success," depicts the hard working habits of famous Song general Yue Fei. "岳飛的成功" [Yue Fei de chenggong, Yue Fei's success], *Harvest* [Fengnian], July 15, 1951.

Harvest targeted four million rural farmers in Taiwan through bimonthly issues with "agricultural and health guidance, government and marketing announcements . . . with broad appeal to all segments of rural life, so interesting and useful that each issue will be eagerly awaited."[44] *Harvest* was distributed to rural areas at subsidized prices and had articles in both Chinese and Japanese, which was the more familiar language for many who had been educated only under Japanese colonial rule. (However, Japanese language was to be secondary to Chinese, usually provided as summaries instead of as equal languages, and eventually phased out as Chinese language education took root. This was part of Guomindang efforts to decolonize and de-Japanicize Taiwan.)[45] *Harvest* possessed both push and pull factors. On the one hand, it would push new techniques through illustrations and photographs in its issues, describing how they produced better results for farmers. On the other hand, it also demonstrated successful cases of these new practices, providing incentive for readers to also want to achieve the bountiful harvests shown in the publication.

Harvest was intended to showcase ideals of social and personal livelihood for rural populations. JCRR chairman Jiang Menglin, a former minister of education during the Republican era on the mainland, was keen to use media like *Harvest* to counter Communist ideology, which had "ideals behind it." Though Taiwan was ruled under Guomindang martial law and Communist insurrection was less likely on the island, the loss of the mainland was likely behind concerns of potential Communist sympathy and ostensibly counter-Communist idealism would prove useful for Chiang Kai-shek's future retaking of the mainland. Thus, *Harvest*, too, needed to "get through . . . the hope and inspiration, [to] let people visualize

FIGURE 13. Titled "Good Habits," this short cartoon depicted daily health and hygiene practices for children to follow in the youth section of *Harvest*. "好習慣" [Hao xiguan, Good habits], *Harvest* [Fengnian], July 15, 1951.

[a] better life."[46] This translated through positive messages and idealized roles, through inspirational news stories and fictional accounts that read like morality tales. In this sense, it also served as propaganda, to champion the benefits of state-led agricultural development and to bring back to the rural populations news of successes across Taiwan and elsewhere in the world. As chapter 6 will show, these

included the eventual international missions where Taiwanese agricultural technicians aided developing nations in Africa, Asia, and Latin America.

Harvest consisted of various sections designed to educate rural residents in new agricultural methods and techniques, news reports, sanitary health and well-being practices, and inspirational stories. Various sections targeted different segments of rural populations, and among the youth sections, "stories" (故事) were commonly told to model good behaviors and moral norms. One such story was titled "Yue Fei's Success" and depicted the hard-working habits of famous Song general Yue Fei, who has served as a historical exemplar of loyalty in China. The story began with the contributions of Yue Fei to society, first fighting off invasion, then reviving the people (復興民族, *fuxing minzu*), and finally sacrificing "his life for the great cause of a war of resistance and reviving his nation." But, the parable continued, Yue Fei's greatness did not begin on the battlefield; it began at home, as a child. Yue was raised in a poor family that was unable to purchase paper or brush for learning to write, and so "one day he returned home with a bucket of sand and some tree branches and thus resolved the problem of his lack of paper and brush." The story was meant to illustrate the determination of Yue Fei to study and thus achieve greatness. Thus, the story concluded with a reminder to the youth audience that just as Yue achieved his "noble moral character" and "accepted his excellent training," so too can children become a "contemporary Yue Fei that our China today needs!"[47]

As indicated by the original objectives of *Harvest*, its architects, Jiang Menglin and Americans Willard Rappleye and Robert Sheeks, envisioned targeting the language and medium of the magazine toward the literacy and interests of a rural audience. This included visual and literary elements that would draw interest, including art and comics. Another image depicted above demonstrated this with illustrations of proper hygiene for village youth. In the six-panel animation, a child is shown performing various habits that encouraged healthy living, from washing hands before eating, to daily bathing, to sleeping with the windows open. These were continuations of public health campaigns that originated in Repubican-era China and were seen as important for eradicating disease and improving rural livelihoods.

4-H

To supplement the work of farmers' associations in public health and youth education and continuing a trend of such community development from efforts like the North China Rural Reconstruction movement on the mainland (see chapter 1), the JCRR established 4-H clubs throughout rural Taiwan. 4-H were rural community youth clubs that originated in the United States, administered by the United States Department of Agriculture (USDA) beginning in 1914. The four "h's"—

hand, heart, head, and health—represented the club's dedication to inculcating work ethic combined with modern practices of public health and education. As historian Amrys Williams has written, the USDA Extension Service encouraged the founding of 4-H clubs for two objectives: "the immediate improvement of rural conditions through the teaching of new practices to young people in the context of the farm home, where other members of the family would take notice and follow their lead; and the long-term future development of agriculture that would result from children learning and internalizing these methods as they grew into adults with their own farms and children."[48] More importantly, 4-H was integral in rural governance in the United States, as Gabriel Rosenberg has argued, in creating a political economy of agriculture and a "biopolitical apparatus" that incorporated the bodies of rural youth.[49] These same objectives translated to Taiwan, where a history of rural youth education traced back to Yan Yangchu's Rural Reconstruction movement and Jiang Menglin's work as the minister of education in the Republican era (see chapter 1).

The JCRR produced an English language promotional video on 4-H titled *Lee Yu's 4-H Banner* in 1974.[50] Filmed in Bifengli (碧峰里), a village in Nantou County (南投縣) in rural central Taiwan, an unnamed narrator follows the story of a young Taiwanese boy, Lee Yu, as he accidentally happens upon a local 4-H chapter vegetable demonstration field (see figure 14). The opening scene depicts Lee Yu and his friends playing in the fields, in a scene implied as representative of unproductive village youth. They chase a rabbit into a nearby 4-H demonstration field, which then provides a stark contrast: men dressed in standardized 4-H uniforms, complete with the four-leafed clover symbol of 4-H emblazoned on green jackets and white caps, applying chemical fertilizers or pesticides across a field burgeoning with green vegetables. The uniformity, application of modern technology, and stunning results in the color video are clear—this is modernity in action.

The rest of the video then proceeded to demonstrate the various activities sponsored by 4-H chapters in Taiwan. The local 4-H chairman showed Lee Yu and his friends to the 4-H administered village. In one scene, ballots were handed out to 4-H members for elections of the local 4-H chapter chairman (see figure 15). These demonstrations of democracy in action were representative of community development aims to inculcate democratic practices and ideals at rural and youth levels. The JCRR sought to leverage local-level democratic processes as a form of self-administration and also as an ideological form of agrarian development that emphasized community democracy.

In another scene, village women are shown working on handicrafts, an example of how gender affected agrarian development (see figure 16). As historian Kenneth Pomeranz has observed, rural handicrafts have served a valuable economic function in China dating back centuries.[51] Women, who did not always work in planting, maintenance, or harvesting in the fields, have supplemented household

FIGURE 14. (*top left*): After first happening upon a 4-H demonstration field, local village children in the film *Lee Yu's 4-H Banner* witness the usage of modern chemicals and lush, green fields attended to by 4-H workers in uniform. Figure 15 (*top right*): 4-H worker administering ballots for local 4-H chairperson elections. Figure 16 (*bottom left*): 4-H young women working on textile handicrafts. Figure 17 (*bottom right*): Youth recording egg production from hens. *Lee Yu's 4-H Banner*, February 1974, records of USAID, RG 286.95, US National Archives at College Park.

income by producing handicrafts for sale in local markets. 4-H similarly encouraged such activities. In the scene from *Lee Yu's 4-H Banner*, rural women are shown in a central village location working on handicrafts under the instruction of a 4-H worker. Though this aspect is not heavily emphasized in the film, it nonetheless demonstrates a gendered division of the rural family: children participating in youth 4-H activities, men working in the field applying pesticides and fertilizers, and women at the village working on handicrafts.

Explicitly "modern" practices were also emphasized by 4-H in Taiwan. Another scene demonstrates an example of how Taiwanese youth could be productive for their villages, showing how raising fowl for sale and hens for eggs can be fun and also generate income. In demonstrating youth agrarian activities, a 4-H female worker is shown with a young boy, who is holding a pencil and paper pad (see figure 17). As the woman collects eggs from hens in the chicken coop, the boy records these numbers in his journal. This method of quantification provided youth training for rural farmers to become more scientific, in a Taylorist sense.

Though left implied, the idea of quantification would prove to be useful for farmers later, in calculations such as amount of fertilizers, pesticides, or seeds necessary for ideal production, as well as financialization of production and sales. These practices of quantification were in line with other efforts by the JCRR to reduce waste, increase precision, and improve knowledge of agrarian processes for better implementation and planning.

AGRICULTURAL SCIENCE AND TECHNOLOGY

Chapter 1 discussed the rise of agricultural sciences in Republican China, including the experiences of agronomist and plant breeder Shen Zonghan. In 1949 the Guomindang regime retreated to Taiwan following its defeat to the Chinese Communist Party on the mainland, and Shen and numerous other scientists affiliated with the JCRR and the Ministry of Agriculture and Forestry also accompanied the move to the island. With them, they brought over not just their scientific expertise, with a significant number having been trained in the United States, but also accumulated experiences of crop selection and improvement methods in the varied natural and social ecologies of China.

Yet Guomindang agricultural scientists and officials found a Taiwan that was already significantly developed as an agricultural economy under the Japanese empire. Colonial administrators established significant advances in agriculture, ranging from agricultural research stations throughout Taiwan to farmers' associations and agricultural infrastructure such as irrigation canals. Japanese agricultural universities such as the Taihoku Imperial University (臺北帝國大學), reorganized as National Taiwan University after the Nationalist takeover, and the Taiwan Advanced Academy of Agronomy and Forestry (臺灣總督府高等農林學校), later renamed National Chung Hsing University (國立中興大學, Guoli Zhongxing Daxue), trained future generations of Taiwanese agronomists and scientists that remained after retrocession. By 1945, the Nationalist government had inherited an island that in some cases had been run under a more productive, scientific, and profitable regime than many of the counties and provinces from which the Guomindang fled.

The JCRR encouraged institutionally driven agricultural science research. This policy entailed the development of Taiwan's university system to supply the research talent necessary for new research institutes and support from the Guomindang state bureaucracy to prioritize science and technology as a growth industry.

In one example of the dozens of new agricultural research institutes that emerged from the postwar development period, the Plant Protection Center was established in Taichung in 1960. The goal of the center was to provide research to battle plant diseases and pests. It combined the biological sciences—taxonomy, physiology, pathogenicity, and histopathology of microorganisms—with field trials to bring basic science to agricultural application. It employed field trials of chemical based pesticides as well as non-chemical, natural pest deterrents.[52] By combining scientific research with an applied goal, the Plant Protection Center was representative of twentieth-century changes to agricultural science that have been associated with the Green Revolution, as well as its negative consequences of over reliance on toxic chemicals and polluted runoff.

In another example of the marriage of science and industry, the Taipei District Agricultural Improvement Station requested funding from the JCRR for a study titled "Post-harvest Physiology, Handling and Storage Techniques for Fresh Vegetables and Fruits." Science and technology was not limited to improving productivity yields from crops. Technocratic planners also ensured that science and research be applied to industrial operations, sales, and exportability—in this case, distribution. The report remarked that "due to inadequate handling, transit, and storage of fresh vegetables, the losses during the handling and marketing stages in Taiwan are tremendous. Inadequate handling and transit were also responsible for the poor quality and low market value of fresh fruits on the foreign markets as reported in the past."[53] Benefits of distribution research were twofold. Proper handling of vegetables during distribution would minimize direct losses due to damage and lack of refrigeration, and indirectly, an increase in quality at distribution destinations throughout Taiwan would result in a higher market value for vegetables. The proposed study researched post-harvest physiology of vegetables and fruits to discover new transport methods and practices to ensure that they would reach destinations at optimal ripeness and condition. The application of research thus was broadly applied to many aspects of the agriculture industry.

The JCRR saw dozens of funding requests on a monthly basis that were not just limited to traditional rice and sugar crops. In September of 1968, it received requests for research into a variety of agricultural-related industries, reflected a vast diversification of the agriculture industry. This spectrum included breed selection for peanuts, farm mechanization, cropping patterns, fruit diseases and insects, forest management systems computer simulations, watershed management, tree breeding and bamboo research, kiln drying for hardwoods, fisheries development, and management of farmers' associations.[54] By the late 1960s, development that had previously been focused on rice had expanded into tuna fisheries, highland timber, and tropical fruits.

Applied scientific research was practiced with fervor for an increasing variety of domestic products and needs, furthering a capitalist directive for industrialized agriculture. Ducks raised and sold for human consumption are typically a cross of two duck breeds, one used for its low fat content and the other for its distinctive meat qualities. The hybrid offspring, however, are sterile. Typically, breeding the Pekin duck hybrid involves a lengthy process of mating, but by the 1960s, Taiwanese scientists perfected artificial insemination to a process of mere minutes per female duck.[55] The resulting breeding program allowed for an enormous boost in Pekin duck breeding. In another display of applied research methods and attempts at innovation, in 1969 a request was made to the JCRR for funding to research the use of bamboo as a replacement for steel in reinforced concrete.[56] The broadening application of science research resulted in productivity increases across the island.

Aside from this marriage of applied scientific research to agriculture, the JCRR also served a second yet important purpose—facilitating professional exchange and educational development. The JCRR largely sought experts abroad when the appropriate expertise could not be found in Taiwan or when domestic research institutes sought to bring in international experts for educational purposes. The majority of these experts were from "developed" nations such as United States, Japan, and Germany. The exchange of personnel and training across many different nations demonstrates the transnational nature of agricultural development of the time. Many of the agricultural experts who lectured or participated in conferences in Taiwan were also commonly invited to other developing nations.

Conference participation by agricultural scientists sponsored by the JCRR demonstrates a wide range of agriculturally related pursuits. Applied research using cutting-edge science and technology was the theme for international educational exchanges as well. In one interesting example, the FAO and the International Atomic Energy Agency (IAEA), through a joint division between the two, hosted a meeting for the rising field of radiobiology. The JCRR sponsored one scientist, C. H. Huang, to participate in a November 1969 meeting of the FAO/IAEA at Knoxville, Tennessee, titled "Use of Seeds as Biological Monitors for Neutron Irradiations."[57] The goal was to further study the use of neutrons for seed irradiation.

In another example, the JCRR facilitated two Taiwan representatives to the Rural Youth in Agricultural and Rural Development conference held February 18 to March 15, 1969. Sponsored by the German Foundation for Developing Countries in close collaboration with the FAO, the conference encouraged planning for "the design of nationally integrated programmes suitable for a more massive mobilization of the resources of youth for agricultural and rural development." Taiwan was just one of many developing countries that participated, and while traveling to the conference, the JCRR also approved a stop for the two delegates in the Netherlands and Denmark to "observe their agricultural extension work which has been successfully carried out or strongly supported by the farmers' cooperative organizations."[58]

Finally, the JCRR institutionalized a trend of sending its own scientists abroad for training and education in the centers of agricultural innovation, which by the postwar was usually the United States. The JCRR's own commissioners, including Jiang Menglin and Shen Zonghan, underwent graduate education in the United States (at Columbia University Teachers College and Cornell, respectively). One of the more prominent examples was Lee Teng-hui. Lee had written his dissertation, titled "Intersectoral Capital Flows in the Economic Development of Taiwan, 1895–1960," on the importance of resources flowing out of and into the rural and agricultural sector, as discussed in the previous chapter.[59] Writing in the foreword of the 1971 book edition published by Cornell University Press, Lee's doctoral dissertation adviser and prominent Cornell professor of agricultural economics John Mellor explained that Taiwan "offers an unusual opportunity" to examine a model of development where "first, substantial investment in agriculture and development of the agricultural sector, and then, form that base of agricultural development, major transfers from the agricultural to the nonagricultural sectors." Lee's intervention comes in because "there seems little evidence that such a pattern has in fact been followed by presently developed countries," implying that Taiwan was one of the first to successfully implement this theory of agriculture-led economic development.[60]

At the time, Lee had been an agricultural economist working in the JCRR and publishing numerous articles and books demonstrating the importance of the JCRR's impact on the overall economic development of Taiwan.[61] After returning to Taiwan with his PhD, he quickly progressed through the ROC bureaucracy, eventually being chosen as vice president by Chiang Ching-kuo, son of Chiang Kai-shek, and then being elected as Taiwan's first democratically elected president in 1996. That such an important figure in Taiwanese history rose from the roots of agricultural success in Taiwan was not coincidental. For Lee's contemporaries, agricultural development became the primary question of his generation.

FERTILIZERS AND THE GMD STATE

By 1962, one out of every twenty individuals in Taiwan was in the military. Chiang Kai-shek's desire to maintain what *Time* then called "one of the world's costliest military machines" was a direct result of his mandate to build up Taiwan for the eventual counterattack and elimination of the Communists in mainland China.[62] The vast size of Taiwan's six hundred thousand military personnel in relation to its general population of eleven million translated to a massive agricultural burden. Five percent of the population needed to be supported entirely by the state. How did the GMD state feed its vast military?

It was GMD state power, enabled by authoritarianism and the exercise of state-backed violence, that empowered the state to monopolize fertilizer supplies that imposed what was, in effect, a tax on Taiwan's rural farmers. This was the "rice-for-fertilizer" barter system. What initially served as a form of indirect taxation eventually became embedded into a sociotechnical system that encouraged the rapid development of industrialized fertilizer processes and technologies that became crucial for Taiwan's agricultural productivity during the 1960s and 70s, forming a cornerstone of Taiwan's Green Revolution and its eventual Taiwan model represented abroad. Through examining the fertilizer system, we see how Taiwan developed a system blending state power, economy, technology, and food.

Chemical fertilizer was a key factor responsible for twentieth-century increases in agricultural productivity, both globally and in Taiwan. Under the prewar imperial economy, Taiwan first imported chemical fertilizers from Japan in 1902, which were crucial for rice productivity, especially for the selected high-yield varieties that became increasingly important under Japanese colonial rule and the Guomindang.[63] Chemical fertilizer use (as opposed to human waste, so-called night soil) was so prevalent in colonial Taiwan that a fertilizer advisor for the United Nations Relief and Rehabilitation Administration (see chapter 1) in 1946 calculated that Taiwan, with a population of 6.5 million, used more commercial fertilizer than all of China, with a total population of 485 million.[64]

World War II disrupted the import of chemical fertilizers and impacted rice production yields under Guomindang control. Resuming imports of fertilizer became a top priority for postwar rehabilitation immediately after retrocession for both the Guomindang administrators of the island as well as UNRRA. In 1946, rice production yields were at near historic lows, bottoming around thirty-five kilograms per hectare. In the years of 1946 and 1947, the 136,300 metric tons of fertilizer acquired by UNRRA in Taiwan resulted in an increase from 630,000 metric tons of rice to 1.06 million, an almost 40 percent increase in yield.[65] In 1949, when the JCRR took over, a significant portion of funds were directed for acquiring fertilizer. By 1949, effective fertilizer distribution resulted in a production of 1.2 million tons of rice, and by 1952, fertilizer usage resulted in a two-million-ton yield, well surpassing the highest prewar output level of 1.4 million tons in 1935.[66]

How did the ROC state address the limited supply of fertilizer? State power is often exercised through monopolies on critical agricultural commodities, such as salt.[67] The ROC state also monopolized fertilizer supplies in Taiwan, through the rice-for-fertilizer system, first established in September 1948. The government controlled all fertilizer imports and manufacturing and monopolized its distribution to local farmers' associations. Farmers who required fertilizer needed to pay for it not with New Taiwan dollars but rather with rice from their own annual production. This rice was then passed from the farmers' associations back to the state. The exchange ratio of rice for fertilizer naturally favored the state. In a hypothetical free market, farmers would have been able to obtain more fertilizer for the value of their rice than through the state-mandated rice-for-fertilizer system. In their 1975 study of Taiwan's economy, Frank and Mei-Chu Wang Hsiao estimate that the ROC state acquired 19 percent of Taiwan's total rice output through this system.[68]

The JCRR provided oversight to the distribution of fertilizer but did not administer distribution at the village level. Instead, fertilizer was distributed to the Provincial Government Food Bureau and from there to local level farmers' associations. To ensure that fertilizer was being efficiently distributed and properly utilized, the JCRR employed inspectors, who were usually young, recent Taiwan college graduates proficient in speaking the local languages (Minnan or Hakka) or

Japanese, the languages most farmers would have understood.[69] These inspectors surveyed villages judging the reactions to reception of fertilizer. This system later developed to employ permanent extension workers, predominantly farm advisers who were responsible for educating approximately one thousand farm families in agricultural practices. Each township usually had one or two farm advisers, and farm advisers reported directly to district (縣, *xian*) extension supervisors. Specialist training came from the Provincial Department of Agriculture and Forestry (PDAF), agricultural technical schools, training centers, research institutes.[70]

William I. Myers, the Cornell agricultural economist, took critical aim specifically at the fertilizer-for-rice system.[71] His 1962 report to the JCRR outlined the "discourag[ing] intensive fertilizer use by overcharging for fertilizer and paying less than the market price for rice," which amounted to a "hidden tax" on Taiwan's rural population.[72] He called the system the "most serious handicap" to Taiwan because of the burden it placed on farmers and that it made "no consideration of the desires and needs of farmers. . . . There is no hope of achieving optimum yields and production as long as this practice is continued."[73]

Myers urged Taiwan policymakers to do away with the system by allowing farmers to purchase fertilizer at market prices through the farmers' associations that were present throughout the countryside and to sell rice at global market prices. The issue for Myers was not just one of fairness but one of economic rationality. The fertilizer-for-rice barter system artificially depressed rice prices and elevated fertilizer prices, which in turn discouraged farmers from utilizing chemical fertilizers to their optimal efficiency. Myers argued farmers could gain significantly increased intensive productivity simply by being allowed to pay market prices for fertilizer. He suggested instead that the ROC state rely entirely on a regular tax levied on the rural population instead of the exchange system that distorted incentives and prevented efficient allocation of fertilizer usage.

In his correspondences with Myers, Shen Zonghan acknowledged Myers's position and believed that replacing this fertilizer-for-rice system would have been politically difficult for the Guomindang regime.[74] Though not spelled out, Shen understood rice payments were requisitioned for feeding Taiwan's significant and expensive armed forces.[75] Shortly after the report in 1960, the JCRR instead secured from the government, after discussions rising all the way to vice president Chen Cheng, a reduction in the exchange price of fertilizer for rice from a 1:1 (metric ton) exchange ratio of ammonium sulfate to paddy rice to 1:0.9, a modest improvement yet far short of Myers's recommendations.[76] The barter system only ended in 1973, after Lee Teng-hui was appointed minister without portfolio and negotiated with Taiwan's farmers' associations who had long opposed the system.[77]

The rice-for-fertilizer barter system constituted a tax on rural peoples exercised by the ROC regime in order to support its military, and by extension, its own state power. In the fertilizer industry, too, state power dictated changes in technological systems. When the ROC took over Taiwan, it established a monopoly in fertilizer manufacturing through the state-owned enterprise founded in 1946, the Taiwan Fertilizer Company (台灣肥料公司, Taiwan Feiliao Gongsi). Taiwanese policymakers during the 1950s and early 1960s sought to achieve fertilizer self-sufficiency to produce enough chemical fertilizers to meet domestic demand. Yet these goals to maximize fertilizer usage and achieve higher agricultural yields encountered economic, political, and social obstacles that shaped how these technologies evolved.

The first issue involved fertilizer types. There are three main components of chemical fertilizers: nitrogen, phosphorus, and potassium. The ROC four-year economic plans sought to produce key chemical fertilizers, such as urea and ammonium sulphate, through the construction of new Taiwan Fertilizer facilities, such as the No. 6 plant built in Nangang, on the outskirts of Taipei, in 1960. Yet the focus on production numbers as part of Taiwan's planned economy did not match the actual environmental needs in fertilizer application.

A series of reports from the US Agency for International Development mission based in Taipei illustrated some of the issues. Specific fertilizer usage, whether nitrogen-, phosphorus-, or potassium-based or a combination of those, depended on specific soil composition, crop type, climate, and other ecological conditions. Such knowledge required significant field surveys and tests to collect soils, test irrigation water to ascertain fertilizer nutrients, test different types of fertilizers (nitrogen, phosphorus, or potassium) on different types of crops, and so on. To do this, the Taiwan government commissioned scientists from National Taiwan University, Provincial Chung Hsing University (台灣省立中興大學, Taiwan Shengli Zhongxing Daxue), and the Taiwan Agricultural Research Institute (TARI) and contracted chemical engineers from the J. G. White Engineering Company.

But industrial production, as a result of the economic four-year plans and the goals of the developmental state, was set by top-down logic and not by the results of these field surveys. For example, in 1961, a different Taiwanese state-owned enterprise, the China Petroleum Corporation (CPC), launched a joint venture with the international petroleum giants, Mobil and Allied Chemical, to build a new US$22.5 million plant in Miaoli to produce urea from natural gas. The new jointly owned plant and corporation, called Mobil-Allied, was part of high-level Taiwanese economic goals to decrease its reliance on foreign exchange by encouraging foreign investment in Taiwan's new "free trade zones," which ballooned in popularity during the 1970s and remain an integral part of the international economy today.[78] In 1962, however, at the time of the USAID report, the result was that both urea production facilities from Mobil-Allied and Taiwan Fertilizer's No. 6 plant contributed to significant overproduction in the urea market, almost double what was needed domestically.[79] This resulted in twenty thousand metric tons of urea being donated to Taiwan's Cold War allies, the Republics of Korea and Vietnam, in another instance of state power reinforcing geopolitics. The end result was that both CPC and Taiwan Fertilizer produced urea in accordance with high-level economic planning without considering the local requirements for fertilizer application.

Fertilizer use was further complicated by farmer predilections. Results in Taiwan demonstrated that during the 1950s and 60s, nitrogenous fertilizer provided generally better yields than phosphorus or potassium.[80] But farmers tended to favor only one nitrogenous fertilizer, ammonium sulphate, at the exclusion of others, which prompted a USAID report to lament the "inadequate education of farmers on fertilizer use."[81] Of course, fertilizer usage was an integral part of Taiwanese efforts to educate farmers in Green Revolution methods and was implemented through color print media and film like *Harvest*.

The problems of Taiwan's fragmented production goals and its actual needs led them to new technological solutions intended to close the gaps in the system. In April 1962, the American chemical engineers from J. G. White Engineering Corporation hired by Taiwan and the US government suggested that Taiwan develop and utilize compound fertilizer production facilities and distribution.[82] Compound fertilizers consist of not just one type, meaning just nitrogen, phosphorus, or potassium, but rather a combination. Compound fertilizers would seemingly resolve both aforementioned problems. By utilizing a combination of more basic inputs, it could potentially resolve the oversupply issue exemplified by the Mobil-Allied plant. Moreover, phosphorus and potassium could be easily added to compound fertilizers to compensate for the overutilization of nitrogenous fertilizer, especially ammonium sulphate, preferred by Taiwanese farmers.

American observers lamented the "rigidly controlled agricultural system" of Taiwan, which they warned would fail as had been seen in the examples of Communist China and Soviet Russia.[83] They clung to their ideals of an agricultural society undergirded by a free market. Yet what the American observers failed to understand was that systems of economic production were deeply tied to the political system in Taiwan that both enabled and necessitated state power in markets, rural society, and technological systems. Even in their ideal "free play of private market forces" in the United States, we see instances of state power as well, such as the land-grant university or the technocratic US Department of Agriculture, as argued by historians like Ariel Ron.[84]

Taiwan's political, social, and economic conditions shaped how agricultural technologies and science was carried out in its rural spaces. The authoritarian Guomindang state, seeking to prioritize its own military needs that buttressed its state power, utilized exploitative economic systems such as the rice-for-fertilizer barter system to control food systems. The same desires to maintain and exercise state power through top-down planning and attracting foreign capital also shaped how fertilizer production, application, and technologies were carried out in Taiwan during the 1950s and 60s. When combined, these created a cycle of state power-technology-food that reinforced each other in martial-law era Taiwan. State power enabled agricultural technology in the Taiwan case, providing its funding and impetus, which in turn fed the troops and agricultural surpluses that fueled authoritarianism.

CONCLUSION

By 1965, Taiwan was classified by the United States as a "developed nation" and a "graduate of [US]AID." [85] Although this resulted in the cessation of US funding, the JCRR continued operating until 1972, disbursing leftover USAID funds and ROC government funds that took the place of USAID funds. In 1978, the JCRR ceased to function as a joint institution as the last American commissioner, Bruce Billings, returned to the United States and was not replaced. The JCRR was then renamed the Council for Agricultural Planning and Development. By the 1970s, the story of Taiwan's economic growth had shifted from agriculture to industry, and industrial growth became the face of the Taiwan miracle.

Nonetheless, the agricultural history of Taiwan's miracle was a crucial precursor for Taiwan's economic growth and emergence as a modern society. Unique elements of Taiwan's agricultural planning and circumstances emerged both domestically and abroad. Farmers' associations, established under Japanese colonialism but reformed under the Guomindang, allowed top-down centrally planned policies, technologies, and practices to reach rural spaces. Development planners created new pathways for knowledge dissemination, including visual media like *Harvest* magazine that focused on rural audiences through accessible language and relevant knowledge. The JCRR also imported American ideas, like 4-H, combined with experiences of community development from the Republican era. Organizations like 4-H and farmers' associations inculcated ideals of community-based democracy and public health that attempted to reshape rural norms and practices.

In the agricultural sciences, the JCRR heavily invested in the system of agricultural universities, research institutes, and experiment stations that would generate Green Revolution methods of high-yield crop cultivars, chemical fertilizers, and pesticides. Though this narrative is familiar, basic science was also oriented toward applied uses, such as fruit marketing or produce transportation. These new fields of scientific research emphasized practical applications and non-laboratory forms of scientific knowledge in line with rural needs. Combined with this was a focus on international exchanges, particularly drawing upon foreign expertise and centers of training.

Chemical fertilizers were an example of how emerging, industrialized agricultural technologies were embedded and made possible by the authoritarian GMD system that exerted martial law to extract economic value from Taiwanese rural society. These extractions enabled the fueling of Taiwan's military manpower, which depended on Taiwan's agricultural productivity to provide caloric sustenance and state revenues to reinvest in further development of new chemical fertilizer production.

Individually, these practices were not unique to Taiwan, but taken together, they contrasted with practices elsewhere. In general, higher-cost approaches like dam building and infrastructure were eschewed in favor of privileging knowledge and technology. This approach played to the strengths of development in Taiwan—the preexisting social organizations and infrastructure left by Japanese colonialism, the experiences of Guomindang technocrats, and the availability of US-based expertise and funding—and more importantly, it was successful, as proven by agricultural productivity numbers.

Though Taiwanese development practitioners at that time did not think of their work as engaging in a Taiwanese-specific manner, by the 1960s, Taiwanese technocrats and intellectuals began to market the uniqueness of Taiwan's methods and successful record abroad. This marketing evolved in different cases to a package of ideas that could be easily understood as a model for other nations to follow. This "Taiwan model" most often included the utilization of agricultural science, the dissemination of better methods and practices to the rural populace through agricultural extension, and the fostering of rural social organizations like farmers' associations. As the next chapters will explore, these specific aspects also possessed particular political utility, as they echoed with the needs and limitations of developing nations in Africa, Asia, and Latin America, where Taiwan sent its agricultural technical teams.

4
___

Martyrs of Development

Taiwanese Agrarian Development and the Republic of Vietnam, 1959–1975

Under your great leadership the Vietnamese nation has made remarkable achievements in its fight against communism and in the task of national reconstruction—to the great admiration of the Chinese people. As partners in our common struggle against communist aggression and by working closely together, both our nations shall be able to hasten the triumph of our common cause.

—CHIANG KAI-SHEK

INTRODUCTION

On November 13, 1963, Taiwanese rice technician Zhang Dusheng (張篤生, Chang Tusun) was in a jeep returning to Saigon after visiting a rice experiment station approximately seventy kilometers outside the city when his convoy was ambushed by Vietnamese Communist forces and he was killed by gunfire.[1] In the subsequent months, Zhang was made into a martyr, not of war but, rather, of development. *Cheng Hsin Daily News* (徵信新聞報, Zhengxin xinwenbao, later renamed *China Times* [中國時報, Zhongguo shibao]), a pro-government and pro-Guomindang newspaper in Taiwan, wrote that Zhang was "one of the many technical experts who are away from their homes to help foreign nations, as under-developed as or more under-developed than ours, in developing their resources. They have enabled many [foreign nations] to understand more correctly of [*sic*] the industrious spirit and the scientific knowledge of our countrymen. Their contribution[s] in foreign countries are as great as in their own country."[2]

In the dozens of newspaper articles, interviews, and speeches that followed, Zhang's martyrdom forged a new narrative of Taiwan's engagement with the world. Following its defeat at the hands of the Chinese Communist Party, the ruling GMD regime framed the Republic of China's (ROC) international affairs around an existential battle with Communism and the People's Republic of China (PRC) regime. As I show in this chapter, agrarian development missions to Vietnam beginning in 1959 expanded this narrative beyond retaking mainland China from the Chinese Communists to include development. The ROC was demonstrating its technology, perseverance, and modernity to the Global South. In the rural villages of Vietnam, dozens of Taiwanese teams worked side by side with Vietnamese farmers to showcase greener, lusher vegetables, more efficient and practical farm implements, and stronger Taiwanese rural organizations. The fervent anti-Communism of the Cold War was present, but it was complemented by a new narrative of development rooted in the discourse of modernity and strength through economic self-sufficiency. By the 1970s and 1980s, with the thawing of the Cold War in East Asia, economic growth and success increasingly became an important point of legitimacy and state power for the GMD to the extent that they eventually eclipsed the Cold War anti-Communism as predominant subjects of state discourse.

International development marked a new frontier for Taiwan's interactions with the world. The 1959 Vietnam mission was the first such effort that placed Taiwanese technicians and experts in rural areas outside the island. This initial mission was modest in scope, just over a dozen technicians specializing in plant breeding, fisheries, and farmers' associations, who were then tasked with aiding Vietnamese state-led efforts in crop improvement and rural welfare. From the ROC perspective, anti-Communism and GMD leader and dictator Chiang Kai-shek's quest to form Cold War alliances provided geopolitical incentives for offering assistance. By the mid-1960s, technical assistance to the Republic of Vietnam (RVN) and other non-Communist Asian regimes became a significant complement to military assistance.[3] Chiang incorrectly believed that North Vietnam was completely controlled by the PRC regime. He viewed actions in Vietnam as part of a greater international anti-Communist strategy that could not be limited to the borders of any one country and development offered an additional means to stop Chinese Communist advances.[4] Development became an increasingly vital tool in ROC international diplomacy. In turn, development grew more influential in shaping the Taiwanese state and national identity.

The Vietnam missions beginning in 1959 were especially significant as the first international development missions undertaken by Taiwan. Over the course of the 1960s and 1970s, Taiwanese agrarian missions expanded from one to two dozen, covering every corner of the developing world—Asia, Africa, the South Pacific, and Latin America. The African missions during that period were a form of development diplomacy and a cornerstone of ROC foreign policy, especially in the context of PRC-allied Communist-bloc pressure in the United Nations. ROC officials traded agricultural development assistance for votes from newly decolonized, UN-voting member-states from the African continent. There, they deployed many of the lessons learned in the Vietnam missions, including evoking the discourse of Third World solidarity and commonality through non-whiteness and the strength of non-Western knowledge and methods for achieving postcolonial strength and independence, as the following chapter will explore.

From 1959 until the end of the Second Indochina War (Vietnam War) in 1975, the once limited Vietnam teams represented a new means of legitimacy for the ROC regime. Through development missions, ROC planners demonstrated that they were developed enough where they could assist foreign nations to achieve the same wealth and rural livelihood of Taiwan. At home, this evidence of technical mastery reinforced a new facet of ROC authoritarianism and state power—the celebration of the modern, economically independent nation that staked its claim internationally as much as domestically and on equal grounds with the West. No longer was the ROC a developing nation but a nation whose advanced agrarian development brought demand for its expertise globally and put it at the global vanguard.

In the English-language literature, political scientist John Garver had written about ROC assistance to the RVN, albeit briefly and only within a diplomatic context.[5] Historian Hsiao-ting Lin has written on the ROC-RVN diplomatic relationship, focusing mostly on military assistance.[6] More consequentially, historian Simon Toner has written about how RVN officials under President Nguyễn Văn Thiệu looked to Taiwan and South Korea as potential development models.[7] Toner makes the important claim that Vietnamese officials found relevance in their Asian neighbors instead of the United States or the West because "Taiwan and South Korea offered an alternative model of governance that appealed to the [RVN government]: depoliticized masses, loyal to the authoritarian state and mobilized for economic development."[8] Like Taiwan, South Korea and Japan also engaged in international development, especially in Southeast Asia, where they were present for decades rendering agricultural, medical, and infrastructural development.[9] For RVN leaders, states like Taiwan represented a "romance" or "imagining" of what an idealized RVN could be: a developed, authoritarian state.

This chapter, integrating archival sources from Taiwan, Vietnam, and the United States, traces how Taiwanese experts attempted to transplant elements of their own modernity abroad. It then shows how the development project in Vietnam became an imaginary for the Taiwanese. The purpose of development was as much performative as modernizing, and that performance was in furtherance of ROC objectives to portray itself as a modern, technologically advanced, humanitarian, and prosperous society to the Global South and especially at home.

WHY TAIWAN?

In 1955, Ngô Đình Diệm took power as president of the newly declared Republic of Vietnam in a coup that deposed Bảo Đại, the head of the State of Vietnam. Diệm was a fervent nationalist and anti-Communist opposed to both French colonial presence in the State of Vietnam and Hồ Chí Minh's Democratic Republic of Vietnam regime that occupied Vietnam north of the seventeenth parallel. By then,

US aid had been increasing after French losses to Communist insurgency in Indochina, and Vietnam was seen as a crucial territory that required US guidance and tutelage.[10] Several prominent American development experts were appointed to serve in Vietnam, including the land reform expert attached to the US Department of Agriculture, Wolf Ladejinsky. As historian Edward Miller has observed, experts like Ladejinsky and others in charge of technical aid and rural development policy in Vietnam all had prior experience in other Asian countries.[11] This was certainly the case for William H. Fippin, director of agriculture for US Operations Mission to Vietnam (USOM/Vietnam).

Before he served as director of agriculture for USOM/Vietnam, Fippin was one of two American commissioners from 1952 to 1957 on the Sino-American Joint Commission on Rural Reconstruction (JCRR) in Taiwan. Consisting of five commissioners—three Taiwanese and two American—the JCRR was tasked with formulating agricultural policy for the entire island. Fippin was a farmers'-organization specialist who had overseen several of the farmers' association reforms in the early years of JCRR tenure.[12] As a result of his five years in the JCRR, Fippin was not only intimately familiar with the operations and specialty of the JCRR in farmers' associations but also held that Taiwan was a particularly successful case of agricultural development.

In 1957, the International Cooperation Administration (one of the predecessors to the US Agency for International Development) moved Fippin to Vietnam, an area of increasing security concern. For the RVN, agricultural development became a key concern of not just the Americans in Vietnam and in Washington but also for the Diệm government. Shortly after his arrival, Fippin wrote to former colleague JCRR commissioner Shen Zonghan (沈宗瀚) that "the agricultural program is the largest and in their eyes most important (except of course the military)" for the Vietnamese, especially in the context of seeking American aid to fight the growing communist threat.[13]

On April 4, 1959, in a memorandum to the deputy minister of foreign affairs, a Taiwanese foreign affairs official in Vietnam wrote that "in discussion with USOM Agricultural Director Fippin and RVN Agricultural and Forestry Minister Lê Văn Song, the US has prepared $300,000 USD, to invite twenty or thirty foreign agricultural experts to direct and assist."[14] The initial decision to invite Taiwanese experts was made on the recommendation of Fippin, stemming from his experience as JCRR commissioner. "Because of Fippin having been in Taiwan for many years," the Taiwanese official in Vietnam continued, "and having worked well with many people within our agricultural circles, he has strongly advocated to invite [experts] from our side. The RVN Agricultural and Forestry Minister, however, is interested in hiring French experts."[15] The RVN preference for French experts was unsurprising given the long colonial relationship between France and Indochina. The decision to choose Taiwanese experts was unusual because it broke with colonial preferences for French experts, marking the power of American advisers under Diệm. It was not Vietnam's first exposure to Taiwanese development, however.

Vietnamese officials in Bảo Đại's State of Vietnam (1945–54) that preceded Ngô Đình Diệm's Republic of Vietnam government had as early as 1949 been observing the developments of the JCRR in China and Taiwan. In a document from the State of Vietnam Ministry of Public Works and Transportation (Bộ Công Chánh và Giao Thông), possibly a translation of English-language JCRR documents by Vietnamese officials, the JCRR was described as focused on "bringing earnings to the rural population" and "also recognizing the value of long term research and education."[16] It continued to explain that the JCRR was not a program designed to funnel large amounts of US currency, "because experience has shown in Asia, it was difficult, at least in the beginning, to expend large sums quickly and in a reasonable (wise) manner. On the contrary, it is a lively, dynamic program that begins by finding what is necessary for an ordinary farming family."[17] Though it is not entirely clear where this translation originated, it was most likely read by officials of the Ministry of Public Works and Transportation. In contrast with development programs that are seen as highly capital intensive, a picture emerges of JCRR as being more attuned to the needs of the rural peasant.

Nonetheless, the decision to invite Taiwanese development experts in 1959 should mostly be attributed to the presence of William Fippin. Fippin's position as head of USOM/Vietnam Agriculture and as former head of the JCRR gave him a direct link to the Taiwanese, but there were also intellectual reasons behind the choice beyond mere coincidence and convenience.

Vietnam's agrarian "problem" was construed at the time as social and economic, with significant political consequences for the RVN government. The countryside was where the National Liberation Front (called "Việt Cộng" or Vietnamese Communists, by anti-Communists in the South) operated and drew support. Both the RVN and the US thus targeted rural areas, leading to "pacification" counterinsurgency campaigns beginning in 1954 (and even earlier under French colonial rule and the State of Vietnam), and the Strategic Hamlet Program of 1961 designed to bring counterinsurgency military tactics to the countryside.[18] However, approaches for programs to counter Communist insurgency differed between the two allies. Fippin and other US officials realized that Diệm's demands were centered on amassing as many US dollars with as few strings attached as possible. Fippin sought to discourage this by emphasizing low-cost, high-impact solutions that could be realistically achieved with American assistance. Translated into policy, this meant focusing on projects that could be easily implemented and would not require significant capital or labor resources. "Water," he wrote, was the "biggest, and most difficult problem, but one that we can do relatively little about. Problem is too large. Have seen an old French estimate that control of the Mekong would run to the magnitude of several billion US dollars. Will be a long, long time before anything much is done in that direction so all we can do is a

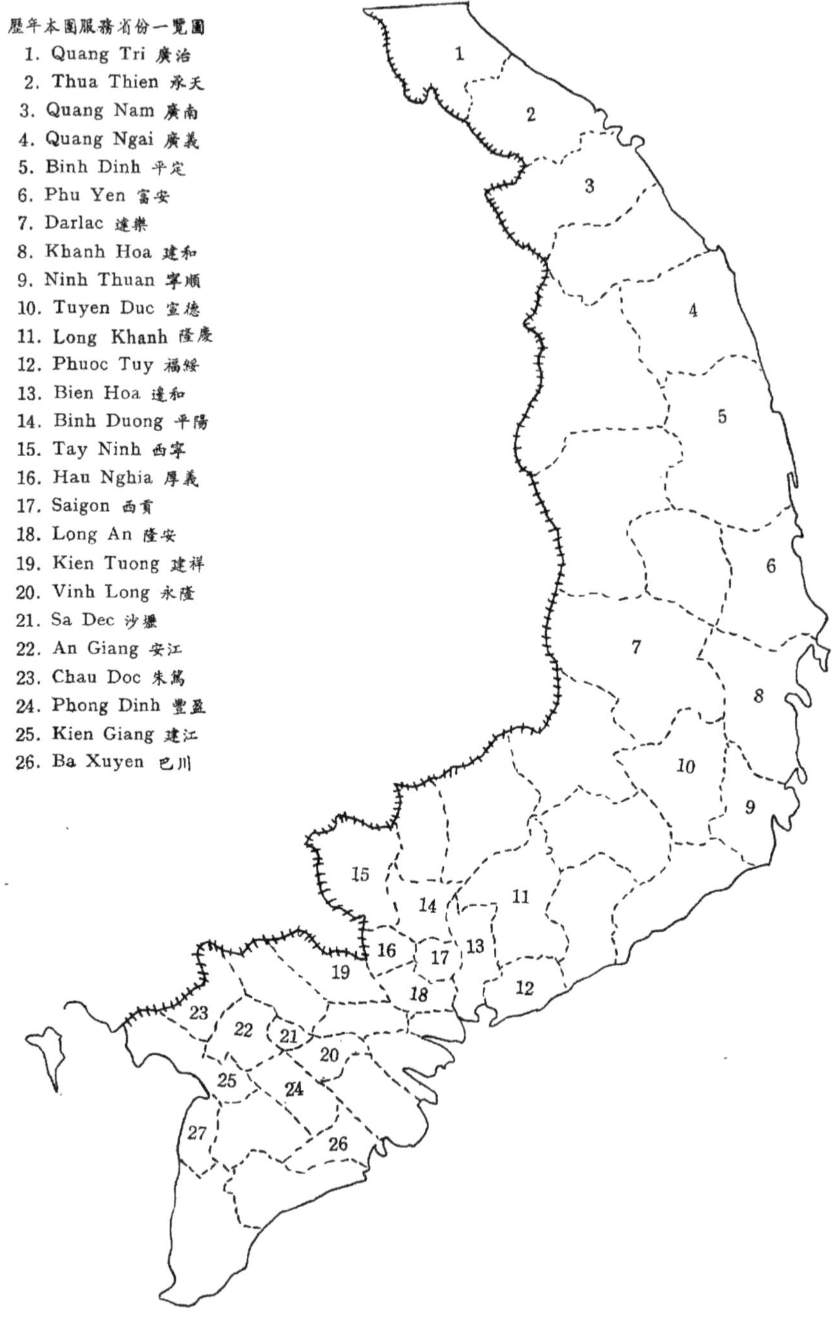

FIGURE 18. A map of the Republic of Vietnam showing provinces where Taiwanese technical assistance was rendered from 1959 to 1973. Zhang, "Twelve Years in Vietnam."

dab here and a dab there."[19] Water was indeed a major topic of discussion among twentieth-century development experts, and the Mekong in particular was a target of the US Bureau of Reclamation as well as Japanese overseas development.[20] Fippin, however, was more concerned with factors he could invite the Taiwanese to assist with.

Instead, Fippin homed in on practices that the Taiwanese excelled at: "varietal improvement, fertilization, pest control and cultural practices." These four were core practices of the JCRR dating back to the Nanking-Cornell cooperation and National Agricultural Research Bureau in Republican-era mainland China. Taiwan benefitted from an extensive hydrological legacy left by Japanese colonialism and water infrastructure projects continued under the JCRR with US funding. However, Taiwan's innovations in cheaper and more easily transferable forms of development were more prominent and were certainly noteworthy for Fippin. Finally, Fippin also observed that for "very much of the southern area floating rice is all that can be grown, and yields are pitifully low—slightly over one metric ton per hectare. One crop."[21] Taiwanese teams were well versed in high-yield rice selection and breeding, having contributed the semi-dwarfing parent, 'Dee-Geo-Woo-Gen' (低角烏尖, 'Dijiao Wujian') to the miracle rice IR-8 (see chapter 7). Taiwanese were also observant of soil conditions and climate that would welcome non-rice crops, such as corn or mustard greens, which were planted by Taiwanese teams in Vietnam.

TRANSPLANTING TAIWANESE SCIENCE
TO VIETNAMESE CONTEXTS

In December 1959, the ROC began its development assistance missions to the RVN. The Vietnam missions consisted initially of technicians and scientists in farmers' organizations (associations and cooperatives), crop improvement, fisheries, and sugarcane. Over the course of its roughly fifteen years, it expanded to include plant breeding, veterinary medicine, entomology, soil science, and irrigation.

A major portion of the 1959 mission focused on crop improvement, with renowned plant breeder Ma Baozhi (馬保之, Paul C. Ma) at its head.[22] Ma began his career as an agricultural scientist in China, graduating in 1929 from one of the preeminent centers of agricultural science, University of Nanking, followed by his doctorate in plant breeding at Cornell University on fellowship and a year doing research at Cambridge University.[23] Upon returning to China in 1934, he took a position with the National Agricultural Research Bureau (NARB), in charge of operating the NARB Guangxi Extension Station. In 1944, he was appointed the head of the Agricultural Division within the Ministry of Agriculture and Forestry (MOAF) of the Republic of China, as well as later the deputy chief for the Agricultural Rehabilitation Commission established by the MOAF to work with the United Nations Relief and Rehabilitation Administration in China. After moving to Taiwan with the Nationalist regime, he became the dean of the College of Agriculture in the preeminent National Taiwan University. In choosing Ma as the leader of the first Crop Improvement Mission to Vietnam, the ROC sent one of its most experienced and respected plant breeders abroad. A well-traveled scientist, Ma was likely as highly regarded as far as technocrats went, and after his brief time as head of the Crop Improvement Mission in Vietnam, he spent over a decade employed by the UN Food and Agriculture Organization as the dean of the College of Agriculture in the University of Liberia (see following chapter).

Under Ma's guidance, the Crop Improvement Mission produced lengthy reports on the state of Vietnamese agriculture. Rice was a key concern given that like Taiwan, Vietnam was primarily a rice-consuming culture. In 1964, Taiwanese experts approximated that 2.5 million hectares produced 5 million metric tons of rice annually in Vietnam.[24] One of the key reports was published in February 1960, titled *Rice Seed Production in Vietnam*.[25] It surveyed and summarized rice production in the RVN, examining each step from production to district farmers, including inspection, storage, distribution, financial subsidies, and dissemination of information. The broad scope of the report mirrored 1950s JCRR reforms in Taiwan, where in addition to focusing on plant breeding and application of new agricultural seeds and technologies, JCRR technicians also developed farmers' associations that served as intermediaries for providing agricultural credit and selling agricultural products to wholesalers and the market. Taiwanese studies in Vietnam also considered new ideas of applied economics and agricultural extension that worked hand in hand with surveys and policymaking. The focus on the full cycle of production to consumer reflected a lesson learned from the JCRR experience on Taiwan, that basic science was inseparable from the society in which it operated. Thus the application of science also considered new ideas of applied economics and agricultural extension that worked together with policymaking and social observations. Most of the report recommendations fell into this category.

The report's primary concern was plant breeding. The Crop Improvement Team observed that rice produced in Vietnam originated mostly from government-run primary-seed multiplication farms. The rice produced from the primary farms was sent to secondary-seed multiplication farms that then produced enough seeds to be distributed to farmers to plant for the season. One significant problem was that at the primary level, multiplication seed was filtered only for off-types, rice varieties not intended for distribution onward. As a result, the team wrote that "the desirable level of purity can hardly be thus maintained," implying that standards for multiplied rice were too lax.[26] Furthermore, selection for the primary-seed multiplication farms was made fifteen years prior to the report, in 1945, and no further selection was performed on a regional basis at the secondary-seed multiplication farm level. The report implied that Vietnam was relying on outdated rice and that selecting newer varieties would likely improve production. The team suggested instead that the government agencies responsible for rice breeding work

FIGURE 19. Taiwanese technician showing a Vietnamese farmer how to use a rolling marker to maintain ideal distance while transplanting rice seedlings. "嚴家淦總統數位照片—臺灣農技團在越南工作成果," April 1965, archival collection number 館藏號 006-030202-00011-001, Yan Jiagan Papers, Academia Historica, Taiwan.

closely with the seed multiplication farms in order to select and produce seeds that were suitable for the local regions they supplied.

This recommendation on seed multiplication was in line with the fundamentals of agricultural science of the twentieth century—with its focus on production using disciplined, rationalized practices—that helped define the Green Revolution. In this case, improving the national seed production system adhered to the goal of scientific selection and breeding, which was to create higher-yielding seeds rather than allowing the multiplication of lower-yielding varieties. Localization was also a part of selection, which involved ensuring that varieties accommodated the specific soils, climates, growing seasons, and other conditions in the wide rural areas where seeds would be distributed.

Rationalization also extended to cultural practices, such as maintaining precise and consistent distance between rice seedlings to ensure enough room for growth without underutilizing much needed land. Taiwanese farmers introduced new agricultural implements that could aid Vietnamese farmers in easily marking distances through imprinting grids in the soil (figure 19).

In the following years, the Chinese Agricultural Technical Mission (CATM), as the Taiwanese teams to Vietnam were collectively known early on, established a rice experiment center in Mỹ Tho, located in the Mekong delta, with experiment stations located throughout Vietnam, including Long Xuyên and Cần Thơ in the Mekong River delta and Phan Rang in southern Vietnam.[27] The 1968 annual report from the CATM indicated that the Mỹ Tho Experiment Center had collected 710 varieties for comparative trials, including 84 newly-introduced foreign varieties from the International Rice Research Institute (IRRI) in Los Baños in the Philippines, and 37 varieties from Cambodia and Thailand. These were then distributed to the regional experiment stations for field trials to determine which varieties would perform best for each region. The seeds sourced from neighboring Southeast Asian nations reflected the belief among Taiwanese scientists (and IRRI scientists, too) that different areas of Vietnam shared ecological similarities with much of Southeast Asia. Indeed, terrain and geography as varied as central and southern Vietnam, which spanned not just latitude but also topographical, precipitation, and soil differences, made seeds one way in which development was seen spatially, not just nationally.

IR-8 rice produced by IRRI showed impressive yields, nearly doubling the native check variety (used as a control) at 5,744 kg per hectare compared with 3,049 kg per ha. IR-8, often called "miracle rice" because of its high yields or sometimes "god of agriculture" (*thần nông*, or TN-8) in Vietnam, implying supernatural power, was the most famous product of IRRI.[28] Bred in the early 1960s as a cross of two varieties, Indonesian Peta and Taiwanese 'Dee-Geo-Woo-Gen', its global dissemination allowed for significant improvements in yield across many South and Southeast Asian rice-growing regions. IR-8 became an integral contributor to the Green Revolution in Asia, though along with monoculture and reliance on chemical fertilizers, it also led to dependence on chemicals and commercialized agriculture with potentially disastrous ecological consequences.[29] Assistant director for USAID/Vietnam, James P. Grant, who was born and raised in Beijing as the son of Canadian missionaries and became a longtime development advocate, wrote to Shen Zonghan of his visit to a Taiwanese demonstration plot near Biên Hòa where IR-8 was being planted. He remarked of "the fine work done by your JCRR technicians in Vietnam" in helping to transform the formerly "crude demonstration plot" to "a major rice research center" on his second visit a year later. He included to Shen a *New York Times* clipping showcasing the gift of IR-8 from Vietnam to the United States, a symbol of its gratitude as appreciation for the US introducing the new cultivar in Vietnam.[30]

IR-8 did not perform well in all field tests. One of IR-8's differentiating characteristics was its semi-dwarfing allele, *sd1*, which it inherited from its Taiwanese parent, 'Dee-geo-woo-gen'. Dwarfing allowed IR-8 stalks to be short and stocky and resist toppling, which would submerge rice under water, making it impossible to harvest and thus reducing yields. But IR-8 in Định Tường and Phong Dinh

FIGURE 20. Comparison of the American variety 'Dixie Queen' watermelon (*left*) at 14 kg introduced by the Taiwanese agricultural team compared to a native variety (*right*) in Định Tường. "嚴家淦總統數位照片—臺灣農技團在越南工作成果," April 1965, archival collection number 館藏號 006–030202–00011–001, Yan Jiagan Papers, Academia Historica, Taiwan.

suffered from the opposite problem. There, due to higher rainfall, water levels in paddy fields were high enough to submerge the shorter dwarf-type rice. The CATM instead suggested earlier plantings in April and November to harvest in July and March and thus avoid flooding in the later season.[31] Taiwanese efforts to distribute field tests of different varieties was in recognition of the difficulties of national-scale development across different cultural, social, and ecological contexts. As historian David Biggs has argued, the specificities of place and locality had outsized consequences for American development on the ground in An Giang province.[32] In the Taiwanese missions, the downsides of using IR-8 were avoided by adjusting planting seasons to account for local hydrological conditions. Nonetheless, the unexpected obstacles facing IR-8, known for its universal applicability and extraordinary yield, exemplified the issues facing development not just by Taiwanese teams in Vietnam but everywhere in the world.

Taiwanese teams expanded beyond rice to include other food crops, including onions, carrots, garlic, sweet potatoes, watermelon, soybean, cabbage, lettuce, peanuts, sorghum, corn, and mung bean. Varieties were sourced from countries throughout the Global North and South, from the United States, Australia, and

Korea. Experiment stations run by Taiwanese compared varieties, which could include up to twenty-eight varieties as in the case of onions ranging from 'Texas Early Grano 502' to 'Early Lockyer Brown'.[33]

Simultaneously with seeds, another aspect of Green Revolution methods was also touted by Taiwanese teams: chemical fertilizer. In a 1964 report written by the Taiwanese mission to Vietnam to the JCRR, chemical fertilizer was identified as being used "very little" because "rice farmers are not familiar with chemical fertilizers." Their conclusion was of course that increased usage was "absolutely necessary." This conclusion is unsurprising, given the Green Revolution paradigm of the 1960s that relied heavily on chemicals and varieties that responded well to chemical fertilizer, despite its being short-sighted due to the environmental consequences. Taiwan had utilized chemical fertilizers extensively for decades, dating back to the Japanese colonial era, and relied heavily on chemicals for its own agricultural miracle in the 1950s and 1960s (see chapter 3). In the resulting solution, implemented at the recommendation of the Taiwanese team in Vietnam, newly established Vietnamese fertilizer committees (one central and eighteen provincial) sold fertilizers on credit through farmers' associations and cooperatives, similar to the system in Taiwan. The report detailed that logistical issues (tardiness and confusion) were problematic but excusable given how "new" fertilizer was.

Fertilizer usage similarly followed after rigorous field trials across the rice experiment stations. Across Ba Xuyên, Cần Thơ, Huế, and Phan Rang experiment stations, three types of chemical fertilizers were tested in growing rice at various ratios: Nitrogen (N), Phosphorus Pentoxide (P_2O_5, or phosphoric acid), and potassium oxide (K_2O, or potash). Responses differed dramatically, with some showing a near two-fold increase in yields, while rice grown in Huế responded negatively to fertilizer compared to use without fertilizer.[34]

In the language of the 1964 memorandum, the Taiwanese team leader described how "fertilizer distribution and utilization in Taiwan, Republic of China, has won praises of countries in Southeast Asia." This self-affirmation served to encourage Taipei to accept a team of four Vietnamese fertilizer distribution specialists to observe demonstrations of fertilizer distribution and usage in Taiwan, but it nonetheless reinforced a narrative of Taiwan's success being welcomed and recognized by receiving countries like Vietnam in the Global South.[35]

RURAL ORGANIZATIONS, GENDER, AND AGRICULTURAL EXTENSION

The ROC team recommended a series of measures centered on agricultural extension and demonstration. An early suggestion during the first year of the mission in early 1960 was to establish demonstration fields for proper planting and care of seeds selected by the state. To complement demonstration, the team suggested providing training in conjunction with 4-T, the Vietnamese equivalent of 4-H in the United States that was also funded by US agricultural development missions in Vietnam. 4-T and 4-H were both rural organizations that integrated agricultural and public health practices as a means of community youth activity (see chapter 3). In the context of the ROC recommendations, 4-T club members would be utilized along with village leaders to disseminate information about seed planting. Other suggestions to help knowledge dissemination included printed materials, similar to *Harvest*, which was written and distributed in Taiwan by the JCRR in conjunction with the US Information Service. Finally, the report also suggested that Vietnamese officials establish contests for the highest per-unit area of rice production, in which the "winning farmer will receive [an] award and will be asked to tell other farmers the ways and means by which he achieve[d] [his] goal."[36] By incentivizing demonstration through informal competition, Taiwanese experts were hoping to create new information venues for rural Vietnamese farmers to learn from their own.

Zhang Lianjun (張廉駿), who led the farmers' association team and later the entire CATM, reflected on his time in Vietnam. He wrote, "Vietnam's agricultural environment, cultivation methods, and cultural habits on the whole are very close to that of Taiwan's those who are knowledgeable on the issue all believe that to develop agriculture one must draw upon the experiences of Taiwan (以台灣為借鏡 *yi taiwan wei jiejing*)."[37] This perspective of Taiwan providing an invaluable model for other Global South nations to follow because of its similar ecological and cultural characteristics was pervasive in writings on Taiwanese development.

The Vietnam mission was not just focused on the agricultural sciences. Among the greatest needs of Vietnam were perceived to be social in nature. With the expansion of the Vietnamese Communists in northern Vietnam, the Republic of Vietnam prioritized the needs of its farmers, the most vulnerable to Communist organization. Despite attempts to replace French colonial administrators with Vietnamese administrators under Diệm's government, Communist insurgency was not stemmed by pacification campaigns. Diệm and other RVN officials turned to rural and community development, which emphasized the community as a durable unit of governance from which positive social change could be replicated from the bottom-up and thus throughout rural Vietnam.[38] It was here that Fippin's aforementioned connection with Taiwan was fateful. In May 1959, approximately one month after Fippin's suggestion to invite Taiwanese experts on farmers' associations, Trần Ngọc Liên, the commissioner general for cooperatives and agricultural credit, traveled to Taiwan with Fippin and several other RVN officials to observe Taiwanese farmers' associations firsthand. After the trip, Liên formally requested Taiwanese experts in farmers' associations and cooperatives. Ten Taiwanese agricultural experts were requested to be sent to the RVN on a six month provisional basis, to "work especially at village levels, he said, encouraging, guiding, training, and assisting Vietnam's newly formed farmers' associations to get firmly established and operating."[39] Along with teams from other "Free World"

FIGURE 21. Vietnamese farmers visit a Taiwanese demonstration farm. My interviewee, Taiwanese technician Zhang Jiming, noted that by his arrival in Vietnam in 1968, a large number of farmers consisted of women, which he attributed to the drawing away of men to fight in the ongoing war. "嚴家淦總統數位照片—臺灣農技團在越南工作成果," April 1965, archival collection number 館藏號 006–030202–00011–001, Yan Jiagan Papers, Academia Historica, Taiwan. Zhang Jiming, retired agricultural technician, interview by author, Taichung, Taiwan, January 14, 2019.

nations brought in through US mediation, the work of the Taiwanese technical mission would help form the basis of counter-communist insurgency efforts that were designed to win the hearts and minds of the Vietnamese peasants.

On October 27, 1959, Republic of Vietnam vice president Nguyễn Ngọc Thơ sent to eleven province chiefs the objectives and scope of the Taiwanese assistance mission in farmers' associations.[40] The October agreement increased the Taiwanese technicians to eleven, among whom eight were to focus on establishing farmers' associations and cooperatives, two on fisheries and crop cooperatives and the remaining technician on training. The eight were split into three teams and were responsible for vast territories of central and southern Vietnam, roughly four to five provinces per team. After familiarizing themselves with local conditions, the RVN regime placed the onus upon local governments "to let these specialist conduct their activities without hindrance" and furthermore to "must have new ideas and make clear problems that require specialists' help and investigation" to send up to the Central Farmers' Association Committee and central government authorities.[41] Though spread thin, the Taiwanese advisors were meant to encourage new ideas within the local governments that would be actionable, and thus contribute toward the South Vietnamese regime's efforts in a national rural policy.

FIGURE 22. Chiang Ching-kuo (蔣經國, Jiang Jingguo), premier of the ROC and son of Chiang Kai-shek, visits a 4-H chapter in Biên Hòa Province, Republic of Vietnam. Zhang, "Twelve Years in Vietnam."

FIGURE 23. As part of the agricultural extension and demonstration program, Taiwanese technicians trained selected Vietnamese farmers to serve as demonstration supervisors. This picture shows the Taiwanese-trained supervisors teaching soybean planting methods to other Vietnamese farmers. "嚴家淦總統數位照片—臺灣農技團在越南工作成果," April 1965, archival collection number 館藏號 006–030202–00011–001, Yan Jiagan Papers, Academia Historica, Taiwan.

From the Taiwanese side, these objectives needed to be translated from diplomatic objectives, defined by the realities of anti-Communist warfare, into development policy objectives, defined by organizational directives. On April 9, 1959, the Ministry of Foreign Affairs sent a memorandum to the Ministry of Economic Affairs, which oversaw the JCRR and agricultural development policy in Taiwan. In the memo, MOFA outlined the work details. First, "work comes into contact with broad social strata, including central and local, to the lowest stratum of village farmers' associations."[42] Following that, "work scope includes matters related to leading, extension, and training, with achieving farmers association self-sufficiency and independence as the objective."[43] These objectives were supplemented by goals of the farmers' association to "produce agricultural products."[44] The focus on the lowest levels of Vietnamese social strata reflected the rural emphasis of development from the Taiwanese model and also the diplomatic desire to engage at the village level. The Taiwanese success at organizing farmers' associations and using them as the unit by which to distribute fertilizers and engage in distribution of knowledge via extension in this case dovetailed with Vietnamese and American objectives.

In defining how these projects would be carried out, Taipei chose a different approach from the United States. Whereas the ICA and its predecessors chose to send experts with extensive scientific training for its missions abroad, Taiwanese planners instead sought blue-collar technicians. The same April 9 memo continued that Taiwanese "workers do not require higher education, but rather require long term service in farmers' associations or related organizations as well as wide ranging practical experience managing farmers' associations or related organizations."[45] This change was pragmatic, reflecting the importance of on-the-ground experience interacting with "the lowest stratum" of rural society. It also saved on costs; technicians received significant hardship bonuses for working abroad in Vietnam, and many were eager to take the salary bump. Even the relatively few scientists who led the technical teams were represented as working in the rural countryside and with Vietnamese farmers. In reports written for audiences outside of Taiwan, especially for Americans and "Free World" allies like Vietnam, Taiwanese documents presented university science professors as working "shoulder to shoulder" with Vietnamese farmers.[46]

My interview with a retired technician, Zhang Jiming (張基明), who worked in Vietnam from 1968 to 1969, indicated that the majority of technicians were recruited from agricultural vocational schools (農校, *nongxiao*). Zhang's own background was from the Taichung Agricultural Vocational High School (台中高農) in agronomy (綜合農藝, *zonghe nongyi*). He underwent two months of training designed by the JCRR for technicians performing technical work abroad and was assigned to a four-person team approximately 35 km northwest of Saigon. Zhang engaged in all manner of work, from demonstration to extension, thus showing local Vietnamese farmers how to plant rice, grains, vegetables, and use agricultural equipment. At each stage, representatives from local Vietnamese

FIGURE 24. National Taiwan University professor C. I. Lin (*left*) demonstrates transplanting rice "shoulder to shoulder" with Vietnamese farmers. "嚴家淦總統數位照片—臺灣農技團在越南工作成果," April 1965, archival collection number 館藏號 006–030202–00011–001, Yan Jiagan Papers, Academia Historica, Taiwan.

farmers' associations would be invited to their Taiwanese team demonstration farm. Usually, each day after dinner, Taiwanese technicians would hold meetings for one to two hours to teach usually around ten Vietnamese farmers different agronomic techniques.[47]

Taiwanese extension and demonstration teams in Vietnam worked not only in agricultural sciences and farmers' associations but also in "home improvement." Demonstration centers included rural handicraft production equipment that could be utilized within "home economics," a gendered notion that home-based labor was also productive labor. In Taiwan beginning in the 1960s, rural organizations like 4-H had begun to organize women to produce handicrafts that could then be sold in markets. This was tied with 4-H in the United States, where 4-H originated, and its gendering of boys and girls.[48] It continued into Taiwan, along with work on community development, and persisted well into the 1970s, 80s, and 90s with Taiwanese government promotion of married women labor to fuel rural home-based production that formed the "satellite factories" of Taiwan's later industrialized economic growth.[49] In Vietnam, women played a prominent role in rural areas. Zhang Jiming indicated that by his arrival in Vietnam many men were involved in the ongoing war, and thus women often participated in extension and demonstration activities.[50]

FIGURE 25. "Home improvement agents" shown here are using straw-rope-making machine at a Taiwanese demonstration center in Biên Hòa. "嚴家淦總統數位照片—臺灣農技團在越南工作成果," April 1965, archival collection number 館藏號 006–030202–00011–001, Yan Jiagan Papers, Academia Historica, Taiwan.

Though most extension and demonstration were performed in person at demonstration centers and farms, they were also complemented with written materials. In Taiwan, magazines, pamphlets, and other materials were distributed by farmers' associations and government agents as a core strategy in extension. *Harvest* included morality tales, comics, and other means of attracting a wide swath of Taiwanese rural society.

In Vietnam, Taiwanese development included written materials as well. In one instance in 1973, a Vietnamese request for an emergency shipment of Taiwanese fertilizers and seeds was accompanied with literature on proper usage of fertilizer in Vietnamese. Simply titled "Seed and Fertilizer Usage Guide," the cover also indicated that the seeds and fertilizers were a gift of the Republic of China ("中華民國敬贈") with a short message that wished "peace and happiness" to "the prosperous village farmers of the Republic of Vietnam."[51] The guide elaborated the technical contents of fertilizer, including chemical composition, but was also a means to showcase humanitarian actions and goodwill of Taiwanese assistance. Boxes containing vegetable seeds were adorned with both flags of the Republic of China and Republic of Vietnam side by side, showing the origins of the gift along with partnership for the RVN peoples.

In the official ceremony handing over the roughly fifty thousand packages of seeds and fertilizer, ROC ambassador to Vietnam Xu Shaochang (許紹昌)

presented a speech that outlined ROC perspectives on the alliance. Throughout the speech, he emphasized that the ROC was similar to the RVN in social and cultural terms; the gift, he affirmed, was "from one farming people to another." In relaying the hopes of the ROC, the ambassador's speech also evoked modernist language of economic prosperity as well as valorization of the rural. The seeds and fertilizer were intended to give "a helping hand to the individual small farmer to stand on his own feet again." These packages to individual farmers were then accompanied with a large number of "high-yielding hybrid corn seed" that were "designed for the purpose of demonstrating profitable corn-growing in various provinces in Vietnam to pave the way for large-scale production of corn both for domestic use and for export in the future."[52] The capitalist language focused on scientific modernism of high-yielding hybrids in order to achieve high productivity and large export numbers, which would then resolve both problems of basic human need as well as national economic prosperity.

REPRESENTING DEVELOPMENT AT HOME

In Taiwan, the continued demand for Taiwanese development assistance abroad was continually reported on domestic news outlets. On a regular basis from 1959 until 1974, newspaper articles delivered updates on the progress and incidents of the Taiwanese team in Vietnam. Though often short, they compensated for their brevity with regularity. Changes in team leadership, project accomplishments, and particularly contract renewals were all reported on by major Taiwanese newspapers. These newspapers, which at the time were run by or closely affiliated with the Guomindang regime, served official state interests, to report on the efforts of the ROC abroad helping other developing nations.

The aforementioned 1963 death of agricultural technician Zhang Dusheng demonstrated the importance of overseas development to ROC foreign policy officials. Zhang was a Taiwanese rice technician who was killed in the line of duty by Vietnamese communist forces near Saigon. He was born in 1935 and raised in Tainan, in southern Taiwan. After graduating from Tainan No. 1 High School, he enrolled in the Taiwan Provincial Agricultural College in Taichung (today National Chung Hsing University, 國立中興大學) for his secondary education. Upon graduation, he underwent training as a reserve officer and was assigned to grassroots political organization work. After completing his military service, he taught at the Yuanlin Agricultural School (員林農校, Yuanlin Nongxiao) briefly in 1961 before moving on to work at the Taichung District Agricultural Improvement Station (台中農業改良場, Taizhong Nongye Gailiang Chang), where he worked for two years in rice improvement. On October 10, 1963, he left Taiwan to join the Taiwanese Agricultural Technical Assistance Team to Vietnam.

On November 13, 1963, Zhang was in a jeep returning to Saigon after visiting a rice experiment station approximately forty *li* (seventy kilometers) outside of Saigon when his convoy was ambushed by Vietnamese Communist forces and he was killed ("遭越共伏擊死亡") along with a Vietnamese translator.[53] Based on an interview I conducted with a Taiwanese rice technician who had also participated in Taiwan's later development missions abroad, it seems likely that Zhang's death was collateral and accidental and that Zhang was not the intended target of the ambush. Taiwanese technicians would on occasion be caught in the middle of military operations. Another incident involving three Taiwanese technicians being surrounded by Vietnamese Communist troops occurred in Huế in 1968, but usually the Taiwanese technicians emerged without issue due to intervention by allied forces.[54] My interviewee expressed that it was likely Zhang's group may have panicked and attempted to flee upon being ambushed by Vietnamese Communists, who usually did not explicitly target Taiwanese agricultural technicians for attacks, and Zhang was unfortunately killed as a result. One memorandum sent by the Taiwanese technical team to a Vietnamese agricultural official referenced "Vietcong snipers" as being responsible for Zhang's death.[55] Yet newspaper portrayals of the incident left out details of the incident, instead pointing to the patriotic nature of Zhang's work and the work in general conducted by the Taiwanese agricultural technical teams.

Newspaper editorials, especially those from Guomindang-affiliated papers, *United Daily News* (聯合報, *Lianhe Bao*) and *Cheng Hsin Daily News*, provided venues for the Guomindang to use development as a means of propaganda.

One *United Daily News* article cited Provincial Department of Agriculture and Forestry director Zhang Huiqiu (張慧秋, H. T. Chang), who after being interviewed following Zhang Dusheng's death stated that Zhang Dusheng was "exactly the type of youth that our country needs [正是國家所最需要的]." Elaborating further, Zhang Huiqiu explained that young technicians like Zhang Dusheng served a crucial role. Since 1953, Taiwan's agriculture "had primarily relied on practical and relatively simple experimental research results [主要依賴實用性的 比較簡單的試驗研究的結果]" but by 1963 "had already attained such high levels that in order to further develop, it requires engaging in even more refined and profound research [但現在本省的農業已達到很高的水準，再要改進，必 須從事較精密高深的研究]." Thus, going abroad to Vietnam represented positive opportunities for experts like Zhang, where work in Taiwan was often poorly compensated ("待遇菲薄"), so that they could "on the one hand accomplish our national mission of assisting our allies, and on the other hand, after accumulating savings, return home to work with peace of mind [一方面達成我國協助友邦的 任務，一方面可於略有積蓄後返國安心工作]."[56]

Zhang Huiqiu's goal in emphasizing aspects of pragmatism and advanced research not only reinforced that Taiwan possessed unique and useful expertise but also informed the domestic Taiwanese audience why Taiwanese youth needed to be abroad in Vietnam to benefit both their own careers and their nation. Zhang Dusheng's status as *benshengren* (本省人), or native Taiwanese, was never explicitly mentioned in these accounts, as official accounts would not acknowledge such ethnic divisions under official GMD policy that treated the *benshengren* as Chinese. However, Zhang's birthplace of Tainan was mentioned on occasion, and combined with his birth year of 1935, which predated the arrival of the GMD, the reader could easily deduce Zhang was *benshengren*. Many of the blue collar technicians who worked in rural areas in Taiwan and then were sent abroad to Vietnam and other foreign locales in the 1960s were *benshengren* like Zhang Dusheng, as opposed to the bureaucrats and scientists in positions of power like Shen Zonghan and Ma Baozhi, who were *waishengren* (外省人), "mainlanders" who arrived in Taiwan with the Guomindang in 1949. This common background of Zhang perhaps made international development more sympathetic to *benshengren* audiences, tying in the political and diplomatic objectives of the *waishengren* Guomindang with the sacrifices made by *benshengren* on behalf of representing Taiwan abroad.

Most importantly, development legitimized the GMD state in the eyes of *benshengren*. The need for Taiwanese aid abroad and Taiwanese willingness to put their lives on the line to help other nations gave the Taiwanese a sense of nationalistic pride, demonstrating superior Taiwanese qualities of "industriousness" and "scientific knowledge."[57] Economic growth, humanitarian largesse, and expertise in modern science and technology were the characteristics that the GMD sought to cultivate in their public image to maintain their authoritarian grip on Taiwan.

REPRESENTING DEVELOPMENT ABROAD

While Zhang Dusheng was crafted into the image of the idealized Taiwanese under the developmentalist Guomindang at home, the targeted audiences were not just limited to Taiwanese and the rural Vietnamese. The GMD portrayed itself as the leaders of "Free China" internationally—the legitimate Chinese regime. This included the overseas Chinese (華僑, *huaqiao*) diaspora. For late Qing revolutionary activists such Sun Yat-sen, overseas Chinese had played an important role, from funding early GMD revolutionary efforts to providing the technical expertise for nation-building.[58] During the Cold War, the overseas Chinese became a particularly important demographic for the GMD in order to substantiate its own claims of legitimacy as the true guardians of "China." Without the majority of its territories prior to its retreat in 1949, the GMD made extensive efforts to garner support in major overseas Chinese communities abroad in places like Southeast Asia, as historian Chien-Wen Kung has argued, to "mobilize a deterritorialized Chinese nation and destroy Chinese Communism in pursuit of a unified China under its leadership."[59]

Vietnam was certainly no exception. Vietnam and greater Southeast Asia were home to a large Chinese population that had begun emigrating in the seventeenth century with the end of the Ming dynasty. Many overseas Chinese originated from south China, particularly speakers of Cantonese, Chaozhou (Teochew), and Minnan (Hokkien). A large number settled into the southern Vietnam city of Chợ Lớn just outside of Saigon and later integrated and merged into Saigon. ROC official diplomacy targeted these Chinese populations as part of their global efforts to build a *huaqiao* identity under ROC patronage. Historian Mei Feng Mok argues that the Chinese community in Chợ Lớn in particular developed transnational diaspora ties with Chinese outside of Vietnam, in Taiwan, Malaya, and Hong Kong, partially through the connections fostered by the ROC state.[60] The ROC, for example, encouraged Vietnamese-Chinese to attend universities in Taiwan by offering scholarships and reserved spots for overseas Chinese as incentives.[61]

Chinese communities in Vietnam thus became another discursive battleground for the GMD to win over. Utilizing the same language and imagery, GMD development was covered in Vietnamese newspapers serving Chinese communities in Chợ Lớn and elsewhere in Vietnam. One of the largest Chinese newspapers by circulation in Vietnam was the *Yuen Tuong Jih Pao* (遠東日報, *Yuandong Ribao*, "Far Eastern daily"), founded in 1940 by Zhu Jixing (朱繼興), a *huaqiao* businessman of Chaozhou descent, and distributed as far as Laos and Cambodia.[62] *Yuen Tuong*'s regular columns discussed matters of everyday life, such as education, gender, literature, and film, along with coverage of ROC actions in Vietnam. In the July 14, 1960, issue of *Yuen Tuong*, a journalist interviewed Crop Improvement Mission head Ma Baozhi and relayed the goals of the Taiwanese team in beginning technical assistance to Vietnam.[63] Thereafter, *Yuen Tuong* reported with regularity the actions of the Taiwanese teams, ranging from visits of irrigation experts to contract renewals.[64] In the aforementioned instance where Taiwan gifted seeds and fertilizer in 1973, *Yuen Tuong* reported on the consequences of the gift by borrowing the same language and phrasing as utilized in Ambassador Xu Shaochang's speech. In detailing the goals of the gift, *Yuen Tuong* wrote that gifted seeds were intended "in the future not only to supply the food needs of this nation, but also to expand its crop exports."[65]

The ROC portrayed the Taiwanese-Vietnamese alliance in nationalist, Asian-centric, and anti-Communist terms that appealed to the anticolonial legacy of RVN and of Ngô Đình Diệm. Diệm came to power on what Ed Miller has called "an unimpeachable reputation as a nationalist" that culminated with deposing the French-backed Bảo Đại and ended French colonial influence in Vietnam.[66] Though fiercely anticolonial, he also gained US support for his regime through his vehement anti-Communism as well, particularly against Hồ Chí Minh's Democratic Republic of Vietnam. As historian Nu-Anh Tran has argued, the RVN engaged in an anti-Communist internationalism imagining the RVN in friendships with Cold War allies and as a member of the "Free World."[67] This included participation in the Asian People's Anti-Communist League, of which the ROC was a founding member, along with delegations from South Korea, Thailand, Macau, Hong

Kong, the Ryukyu Islands (Okinawa), the Philippines, and the RVN.[68] RVN anti-Communists "conceived of anticommunist internationalism as the natural response to communist imperialism" and as a result the RVN emphasized its international relationships.[69]

A 1960 document from the RVN Ministry of Public Works and Transportation (Bộ Công Chánh và Giao Thông), most likely a Vietnamese translation of an ROC official report of Diệm's visit to Taiwan, likened the two nations as being "two peoples [or nations, *dân-tộc*] that share the same cultural root which communism is destroying now."[70] It elaborated on the existential threat ("the existence of two countries is also currently in danger") from Communism to both nations. The report praised the accomplishments of the Guomindang's 1911 revolution that led to the establishment of the Republic of China and Diệm's founding of the Republic of Vietnam.[71] The struggles of the "free" peoples of Asia became a point of pride and of common history. Both sides perceived themselves to be linked with a recent revolutionary past, rooted in their violent opposition to Communism.

The translated ROC report furthermore favorably compared the nationalist ideologies espoused by both leaders, the Three Principles of the People of Sun Yat-sen adopted by Chiang Kai-shek as the political ideology of the Republic of China, and Diệm's personalism theory (Thuyết Nhân vị).[72]

Both personalism and the Three Principles shared basic tenets. Personalism was Diệm's answer to finding a path between radical Communism and French colonial–defined liberalism. Personalism can be traced back to the writings of French Catholic philosopher Emmanuel Mounier, who critiqued liberal capitalism and individualism in the wake of the 1930s Great Depression, while also rejecting Marxism and its tendency toward oppression of individuals.[73] Diệm's brother Ngô Đình Nhu, who played a crucial advisor and political role in the Diệm regime, was exposed to personalism while studying in France as an archivist. As argued by historian Jessica Chapman, personalism eventually became the "official state philosophy" of the RVN under Diệm.[74] Phi-Vân Nguyen and other historians have shown that the RVN constitution of 1956 reflected personalist principles.[75]

Yet personalism as articulated by Diệm's brother Ngô Đình Nhu and adopted in the RVN context was also, in Ed Miller's words, "maddeningly opaque."[76] This was in part due to its role as an indigenous ideology and to serve as a platform for postcolonial consolidation. As Geoffrey Stewart has put it, the Ngôs needed an "authentic Vietnamese 'cultural formula' to imbue the population with the appropriate sense of national spirit to willingly participate in the nation-building process."[77] Personalism was this formula. In imagining the ideal Vietnamese village, the Ngôs believed that conservatism and spiritualism of personalism were needed to enact the social ties between community and the modern Vietnamese nation.[78] Through his examination of the resettlement of northern refugees into southern Vietnam, Jason Picard has argued that the Ngôs saw in traditional northern villages their ideal of "a corporate, close-knit community" that needed to be replicated across rural Vietnam.[79] Personalism tied into this vision, and hence the emphasis on the rural village.

Like personalism, Sun Yat-sen's Three Principles as an ideology provided justification for a revolutionary regime without being too dogmatically onerous. Beginning in 1905, Sun had elaborated publicly on the Three Principles—Minsheng zhuyi (民生主義, usually translated as "livelihood of the people" or less often as welfare), Minquan zhuyi (民權主義, usually translated as democracy), and Minzu zhuyi (民族主義, usually translated as nationalism)—as an organizing principle for his revolutionary platform, culminating in the 1924 published eponymous work. Sun was a pragmatist, and the Three Principles served as a malleable political tool to allow Sun and the ROC to garner popular political support in an anti-Manchu and anti-imperial sentiment in early twentieth-century China. In the words of Sun Yat-sen biographer Marie Claire-Bergère, the Three Principles were "a work of propaganda, a long political tract designed to win followers rather than to instill conviction, an appeal to action rather than to thought" aimed to "diffuse a number of ideas rather than to analyze them."[80] As discussed in chapter 2, some of the concepts, such as Minsheng zhuyi, entailed specific references to taxation policies. Continuing under Chiang Kai-shek's ROC, the Three Principles were largely used as a symbolic platform, deployed to demonstrate the ROC's welfarist or revolutionary roots when convenient. Integrated into curricula across schools and military academies, for example, the Three Principles were meant to build loyalty to and support for the authoritarian ROC regime.

Though personalism and the Three Principles were both often used for propaganda purposes, its deployment often resulted in real networks, movements, and institutions, such as the Asian People's Anti-Communist League and Moral Re-armament, that affected perceptions and foreign policies. As Mitchell Tan has argued, "The production and proliferation of a national ideology was an important way in which nascent Asian nation-states like the RVN sought to define themselves not just to their people but also in relationship to a Region divided, at least in part, by a conflict of ideas."[81] In the ROC-specific Cold War, the defining and legitimation of the Guomindang regime was unquestionably of the highest priority. In this sense, the Three Principles expressed not only a political or social ideology but a developmentalist one as well. Economic welfare, the providing for the well-being of the Taiwanese and global peoples like the Vietnamese against Communism, became crucial.

Alluding to common political ideologies and revolutionary origins was inherent to Taiwan's imagining of its development missions to Vietnam and the rest of the Global South. Taiwan's missions to Africa and land-reform training of Third World bureaucrats also reflected how the Guomindang became adroit at using the language and discourse of decolonizing nations to demonstrate solidarity and commonality. In Vietnam, the ROC seized upon personalism, the founding of the

RVN, and the background of Diệm and his family to enable the representation that it found most ideal, centered on Taiwan's revolutionary and technical modernity and steadfast anti-Communist solidarity.

CONCLUSION

The Vietnam mission proved to be a success for the Taiwanese, at least in terms of continued demand from the RVN. The original six-month mission was extended to three years. In 1961, the JCRR attempted to reassign the leader of the farmers' association team, Yang Yukun (楊玉昆, Y. K. Yang) back to Taiwan, where work related to farmers' associations needed his attention. But this resulted in a deeply impassioned plea from Trần to the JCRR chairman at the time, Jiang Menglin:

> The establishment of numerous Strategic Hamlets has greatly improved security conditions in the rural areas and will afford greater opportunities to more effectively expand the services of our [farmers' associations]. This situation intensifies the urgent need of the specialists who have become familiar with our conditions. . . . Mr Chairman, I must earnestly request that you reconsider your three year service policy in the light of the present situation in Vietnam. We are deeply engaged in an active war, and our resources are stretched to the maximum. The focus of this war is in the country-side and among the rural people. Experienced direction and leadership is of special importance at this time.[82]

With the implementation of the Strategic Hamlet program that sought "pacification" of rural villages by increasing support and thus ostensibly lessening rural ties with Communist insurgents, the Republic of Vietnam sought Taiwanese expertise in rural organization.

By 1970, the United States had expended US$2,036,088 for the Taiwan missions, paying for capital costs involved in technical assistance.[83] In a 1972 evaluation of the contract with the ROC, Ralph Gleason, USAID deputy associate director for food and agriculture in Vietnam, described the Taiwanese mission as attaining mission goals "in a very practical manner . . . for instance, demonstration fields were elaborately set up and operated by the contractor as an intermediate goal towards attainment of the final goal of widespread extension of improved varieties and cultural practices." As a result, "farmers benefiting from CATG assistance have experienced substantial increases in income through increased harvests of crop produce of high value." However, Gleason cast doubt on the ability of the Republic of Vietnam to fulfill its end of the agreement, stating that "final goal of nationwide extension rests in the capacity and competence of the cooperating country" and lamenting that "more could have been accomplished if host country support were more adequate." In a matter of a few years, Gleason was proved correct.[84] Despite the "intermediate" success of the Taiwanese technical mission in realizing higher incomes and a system of extension and demonstration, these efforts were ultimately unable to save the Republic of Vietnam regime. Taiwanese missions were continually renewed until 1975, until the demise of the Republic of Vietnam ended Taiwanese missions to Vietnam.[85]

Taiwanese development to Vietnam began a decades-long project to portray itself as leading a vanguard of the development world. After having achieved success in agricultural science, farmers' association, and rural improvement in Taiwan, GMD planners sent Taiwanese scientists and technicians abroad to develop other nations. Taiwanese missions deployed specific practices of modern high-yielding seeds and chemical fertilizers to reproduce Taiwanese success. At the same time, it also emphasized its rural modernity as accomplished through a history of farmers' association success. In representations of Taiwanese development through public diplomacy, Taiwanese planners portrayed Taiwan as a primarily rural society that succeeded through achieving modern science (of developing high-yielding seeds), ingenuity (through agricultural machinery), and hard work (of farmers and technicians). This imaginary of Taiwanese modernity marked a larger shift within the GMD technocracy and ROC state itself, which saw its development success deployed for diplomatic objectives as well as to strengthen its domestic rule. Not only did the ROC demonstrate its anti-Communist conviction to a "Free World" ally, Vietnam, but it also burnished its developmentalist credentials at home and diverted from a repressive authoritarian regime. As shown in the official speeches and writing of Zhang Dusheng, the GMD imagined a modern and humanitarian ROC that sacrificed its youth to save other nations. This undergirded the emergence of a developmentalist platform that continued to define the GMD for decades to come.

5

"Straw Hat Diplomats"

Taiwanese Agrarian Development and Africa,
1961–1971

The colonial powers can no longer use the methods of the past to continue their plunder and oppression. The Asia and Africa of today are no longer the Asia and Africa of yesterday. Many countries of this region have taken their destiny into their own hands after long years of endeavours.

—ZHOU ENLAI

After the Second World War, there occurred a number of events of historic importance in the community of nations. One of these was the awakening of the peoples of Asia, Africa and other areas of the world. Hundreds of millions of people have emerged from colonial rule and freely formed themselves into new independent States which now exercise considerable influence in the United Nations.

—SHEN CHANG-HUAN, ROC MINISTER OF FOREIGN AFFAIRS

INTRODUCTION

On a chilly December evening in 1978, deputy minister of foreign affairs Yang Xikun (楊西崑, Yang Hsi-kun) presided as the flag of the Republic of China (ROC) was lowered amid a light drizzle in the grounds of the ROC embassy, Twin Oaks, in Washington, DC.[1] An eighteen-acre estate located in the wealthy Cleveland Park residential neighborhood of Washington, Twin Oaks served for over forty years as the residence of the ROC diplomat to the United States from 1937 to 1978. In 1979, with the severance of diplomatic relations between the ROC and the United States, Twin Oaks ceased to serve as the official embassy for the ROC.

Yang's presence at that fateful moment was befitting of the irony of Taiwanese history. Taiwanese and African newspapers dubbed Yang "Mr. Africa" (非洲先生, Feizhou Xiansheng), a reference to the internationalization diplomacy of Taiwan

119

during the 1960s aimed at obtaining United Nations allies among the newly decolonizing and vote-carrying nation-states of Africa and Asia. On the ground, this diplomacy consisted of the ROC sending agricultural technical teams abroad, beginning with South Vietnam in 1959 (see previous chapter). These were a concerted effort by the ROC to leverage its success at agricultural technology and science as a form of diplomacy, buoying its international prestige via humanitarian action, and in some cases directly trading development assistance for votes.

In 1961, these efforts were organized into Operation Vanguard (先鋒計劃, Xianfeng Jihua or 先鋒案, Xianfeng An) under the direction of the ROC Ministry of Foreign Affairs (MOFA).[2] These newly emerging Third World allies were crucial for the ROC's continued international existence. When the ROC regime was defeated by Communist forces in 1949 and retreated to the mainland, it continued to be recognized as the legitimate government of all of China and thus retained control of its crucial seat in the UN. Almost immediately after its victory, the PRC, led by Foreign Minister Zhou Enlai, sought that UN seat. Albania, at the time one of the closest international Communist allies of the PRC, continually introduced resolutions in the UN to recognize the PRC as the official representative of China, which would delegitimize the ROC and force the ROC to forfeit the seat it held. This led to a unique global Cold War, battled between the PRC and ROC, waged culturally, economically, and developmentally in order to win influence among vote-carrying nations that would support their respective UN positions. Yet efforts to curry favor among African and Asian nations ultimately proved a failure for the ROC. In 1971, the ROC lost its seat in the United Nations, and by 1979, the United States formally extended diplomatic recognition to the PRC in lieu of the ROC.

The efforts of the ROC amid a diplomatic proxy war with the PRC is largely told as one of states and statesmen—secret deals made behind closed mahogany doors, Nixon and Kissinger, and Zhou Enlai and Deng Xiaoping. Though the Cold War is crucial throughout this history, what is lost in this narrative of high diplomacy was a little known yet robust development campaign launched on the part of the MOFA to secure its international position. This campaign of development diplomacy reached over two dozen African, Latin American, and Asian nations at its peak, and it continues into the present. The United States provided partial secret funding. Postcolonial leaders across the Third World welcomed Taiwanese technical missions. All the while, Taiwanese technocrats outlined a vision of the developing world as following in the footsteps of Taiwan's own modernity.

This chapter recovers a lost history of Taiwan's development—its agricultural technical missions abroad to the developing world. It focuses specifically on the agricultural technical missions to Africa, Operation Vanguard, and it discusses the visions of modernity contained within the missions as shaped by the Chinese technocrats in charge of their implementation. The chapter simultaneously explores the international and global circumstances constraining the actions of the ROC leading it toward "development diplomacy" as well as consequences of this diplomacy on the ground. In other words, it is necessary to unpack the meanings of modernity, the Third World, and the Cold War to understand how they influenced what types of agricultural technologies and practices Taiwanese technicians were implementing in places like Chad, Côte d'Ivoire, and Gabon. I argue that ROC foreign-policy officials and scientists packaged elements of Taiwan's agricultural development "experience" into a Taiwanese model that they portrayed as being better suited for the tropical and subtropical agrarian societies of Africa and shows that this portrayal became essential to the ROC's search for an identity after losing the mainland.

The history of Taiwan's development missions abroad is important for our understanding of the waging of the Cold War on the ground, the transformation of development toward South-to-South connections, and the evolution of international worldviews among postcolonial societies like Taiwan. Funded by US dollars, Operation Vanguard was seen by US planners as an avenue to generate support for its ally, the ROC. Simultaneously, the United States also sought to attract decolonizing nations into its orbit and away from the allure of Communism. Taiwan served as a front, a guise under which the United States could attain its Cold War objectives.

However, Vanguard's serving as a proxy for funneling US dollars did not detract from the robustness of the theories and practices embedded within Vanguard missions; nor did it remove the agency of Taiwanese development practitioners who co-opted Vanguard to demonstrate the superiority of Taiwanese development. Since its funding status was kept secret, Vanguard planners possessed significant leeway to exercise intellectual freedom in constructing their model of development. Drawing on their own technical expertise, Taiwanese development goals reflected an idealized image of Taiwan itself. This reflection was deeper than a matter of technical comparative advantage. Many of the Taiwanese elites who had overseen the rapid growth in agricultural production in Taiwan took particular pride in its success, especially vis-à-vis other decolonizing nations internationally. Furthermore, by the 1960s, Chiang Kai-shek's repeated rhetoric of retaking the mainland began to appear increasingly unrealistic as the PRC consolidated its regime and built up its military force. The reality of possible permanent separation from the mainland began to set in. In staking their international interactions on a rising international standard of nation-building—economic development—Taiwanese intellectuals were beginning to locate a postcolonial identity through South-to-South aid.

Despite that language of aiding the Global South, these missions were largely performative. Taiwanese agricultural technicians were well intentioned and technically capable, but teams were deeply limited in terms of human and physical capital. Ironically, the Taiwanese touted the benefits of modern science that obviated the need for capital intense approaches like the United States or the Soviet Union. In conferences, study tours, and demonstration farms, Taiwanese technicians and scientists emphasized how a poor and postcolonial society could achieve rapid agrarian development. But the massive countries of Africa, especially compared to Taiwan, meant that a dozen or even a hundred technicians made relatively little impact. These missions reinforced the contradictory nature of development, argued by anthropologists such as James Ferguson and Arturo Escobar, that its apolitical claims and faith in modernity and technology were usually counterproductive. Indeed, Taiwanese development in Africa was more about the Taiwanese themselves. For the ROC elite, this was coming to terms with an impending existential crisis.

Relatively few scholars have written about this history.[3] Although diplomacy explains why these missions were initiated, this chapter seeks to examine not just foreign policy and geopolitical calculations but also the content of Vanguard missions and what they meant to those practicing development. Within the policy blueprints, mission reports, and even propaganda articles and speeches, a picture emerges of Taiwan's efforts at utilizing its development expertise as a means of postcolonial identity. This chapter illuminates why development and postcolonial thought converged in this era, and what it meant for the evolution of development history and Taiwan.

THE UNITED NATIONS

The founding of the United Nations in 1945 from the ashes of World War II saw the Republic of China included as one of the permanent members of the United Nations Security Council. Serving as a permanent member on the Security Council proved valuable to the ROC's international interests. In 1955, the ROC used its Security Council veto power to prevent the admission of Mongolia as a member of the United Nations, pursuant to its claim over Mongolian territory from the founding of the ROC in 1912 as a continuation of Qing territory. In 1949, after the Communist victory over the Guomindang, the Republic of China became a government in exile, exercising de facto governance over the island of Taiwan and governing the rest of China in name only. The Chinese Communist Party established the People's Republic of China on the mainland. Despite losing control of the majority of its previously governed territory, the ROC retained its seat in the United Nations, though this would not last long.

Shortly after the establishment of the PRC, beginning in January 1950, Chinese foreign minister (and later also premier) Zhou Enlai sent messages to the United Nations General Assembly contesting the legitimacy of the Guomindang regime ("Chinese Kuomintang reactionary remnant clique.")[4] By the 1960s, PRC ally Albania began submitting resolutions to the United Nations General Assembly to recognize the PRC in lieu of the ROC. These received the support of the Communist bloc of nations. In response, the United States and its allies in the United Nations put forth in 1961 UN General Assembly Resolution 1668, which dictated that any change stemming from two governments contesting legitimacy over a seat be regarded as an "important question," thus requiring a supermajority vote of two-thirds of the General Assembly before any action is taken.[5]

Resolution 1668 gave the ROC a temporary respite, but with decolonization coming into full force, new nations among the former European colonies in Africa were joining at a rapid rate. Western nations that voted predominantly with the United States and that outnumbered the Communist bloc, in contrast, were fixed in number. Given the arithmetic reality, ROC Foreign Ministry planners understood that they needed votes among the newly decolonizing nations in order to prevent a supermajority from forming on behalf of Beijing to oust the ROC.

OPERATION VANGUARD

In 1961, the MOFA officially inaugurated its various international development missions under the Operation Vanguard project. Officially, it consisted of technical missions, like the one to Vietnam, except under Vanguard, it had expanded its scope from one mission to one country to what would eventually be over two dozen. Unofficially, with the rise of the People's Republic of China as an international power and the scant likelihood of the GMD wresting the mainland back from the Communists, the Vanguard program was the Foreign Ministry's attempt at agricultural development diplomacy. It offered technical missions, with Taiwanese technical expertise and American funding, to African nations in exchange for diplomatic support, especially in the emerging global Cold War against the Soviet Union and PRC. The United States funded Vanguard with the hopes of using its proxy ally to build an alliance among developing nations—a Global South ally in the Global South. This means of currying international favor became more important as the Communist bloc in the United Nations attempted to replace the seat of the Republic of China with that of the People's Republic of China on the mainland, which was increasingly being viewed as the legitimate and rightful representative of China.

Based on oral history interviews with many Taiwanese agricultural technicians who worked on the ground in Africa, ranging from two to over two dozen years of experience, as well as archival documents from the ROC Ministry of Foreign Affairs and the United States National Archives, a picture emerges of attempts to bring a unique Taiwanese experience, rooted in science and practical, low-capital methods of the bootstrapping ethic of hard work, free from the colonial trappings and elite-centered development legacies from the West.

RACE

In Africa, Taiwanese teams met political circumstances in which they could take advantage of their status as outsiders unburdened by the colonial legacy of the West. ROC foreign minister Shen Changhuan (沈昌煥, Shen Chang-huan), recounted an anecdote to US vice president Hubert Humphrey. In 1963, Shen was near Brazzaville. He was crossing the Congo River when he was stopped,

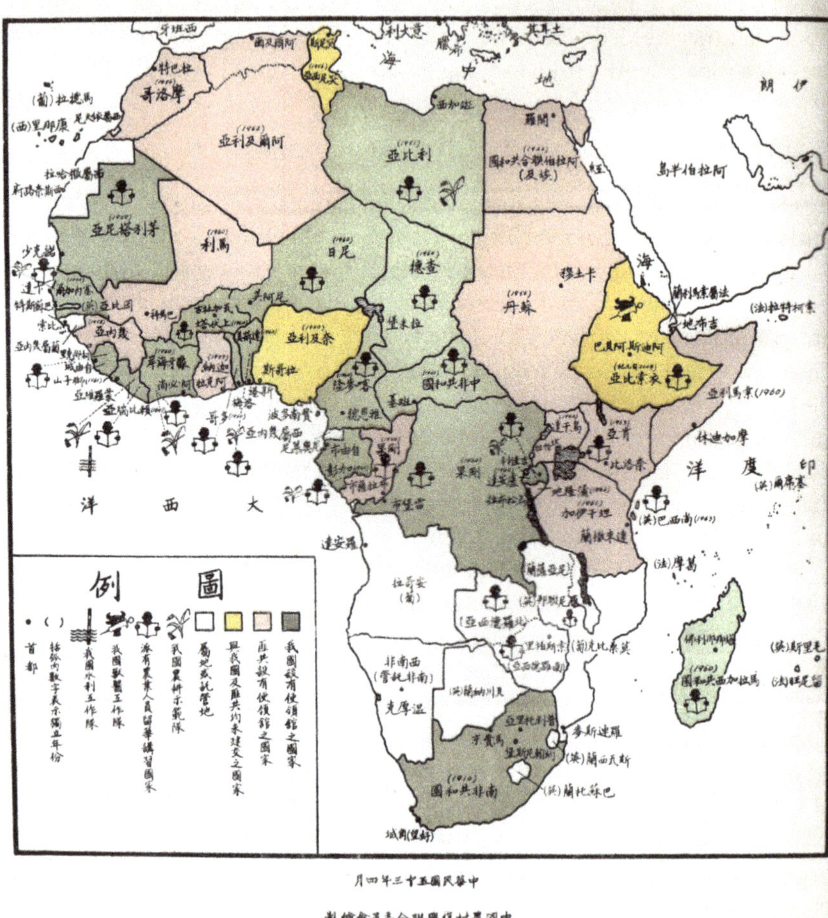

FIGURE 26. A 1964 Taiwanese map showing African countries receiving ROC agricultural technical assistance missions (*in green*), PRC missions (*in red*), and both (*in yellow*). Jin Yang-gao, "Sino-African Agricultural Technical Cooperation Summary."

presumably by non-government armed soldiers, and "would have been shot had he not been able to point out that his skin was neither white nor black." The lesson of this anecdote, Shen related, was that everywhere in Africa, "he found suspicion of all white people."[6]

Race was almost never openly discussed in development documents, but the language of postcolonial solidarity was present throughout public speeches, conferences, newspapers, and other published media. Whereas in Vietnam, race was coded as having "similar cultures" or "similar peoples," commonality in Africa was coded from the Taiwanese side through shared socioeconomic, historical, or cultural markers. This included, for example, the legacies of colonialism referenced privately by Shen Changhuan. Publicly, solidarity was established through assertions of shared perseverance and hard work, implying a commonality within the basic human condition of subsistence or rural societies. In front of Humphrey, Shen was likely aware that his audience was an American one, and Shen was possibly justifying the continued US financial support of Operation Vanguard by emphasizing what the Taiwanese offered that the Americans could not in Africa—freedom from a white colonial legacy. Nonetheless, Taiwan's portrayals of its unique position as a Global South development power in fact integrated an anti- or postcolonial sentiment at times.

In the same example, Shen also conveyed that there was also little patience for "American red tape and other difficulties" that produced results too slowly. This perhaps hinted at the more pragmatic elements of development diplomacy. Given the relative lack of democratic oversight on budgets, the authoritarian ROC was more likely to oblige with gifts. Humphrey emphasized that "cultural, technical assistance and information activities are not expensive and the [Republic of China] can perhaps do better in these activities than the U.S."[7] It was this postwar moment that the ROC hoped to take advantage of, where the development plans of American experts carried the legacies of European colonialism and provided an opportunity for Taiwan to seize the global stage.

ON THE GROUND

The Vanguard program sent technical missions to over a dozen African nations, beginning in 1960 with Liberia.[8] While Operation Vanguard was imagined from the heights of MOFA as a Cold War project, its actual implementation on the ground involved different concerns, centered on translation of technologies from Taiwan to Africa, on the contestation between labor and environment, and most importantly on the actions of the crucial intermediaries: the Taiwanese agricultural technician. In the words of one agricultural technician interviewee, Peng Ruiduan, "Diplomacy is diplomacy. What we did was actual work."[9]

In the 1975 document on technical cooperation, Vanguard missions were described as following five steps:

1. Land reclamation work: Reclaiming a predetermined area of jungle, swamp, wilderness, hills, inside the city into usable farmland for tillers.
2. Experimentation work: In accordance with local climate, water resources, land type, and other natural environmental factors, implement variety, planting

season, fertilizer amount, and planting methods comparative experiments. Use these selected improved varieties, most suitable planting seasons, and appropriate planting methods for the usage of demonstration and extension.

3. Demonstration work: Using improved varieties, appropriate planting techniques, and new agricultural implements to perform demonstrations of plantings. To increase production results, farmer viewing and emulation meetings are held to initiate local farmers' interests and to build their confidence.

4. Training work: Our tilling teams in Africa utilize a "learning while doing" (做中學習, *zuozhong xuexi*) method, while working on a field, using practical manual work methods, leading African farmers in using agricultural implements, and to familiarize them with our planting methods.

5. Extension work: Uses the agricultural production techniques and experience obtained from each step of experimentation, demonstration, and training, to encourage African farmers to practically adopt these in order to improve farmers' lives and agricultural development.[10]

Experimentation, demonstration, training, and extension formed the core principles constituting agricultural development for Chinese and Taiwanese planners as far back as 1920. In both mainland China in the early Republican era (see chapter 1) and in Taiwan under Japanese colonial rule (see chapter 3), state-led agricultural policies led to an expansion of experimentation centers that produced both seeds and technologies. Experimentation was followed by demonstration and extension through a variety of channels, including farmers' associations, 4-H youth groups, and printed media.

Across the dozens of missions in Africa, missions in actuality differed greatly depending on the specific needs of the government receiving assistance, the local social and economic conditions, environmental and ecological considerations, and diplomatic negotiations between the ROC and their African counterparts. Given that most of the missions were often limited in terms of capital and human resources, with most teams averaging between a half dozen and a dozen members, Taiwanese leaders chose to focus on demonstrating the potential of newly introduced Taiwanese varieties or Taiwanese-selected local varieties of crops as well as Taiwanese methods of planting, fertilization, harvesting, and so on. The overall goal was to show first of all that Taiwanese methods could grow far more quantities of crops through demonstration farms and that once local farmers saw the results firsthand, they would be open to learning about these techniques through extension. Taiwanese agricultural technicians I interviewed between 2012 and 2019 often claimed that local African farmers were intrigued by the results of Taiwanese demonstration farms, and many were eager to likewise reproduce those results on their own farms.

Most Taiwanese technicians sent to Africa came from modest, rural backgrounds in Taiwan. When the Vanguard program was introduced, a search for technicians focused on the state-owned enterprise Taiwan Sugar Corporation and agricultural experimentation stations. Ecological considerations played a role, too. According to one former technician, recruitment focused on southern Taiwan with the belief that southern Taiwanese climate made technicians hailing from the south more able to acclimate to the tropical climates of sub-Saharan Africa. Because Vanguard missions were expected to involve significant physical hardship, candidates were required to be between twenty-five and thirty-five years of age and in good health, with sufficient stamina to endure the challenges of field work. Technicians were limited to graduates from technical agricultural schools (農校, *nongxiao*), technical schools that trained agricultural technicians to perform the labor of experimentation, farming, and extension work. However, unlike in Taiwan, where monthly salaries for young technicians was often limited to 350 New Taiwan Dollars (NTD) per month, Vanguard salaries offered at least $270 USD per month (this would increase each year that Vanguard operated), which at the exchange rate of the time, was approximately 10,000 NTD, or a thirty-fold increase in salary. Despite the hardship, young Taiwanese technicians jumped at the opportunity.[11] Over the course of Operation Vanguard's history, according to Yang Xikun, around six hundred Taiwanese technicians in total worked in Africa, and many stayed six to seven years during their deployments.[12]

In Africa, Taiwanese technicians indeed faced significant challenges. Yang Xikun called technical labor in Africa "extremely arduous."[13] In many Vanguard missions, including the first 1961 mission to Liberia, Taiwanese were sent to rural areas that lacked infrastructural development. The Liberian Vanguard team on arrival was thus forced to begin with the difficult work of land reclamation, clearing forested jungle to develop suitable land for agriculture. It was only after a full season of clearing land, planting crops, and nearing harvest that the Vanguard team was able to begin its demonstration work for neighboring villagers. Most Vanguard teams operated in rural areas without electrification, running instead on generators, which limited their usage of irrigation pumps to gas-powered generators and required that most of their irrigation infrastructure be constructed by their own teams. This extended to personal living conditions too, where many Vanguard teams depended on generator-powered electricity, if there was electricity at all, in their dormitories. If lucky, some teams were given prefabricated accommodations by the local government. In the case of Liberia, the Vanguard team was considered fortunate for having chosen a location where an American agricultural team had recently built a small dormitory and abandoned it just prior to the Taiwanese arrival, which the Taiwanese promptly took up as their own. In Chad, the Taiwanese team set up their own *siheyuan* (四合院), a classic courtyard house, though my interviewee conveyed that when it rained, conditions inside their poorly constructed *siheyuan* were not too different from being outdoors.[14] In their free time, Taiwanese technicians resorted to basic activities of playing cards or basic outdoor sports for their leisurely activities. Many Taiwanese technicians, all men, fathered a number of mixed race children, many of whom were tragically left behind when technicians returned home to Taiwan, similar to the mestizos legacy of colonial regimes around the world.[15] For the most part, Vanguard technicians operated as farmers would in Taiwan, with the goal of demonstrating how farming techniques from Taiwan could help their African counterparts.

With limited capital resources, many Taiwanese technicians emphasized ingenuity and practicality as characteristics of Taiwanese development in African contexts. Vanguard funds did not provide for a significant budget for capital expenditures, much less equipment such as power tillers that were then expensive even for Taiwanese farmers. This left the Taiwanese technicians to piece together their own tools from everyday, common objects. Another interviewee, Chen Dianxin described how Taiwanese teams managed. In Côte d'Ivoire, Taiwanese teams welded a metal plate onto a gasoline barrel, then attached wheels, to create a makeshift plow. A tree trunk would be dragged across land to smooth out tilled soil.[16] The focus on pragmatism, which became a key aspect of representing Taiwan's development model in Africa, took prominence in many of the Vanguard missions, where Taiwanese teams were not able to set up experiment stations to select suitable local cultivars.

Vanguard demonstration farms included local training centers, which were responsible for the important aspect of technological translation typically practiced in agricultural extension. One Taiwanese team member was responsible for each training center and set up a class schedule for local farmers. In the case of Sierra Leone around 1967, each class had about ten local farmer participants, sent by their home village and each representing a different village from the vicinity. Training instructors would distribute seeds to class participants, though farmers still needed to procure their own fertilizer. Training centers focused primarily on showing practices using demonstration plots that were a priority for the local Vanguard teams. In Swaziland (today Eswatini) in 1971, Peng Ruiduan conveyed that initially, a training class recruiting participants even with help of the local village chief was only able to recruit ten locals. That initial class assigned two plots of land to each participant and guided them to plant Taiwanese-provided cabbage. After a short two-month growing season, according to Peng, the sales of cabbage to local markets netted such profit for the ten locals that the next class enrolled forty participants.[17] The Taiwanese ability to showcase the value of producing and consuming Vanguard-grown crops on demonstration plots was crucial to their mission in Africa.

The politics of crops and planting demonstrated the intertwined nature of Taiwanese diplomatic objectives, colonial legacies, technician expertise, and local environmental conditions. In one example, Taiwanese diplomats promised officials in Chad that the Taiwanese mission could develop paddy rice agriculture. Upon arrival in 1965, Taiwanese technician Peng Ruiduan discovered that this was impossible. The local environmental conditions were too dry to practice paddy rice cultivation, yet the ROC embassy took no interest in addressing their promises made without reference to ecology. Peng's team instead introduced sugarcane, a crop that Taiwan produced in abundance and that was deeply intertwined with Taiwan's own colonial history dating back centuries. Yet French agricultural experts, who continued to hold significant influence even in postcolonial Chad, objected to Taiwanese efforts to introduce sugarcane. (Peng states that French agricultural experts had never seen sugarcane in the field prior to encountering them in Taiwanese demonstration farms, indicating complete unfamiliarity.) Peng believed that this opposition stemmed from French vested interests in maintaining tangerine exports to France.[18] As historian Tiago Saraiva has argued, citrus groves in Algeria, bringing together white French settlers and cloned California citrus fruit, demonstrate the materiality of colonialism through "movements of thick technoscientific things that bind science, technology, and politics together in a continuum."[19] The contestation between Taiwanese and French influences in Chad, played out through competing colonial-era crops of sugarcane and citrus, represented how development in postcolonial Africa was often constructed through legacies of colonial science, economics, and politics.

BY THE TAIWANESE "METROPOLE" FOR A GLOBAL AUDIENCE

In Taipei, missions in Africa became integrated into a narrative about Taiwanese development abroad that was then represented to global audiences. *Free China Review*, a monthly English language publication from the information service of the Ministry of Foreign Affairs, served as a public media platform for the ROC regime targeting foreign observers. Though it was a state-published media venue under an authoritarian regime, thus likely tightly controlled in terms of how it presented information and narratives, reading *Free China Review* as a form of public diplomacy and as visual and discursive representations of Taiwan's developmentalist visions still renders valuable insight for understanding what Taiwanese postcolonial development entailed.

The May 1962 issue of *Free China Review* underscored how ingenuity and hard labor were deployed across Africa. Titled "Straw Hat Diplomats," the article reported on the 1962 Seminar on Agricultural Techniques for Africans, which invited African trainees from Central African Republic, Congo, Dahomey, Côte d'Ivoire, Libya, Madagascar, Mauritania, Niger, Senegal, and Togo to Taichung and Tainan to see Taiwanese demonstration farms and learn agricultural methods in upland crops and rice cultivation (figure 27).[20]

Taiwanese technical ingenuity with everyday implements and blue-collar willingness to roll up sleeves and dig trenches became centerpieces in representations of Taiwanese development in Africa. Aside from showing invited African trainees donning "Taiwan hats" (straw hats), *Free China Review* also showcased

FIGURE 27. "Straw Hat Diplomats," an article in *Free China Review*, a monthly English-language magazine published by the ROC Ministry of Foreign Affairs, reported on the Taiwanese agricultural technicians engaging with African nations. Pictured here are African invitees participating in the 1962 Seminar on Agricultural Techniques for Africans in Taiwan donning "Taiwan hats." Wang, "Straw Hat Diplomats."

pictures from the early Taiwanese agricultural team in Liberia utilizing a makeshift land level, with a Taiwanese technician lying flat on the ground with his level atop an ordinary wooden stool, a similar instance of achieving agricultural technical needs with everyday implements as described by retired agricultural technician Chen Dianxin (figure 28). In another picture, Taiwanese technicians are shown digging a drainage ditch alongside African farmers when machine labor was too expensive or inaccessible, an example of the labor that *Free China Review* was eager to valorize, epitomizing the hardworking nature of Taiwanese technicians sent to help Africans. In a final photograph two Taiwanese technicians are shown bare chested, wearing work trousers or jeans and a baseball cap while holding a shovel (figure 29). In contrast with the formal suits and ties of agricultural scientists and economists, these technicians are represented in a blue-collar fashion, likely denoting their rural backgrounds and willingness to undertake difficult labor.[21]

Demonstration was a central defining feature of Taiwanese methods. Through printed media, documentary films, and actual farms, demonstration allowed Taiwan to showcase its carefully curated modernity. Agricultural extension requires the utilization of demonstration sites in rural areas for easy access to rural farmers, but Vanguard also integrated perhaps the ultimate form of demonstration—the tour of Taiwan. A select few were given roundtrip airfare, lavish hotel stays, extravagant banquets (often featuring shark fin soup among other delicacies), and packed

FIGURE 28. "Straw Hat Diplomats" exemplified the ingenuity of Taiwanese technicians in conditions where state-of-the-art tools were too expensive or difficult to acquire. The one pictured here was a member of the Taiwanese team in Liberia shown with a "makeshift level" on an ordinary stool. Wang, "Straw Hat Diplomats."

FIGURE 29. This photo from *Free China Review* features Taiwanese technicians, shown bare chested and wearing jeans and a cap or work trousers, side by side with a Liberian woman and children. Though reminiscent of colonial photography, the Taiwanese technicians are attired in a way that signals their working-class background. Wang, "Straw Hat Diplomats."

FIGURE 30. *Free China Review* featured on its cover of the April 1962 issue Malagasy Republic president Philibert Tsiranana sitting atop a glossy, Taiwanese-made power tiller. "Farmer-President" Tsiranana, the title given to him in the *Free China Review* article, was the first chief of state from the African continent to visit Taiwan. Chu, "Free China Receives a Farmer-President."

full island itineraries. Taiwanese tours were, above all, performative. Regardless of whether guests were chiefs of state or young agricultural extension agents, visits incorporated stops throughout the Taiwanese countryside and agricultural centers of knowledge to showcase the modern ideal-type in person.

One of the earliest African state visits to Taiwan was from President Philibert Tsiranana of the Malagasy Republic, an anti-Communist ally of the ROC, in 1962. The visit was a regal matter. Published in the April 1962 volume of *Free China Review* was a vivid color photograph of Tsirinana, sitting atop a new, glossy, bright orange power tiller produced by Taiwan-based firm Zhongguo Nongji (中國農機). In 1962, the power tiller was still relatively rarely used in Taiwan, with only 6,154 total counted throughout the entire country, thus showcasing some of the most modern and expensive pieces of agricultural machinery.[22]

The language within *Free China Review* evoked the Afro-Asian postcolonial solidarity of the Bandung Conference, except expressed with a subtle pro-Taiwanese spin. Tsiranana was praised for his leadership in the decolonization transition that resulted in a peaceful and implicitly strong nation-state:

> Such leadership is rare, especially among the emerging Afro-Asian nations. Many of these countries gained their independence after bloody struggles with the old colonialists. A few of them even turned to the Communists for help. Not so with the Republic of Malagasy. Under the guidance of their patriotic President, the Malagasy people achieved their independence speedily and in peace, thereby preserving strength for the building of their new nation.[23]

Within this praise for foreign nations was a reflection of Guomindang political discourse. Despite the militant nature of Guomindang authoritarianism under martial law utilizing surveillance tactics and executions without trials, outward public diplomacy emphasized the pacific nature of the Republic of China. Nation-building in peace meant that its citizens would benefit economically and would profit, a point in favor of Guomindang legitimacy as it began to be increasingly defined by its agrarian transformation and nascent economic success in the early 1970s. The emphasis on peace and prosperity at home engendered an internalization of the regime's patriarchal duties, such that many Taiwanese in Taiwan saw themselves as beneficiaries of a form of capitalist state welfare, despite the violent repression of political liberties.

Commonality and solidarity once again reached across historical and socio-economic ties, not just political and postcolonial ones. *Free China Review* emphasized the rural roots of both Tsiranana (and by extension, the Malagasy Republic) and the Republic of China. "Some," the article referenced, perhaps apocryphally, "have attributed President Tsiranana's wise leadership to the fact that he comes from a rural area and is long on horse sense and short on impetuous bluster."[24] Here, the valorization of Tsiranana's social origins from the rural countryside reinforced Taiwan's ongoing emphasis on rural modernity. Taiwan's own expertise in rural development needed emphasis, and bringing to the fore Tsiranana's rural roots offered another means of demonstrating similar historical narratives in the ongoing rural-colonial to modern-nation transition among both postcolonial states. This type of identification extended to most Vanguard recipients.

More unique to the Malagasy Republic was an emphasis on diasporic and migration ties. "Although separated by an ocean and sub-continent, the two established contact more than a century ago when Chinese emigrants settled in Madagascar." The article continued, "Today there are about 8,000 Chinese residents among the 5.5 million Malagasy people. Many Chinese settlers have married into Malagasy families and are actively participating in the economic development of the host country."[25] Again the importance of economic development took priority, where the presence of Chinese migrants in the Malagasy Republic were seen as a positive sign because of the economic contributions to its development.[26]

Like *Free China Review*, the magazine *Xinwen tiandi* (新聞天地) featured news of Taiwanese development missions. Originally published in the mainland during the Republican era, after 1949 *Xinwen tiandi* moved its publication office to the British colony of Hong Kong, outside of the control of the Communists, but still able to reach Chinese reading audiences in Hong Kong, Taiwan, and elsewhere in the Sinophone world. The March 31, 1962 issue *Xinwen tiandi* featured on its cover a picture of six of the technicians within the seven person Taiwanese team to Libya. One of the articles in the issue was titled "Going to the Sahara Desert to Plant Rice."[27] The photographs of the technicians, again plainly dressed in rolled up pants and in the fields, represented the down-to-earth nature of Taiwanese assistance. The article title also conveyed a sense of environmental miracle: planting rice, typically requiring wetlands or irrigation, in the desert.

REPRESENTING THE TAIWAN MODEL

For the agricultural scientists in the Joint Commission on Rural Reconstruction (JCRR, 中國農村復興聯合委員會, Zhongguo Nongcun Fuxing Lianhe Weiyuanhui) who were tasked with planning the missions, the Vanguard program became a point of pride. Taiwan, like many of its Vanguard targets, was a colony just three decades prior to the start of Vanguard. In the eyes of the development planners, Taiwanese ingenuity, determination, and skill allowed it to not only resume exporting agricultural products, by the late 1960s becoming a heavyweight exporter in canned fruits and mushrooms, but also to have the unique insight of what it is like to rapidly succeed as a developing nation. JCRR commissioner Shen Zonghan, in correspondences with his American agronomist colleagues, would often reiterate proudly that Taiwan had a lot to teach the world. In the context of the ongoing Cold War, this representation of success was necessary in order to contrast its model of development with the Communist model from the PRC, which also competed on the notion of Third World solidarity. As a consequence, Taiwanese technical missions attempted to duplicate the Taiwanese agricultural miracle.

This became evident in the Sino-African Agricultural Technical Cooperation Conference (SAATCC) (Séminaire Afro-Chinois pour la Coopération Technique Agricole), hosted from July 26 to 30, 1965, in Côte d'Ivoire. Organized by the ROC Ministry of Foreign Affairs, it invited agricultural experts and bureaucrats from Taiwan and over a dozen African nations, including Ivory Coast, Liberia, Cameroon, Senegal, Sierra Leone, Congo, Gabon, French Upper Volta (Haute Volta, today Burkina Faso), Congo-Leopoldville (Zaire), Madagascar, Niger, Rwanda, Chad, and Togo. ROC officials included Shen Zonghan, Ministry of Foreign Affairs diplomats, and heads of experiment stations, crop improvement stations, and fertilizer associations in Taiwan. Also included were the Taiwanese team leaders of the various Vanguard missions, including Vietnam Crop Improvement Mission head and later FAO official Ma Baozhi and his successor as the Vietnam Mission head, Jin Yanggao (金陽鎬).

The conference began with an opening speech by an ROC diplomat describing the importance of agriculture, both for humankind and for their respective nations. The speech began with hope and praise: "Africa is expansive and possesses ample resources, its soil fertile, and possesses optimal conditions for agricultural development; that is to say, it possesses the fundamental conditions to build a strong and prosperous nation" (建立富強國家的基本條件).[28] He further exhorted that if Africa were to "increase research and improvement in agricultural techniques, each African ally's future would be limitless."[29] The ROC's goal was to "contribute all of its agricultural knowledge, experience, and techniques . . . under a common desire and objective, to assist our African allies to fully utilize their own manpower, intelligence, and resources, to increase production, improve the environment, and raise citizen living standards."[30] Under the Vanguard program, Taiwan emphasized its friendship as well as its experience, using its role to educate and lead African nations toward self-reliance and success.

After establishing their vision for how Taiwan would benefit African nations seeking to improve their respective citizens, Taiwanese leaders then moved on to qualify Taiwan's bona fides and to describe what constituted Taiwan's success in agrarian development. Shen Zonghan, who in 1965 had recently been promoted to chairman of the JCRR after the passing of Jiang Menglin, presented a detailed analysis of Taiwan's development history as an introduction for African dignitaries in the first substantive speech of the conference. Shen began immediately by drawing parallels, pointing out that Taiwan's "environment and agricultural development are, in many respects, similar to those of the African countries."[31]

Shen continued on to describe most tropical and subtropical countries in the world as "confronted with somewhat similar problems," that "they have not yet adequately developed their natural resources and their economies are primarily agricultural." As a result, "poor and dissatisfied, they are easily taken in by Communist propaganda." Shen was referring obliquely to the rival diplomatic efforts by the PRC and by the USSR to likewise sway the Third World.[32] In associating

Communism with propaganda, he was dismissing the legitimacy of Communist methods in actually creating better livelihoods: "Only with increased farm production and increased income can their livelihood be bettered and the social and political order be stabilized and democratic institutions strengthened."[33] Discrediting Communist methods were important to Shen, as in fact many of the reasons to which Shen would later appeal regarding the suitability of Taiwanese methods in some respects appeared similar to Communist agricultural development. Specifically, themes of self-reliance, low capital investment, and utilization of native resources and labor resembled agricultural development policies in the PRC.[34] Taiwanese officials pointed out that Communist methods were often far more violent and radical, relying on forced collectivization and sometimes the loss of lives, though these were more often raised in discussions of land reform as opposed to agricultural improvement.

Following a history of agriculture in Taiwan first under Japanese colonialism and then under the transition to the Nationalist government, Shen went on to describe the contributions of the JCRR and its role in guiding agricultural development, starting by:

> [Building] up a small but highly qualified technical staff, put its fingers on the most important production and marketing problems, established priorities among them, and made grants to stimulate the expansion of agricultural research, education and extension in order to solve those problems. It has also assisted the government in implementing land reform, reorganizing farmers' associations, and planning and co-ordinating agricultural programs for the economic development of Taiwan.[35]

This story of agricultural development being led by certain state policies focusing on research, education, extension, land reform, and farmers' associations reflects the unique aspects of the Taiwanese approach to agricultural development. These aspects were indeed grounded in reality (see chapter 2), but by the 1960s, these characteristics began to be solidified into what I have termed the "Taiwan model" that was packaged and marketed throughout the Third World, at conferences like SAATCC, by officials such as Shen Zonghan.

Shen laid out the benefits of the Taiwan model. Complemented by graphs and projections, Shen listed off the impressive statistics of the Taiwan miracle (see figure 1). "Aggregate agricultural output of crops, livestock, fisheries and forest products in 1964 almost doubled that of the 1950–1952 average or that of the prewar peak year. The average annual growth rate of agriculture was 6.0 percent under the First Four-Year Plan, 4.6 percent under the Second, and 4.9 percent under the Third." Most impressive was the growth in rice productivity, which increased in "per hectare yield from 1,998 kg of brown rice in 1952 to 2,937 kg in 1964." These figures supported "an expanding population" as well as the maintenance of "a large military force."[36]

Shen attempted to collate the concrete steps of the Taiwan development model that would be replicable for his African audience, breaking them down into

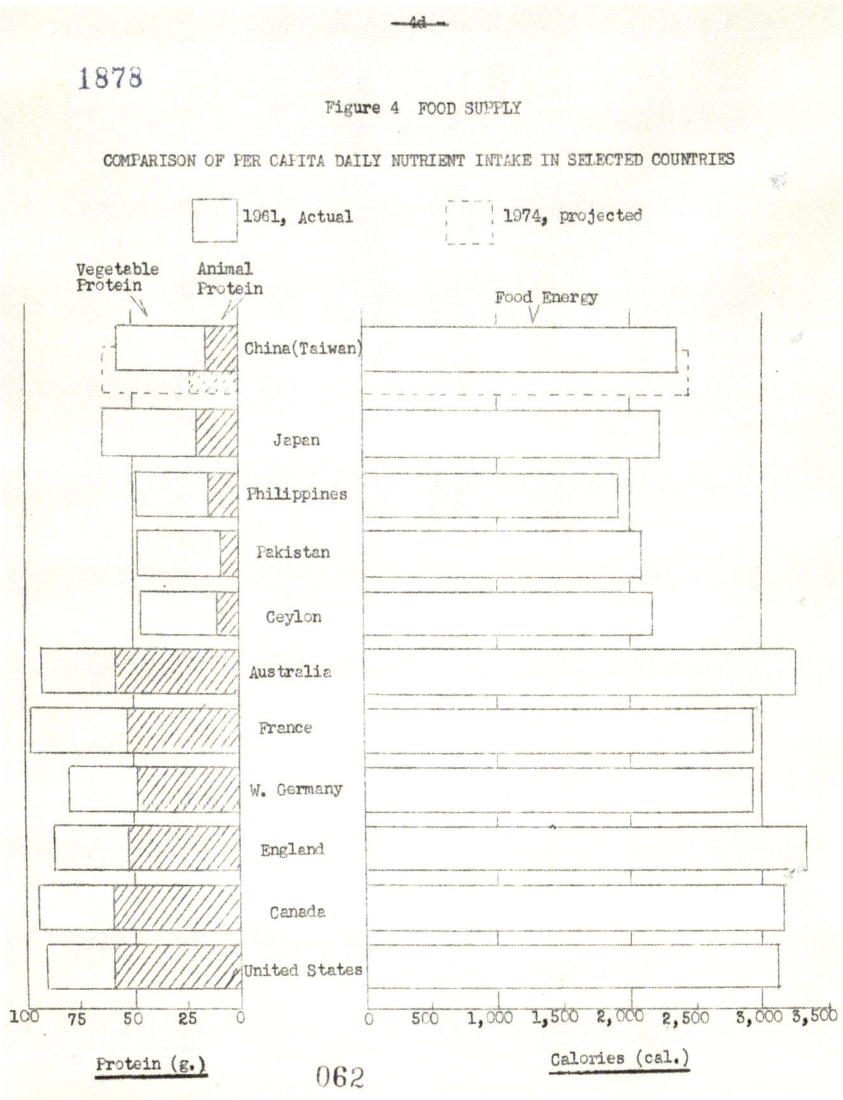

FIGURE 31. A comparison of per capita nutrient intake in Taiwan compared to other developed and developing countries, demonstrating Taiwan's accomplishments in achieving high average caloric intake. Included and likely shown to audience members in Shen Zonghan's speech to the Sino-African Agricultural Technical Cooperation Conference held in Ivory Coast, July 26–30, 1965. 中非農技合作討論會 [Sino-African Agricultural Technical Cooperation Conference], July 16, 1965, page 1878, archive number 020000039124A, Ministry of Foreign Affairs Collection, Academia Historica.

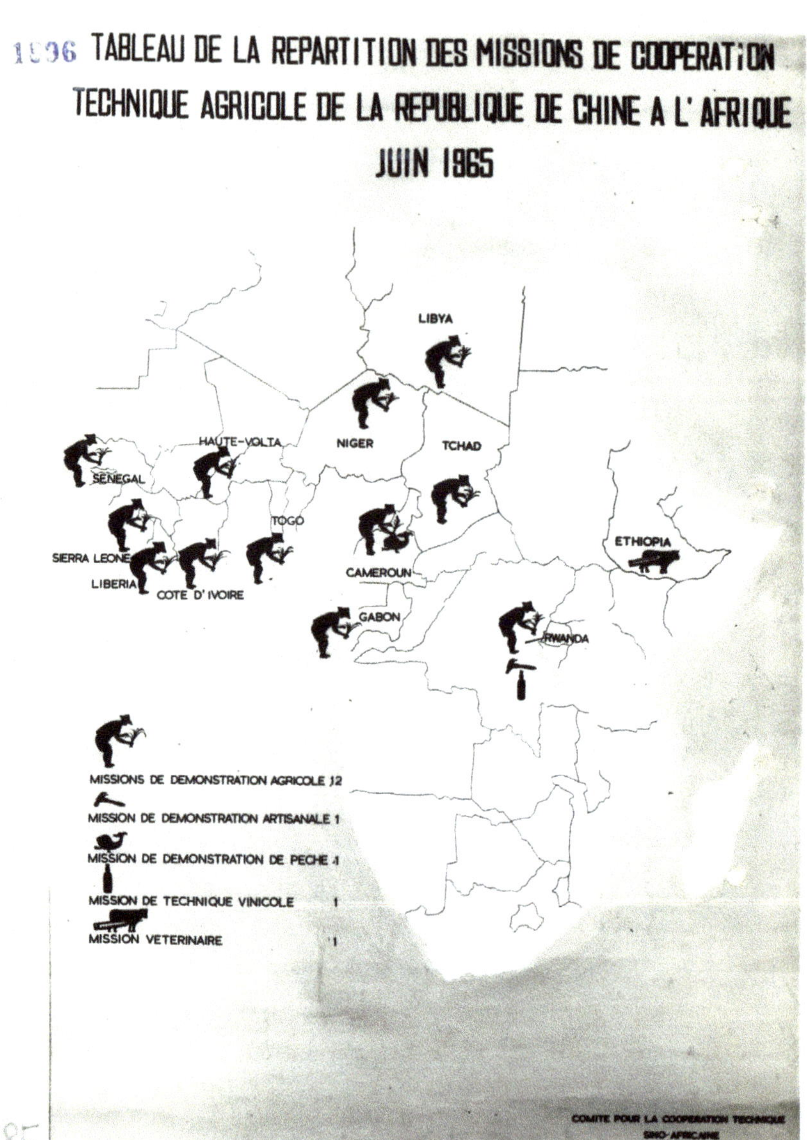

FIGURE 32. A French-language map visualizing Taiwanese development missions throughout the African continent in 1965. Included and likely shown to audience members in Shen Zonghan's speech to the Sino-African Agricultural Technical Cooperation Conference held in Ivory Coast, July 26–30, 1965. 中非農技合作討論會 [Sino-African Agricultural Technical Cooperation Conference], July 16, 1965, page 1896, archive number 020000039124A, Ministry of Foreign Affairs Collection, Academia Historica.

"(1) resources endowment, (2) technological factors, (3) organizational factors, (4) economic incentives, and (5) human incentives." Among these, Shen homed in on those aspects that once again characterized the Taiwan model. Shen rapidly dismissed resource endowment, even going so far as saying that the resource endowment of Taiwan "is only moderate," which was a fair assessment. Technological factors were attributable to basic and applied research, in improved varieties of plants and livestock, cultivation, fertilizer, and pesticide methods, and usage of irrigation and soils. Organizational factors reflected the other end of the Taiwan model spectrum, also dating back to the Republican era in China, where special focus was paid to social organizations such as farmers organizations and extension "for channeling the resources and the technology down to the village and farm level for increasing output."[37] In other words, Shen was describing the marriage of science and society that was at the heart of the Taiwan model.

Economic incentives demonstrated the qualities of Taiwan's state-capitalist approach to development that more sharply divided it from Communist development. Shen elaborated that economic incentives involved capitalistic mechanisms that provided stable markets and subsidies for farmers, including "land reform," "supported . . . guaranteed, or negotiated prices," "improved marketing systems of export crops," "adequate supply of farm requisites such as fertilizers, pesticides, farm implements, and feeds," and "the supply of agricultural credit."[38] These were all elements of Taiwan's approach to state-sponsored capitalism, combining elements of free market principles, such as credit mechanisms for private farmers and compulsory but financialized sales of land holdings (see chapter 2 for more on the capital raising techniques used in Taiwan's land reform), combined with state subsidies, aid, and regulatory oversight in order to provide stability and availability of critical supplies and market access.

The final element, human incentives, conveyed something that the previous elements did not, which was the closest to a direct political intervention into the state level. Though the state was closely involved in setting economic incentives and structuring markets, these policies are set from the top-down. In contrast, in describing human incentives, Shen began to describe the elements that constitute a developmentalist state: "a progress-oriented stable government," "a small group of agricultural leaders with advanced training and long experience," "a large number of graduates from agricultural colleges and vocational schools working in government and private organizations," and "an intelligent and literate farming population."[39] These factors were indeed crucial for Taiwan's own miracle. However, these elements were the most difficult to accomplish, as they would necessitate large-scale mobilization of resources and restructuring of government, institutions, and society, perhaps sustained over decades. Members of Shen's audience were neither equipped nor empowered to enact such changes. Instead, here and in other instances of development, these issues are depicted as technical, when in fact they are fundamentally political and require structural change at all levels of state and society.

Wrapping up his speech, Shen pointed to the signs of success and encouragement from the missions established in the early 1960s up until 1965. In the Ivory Coast, he proudly presented results of the Taiwanese assistance team planting 93.97 hectares of rice "according to Chinese cultural practices," with some teams even reporting "that the per unit area yield of various crops planted in the demonstration fields is even higher than the highest per unit area yield achieved in Taiwan itself." Shen attributed this "to the fact that most of your lands are virgin lands which have never been cultivated before and, therefore, are rich in plant nutrients." This was cause for immense optimism for Shen, who added that "such being the case, if your lands properly utilized, their productivity will certainly be very high." Thus, Africa's natural fertile soils, its "plentiful supply" of labor, combined with Taiwanese guidance to bring an "emphasis on trial and extension so as to make it easier for the local farmers to accept Chinese cultural practices" would bring "very bright" prospects. Taiwanese methods, combined with the natural African abundance of fertility and labor, could overcome other obstacles, such as the lack of capital, since in "the initial stage of agricultural development not much capital is needed anyway."[40] For Shen, the Taiwan model was the pathway for Africa to greater productivity and better livelihoods, as its strengths suited the strengths of Africa, and its low-capital methods compensated for its weaknesses.

VANGUARD AT HOME

By 1969, Operation Vanguard missions were ongoing in twenty African countries: Liberia, Côte d'Ivoire, Gabon, Rwanda, Senegal, Sierra Leone, Niger, Cameroon, Upper Volta (Haute Volta, today Burkina Faso), Chad, Togo, Malawi, Gambia, Congo-Kinshasa (Democratic Republic of the Congo), Dahomey (Benin), Malagasy Republic (Madagascar), Botswana, Lesotho, Central African Republic, and Ghana. Vanguard at that point also included three missions to Latin America (Chile, Brazil, Dominican Republic) and one to Asia (Thailand), with annual PL480 allocation from the United States to Vanguard exceeding $650 million New Taiwan Dollars.[41]

Behind the scenes of Vanguard was the tireless politicking of Yang Xikun, "Mister Africa," the vice minister of foreign affairs. Yang had studied international relations at Columbia University and then served as a bureaucrat with the Guomindang in various roles within the Ministry of Foreign Affairs. By 1958, he was participating in the ROC delegations to the United Nations, and by 1959, he had been appointed director of the West Asian Department of the MOFA, then director of the African Affairs Department. American observers in the State Department credited Yang as the "initiator and executor" for the MOFA's United Nations diplomacy strategy in Africa.[42]

In 1969, Yang Xikun penned two letters. The first was to the Taiwanese agricultural experts, copying several important technocrats in the JCRR and across

ROC government bodies, expressing his appreciation and reflections on the value of the Vanguard missions. On May 24, 1969, Yang wrote that Vanguard missions "were not only establishing a historical example by the Chinese people for the African people . . . but furthermore have redressed the mistaken impressions of the Chinese people due to the infiltration and subversion caused by the invasive nature of the Maoist bandits (毛匪, *maofei*)."[43] To that end, he wrote a second letter directed to the agricultural development team leaders and technicians on the ground in Africa to further encourage their work in assisting their "African allies."

The internal letter to the agricultural technical teams repeated several of the principles that Shen had presented to his African audience: the uniqueness of Taiwan's contributions, the importance of their work, and the success they achieved. Yang emphasized that "industriousness and frugality [克勤克儉]" was a "traditional virtue of us Chinese people" and "African countries were just like ours, we are all developing countries," hence it was necessary to practice the same industriousness and frugality agricultural work in Africa. The goal was to "spend as little in order to achieve the greatest results" so that "after leaving Africa, our African friends could also accomplish what we did."[44] These points emphasized the uniqueness of Taiwan's development approach and also reiterated that Taiwan's successes made that approach more easily taught and implemented in other similar developing contexts.

The letter also revealed Yang's insight into the purpose of agricultural technical cooperation and how it benefitted Taiwan as well as a greater humanitarian mission. He wrote:

> We are a developing nation [開發中的國家]. In these past few years, that we can unexpectedly participate in the economic development of other developing countries, especially with regards to agricultural productivity, and serve the people of our allied African nations, win their trust, and furthermore attain such ardent support and approval in our country and abroad, ought to be the greatest honor that all of those working in agriculture can hope to achieve.[45]

Yang appealed directly to the sense of pride among the Taiwanese for working from humble beginnings and with modest resources to accomplish enormous tasks abroad. These tasks were not merely to further diplomatic objectives, but also to serve the betterment of peoples internationally, and to bring meaning to agricultural work.

CONSEQUENCES

However, in many of its African missions, the replication of the Taiwan experience met significant obstacles. As historian Philip Hsiaopong Liu has written, with faith in the production capabilities of its rice seed and technology, one Taiwanese MOFA official wanted to replace African diets of maize and cassava with rice. For the average Taiwanese, rice formed the backbone of daily diet. But Taiwanese rice, usually of the starchy, sticky ponlai (蓬萊, *penglai*) variety, was bred for a Taiwanese consumer, meaning that it suited Taiwanese cultural taste preferences. When Taiwanese technical teams produced rice in Liberia, for instance, local market conditions meant that imported rice was often cheaper than the rice that the Taiwanese were able to produce locally.[46] This was a consequence of both the low cost of imported rice and its higher demand vis-à-vis rice brought over by the Taiwanese for local production. Cultural affinities for particular foods and its effect on food markets have of course been an issue in China, Taiwan, and elsewhere in the world for centuries, including in reaction to the Green Revolution and monocultures, and should not have come as a surprise for the Taiwanese teams in Africa.[47]

Furthermore, the success of Taiwanese rice depended in part on conditions that were fairly unique to Taiwan's economic and social circumstances: the availability of capital to purchase agricultural machinery and chemicals and a relative surplus of available agricultural labor that allowed for cheap, labor intensive processes like planting and harvesting rice. Without the ability that the JCRR had possessed to shape the political economy through state policies and access to the top echelons of government to implement changes and intervene in society, Taiwanese technical missions could rely on success only within their small, contained demonstration plots, such as aforementioned training centers in Sierra Leone and Swaziland. Taiwanese teams tended to cherry-pick locations with high fertility potential for their demonstration funds, and with an abundance of American funding through Vanguard, they were able to purchase irrigation pumps, fertilizers, pesticides, and labor that would not have been sustainable for locals without access to foreign capital. Thus, after Taiwanese teams left and the equipment they left behind fell into disrepair, many of these demonstration farms reverted to old farming methods used prior to Taiwanese arrival.[48]

In other instances, Taiwanese teams achieved limited success. Liu provided Rwanda as a counterpoint, where a relatively cheaper cost of agricultural labor and the use of Malagasy rice as opposed to Taiwanese rice allowed for more successful rice production.[49] In another example, Foreign Minister Shen Changhuan related how the Taiwanese team to Dahomey allowed it to "save $500,000 a year by producing itself materials for packing bags which it had previously had to import."[50] Yet productivity gains and cost savings often did not translate to lasting impact or long term improvement in livelihood. Former JCRR commissioner Bruce Billings reported on his trip to Africa in 1969 that successes were often complicated. In Sierra Leone, the farm supervised by Taiwanese technicians was "able to sell veg[etables] at a lower cost than those produced on other native farms" which led to native farmers being "not happy" with the Taiwanese for introducing unwelcome competition. Because Taiwanese teams were limited largely to supervising a handful of farms for demonstration purposes, they were not able to extend the technologies and methods on a broad scale to insure equitable distribution like in Taiwan, and conversely inspired counterproductive jealousy.[51]

In Côte d'Ivoire, politics and diplomacy also limited the ability of Taiwanese teams. From 1964 to 1965, Côte d'Ivoire was one of the rotating temporary members of the UN Security Council and thus a particularly important target for the Ministry of Foreign Affairs. Like most Vanguard missions, the Côte d'Ivoire mission was limited in resources and manpower. In part because of these limitations, the Vanguard mission selected the personal farm of Côte d'Ivoire president Félix Houphouët-Boigny as a model farm. Billings argued this was because "the fact that the President does have a farm with Chinese technicians is important in gaining the cooperation of the natives." However, this justification obscured the ultimate goal of the Vanguard missions, which were fundamentally political in nature—to secure votes for the ROC in the UN. In Côte d'Ivoire, the benefits brought by Taiwanese techniques were not seen by Côte d'Ivoire farmers. "The rice produced by the presidential farm is given over to the Army," or in other words, directly supported President Houphouët-Boigny's regime. Billings furthermore wrote that most farm labor in Côte d'Ivoire was imported from Mali "due to the affluence of the natives," referring to the relative wealth of Côte d'Ivoire compared to its poorer neighbors.[52] Though investments in agricultural cash crop exports continued to bring wealth to Côte d'Ivoire in the decades to follow, Taiwanese development did not always bring techniques to the bottom rungs of subsistence farmers as might have been implied when Vanguard was reported by the media within Taiwan.

Indeed, though development proved to be successful in raising incomes among Taiwanese farmers, increasing caloric intake among Taiwanese rural populations and freeing up agricultural labor for industrialization, in Africa these long term changes were far less pronounced. Vanguard missions were hamstrung by politics in most instances, where the supposedly apolitical techniques taught by Taiwanese teams could not overcome structural issues such as inequitable distribution of resources, limited native government support, and the politics of diplomacy. The United States also limited the scope of Vanguard mission, discouraging its providing technical assistance outside of agriculture.[53] Billings also lamented this, implying that "if the Vanguard project could include projects other than those directly tied to agriculture" then perhaps even greater results could have been achieved.[54] As described by anthropologist James Ferguson, this "anti-politics machine" of development touted its technical ability to transcend politics, but successful development more often than not required not just technical capability but also political will and reform.[55]

By 1971, support for the PRC taking over the seat of the ROC as "China" gained enough traction such that the ROC no longer could trade favors for votes. The pro-PRC bloc gained a supermajority, and the US, the ROC's staunchest ally, had acquiesced to this reality. United Nations General Assembly Resolution 2758 passed, formally recognizing the PRC as the legitimate government of China. The ROC had withdrawn its representative just prior to the vote, due to Chiang Kai-shek's perception that withdrawing would save face and prove less damaging to the international prestige of the ROC than being forced out by a vote, effectively ending its campaign to remain in the UN.[56]

As a consequence of the resolution, the United States ceased to fund the Vanguard program through its PL480 counterpart funds. Missions to most Vanguard nations were withdrawn or significantly reduced, though they would continue for certain allies who continued diplomatic recognition of the ROC under a different government agency, the Council for International Economic Cooperation and Development.

CONCLUSION

Despite the short-lived status of Vanguard, its efforts nonetheless marked an important turn in light of greater histories about decolonization, the Global South, development, and knowledge. By the 1960s, the elite of the Guomindang had begun to lose sight of regaining the mainland. For Chiang Kai-shek, military reconquest was always at the fore, but for the mid-level bureaucrats in the Ministry of Foreign Affairs and the JCRR, Taiwan had become a new home and governing reality. The Vanguard missions provided an opportunity to expand that horizon. Abroad, they provided proof of national greatness, that ROC techniques and technology were as useful, if not more useful, than those practiced by the United States or Japan. ROC missions abroad dedicated to these technologies could put these to use for those nations and peoples who needed them because hunger and poverty still plagued them. These humanitarian actions reinforced the notion that because the ROC could afford to be a donor abroad, that it had conquered these issues at home. And carving out this international niche as a groundbreaking nation in agricultural development allowed the ROC to perceive itself as being in the international "vanguard."

The home front was perhaps even of greater importance for many of these intellectuals and bureaucrats. By pointing to the demand for ROC technical assistance abroad and by reinforcing its position as one of humanitarian goodness, agricultural technology became a means of proving the success of the ROC state to a domestic audience. No longer was Taiwan a sleepy colonial backwater that planted rice for others abroad. It became the producer of technologies, the model for others to follow. This sense of legitimacy provided immense propaganda value for a regime that needed continued support from the average citizen to justify its authoritarian rule and Chiang's continued quest for military build-up. It also provided a sense of nationalism for the GMD elites, which by the 1960s, after growing increasingly disillusioned about the prospects of retaking the mainland, also began to show signs of agitation against Chiang.[57]

The idea of being in the vanguard and providing a model for others to follow was also unique from a historical perspective because of the Cold War in Asia and the state of development at the time. Unlike the Cold War in Europe or in the United States, Taiwan's Cold War was waged primarily for its international legal status, an almost existential question of whether it was a state at all. Development was one field in which this unique Cold War produced rival scientific and technical regimes between the ROC and PRC. While development had largely been practiced by what were considered First World and Second World powers like the United States and the Soviet Union, the engagement of a former colonial territory like Taiwan in the field marked a significant shift. Today, South-to-South cooperation is far more commonplace, but in the 1960s, Taiwanese aid to Third World countries was novel and a source of pride for both Taiwanese and Americans (who saw Taiwan as an Agency for International Development "graduate"). The introduction of practices from a former colonial space also meant technologies and practices evolved from social settings quite different from US and Soviet development. Thus, emphasis on farmers' associations, for example, proved to be a unique area of contribution in many Vanguard missions. Taiwan's contribution in farmers' associations, combining top-down and bottom-up knowledge techniques, demonstrate that knowledge can coalesce in different ways when constructed in South-to-South networks.

6

———

Capitalism with Socialist Characteristics

The Land Reform Training Institute, 1968–1979

On the other hand, many poor peasants are still living in poverty for shortage of the means of production, with some getting into debt and others selling or renting out their land. If this tendency goes unchecked, it is inevitable that polarization in the countryside will get worse day by day. Those peasants who lose their land and those who remain in poverty will complain that we are doing nothing to save them from ruin or to help them out of their difficulties.

—MAO ZEDONG

A great economic accomplishment of the past ten years was your program in land reform. Due to its fair and democratic conception and execution it has become a model for similar reforms in other lands. It dealt successfully with one of the fundamental problems the Chinese people have faced throughout history. Moreover, in it you achieved much more than a fair and equitable adjustment—you produced both social dynamism and economic growth. That reform, founded on Sun Yat-sen's three peoples principles and executed with due regard for law and for private property, stands in sharp contrast to the brutal regimentation of your countrymen on the mainland. There they are often herded into the soul-destroying labor brigades of the Commune System. But free China knows that a system in which the farmer owns the land he tills gives him the incentive to adopt advanced fertilization, irrigation and other farming techniques.

—DWIGHT D. EISENHOWER

INTRODUCTION

US President Dwight D. Eisenhower, on a visit to Taiwan in 1960, extolled the land reform performed by the GMD in Taiwan to a rally held in Taipei. He called GMD-led land reform "a great economic accomplishment" that resolved a long-standing historical problem of inequity. In the speech, he pointed out that Taiwanese land reform offered not only fairness and "equitable adjustment" but also "due regard for law and for private property," in direct contrast with land reform across the strait under the PRC. Like language that was wielded by Chen Cheng (see chapter 2), Eisenhower pointed to capitalistic principles of "incentives" and "techniques" that would be fostered by respect for property rights and contracts. In doing so, he was establishing a sharp contrast between GMD-led land reform and PRC land reform that centered on the importance of capitalist technocracy: proper management of rights, law, and markets for the prosperity of all.

Together with the publication of Chen Cheng's *Land Reform on Taiwan* in English, Eisenhower's speech marked the beginning of a GMD turn to showcase Taiwanese land reform for a global audience. Compared to the previous two chapters that have discussed Taiwanese agricultural science and technology and social groups such as farmers' associations in the developing world, Taiwanese land reform demonstrated a different facet of its development experience. Land reform shared the same emphasis on Taiwanese success at modernity and improving rural lives. The difference was more pronounced in ideology. Land reform especially included discussions of Sun Yat-sen's Three Principles of the People that the GMD co-opted as an anti-Communist ideology and an emphasis on capitalist strategies being more suitable for developing states.

These GMD strategies came to a head with the establishment of the Land Reform Training Institute (土地改革訓練所, Tudi Gaige Xunliansuo, hereafter LRTI), established in 1968 in Taoyuan in northern Taiwan. The ROC partnered with a private philanthropic organization, the John C. Lincoln Foundation. Endowed by an American railroad entrepreneur, the Lincoln Foundation found in the LRTI a suitable vehicle for its propagation of Georgist thought, based on the theories of popular nineteenth-century American economic thinker Henry George. The LRTI, like Operation Vanguard, targeted bureaucrats from developing world nations interested in learning how to enact land reform, either to increase financial revenues for the state or to battle Communist insurgency in their home countries. For the GMD, the LRTI represented another opportunity to "win" its ideological Cold War with the PRC, to build relationships with non-Communist developing world nations, and to showcase its development success globally and at home.

The LRTI-assisted nations that sent technocrats to Taiwan spanned Barbados, Bolivia, Brunei, Colombia, Cook Islands, Costa Rica, Dominican Republic, Ecuador, El Salvador, Fiji, Guam, Guatemala, Haiti, Honduras, India, Indonesia, Iran, Khmer, South Korea, Lesotho, Malaysia, Micronesia, Nicaragua, Panama, Paraguay, Philippines, Solomon Islands, Sri Lanka, Thailand, Tonga, Uruguay, South Vietnam, and Western Samoa.[1] Taiwanese development leadership once again co-opted its narrative of development success in land reform for its efforts at forging ties with other states. Taiwan sought to lead other decolonizing powers in the Cold War world through land reform.

Institutions like the Land Reform Training Institute have not been discussed in any English language literature, as far as I know, and have appeared only in spurts in the Chinese language literature. Utilizing archives that I have not seen used by any scholar—the Lincoln Foundation papers at the University of Hartford and the archives of the Land Reform Training Institute—as well as documents from the Land Tenure Center in the University of Wisconsin, this chapter attempts to "rescue history" from land reform. It does so by contextualizing the role of land reform in the technopolitics of development, or, put differently, disentangling the relationship between political power and the discourse of the "apolitical" and technical.[2] It privileges the performativity of land reform and argues that land reform should be understood as different "keys," namely land reform as historical narrative and as technopolitics.[3]

Land reform as historical narrative refers to the construction of a historical narrative ex post facto in order to support a political goal—the ability to claim unparalleled technical expertise in the field of development attributable to unique historical experiences and success. Land reform as technopolitics refers to the wielding of that claimed technical expertise as a Cold War political strategy. Land reform as technopolitics provided not only an ideological basis for the ROC's diplomatic alliance-building in the Global South but also a shield for its political legitimacy at home, justifying its military dictatorship with a social welfare agenda that contrasted sharply with the Communist foil across the Taiwan Strait.

This chapter also attempts to address land reform as it fit into the larger puzzle of development. For an agricultural miracle that was so heavily promoted as evincing the success of the Guomindang in breaking the power of the landlords, by the 1970s the story of Taiwan's agricultural success had shifted almost entirely to the agricultural tenets of the Green Revolution—high-yield crop cultivars, chemical fertilizers, and irrigation. The marvels of high science and technology, in other words, had buried the anti-Communist origins of land reform. Hidden in this transformation is a discussion of what land reform meant to Taiwan, the United States, the Third World, and the shifting global understandings of modernity.

THE 1966 WORLD LAND REFORM CONFERENCE

In 1963, the United Nations Economic and Social Council's Social Commission undertook studies on land reform, publishing a report on the state of global social development and on land reform in Asia, Africa, the Middle East, and Latin America. Land reform also entered into discussions in the United Nations Conference on the Application of Science and Technology for the Benefit of the Less Developed Areas and to the UN Food Agriculture Organization (FAO), where during a conference convened in its twelfth session, FAO director B. R. Sen was asked to organize another conference specifically on the issue of land tenure and agrarian reform programs. This culminated in resolution 1078 to organize the 1966 World Land Reform Conference, cosponsored by the UN, FAO, and the International Labour Organization and held in Rome.[4] Representatives from eighty-one countries and territories and nineteen international NGOs attended the conference, including a majority from "less developed countries." Sen began the meeting by stating that there was a "veritable crisis in the world food and agriculture situation."[5]

According to one account by a participant from the University of Hartford, historian and political scientist James R. Brown, the conference began with an overall theme of impending Malthusian doom, the idea that population was rapidly growing in the Third World while agricultural productivity was relatively stagnant. In moving toward solutions, speakers like Professor D. G. Kare, adviser to the Reserve Bank of India, argued that the conference should remain a technical one. This raised the ire of the representative from the Soviet Union, Professor Lebanov, as well as Belarussian and Polish representatives, who argued that land reform was fundamentally a social and political subject. The debate ballooned into a miniature Cold War of ideologies. In Brown's words, the Soviet bloc representatives co-opted the conference to serve as a platform for their agenda, attempting to sway representatives from the Third World that land reform was a naive endeavor and "nothing could be done about land reform or changing land tenure unless the whole form of government was changed."[6]

Despite the objections from Communist state representatives, the resolution and discussions of the conference produced a number of tangible discussions regarding best practices of land reform. For example, almost all delegates understood that there was a "complementary relationship" between land reform and community development or "peasant organization" (according to Brown, a wide-ranging definition for groups ranging from "home economic clubs of peasant women" to "highly organized peasant syndicates"), but as Brown portrays it, there was "considerable disagreement" regarding whether community development was a precondition or result of land reform.[7] This chicken-and-egg conundrum seemed to reveal arguments about the social or technical nature of land reform itself. If community development preceded land reform, likely the emphasis was first on the social; community development, as historian Daniel Immerwahr has argued, was "an effort to shore up small-scale social solidarities, to encourage democratic deliberation and civic action on a local level, and to embed politics and economics within the life of the community."[8] Thus, the village and the peasant assumed primacy, and it was through their organization and power that reform could be enabled. In the latter case, if land reform preceded community development, then it appears that the peasants were the objects, formerly locked into untenable situations and now freed through breaking the shackles of tenancy.

The issue received little more than a few sentences of discussion from Brown, but its treatment by Brown was undeniably technical. Instead of reconciling the importance of discussing which preceded which, land reform or community development, Brown provided the analysis that "organized peasant movements have proven helpful in overcoming [legal] obstacles" to land reform that may be initiated by vested interests, and afterward can "also help to integrate the new land holders into their communities and cooperatives."[9] What had been an entire school of thought for a number of rural sociologists about communitarianism and the value of local village communities thus became merely a catalyst for ensuring that the formula for land reform could be carried out more efficiently.

Through its resolution, the conference brought land reform further under the umbrella of technical development practices. After a unanimous vote at the plenary session, the conference recommended that the UN and FAO begin to organize conferences and workshops on land reform, provide assistance to countries requesting it for land reform planning and implementation, publish additional studies and reports on land reform, increase visibility of land reform at future conferences of the FAO, the Social Commission of the UN, and similar agencies, and finally encourage "all the developed nations to extend adequate economic and technical assistance, on request, to the developing countries in land reform and related fields" and "the exchange of experts, personnel, and trainees in the field of agrarian reform" among UN members.[10] The final recommendations of the conference set land reform as one of the major agendas for international development. This internationalization of land reform created new opportunities for "developed nations" to gain a foothold in the international arena, especially in the highly contested political space sensitive to both Communist and non-Communist nations, and was crucial to the struggle for influence within the Third World.

Member countries contributed working papers, usually based on their experiences with land reform, to share with other delegates at the conference. The representatives from the Republic of China submitted a paper based on of the history of land reform in Taiwan. Highly technocratic in nature and resembling an abridged version of Chen's *Land Reform in Taiwan*, it differed not in its basic narrative but in its deviation from Chen's 1961 book through a historical revision of land reform. The report began with the obligatory nod to Sun Yat-sen's Three Principles of the People: "The policies and programs of land reform implemented in Taiwan by the Government of the Republic of China are based on the teaching of Dr. Sun Yat-sen, Founder of the Republic," which advocated that "the State shall have the supreme power in disposing land and that all unearned increment from the land shall be enjoyed by the public."[11] This claim regarding the "principle of the Equalization of Land Rights" was mildly deceptive. Sun's elaboration of land reform was limited to the state purchasing undervalued land from landlords, thus in theory discouraging speculation and underutilization for the greater social good. It continued with obeisance to the dictator of the ROC on Taiwan, Chiang Kai-shek, to claim that these policies were enacted by Chiang in Zhejiang in 1927. Like Chen, it identified the source of land reform as the 1930 Land Law dictating the 37.5 percent rent ceiling and went further than Chen, arguing that the 375 policy, among others of the 1930 Land Law (progressive land taxation, compulsory purchase of excess tenanted land for resale to tenants, maximum size limits of tenanted land, etc.) were implemented in Zhejiang, Jiangsu, Hubei, Fujian, Guangxi, Guizhou, and Sichuan but were "frustrated by the long and continuous wars between the Government on one hand and the warlords, Communists and Japan on the other." It further remarked that "these reforms therefore passed unnoticed by the outside world."[12]

The report from the ROC produced a work that would be useful on a technical basis. The historical narrative contained policy specificities, contingency planning, and thoughts on proper procedures and actions that would allow for it to be replicated in different contexts. As such, the ROC narrative of land reform was deployed not just to shine a positive light on the achievements of the Guomindang on Taiwan but to forge the basis for an international development praxis with attention paid to inequality. In describing the effects of land reform, for example, the economic payoffs were always prominently discussed, but social consequences, too, became salient. "Before land reform, rural poverty had caused social unrest and political disturbance in the rural areas." After land reform, the report continued, "social justice was promoted and social order was stabilized. When the majority of the population are property owners, they eventually show more interest in community activities and social work."[13] "No matter how gradual and peaceful its implementation may be, [land reform] will inevitably involve a revision of the existing social organization and economic structure," it continued. "Wealth, power, and status formerly monopolized by landlords will, after the reform, be shared by farmers who gradually become organized and powerful in the field of production and other activities."[14] To minimize the problem, the report called for the government to actively employ education and training to properly support these social groups as they shifted into their new roles. In other words, land reform was a technical problem that called for a technical solution, and as a consequence of the solutions outlined by the 1966 report, technical solutions also had salutary effects for traditional society as perceived from the perspective of the modernizing state.

Furthering this rationale was the introduction of all sorts of state apparatuses to rationally understand and map traditional societies—through land surveying, accurate counts of acreage and production yields and crop varieties—in a James Scott high modernist imagining.[15] In the case of the 1966 report, it recounted the government agencies that had been created to help administer land reform: "The supporting programs consist of a wide range of activities . . . includ[ing] farm production, farm credit, land use improvement, water conservation and farmers' organizations, etc." These programs required the support of the Provincial Department of Agriculture and Forestry, the Provincial Water Conservancy Bureau, the Provincial Food Bureau, the Land Bank and the Cooperative Bank, among others, all "features" and institutions "common to the government organization in a unitary State. They seem to be one of the factors which contribute to the more effectiveness, efficiency and economy in the administration of public programs of the Government."[16] This transformation of what land meant to the state became subsumed as the defining logic of rationality and modernity under this refashioned land reform narrative.

GEORGISM AND THE LINCOLN FOUNDATION

The 1966 World Land Reform Conference brought not just a platform for the Republic of China to showcase its land reform efforts; it also put ROC land reform in contact with a number of American land reform scholars who at the same time were also collaborating with American philanthropists interested in the issue of land reform both at home and abroad. One was the John C. Lincoln Foundation, named after its eponymous founder whose involvement was crucial in the establishment of the Land Reform Training Institute.

John C. Lincoln was an entrepreneur who founded the Lincoln Electric Company in 1895. He invented the first portable welding machine, and Lincoln Electric became one of the leading firms producing portable welders and innovating arc welding, an industry that boomed during World War II. The result was rapid growth for the company, which rose to become the largest arc welding company in the United States by 1975 and that was the subject of many *Harvard Business Review* cases.[17] Lincoln Electric became well known for its labor practices; despite not having any union workers, the company offered guaranteed employment, employee stock-ownership plans, and bonuses based on company revenues, all practices that were revolutionary at its time.[18]

Outside of the Lincoln Electric Company, Lincoln founded the John C. Lincoln Foundation in 1946, dedicated to "teach and expound the ideas of Henry George, as they appear in his book, 'Progress and Poverty.'"[19] Lincoln was a devout Christian who had written a book on his faith (*Christ's Object in Life*), and biographer Raymond Moley has argued that Lincoln's Christian faith defined his belief in the necessity of a "natural law" for economics, a way to "equalize opportunities" and "eliminate involuntary poverty."[20] Lincoln had read *Progress and Poverty* and subsequently believed in the possibilities of Georgist ideas on land taxation and ownership to help people in this manner. He contributed to the Henry George School of Social Science in New York and published a number of short pieces through the school on land, such as "Should Land Have Selling Value?" and "Stop Legal Stealing."[21] The mission statement for the foundation included a quote attributed to John C. Lincoln stating his belief that the foundation should "through the dissemination of proven truth to change the standards of economic education and of public opinion, and thus contribute to a more just and productive life for free men and women."[22] As such, the Lincoln Foundation's guiding principles included "a broad treatise on the science of economics," an economics, it clarified, that expounded a "liberal" tradition that valued "economic liberty within nations" and "freedom of commerce and trade between nations."[23]

The allure of Henry George for Lincoln and other Americans lay in George's egalitarian vision for economic growth without trampling on property rights or opening the floodgates of exploitation. In the eyes of his followers, George was a middle ground between ruthless laissez faire capitalism and the radical Communism of Marx. But Henry George never took hold in the academic or policy mainstream and instead enjoyed popularity largely among its lay readership—John C. Lincoln among them—who had little influence in Washington, DC.

As economist Phillip J. Bryson has argued, George had been historically marginalized because of his utilization of classical economics at a time when neoclassical economics had become the new paradigm in academic and policy circles. As Bryson has phrased it, "as George presented his theory to the world, classical theory was already doing its best to slip quietly into the dustbin of history."[24] Furthermore, George's lack of formal academic training precluded his being taken seriously by other economists, and some scholars, including Bryson, have even gone so far as to argue that George's professional marginalization was due in no small measure to the envy that his popularity incited among his more academically credentialed peers. But it was the controversial "single tax," what Joseph Schumpeter called a "policy panacea," the "nationalization not of land but of the rent of land by a confiscatory tax," that likely made George such a polarizing figure.[25] The "single" aspect of the single tax made it particularly unappetizing for policymakers; George argued that all taxation should be abolished save that on land, a rather radical solution that became less feasible as the modern nation-state evolved in the late nineteenth and twentieth centuries to depend on multiple sources of taxation for its revenue.

Yet Georgists found that this exact aspect provided an answer to a problem that George first recognized in the 1870s—and from which the title of his book is derived—that poverty increases despite overall progress in wealth. In *Progress and Poverty*, George argued that "poverty deepens as wealth increases, and wages are forced down while productive power grows, because land, which is the source of all wealth and the field of all labour, is monopolised."[26] George came to this conclusion after spending significant time in California and seeing the monopolization of land in advance of railroad construction by the Central Pacific Railroad. In combination with speculation and railroad subsidies, ownership of land granted a select few private parties enormous wealth as railroads increased overall productivity, but the wage laborers saw none of this wealth. The next step, George argued, was the understanding that land should be owned by all: "The equal right of all men to the use of land is as clear as their equal right to breathe the air—it is a right proclaimed by the fact of their existence."[27] Thus, private ownership of land led to what George argued to be "the enslavement of labourers," since the "ownership of the land on which and from which a man must live, is virtually the ownership of the man himself, and in acknowledging the right of some individuals to the exclusive use and enjoyment of the earth, we condemn other individuals to slavery."[28] The idea that private ownership of land is inherently unnatural and exploitative formed the basis for his theory.

The solution that George outlined was the single tax, a method he devised to avoid the dispossession of land from any landowners yet still accomplishing his goal of ending exploitation and inequity. The single tax called for the abolishment of all taxes except for one single tax on land value, and this tax would provide economic fruit for everyone, or as George argues, through this manner in effect "land, no matter in whose name it stood, or in what parcels it was held, would be really common property, and every member of the community would participate in the advantages of its ownership."[29] He believed that the single tax "in every civilized country, even the newest" would produce revenue "sufficient to bear the entire expenses of government."[30] Moreover, taxing landowners would take the burden of taxation off the laboring classes. And finally, a single tax would be simple to collect administratively, reducing the size of government by freeing it from the duties "to prevent and publish evasions, to check and countercheck revenues drawn from so many distinct sources."[31] It appealed to those who like George, harkened to the ideals of Herbert Spencer and Jeffersonian democracy.[32]

George did not make his appeal of a single tax merely for the benefit of the laborers whom he perceived to be suffering under land monopolization. He also underscored a broader social good since "the rise of wages, the opening of opportunities for all to make an easy and comfortable living, would at once lessen and would soon eliminate from society the thieves, swindlers, and other classes of criminals who spring from the unequal distribution of wealth."[33] In other words, George argued that single taxation had the secondary benefit of improving societal welfare through its ability to provide for the basic necessities of those who would otherwise turn to crime. It was a pragmatic argument, on the basis that a rising tide would lift all boats, but also one that appealed to the development experts of the Cold War who were concerned with the betterment of societies in the Third World.

The Lincoln Foundation operated largely within the confines of the United States to implement its vision of applied Georgism. An example of its early projects in disseminating Georgist ideas through education included funding an adult school for economics, the Lincoln School of Public Finance, in Claremont, California. But it was after John C. Lincoln passed away in 1959 that his youngest son, David Lincoln, took over as the president of the Foundation and began to seriously engage university faculty interested in land reform and look outward to bring Georgism to the rest of the world.[34] In 1966, the same year as the first World Land Reform Conference held by the United Nations, the John C. Lincoln Foundation funded a new institute at the University of Hartford for the promotion of Georgist land reform studies. The John C. Lincoln Institute, which initially coordinated to help fund seminars and courses of study, officially became a school in 1974, the Lincoln Institute of Land Policy, before being finally merged with the John C. Lincoln Foundation in 2006 to become a single foundation and research institute.[35]

Selected to run the Lincoln Institute as its director was land economist Archibald Woodruff. Woodruff earned his PhD in economics at Princeton, then taught at the University of Pittsburgh, and became dean of the School of Government at George Washington University. In 1965, just a year prior to the founding of the Lincoln Institute, he joined the University of Hartford as provost. In 1967, he became the chancellor (later reclassified as president) of the University of Hartford, a post he filled until his retirement in 1977.[36] According to land economist Ted Smith, who studied with Woodruff at Claremont Graduate University and worked as a postdoctoral fellow with him, Woodruff was a devout religious person and a true believer in the value of land reform for Asia.[37] An academic and university administrator, Woodruff was in a position to leverage his intellectual interests in Henry George into a position of power, and in partnership with the Lincoln Foundation, into international soft power.

Woodruff was unique for having been an advocate of Georgism as an academically trained economist. By the 1960s, Georgism had fallen to the wayside along with most other classical economic theorists. Yet Woodruff attempted to revive Georgism for the Cold War world, as an American response to Karl Marx and the influence of Communism internationally. In a paper titled "A Comparison between Henry George and Karl Marx in their Approach to Land Reform," first presented at the University of Hartford in 1966 (and in 1970 republished by the University of Hartford in a volume of essays on land reform), Woodruff established an explicit contrast between George and Marx. "Karl Marx and Henry George," he began, "alike in odd ways and totally different in others, were both utopians. Each was deeply outraged at the evil he saw in the world about him, each had a vision of a better society, each prescribed a remedy for the world's ills and each crusaded for his cause."[38] The parallels Woodruff established helped burnish George's credentials as a sympathetic figure whose views on social inequality were similar to Marx's.

Part of Woodruff's paper reads as an exegesis of classical economics. He began with the common theoretical foundation for both Marx and George, which is Ricardo's posited relationship between labor and wages, capital and interest, land and rent, and finally, entrepreneurship and profits. Woodruff explained that George adopted Ricardo's interpretation of the "Iron Law of Wages," that real wages tended in the long run to decrease to a minimum necessary for sustenance, as the primary assumption of the aforementioned relationships. At the same time, Woodruff also crafted a social history of both Marx and George. He argued that "each was inflamed with moral indignation over the fact that the rich grew ever richer while the poor grew no less poor," with Marx witnessing this event in Germany,

Paris, and London and George encountering it in California.[39] This indignation over growing wealth inequality drove both thinkers to consider the underlying economic causes for inequality.

Woodruff portrayed George's heterodox approach to economics as more utilitarian than neoclassical. "The main trouble with economics, George specified, lay in the fact that theory fell short of the natural usefulness of the subject. Worst of all, economics had arrayed its *laisser faire* [*sic*] ideas against improvement and reforms on behalf of the working classes."[40] George, so Woodruff argued, offered a practical solution that would help lower-class people.

Woodruff depicted the contrast between Marx and George as one of prescribed solutions. According to Woodruff, George "opposed revolution just as much as he opposed entrenched landlords."[41] Marx, on the other hand, "left no blueprint for actions," or as Woodruff put it more aptly, "Marx's thinking stopped on the day of revolution."[42] Revolution would lead to utopia in Marx's world, and utopia was in reality left to the hands of improvised revolutionaries like Lenin who were willing "to use almost any tactics to keep control of the revolution."[43] With Woodruff citing fifty years of Communist control in Russia, he concluded that Marxism may have been the "basic scripture of Communism," but actual rule stemmed from the pragmatism of Marxists in power. These resulted in situations where the peasantry who were "hungry" for revolution, instead suffered under autocratic rulers.[44] In other words, Marx may have been concerned about the laboring classes, but his solution left power to those whom history had proven to betray the farmers and laborers who were supposed to benefit.

Woodruff then addressed the critiques of Henry George's single tax. Critics challenged the basic premise of his interpretation of the Iron Law, that progress necessarily entailed poverty and that rent on land did not in fact absorb the benefits of progress, while also arguing that a single tax on land was foolhardy in that it was inelastic and unresponsive for public fiscal needs.[45] Woodruff claimed that though the single tax was not practical in contemporary times, it did effect a number of positive outcomes, including more complicated means of assessing property taxes (based on carefully calculated depth tables and corner influence tables), as well as spawning the social reform movement led by idealists such as Carry Nation, Frances Willard, Eugene Debs, and the Garrisons. And while Woodruff admitted other tax sources were necessary, Georgism was still applicable because it (1) was efficient, (2) discouraged letting land go unused or underused, and (3) encouraged urban land use, thus reducing urban sprawl and speculation.[46] He cited the benefits of a "heavy progressive land tax" as having been responsible for "the breakup of huge estates" in Australia and New Zealand and the "Island of Formosa" (Taiwan).[47]

In short, Woodruff argued that Georgism provided a rational and moderate alternative to the uncontrolled revolutionary radicalism of Marxism for the world. Woodruff believed that Georgism would appeal to elites in power because "experience would indicate that most elite power groups are also intelligent and as such aware that while fiscal reform may indeed curtail some of their privilege, it lacks the total completeness of the guillotine." In other words, where Marx was entering the hearts and minds of agrarian populations, Georgism offered an alternative, allowing developing world elites to keep their heads.

Under Woodruff's guidance, the first seminar funded by the new Lincoln Institute was the Hartford Seminar on Land Taxation, Land Tenure and Land Reform in Developing Countries in 1966.[48] The seminar brought together academics and bureaucrats from a number of institutions and countries—Australia, the Vatican, Denmark, Jamaica, University of Bombay, the United Kingdom, the University of Oregon, FAO, the University of Ghana, Venezuela, the London School of Economics, and government representatives of the ROC—to discuss issues of land taxation, tenure, and reform. And it was at this seminar where an opportunity emerged for Woodruff and the Lincoln Foundation to put their Georgist ideas into actual implementation for their development world ideals.

The ROC representative was Shen Shike (沈時可, Shih-ko Shen), the director of the Taiwan Provincial Government Land Bureau (台灣省地政局, Taiwan Sheng Dizheng Ju). Shen had been a county magistrate (縣長, *xian zhang*) on the mainland with the GMD before moving to Taiwan as director of the Land Bureau there in 1946.[49] From the perspective of Ted Smith, who met with Shen regularly at the Land Reform Training Institute, Shen was a classic GMD bureaucrat, "party line all the way."[50] Yet according to Shen's grandson, Shen's experiences with land reform were deeply shaped by his experiences during the February 28 Incident of 1947, when he hid in the basement of the Land Bureau offices to escape the deadly violence. After the harrowing experience, he advocated for land reform with his boss, Chen Cheng, as an important social policy.[51]

Having overseen the actual administration of the various land reform laws, Shen became an ambassador for land reform abroad by the late 1960s, representing the ROC at conferences like the one held at the University of Hartford by the Lincoln Foundation, as well as land reform missions to countries like Iran in 1967.[52] At the University of Hartford 1966 seminar, Shen presented a paper titled "Land Taxation as Related to the Land Reform Program in Taiwan" detailing the recent history of Taiwan's land reform to a University of Hartford audience. Beyond the value of its content to historical representation of land reform, the presentation was also the beginning of a political and intellectual relationship between the Republic of China and the Lincoln Foundation.

Shen began his presentation paper with an array of remarkable statistics stemming from land reform in Taiwan: an increase in owner-cultivators (as opposed to tenant farmers) from 58 to 87 percent, increase in land ownership by owner-cultivators from 57 to 90.6 percent, a 259.6 percent increase in the average income of farmers, and an astounding rise in standard of living of 346.8 percent (though no methodological footnote provided as to how this was calculated). But farmers were not the only ones to benefit. Landlords saw an equally impressive gain of 307 percent increased income, while overall agricultural productivity grew 110.2 percent. Most importantly, industrial productivity increased 322.4 percent, a result Shen attributed to the increase in number of landlords engaged in commerce and industry of 128.9 percent.[53] The heights of land reform made clear the stakes of Shen's paper—Taiwan was a success story of land reform, and land reform that contributed directly to the industrialization success of a developing nation upon which other success stories could be patterned.

Having already established the bona fides of Taiwan's land reform, the burden on Shen was explaining how land reform was accomplished successfully. To this end, the mythologizing of land reform history was once again deployed to explain the origins of land reform. Shen pointed to "Dr. Sun Yat-Sen's theory of equalization of land rights and his 'land-to-the-tiller' doctrine."[54] The specific phrasing of "land-to-the-tiller" was a neologism anachronistically applied to Sun Yat-sen. While Sun advocated for a more progressive land tax that would allow for income equalization (the theory of equalization of land rights), the Three Principles of the People did not include land-to-the-tiller (耕者有其田, *gengzhe you qitian*) that eventually became the lynchpin policy of Taiwan's 1950s land reforms. Aside from this, Shen's exposition was largely historically accurate. Shen provided the standard narrative of rural land reform in the 1950s, beginning with rent reduction, sale of public lands, and finally the land-to-the-tiller redistribution. In greater depth, he delved into Sun's idea of a land increment tax providing for local reconstruction and the public good, an idea borrowed from Henry George. As such, Shen's paper focused on aspects of land reform dealing specifically with taxation in rural and urban contexts.

In the urban context, Shen laid forth the foundations of taxation policy. True to Sun's design a half-century earlier, the ROC had implemented a policy of self-valuation that allowed landowners to determine the value of their land themselves, with the caveat being that the state was allowed to legally purchase the property at the self-reported taxable value (and indeed, the state performed its own valuations for this purpose). The policy streamlined administration of taxes. This complemented other land taxation policies, including progressive tax rates and varying special case taxes on vacant land, land for public use, and land transferred or sold, that all encouraged land development and maximized revenues.[55]

Shen's paper sparked a rigorous discussion from observers interested in the specifics of Taiwan's success. Woodruff raised the comparison of India to Taiwan, and specifically how Taiwan succeeded where India failed despite the underlying ideas of land reform being largely similar. (This topic would continue to interest him intellectually well into his retirement, as he had been working on a manuscript titled "Comparison of Socio-Economic Structures in Taiwan and India, Effects of Land Reform" that was then compiled and published posthumously in 1984.)[56] Shen replied that it was due to careful planning combined with a cautious and long-term approach. M. L. Dantwala, a professor of economics at the University of

Bombay, then pointed out the difference in size between the two nations, where the "sheer magnitude of the scale of operations makes the task formidable," and noted that the Indian state's need to focus on other urgent governance needs limited their ability to tackle land reform with the determination and focus the ROC government was able to bring to bear on the problem.[57] He also pointed out the disparity in the starting points of farmers.[58] Another participant of the seminar, Yitzchak Abt, an Israeli agricultural counselor stationed in the Israeli embassy in Venezuela, added that "it is proximity to existing urban concentration which counts," emphasizing the importance of urban development to overall national growth.[59] Indeed, additional doubts arose with regard to Taiwan's urban land reform, specifically the policy of self-assessing land valuation. Daniel Holland at the Sloan School of Management at MIT added that in the Latin American contexts, few nations would be able to adopt the self-assessment method because of the lack of "a 'credible threat' of enforcement" that would discourage landowners from underpaying taxes by undervaluing their land.[60]

Despite the issues raised regarding the portability of Taiwan's solutions to other contexts, Shen ended the discussion with a suggestion. "In view of the importance of the seminar and the contributions made by such outstanding participants," he urged the participants, "it would be well to consider the prospects of a permanent organization set-up to follow up these problems and for further research."[61] Though Shen continued to provide suggestions in discussing other papers drawing on Taiwan's experience, the official record did not contain a prolonged discussion of this idea, which would eventually come to fruition as a joint project between the ROC and the Lincoln Foundation—the Land Reform Training Institute.

THE LAND REFORM TRAINING INSTITUTE

A mere two years after the 1966 seminar held in Hartford, the Land Reform Training Institute (LRTI) was established in Taoyuan, Taiwan. Shen Shike, the Provincial Government Land Bureau director who had represented the ROC at the Hartford seminar two years earlier, had been corresponding with Woodruff in April 1968 to establish a "Land Reform Research Institute" (土地改革研究中心, Tudi Gaige Yanjiu Zhongxin) that would "allow other countries planning to undertake land reform or in the process of implementing land reform and experiencing difficulties to send representatives and undertake research."[62] This was realized as a training institute, emphasizing the role the institution would serve in helping other developing nations.

For the Lincoln Foundation, an institute hosted in a developing country that had successfully implemented land reform, one of the few at the time, was a compelling platform for enacting land reform internationally. Woodruff reiterated this, eight years after the founding of LRTI, when he proclaimed that land reform demonstrations held in the United States "would mean little" to those from developing countries. Instead, in Taiwan, they could "point out that twenty five years ago

[the] island was primitive," and thus "if the Republic of China could do [land reform] with the resources it had, [other developing countries] could also do it in their own countries."[63] Taiwan was moreover appealing as the intellectual successor to Henry George. Through Chiang Kai-shek and the GMD regime's continued obeisance to the Three Principles of the People of Sun Yat-sen, the Lincoln Foundation believed that Taiwan carried the torch of Henry George into the modern era. For the ROC state, land reform provided another opportunity to showcase the abilities of the GMD regime in economic development and social improvement. The Lincoln Foundation recognized the political agenda of the ROC as well, and as a consequence influenced the selection of an executive secretary, the de facto director of the institute, whom they perceived to be young, bright, and most importantly, not beholden to the political motivations of the GMD regime—none other than Shen Shike.[64]

Located in Taoyuan, approximately an hour outside of the capital of Taipei, LRTI consisted of several buildings: housing offices, dormitories, classrooms, and a library dedicated to providing formal instruction and training for Third World bureaucrats in land reform. The ROC and the Lincoln Foundation agreed to co-fund LRTI (the ratio ranged from 70/30, respectively, to 50/50 during the first decade, depending on the fiscal year), for a trial period of three years, after which the agreement would be contingent upon votes to renew its status by its board of directors.[65]

The board of directors reflected the importance of LRTI. Its list of associated directors drew from Taiwan's development elites, from land economists in academia and well-known figures associated with land reform of the 1950s. It was co-chaired by Shen Zonghan, then the chairman of the Joint Commission on Rural Reconstruction, and David C Lincoln, son of John C. Lincoln and head of the Lincoln Foundation. Also on the board were Li Guoding (李國鼎, K. T. Li), the famous minister of economic affairs who was the public face of Taiwan's industrial development policy; Xiao Zheng, the aforementioned land economist (*dizheng*) who headed his own institute, the Chinese Research Institute for Land Economics, and who served as chairman of the board of directors for the Land Bank of Taiwan that underwrote the land bonds crucial in land-to-the-tiller reform; and Pan Lianfang (潘廉方, L. F. Pan), former legislator in the Legislative Yuan and also an ROC representative of land reform who had served on the ROC land reform mission to Iran with Shen Shike in 1967. Its executive committee, in charge of administration, was cochaired by Shen Shike, whose official title was executive secretary, and Archibald Woodruff. Also sitting on the committee were representatives from the Lincoln Foundation, the JCRR, the Taiwan Land Bank, and the Council for International Economic Cooperation and Development (CIECD, the economic development agency headed by Li Guoding).[66]

These threads converged at the LRTI. The land economics of Xiao Zheng was rooted in the idea that land reform was the legacy of Sun Yat-sen and the Guomindang revolution. A younger generation of land bureaucrats following Xiao, such as Shen Shike and Pan Lianfang, sought to modernize the world in

FIGURE 33. The Land Reform Training Institute building in Taoyuan, Taiwan, which was renamed the International Center for Land Policy Studies and Training in 2000. Photo taken by author in 2013.

Taiwan's image. Finally, Archibald Woodruff and David Lincoln hoped the legacies of Henry George and John Lincoln could be fulfilled through the Taiwan. The LRTI became the institution that would showcase Taiwan's land reform successes to the world and provide them with the firsthand knowledge necessary to battle radical Communism in their own backyards.

In September 1972, the third year the LRTI ran training classes for international participants, Archibald Woodruff sent Alan S. Wilson, a retired vice chancellor of administration at the University of Hartford (and former director of the Hillyer Institute, one of University of Hartford's predecessor schools), as an outsider with no knowledge of land reform to observe a regular session of the LRTI in process.[67] Wilson had been deeply impressed by the operation and execution of the LRTI. In a report written for the directors of LRTI and the Lincoln Foundation, Wilson wrote "since 1968, several emerging countries in Africa and South America have encountered renewed attacks by Socialists and Communists aimed at taking over their governments. Farmers face a hopeless future without land reform. These countries cannot wait nor can they help themselves."[68] Wilson argued, like his colleague Woodruff, that the developing world was under assault from Communism, and land reform was the solution to this global turmoil.

The LRTI curriculum was structured around sessions of two types: regular, lasting eight weeks (initially eleven) and recurring on a regular basis, and short, one-off sessions that were tailored to special missions, usually of single national origin and similar social/professional background, for example for a group of Vietnamese farm leaders. The regular session served the core mission of the institute in providing training in best practices of land reform for participants from developing nations in Asia, and beginning in 1972, in Latin America. Each session hosted approximately thirty participants, nominated by their home countries.[69]

To take an example, the fifth regular session, held from March 15 to May 15, 1971, consisted of twenty seven foreign participants from Khmer (Cambodia), Brunei, Thailand, Vietnam, (South) Korea, the Philippines, and the US Trust Territory of the Pacific Islands. Participants were a mix of government bureaucrats, farm leaders (usually from farmers' associations), and landlords. Titles and professions varied, but generally were related to land policy, administration, and economics. These included an assistant agricultural officer and land officer from Brunei; assistant chief of the National Tax Administration and a cadastral engineer from the Kyongki provincial government in Korea; a land reform project team leader from the Land Authority in Quezon City and a provincial president of a chapter of the Federation of Free Farmers in the Philippines; a dikes and ditches project member of the Royal Irrigation Department and a second-grade economist from the Ministry of National Development in Thailand.[70]

Shen Shike's annual reports offer a window into what LRTI officials believed they had accomplished. Shen's Third Annual Meeting report claims that "the farmer leaders and priests from the Philippines reacted very favorably and suggested that the Institute invite more farmers to attend the course."[71] Though Shen undoubtedly desired to cast the feedback of participants in a positive light, the manner by which he chose to frame the positivity is telling. Shen's tactic was to emphasize the efficacy of land reform in changing the opinions of farm leaders, priests, mayors, and landlords. These were representatives from crucial social classes whom policymakers sought to win over in order to carry out land reform through cooperation and not by force. These were the same classes that were the ostensible beneficiaries of Taiwan's land reform. The revelations from these attendees, as Shen proclaimed in his annual report, were precisely what the LRTI sought to showcase to the John C. Lincoln Foundation and the rest of the world.

The curriculum of the regular session focused on theories and best practices of land-related topics with a significant number of courses based on Taiwan's own history of land reform. The third session, for example, featured courses on the general purpose and theory of land reform, including "The Importance of Land Reform to Developing Countries" and others discussing general problems in implementation as well as land reform specifically in the context of Southeast Asian countries. The technical aspects of land administration were also taught—cadastral survey, land value assessment, land taxation, and Aboriginal (Indigenous) land, to name a few.

Taiwan's success was featured heavily, especially those aspects that curriculum designers perceived to be unique about the Taiwan case. Five courses were offered specifically on the history of land reform in Taiwan, ranging from a general course on land reform to details on its political background, effects on farm economy, economic development strategy, and changes in the social aspect of Taiwan's land reform. The latter topic, which constituted a discrete course of study, reinforced the point that the primary function of Taiwan land reform was to effect social change, though the terms in which the curriculum was presented invariably made it clear that the practice was technical in nature. The course on political background elucidated the "political principles underlying land reform in China," specifically modeled on the "3-phase implementation of land reform" that Taiwan had used in the 1950s to successfully implement reform.[72] This represented a familiar narrative that all success could be traced back to the ROC's founding father, Sun Yat-sen, and his political ideals.

To complement land reform, a series of courses were also presented on agricultural extension, farmers' organizations, the Land Bank of Taiwan, the Cooperative Bank of Taiwan (responsible for allowing low interest purchasing of fertilizer on credit), and Irrigation Associations. Agricultural extension and the ability of the Taiwanese government to disseminate/extract knowledge and correctly administer the distribution of water, credit, and fertilizer depended heavily on these local social organizations. Agricultural extension was the other interlocking piece with land reform to form the basis of the Taiwan agricultural miracle (see chapters 2 and 3), and important for the ROC planners to convey for foreign participants. These were complemented by observation visits into the field to see land reform in action.[73]

Foreign scholars were invited to teach at the regular sessions. The first few regular sessions featured three scholars associated with the Lincoln Foundation or the University of Hartford, including Archibald Woodruff and Sein Lin, the associate director of the Lincoln Institute. Starting with the third session, in pursuit of further internationalization, LRTI sought to diversify the visiting lecturers, including scholars and officials from the FAO Rural Institutions Office, the Iran Central Organization for Rural Cooperation, the Philippines Federation of Free Farmers, an agricultural economist from Thailand, and Japan's Asian Institute of Economics Affairs.[74] Internationalizing its faculty meant that the LRTI was able to claim greater authority over its land reform methods. Though it was based primarily on the Taiwan success narrative, it was also important to bring in alternative perspectives to demonstrate solidarity and wide applicability throughout the developing world.

Aside from the emphasis on social cooperation and effects of land reform, the curriculum also highlighted and drew on other aspects of Taiwan's 1950s history that put it in contrast with Communist land reform. One course sought to advise how "landlords [could] invest their capital derived from Land-to-the-Tiller Program," an aspect of Taiwan's 1950s land reform discussed in chapter 2 that was publicized as having provided the capital for Taiwan's nascent industries at the time, as well as creating a new social class of industrial capitalists who were rewarded for their "cooperation" in land reform with ostensible wealth.

Complementary to the training sessions, LRTI faculty were also sent abroad to evaluate and advise developing nations in land reform. These were conducted for a number of reasons. One was political, as these missions constituted a form of ROC development diplomacy with developing world nations. Another was to follow up on training that was initiated at LRTI. One example was received by the Republic of Vietnam's (RVN) director general of land reform Bui Huu Tien in July 1970. After the visit, Cao Văn Thân, minister of land reform, agriculture, forestry, and fisheries development, wrote in a letter to RVN prime minister Trần Thiện Khiêm of Taiwanese land reform. Cao described the Taiwanese model in terms laid out by LRTI curriculum. He cited Sun Yat-sen's Minsheng zhuyi (People's Livelihood), the 1950s narrative of three-stage land reform culminating in land-to-the-tiller, and the complementary vehicles to land reform in agricultural credit, farmers' associations, agricultural extension, and so on. In the report, he also attributes the success of Taiwanese land reform to several factors: (1) the state and its ability to mobilize "colossal human and material resources," (2) supplementing with "information, promotion, education at the correct level," (3) peace, and (4) complementary programs (the aforementioned agricultural credit, farmers' associations, etc.).[75] These factors helped spread a particular Taiwanese approach to land reform across developing states.

Just months earlier, in February, the LRTI had hosted a group of fourteen landlords from Vietnam. Shen wrote in the second annual report that the landlords were deeply affected by what they saw:

> After the landlords came back to Vietnam, the Land to the Tiller Act was passed. They told their people how their attitude toward land reform changed from objection to support after their visit to Taiwan. The mayors and the farmer leaders said that they would persuade the government to carry out land reform and arouse the farmers' attention to it.[76]

Shen portrayed the visit as a success in changing not only the minds of the farmers who would nominally be the beneficiaries of land reform but the minds of landlords as well. Though Shen did not clarify the reasons for their change of heart, he implied that landlords saw something in Taiwan that they hoped to replicate in Vietnam (though it seems unlikely that a mere fourteen landlords would have shifted public opinion toward redistributive land reform).

In August 1970, a month after Bui's visit, both Archibald Woodruff and Shen Shike traveled to South Vietnam. As part of their visit, they were present at a land title issuing ceremony in Ba Tri in Kiến Hòa Province as part of the implementation of the new Land to the Tiller Act of 1970. Ba Tri, however, was notable as a model "pacified" district. As part of the US and RVN pacification campaign, Ba Tri received special attention through development support.[77] It was likely that the ceremony in Ba Tri served a performative function, to demonstrate the benevolence of the regime in an attempt to win the hearts and minds of villagers. Though both the US and RVN governments pushed for a nationwide implementation of the 1970 act, it came arguably too late for the RVN.[78] Nonetheless, the report by

Minister Cao still stated that Shen would do his best to make sure "the work that Vietnam had and was carrying out will be popularized/disseminated more effectively in Taiwan by him and his organization to obtain active material and spiritual support of the friendly countries of the free world."[79]

DISSEMINATING THE TAIWAN MODEL

By 1977, LRTI became an important component of Taiwan's overall international development apparatus, and land reform became an integrated part of the Taiwan development model. JCRR commissioner Jiang Yanshi (蔣彥士, Y. S. Tsiang) symbolized this in a 1977 symposium honoring the centenary of the publication of *Progress and Poverty*. Speaking before an audience of the major development bodies of Taiwan, the JCRR and the LRTI, the Lincoln Institute, and Academia Sinica, the prestigious government-funded academic research institute, Jiang reminded attendees that "since its founding, the Republic of China has considered land reform policy to be a major national goal." In a narrative that had become de rigueur, Jiang went on to discuss how land-to-the-tiller and equalization of land rights were two of the key programs of Sun Yat-sen's Three Principles of the People. He highlighted the 15 billion NTD "collected from the incremental tax of land value for social welfare collection" as a sign of the ROC's dedication, and he praised Sun for putting "two different progressive ideas from the Chinese and the West into a concrete workable political principle."[80]

Jiang's comments, in addition to those from David Lincoln, Archibald Woodruff, Xiao Zheng, Lee Teng-hui and other scholars and development experts associated with land economics and the Lincoln Institute were regularly published in Lincoln Institute publications destined for international audiences.[81] As with most of these publications, they portrayed land reform as an essential aspect of developing "economic efficiency and democratic political institutions."[82] One of the papers, by Chen Sun, produced a diagram to demonstrate how Sun Yat-sen's Three Principles integrated the best parts of socialism and capitalism and created a middle path (figure 34).

The same diagram utilized by Chen Sun in the centenary publication later appeared in Li Guoding's 1988 book, *Economic Transformation of Taiwan, ROC*.[83] Li's book reached a greater audience. As the minister of economic affairs (1965–69) and later minister of finance (1969–76), Li presided over the formative period of rapid economic growth in Taiwan and thus became one of the most public figures of Taiwan's economic transformation in the 1960s and 70s. His writings on economics have been well publicized. In his words, the importance of the Three Principles of the People and land reform was important for ensuring an "improvement in the distribution of wealth, increased access to education, and a greater social mobility," an ideal he attributed to Confucius.[84] This diagram illustrated the new ideological norm for the LRTI. Sun Yat-sen and Henry George had effectively

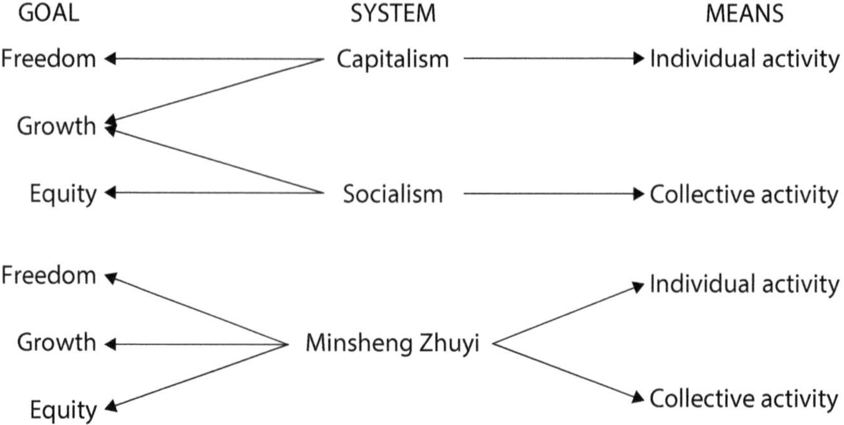

FIGURE 34. According to Chen Sun and later Li Guoding, under capitalist and socialist systems, only two goals could be accomplished: either freedom and growth or equity and growth. Under Sun Yat-sen's Minsheng zhuyi, all three goals—freedom, equity, and growth—could be reached, combining the ideal parts of both capitalism and socialism. Sun, "Land Reform and San Min Chu I," 42–43.

provided a third way for the developing world, one located squarely between the extremes of socialism and capitalism.

The LRTI also functioned as a host to visiting scholars funded by the Lincoln Foundation to perform research on land reform while being associated with LRTI. Theodore (Ted) Reynolds Smith was one of these fellows. Smith had completed a PhD in economics from Claremont Graduate University with funding from the Lincoln Institute. At Claremont, he met Archibald Woodruff, who taught classes there every other week. Upon graduation, Smith was offered a postdoctoral fellowship by the Lincoln Foundation to travel throughout Asia researching land economics, which included time at LRTI in Taiwan in 1969. His time in Taiwan also meant experiencing firsthand the GMD gaze and its disciplining of society. He noted that a visit from GMD police authorities followed a day after a private, politically sensitive conversation between him and his wife in their home in Taiwan. His research assistant was detained by the police as well, and after being released then provided Smith with an official narrative about landowners that was at odds with Smith's own observations.[85] His research was eventually published with the Lincoln Institute at the University of Hartford titled *East Asian Agrarian Reform: Japan, Republic of Korea, Taiwan and the Philippines.*[86] The book was a primer in land reform in Asia. It covered the basics: why bother with land reform, different ways to accomplish it, and an analysis of results from the cases mentioned in the title. Smith's study was representative of a type of literature that sought to publicize the Taiwanese case in the English language scholarship, while also inserting a Georgist-influenced theoretical lens to contextualize its success in the Cold War.

East Asian Agrarian Reform begins, predictably, with Sun Yat-sen and the Three Principles of the People which led to the Land Law of 1930 and its amendment in 1946. It included quotes from Xiao Zheng, referenced as "one of the leading authorities on Chinese land tenure," in a discussion of how the Guomindang had attempted land-to-the-tiller reform in the face of the Communist Civil War. Yet it diverges from more official narratives by offering the reader a realistic assessment of why the GMD turned to land reform, namely, its failure in China when compared to the fervor of the Chinese Communists. For Smith, land reform on Taiwan became a way to reconcile that failure, as well as a means through which the GMD "could remove the landowners from their role of political prominence in village life."[87]

Smith was critical of some aspects of Taiwanese land reform. He expressed skepticism of the official Taiwanese narrative in his analysis of Taiwanese claims that landlords successfully transitioned from landowners to industrial capitalists, citing a study performed by National Taiwan University in 1965 arguing that 98 percent of small and mid-sized landowners and 90 percent of large landowners sold the stock holdings they had received in compensation for seized lands.[88] Smith concluded that "the initial corporation ownership experience of the majority of Taiwanese landowners was much less rewarding than had been the holding of land. To some extent this experience served to alienate many former landlords from an industrial system which actually offered a tremendous potential for economic gain."[89] This observation calls into question Lee Teng-hui's own thesis about intersectoral capital flows (see chapter 2). However, Smith nonetheless indicated as a whole the Taiwan case was a success and suggested its ability to "serve as a model for all those concerned."[90] The example of Smith's writing demonstrates how the LRTI, the Lincoln Foundation, the Lincoln Institute, and their network of Georgist-influenced land economists helped propel Taiwan into academic discussions on land reform.

Disseminating Taiwan's land reform success was also taken on by another Lincoln affiliated individual: John C. Lincoln's daughter, Lillian Lincoln Howell. Lillian Howell founded the KTSF TV station in the San Francisco Bay Area, one of the first stations to focus on Asian language programming directed at the Asian American community. Following in her father's footsteps, she established the Lillian Lincoln Foundation in 1985, funding video media projects on topics of philanthropic interest, such as micro-lending for women in the developing world, primary education in Japan, and land reform in Taiwan.[91] One documentary funded by the foundation and produced in 1987 by Dateline was *Taiwan's Transformation: Winds of Change*. The twenty-seven-minute documentary sought to explain how Taiwan changed from an "economic basket case" to an "economic success" in a mere forty years. It featured interviews with farmers who had benefitted from land reform discussing the social changes it had enacted. In its narrative for the establishment of the Republic of China on Taiwan, land reform naturally followed the principles of Sun Yat-sen calling for democracy, livelihood, and nationalism.

The documentary featured the commentary of Arlo Woolery, executive director of the Lincoln Institute from 1974 to 1986 and a member of the board of directors of LRTI.[92] Woolery pointed out the economic benefits of land reform—farmers have a greater incentive to develop land if they owned it, or in his words, "There is an old saying that the most valuable fertilizer you can have on land is the footprint of the owner." L. Y. Chuang, a former tenant farmer in Taoyuan interviewed in the documentary, stated, "I was overjoyed with land reform. And then I had a right to the land I cultivated. I no longer worried at the end of the year that the landlord might take the land back. I made a more secure life for me and my family."[93] In a scene minutes later, Y. C. Chuang, younger brother of L. Y. Chuang, is shown driving a new Mercedes Benz sedan, with the narrator stating that Chuang had "traded his tractor for this Mercedes" using savings from his family farm that allowed them to start a plastics manufacturing company.

In addition to the social benefit for those below, Woolery made sure to emphasize that landowners were incentivized to sell land because of the potential for "great profit" in the stock in state-owned enterprises they received. The documentary interviewed a former landlord as well, Chenlu Chow, who said that "most of the landlords were opposed to the idea" of land reform and that landlords thought that land reform was "unfair" to the landlords, but "looking back," he thought "land reform was wise" to allow investment for development. Chow is shown in his three-story house playing with his grandchildren, described as "semi-retired" because of the investments he made in a bus company using the capital from his sold land.[94] In the following scene, UC Berkeley sociologist Thomas Gold was interviewed, stating that not all landlords successfully transitioned from landowner to capitalist as Chow and the others did.

The LRTI was extended beyond its initial three-year trial period due to its early successes, and its rapid growth in the 1970s expanded its country participant list to represent a great part of the developing world. It hosted visiting scholars and consultants throughout the 1970s and 1980s from prominent development agencies and universities interested in land reform. But by the late 1980s, land reform began to experience a global decline. Owing in part to the collapse of Communist regimes internationally and also to the decreased emphasis on rural development in favor of urban and industrial growth, land reform became a relic of the earlier Cold War era. Organizations like FAO and the University of Wisconsin shuttered their land tenure centers and rural organization units in the 1990s, as development moved into the domain of the World Bank, and structural adjustment became the new paradigm.

By 2000, the Land Reform Training Institute had changed its name to the International Center for Land Policy Studies and Training (ICLPST). Today, its facilities are in need of repair. There is evidence of water leaks from the ceiling, empty offices, and decaying books in a library that had suffered through a roof collapse. Its curriculum changed as well. Though it still hosts government bureaucrats from the Global South, the ICLPST instead focuses on aspects of land policy with contemporary relevance: land administration and policy in urban settings. Other institutes, like the Land Reform Museum (財團法人土地改革紀念館, Caituan Faren Tudi Gaige Jinianguan) in Taipei that also host short-term courses for international scholars, have likewise undergone the same adjustment. During the mid-2010s, when I conducted fieldwork, they had even attracted a new group of government officials interested instead in rural-to-urban transformation in Taiwan as a model: party cadres from the People's Republic of China.

CONCLUSION

Land reform became the soft-power complement to military interventions, for as long as Communists continued to be a threat in the farming villages of Africa, Asia, and Latin America, the hearts and minds of the Third World mattered more than all the weapons that could be mustered internationally. For the Lincoln Foundation–associated land economists who espoused Georgism, land reform was the shield and sword against radical Communism. Land reform represented the benevolence of capitalism for both farmers and landowners, and philanthropists like David C. Lincoln believed in its power to help complete his father's mission of social deliverance without subjugation to Communism.

This narrative is deeply relevant to understanding development and its relationship with the Cold War. By the 1960s, the global political discourse centered on Communism. The revival of Henry George and the convictions of Georgist economists in proposing Georgism as the solution for oppressed agrarian societies of the world represented a softer Cold War stance. The agricultural miracle of Taiwan in the 1950s and 60s provided thinkers like Lincoln Foundation economists with the ability to tenuously link Georgism, which they retroactively associated with Sun Yat-sen, with land reform under the Guomindang. In contrast to military interventions, development provided an opportunity to stop the halt of Communism with the carrot as opposed to the stick. And by appealing to both protecting land rights and private property as well as providing for the social good of the entire population, Taiwanese land reform sought to find a third way among the extremes of other economic systems to appeal to developing nations.

For Taiwan, land reform provided an opportunity for its political and technocratic elite to reimagine its own history and national identity. The construction of a historical narrative of land reform provided the ROC with the bona fides it needed to demonstrate that it had arrived as a modern nation. According to its land reform pedagogy, the post-1949 Nationalist state was an enlightened, benevolent, patriarchal state. It followed the principles of the founding father, Sun Yat-sen, in supporting the livelihood of the people. Land reform was the proof that all could benefit—farmers, landowners, and the state—in the quest for modernity. It recovered from its mistakes in the fight against the Communists on the mainland and demonstrated that social equality could be accomplished without class conflict, violence, or violation of the sanctity of private property and capitalism. And most importantly, it proved that social equality was compatible with the foremost goal of the developmental state: economic growth, the search for wealth and power that had seemingly eluded the Communists.

Land reform granted the GMD the moral high ground it had formerly ceded to the Communists by demonstrating its commitment to the downtrodden masses and that it was not just the party of the capitalists, the industrialists, and the landlords (though, it was that too). Furthermore, through attempting to internationalize its (constructed) development experience, Taiwan elevated land reform from the realm of historical narrative to reality, through development practices in LRTI's classrooms. From LRTI course materials to economic history research written by US-based economists, Taiwan infused its 1950s agricultural miracle with land reform, constructing a façade for an authoritarian island under martial law with a paradigm of enlightened benevolence for the Third World.

The international arena became the crucial audience through which the ROC could justify its newfound enterprise. Its success with land reform meant that it carried a burden to save other developing nations from the grasp of Communism, a technopolitical version of a *mission civilisatrice*. In this vision, Taiwan, as one of the few successful cases of land reform, understood the unique difficulties of balancing growth with social equality while fighting the rapacious laissez faire capitalists and the radical Communists. Taiwan could lead a crucial coalition of embattled Third World nations on the brink of falling to Communist insurgents back toward a middle path of social betterment and economic growth. In a world where Taiwan had been marginalized as a state dependent on the good graces of the United States and in constant ideological, military, and existential threat from the Communists on the mainland, Taiwan carved out a unique international niche.

7

Green Devolution

Taiwanese Vegetable Science, Nutrition, and the Developing World, 1969–1989

Because the Taiwan story is largely a success story, I believe that profession-als in the development business should spend time studying the development history of the island

—BRUCE H. BILLINGS

I get the feeling that if it were not for the Geo-political factors, the going would not be quite so rough.

—ROBERT F. CHANDLER

INTRODUCTION

In 1968, USAID Director William Gaud coined the term *Green Revolution* to refer to the increased global production of staple food crops (maize, wheat, rice) through high-yielding varieties that responded well to intensive methods of cul-tivation, namely increased inputs of chemical fertilizers and pesticides.[1] Norman Borlaug, the plant breeder who in the 1940s pioneered high-yield, semi-dwarf wheat in Mexico, won a Nobel Peace Prize two years later, in 1970, in recogni-tion of his contributions to agricultural science. The increases in production made possible through high-yield varieties and fertilizers proved a paradigm shift in development practice. Previously, fears of a Malthusian trap, referring to Thomas Robert Malthus's thesis that population growth would always outstrip food sup-ply and thus strain developing economies, preoccupied international develop-ment planners and led to detrimental state-led and international NGO initiatives in population control.[2] The Green Revolution offered states a different solution to their Malthusian concerns by increasing food production beyond the rate of population growth.

At the same time, Green Revolution reliance on chemical fertilizers and pesticides further entrenched the industrialization of agriculture across the world, and with it, new global environmental dangers, including chemical runoff and pollution. The Green Revolution paradigm shift to monocultures—single-crop agriculture to the exclusion of crop variety—created dependencies on improved seeds. In the decades that followed, Global-South states turned away from the development and production of improved seeds and instead ceded this to private corporations located in the Global North, which then patented those seeds and monopolized seed markets. This monopoly in effect locked farmers into a dependent relationship with large agribusinesses. Improved crops emerging from the Green Revolution focused on production above all else. As a result, they were often of lower quality and inferior taste, which limited market demand and reduced their utility to farmers.[3] Despite all these significant problems, during the 1970s, production was king, and the Green Revolution was seen as the key to a promising future of agricultural science and international development. The ultimate consequences of Green Revolution methods were not yet clear.

Equally important was Gaud's contrast of the Green Revolution to what he perceived as "Red Revolution," referring to the Soviet Union, or "White Revolution," referring to Iran. The Green Revolution offered an alternative model based on technology and science that Gaud likened to the Industrial Revolution.[4] As critical scholars have argued, the Green Revolution should be seen instead as a US project to combat the influence of Communism by co-opting agricultural science and industrialized agriculture in the ongoing global Cold War.[5]

For Taiwan, the popularization of agricultural science provided a political opportunity amid an existential crisis. In 1971, UN General Assembly Resolution 2758 permanently banished representatives from the Republic of China from the United Nations. While ROC dictator Chiang Kai-shek bristled at the indignity of being replaced by the Communist regime of the PRC for a few years before he died in 1975, the geopolitical ramifications of the ROC's ouster would be far more disastrous for Taiwan in the long term. For almost a decade, Taiwan had been engaging in agricultural development on a bilateral basis, showcasing its agricultural expertise in the fields of Asia and Africa and its growth curves in academic conferences in an effort to preserve its UN seat. UN Resolution 2758 precipitated the cessation of formal diplomatic relations with many of these countries. With the increasing visibility of agricultural science and its potential to combat the global issues of poverty and hunger, Taiwanese policymakers and scientists seized an opportunity to gain a greater platform for Taiwan's agricultural success and in turn to resolve a political situation that threatened to marginalize Taiwan.

Vegetables and nutrition offered that means for Taiwan to seek geopolitical allies in the midst of its ouster from the United Nations. Whereas the Vanguard missions of the 1960s that sent Taiwanese agricultural technicians to Southeast Asia and Africa emphasized Taiwan's low-capital, practical solutions for other developing nations, the international agricultural research centers of the 1970s symbolized Taiwan's turn to vitamins, proteins, and caloric intake within a discourse and imagination of scientific modernity. This continues a narrative of the co-option of science and technology for Taiwan's political ends. But unlike earlier efforts in the 1960s, by the 1970s, Taiwan's marginalization following UN Resolution 2758 is a discontinuity that marks the decline of Taiwan's international agrarian project.

This chapter explores the construction, politics, and consequences of Taiwanese agricultural science amid global attention to nutrition and industrialized agriculture preceding and following the Republic of China's ouster from the United Nations in 1971. It examines several institutions, the Food and Fertilizer Technology Center (FFTC, 糧食肥料技術中心, Liangshi Feiliao Jishu Zhongxin), founded in 1971, and the Asian Vegetable Research and Development Center (AVRDC, 亞洲蔬菜研究發展中心, Yazhou Shucai Yanjiu Fazhan Zhongxin), founded in 1972. How did Taiwanese scientists seek to leverage Taiwan's expertise in plant breeding, plant physiology, soil science, entomology, chemical fertilizer, and food industry via global networks? Organized through and often funded by the US government and US-based philanthropic organizations like the Rockefeller and Ford Foundations, these multilateral networks connected Taiwan with other American Cold War allies, such as Japan, South Korea, the Philippines, and Thailand for the purpose of regional and global development. For Taiwan, these scientific institutions represented another means to internationalize through an ostensibly Taiwanese-specific approach to agricultural science, which simultaneously served to advance its diplomatic goals. Taiwanese planners turned once again to science, this time as a way to regain a semblance of regional and global power following its UN ouster.

The AVRDC and FFTC also represented a turn to more "high-modernist" science and technology. The marketing success of the Green Revolution made science and technology one of the predominant trends in international development in the 1970s, surpassing and eclipsing, for example, community development and land reform.[6] In contrast with "low-modernist" approaches of organizing farmers' associations and disseminating knowledge to the lowest rungs of society, high-modernist science championed the scientific advances resulting from selective breeding in laboratories and experiment fields and industrial scale production. The FFTC emphasized intensive chemical fertilizers. The AVRDC focused on the other part of the Green Revolution formula—seeds. The idea that seeds selected through experimentation could save millions of lives appealed to popular opinion, at a time when humans were traveling into outer space and possibilities for modern science seemed limitless.

The founding of the FFTC and the AVRDC coincided with a growing international concern for food and food politics. The FFTC and the Food Industry Research and Development Institute, a private research center in Taiwan headed by Ma Baozhi after his return from the University of Liberia, emerged as development shifted away from just resolving basic hunger needs to a focus on the food industry as an important economic sector and food nutrition as a symbol of social progress and economic development. The AVRDC represented a similar effort in international development by focusing on Taiwan's tropical and subtropical climate and its multitude of vegetable varieties. In marketing vegetables, as opposed to rice, maize, or wheat that were developed at the beginning of the Green Revolution, the AVRDC represented another shift, from satisfying basic caloric intake to a more diversified view of nutritional science involving vitamins and minerals.

This chapter also serves as a bookend to the narrative of Taiwanese development. It focuses on the global ramifications of Taiwan's domestic agrarian project but with adverse and permanent consequences for the state and society at home. And it ends with a rapid "fall" of Taiwanese development after its dramatic rise in international development in the late 1950s and 1960s. Taiwan's efforts at disseminating its vegetable and nutrition technologies ultimately succumbed to three headwinds. First, nutrition, as embodied by vitamins, minerals, and proteins, did not receive as much attention as the Green Revolution breakthrough in caloric productivity via cereals. Second, international development begin to shift away from state-funded projects during the Cold War and instead to international agencies and private corporations, especially with the growing move toward market-based solutions. Finally, the geopolitical marginalization of Taiwan following its exclusion from the UN doomed Taiwanese-based institutions like the AVRDC and the FFTC to the global margins instead of the global center. Because of Taiwan's non-country status in the UN, the AVRDC and other centers in Taiwan were not included within the Consultative Group for International Agricultural Research (CGIAR), the group that included the International Rice Research Institute (IRRI) and the International Maize and Wheat Improvement Center (CIMMYT). In effect, Taiwan was forced out of its privileged position at the global vanguard of agrarian development.

RICE

By the 1970s, nuclear weapons, missions to outer space, family-planning contraception, and medicinal advances captured the attention of both governments and the general public. In agricultural sciences, there was also a proliferation in research and public perception in the post-WWII era. Centers dedicated to specific crops emerged, such as CIMMYT for maize and IRRI for rice. Agricultural scientific research centers were not new to the Cold War era. In the United States, Japan, and China, research centers, experiment stations, and universities working in agricultural science had been collecting, comparing, and selecting higher yielding varieties since the late nineteenth century, driven by state objectives to increase agricultural productivity for greater economic profit.[7] Chapter 3 discussed some of the more specialized research centers that emerged in the postwar era on Taiwan, such as the Plant Protection Center, established in 1960, that brought the basic sciences of studying plant diseases to practical applications that could be field-trailed and disseminated through extension. However, CIMMYT's and IRRI's establishment in the Global South (Mexico and the Philippines, respectively) was novel, revealing a shift in how agricultural science began to become integrated into developmental policies throughout the world.

Taiwan was also involved in this specialization of agricultural science, with greater focus on specific agricultural products and technologies and increasingly globalized networks of cooperation and knowledge exchange. In addition to centers focusing on plant protection (discussed in chapter 3), vegetables, and fertilizer, there were proposals for research and demonstration centers in other aspects of Taiwan's agricultural success, such as irrigation.[8] This shift toward an international outlook coincided with the rise of Operation Vanguard and the Land Reform Training Institute, both of which sought to convey the Taiwan model to a global audience. Whereas centers like the Plant Protection Center were primarily looking inward, toward Taiwan as its primary beneficiary, new centers of the 1970s looked outward, first regionally within Asia and then globally to Africa and Latin America.

Research centers began to look outward as early as the 1950s, particularly to areas that possessed similar climates and environments to Taiwan. In 1958, the Taiwan Agricultural Research Institute (TARI) submitted a grant request to the Rockefeller Foundation for a "Program of Studies on the Causes of Low Yield of Rice in Tropical and Sub-Tropical Regions" and the establishment of an "Insect Identification Center for Southeast Asia." TARI, formerly an agricultural experiment station founded in 1895 by the Japanese colonial government on Taiwan, was reorganized as an agricultural research institute. After the GMD took over Taiwan in 1945, the institute was integrated into the Taiwan provincial government. TARI eventually became responsible for eight experiment stations throughout Taiwan ranging in specialties from cotton to tea, which was typical of experiment stations in order to approximate local growing conditions and crops suited for the different regions of the island.

In the grant request, TARI framed their project in terms of the unique environmental aspects of Taiwan: "The Tropic of Cancer passes through the island, and its climate is such that both the *Japonica* and *Indica* types of rice can be grown there. For this reason, Taiwan is an ideal place to undertake studies of rice, particularly with reference to the comparative environmental requirements of these two types." The proposal continued to list the shortcomings of each type, with *Indica* possessing a higher tolerance for low fertility soil and higher temperatures but a low response to fertilizer, while *Japonica*, a shorter-grained rice that was preferred by the Taiwanese, flourished in more temperate climates and seemed to be limited in tropical ones. It framed its research globally, highlighting their stock of 2,285 rice varieties from all over the world. And it referenced efforts conducted by other international organizations in regional rice research, for example, efforts by the UN Food and Agriculture Organization in producing *Japonica-Indica* crosses to select for high fertilizer response in tropical climates.[9]

TARI was not the only institute to which the Rockefeller Foundation and other organizations were looking. Because rice was a staple crop providing basic sustenance for a great portion of Northeast, East, and Southeast Asia, numerous international development organizations sought to increase rice yields to resolve ongoing malnutrition in Asia. As historian Nick Cullather has argued, staple cereals like rice became an intense focus of development organizations like the Rockefeller Foundation due to a focus on providing sufficient calories, a need that was seen as helping to subvert social tendencies to support Communist movements and regimes.[10] Encouraged by positive results from their efforts to improve maize and wheat in Mexico led by Norman Borlaug, the Rockefeller and Ford Foundations helped found the International Rice Research Institute (IRRI) in the Philippines.[11]

The IRRI drew on a diverse group of scientists from Asia and the United States. Ma Baozhi, the agronomist who had served previously as the dean of the College of Agriculture in National Taiwan University and the head of the Taiwanese crop improvement mission to Vietnam (see chapter 5), was a founding trustee. A number of scientists from Taiwan worked at the IRRI, such as plant geneticist Zhang Deci (張德慈, T. T. Chang) and plant pathologist Ou Shihuang (歐世璜, Ou Shu-huang), who served as divisional head at the request of the Rockefeller Foundation.[12] Shen Zonghan later joined later the board of trustees and oversaw training exchanges and cooperation in rice breeding between Ou Shihuang and the JCRR Plant Industry division. Though many of these elite scientists had trained in the United States, they nonetheless carried experience from their work in their home countries.

Taiwan's contribution to international rice research was not just in human capital. It also provided one of the key scientific innovations in the most famous product of the IRRI and one of the most famous of the Green Revolution: miracle rice. Miracle rice was a moniker given to a specific varietal of rice, IR-8, that emerged from the varietal improvement project of IRRI. IR-8, a semi-dwarf variety of rice, was high yielding, produced more grain per stalk of rice, and was more responsive to chemical fertilizers that were crucial to Green Revolution.[13] IR-8 was crossbred from two cultivars. The first was Peta, a fast growing and responsive variety from Indonesia, but it was a tall breed, meaning it was prone to falling over during typhoons and high winds, submerging the rice grains underwater or exposing it to ground-based rodents and other pests. The other was a cultivar from Taiwan, 'Dee-Geo-Woo-Gen' (低腳烏尖, Dijiao Wujian) or more commonly known by its acronym, DGWG. DGWG possessed the key dwarfing gene *sd1* that allowed IR-8 to resist toppling over (figure 35).[14]

Zhang Deci was one of the three main plant geneticists recognized for working on IR-8, and his familiarity with Taiwanese rice varieties like DGWG helped in the development of IR-8.[15] Zhang, in addition to being a graduate of Nanking University and a student of Shen Zonghan, was a JCRR scientist from the Plant Industry division. As much as IR-8 was celebrated for its technical success and

FIGURE 35. A comparison between IR-8 (*left*) and its two parent varieties: Peta (*middle*), an Indonesian variety that was hardy but tall and thus prone to toppling over; and 'Dee-Geo-Woo-Gen', or DGWG (*right*), the Taiwanese variety that possessed the dwarfing allele to allow for the semi-dwarf characteristic of IR-8. Hargrove and Coffman, "Breeding History."

production figures versus local varieties, it was also the international cooperation in advancing science for different global regions that excited so many development practitioners and scientists. The international backgrounds of the key members of the IR-8 team, consisting of scientists from the United States, Mexico, Colombia, and Taiwan, facilitated knowledge of varietals from all over the globe and allowed for the selection of specific genes that they sought. In Zhang's letter to his mentor, Shen Zonghan, he specifically referenced the precedent set by Taichung No. 1, another semi-dwarfing variety of rice from Taiwan, that had already been adopted and grown in India, thus ostensibly paving the way for easier acceptance of IR-8.[16] Bridging scientific knowledge and technologies across borders, which can be traced back centuries to the acclimatization movement of the nineteenth century that sought non-native species for improvement of local environments, seemed to be the future of agricultural science.

NUTRITION

One of the goals of high-yielding rice was applying scientific principles and mass production to increase raw caloric intake and thus resolve social problems of poverty and malnourishment. Though high-yield varieties emerged in the mid-twentieth century, societal concerns over nutrition were not new. Nutrition as an object of policy and public health concern emerged as early as the nineteenth century in Britain, where alimentation arose as a means to intervene into bodies and regimens of the working poor.[17] Historian Jia-chen Fu has written about Chinese scientists and public health activists in the early twentieth century seizing on soybeans "as a miracle plant with which to build modern economies and healthy nations."[18] These activists argued that the soybean, with its high protein content and myriad vitamins, provided the answer to China's modern and developmental needs. These same discussions occurred in Taiwan as well in the early years after the arrival of the Nationalist regime on the island.

In the early 1950s, the ROC government was still searching for new sources of nutritionally rich and cheap sources of food for both its growing human population and the increasingly important animal livestock industry. Historian Nick Cullather has explored the rise of the calorimeter and calorie counting in early twentieth-century nutrition science in the United States as an evolution toward a rationalized treatment of nutrition. This "'scientific eating' based on 'calorie bookkeeping,'" referring to the careful quantification of daily diets and accounting for caloric intake, influenced how policymakers understood public health.[19] For Taiwan, historian Pin-tsang Tseng has shown how the ROC regime, upon taking over Taiwan after retrocession in 1945, implemented strict rationing due to food shortages during the civil war with the Communists on the mainland. This food-rationing regime altered the ratio of consumed staple foods versus non-staple foods, with the former coming from the increase in rice productivity in Taiwan during the late 1940s and early 1950s.[20] Rice could make up for caloric intake, but it was lacking in macro- and micro-nutrients needed for a healthy diet, including proteins and vitamins.

In 1948, the FAO Nutrition Committee met in the Philippines to discuss how to supplement the nutritional intake of rice-consuming societies like Taiwan.[21] Their suggestion was to consider yeast, which provided vitamin B and protein that were usually deficient in rice-consuming societies.[22] Food yeast had been utilized for several decades around the world. In the 1940s, the British colonial government in Jamaica grew Torula yeast (*Torulopsis utilis*) on molasses, plentiful in Jamaica's sugar cane agriculture.[23] Germany also produced Torula yeast in response to food shortages during World War II. In Germany, Torula yeast was predominantly grown on sulfite liquor, a liquid byproduct of wood pulp production that contained 3–4 percent sugar, of which the majority were five-carbon sugars that were not capable of being utilized by baker's or brewer's yeasts (*Saccharomyces cerevisiae*) but could be utilized by Torula. German usage was documented by American observers at the end of the war and disseminated in the US scientific literature, and in the late 1940s, several American plants also adopted the German method of producing Torula using sulfite liquor and sold Torula as an additive to other processed foods like soup and sausage mixes.[24]

Taiwanese authorities sought to follow the same idea and produce Torula yeast using a byproduct of sugar production, as was done in Jamaica. Sugar was a major agricultural commodity of Taiwan dating back to the Qing dynasty, with Taiwan at one point in 1934 being the world's third largest producer of sugar behind India and Cuba.[25] Its production under the ROC was organized under a state-owned enterprise that operated a monopoly on sugar-cane growing and sugar refinement, the Taiwan Sugar Corporation (台灣糖業公司, Taiwan Tangye Gongsi, or 台糖 Taitang for short). In 1954, with funding from a US International Cooperation Administration loan, Taiwan Sugar was contracted to convert an alcohol production plant in Xinying (新營), near the southern port city of Kaohsiung, into a yeast-processing plant.[26] The process grew Torula yeast using blackstrap molasses (糖蜜, *tangmi*), which was a byproduct of the final stage of sugar refinement. Blackstrap molasses was the leftover material that could not be refined any further using economical methods, and it had a high sugar content ranging from 50 to 55 percent, so it could be readily utilized as a cheap source for yeast production.[27]

In 1959, Taiwanese and American experts working on the Xinying yeast plant (officially the Xinying Byproduct Processing Plant, 新營副產加工廠, Xinying Fuchan Jiagongchang) discussed ways to turn Torula yeast into marketable food products. Yeast food products consumed in Western markets became a point of discussion. Xinying Plant Manager Qian Huining (錢輝宁, H. C. Chien) had left a two-ounce jar of Marmite, a British food product created through yeast autolysis (the breakdown of yeast cells) and flavored with salt and other additives, with a food-processing consultant from J. G. White Engineering, John Godston. J. G. White, an American consultancy that specialized in large scale industrial projects, had been advising the Nationalist regime in its industrial economic policy since 1948 when it was still on the mainland, in Shanghai, and moved with the GMD to Taiwan.[28] Godston wrote in reply that Marmite was not the only such product available in Western markets, citing Bovril's competition as a yeast product in the United Kingdom. Godston also raised the potential for yeast in military contexts, especially the need to provide flavor and nutrition in army rations. He suggested that a Marmite-like product could be used to flavor canned beef, pork, and fish, given the "excellent meat-like flavor" of Torula yeast. Godston asked Qian to produce a sample of yeast-flavored army rations for the military from the Taiwan Sugar Corporation laboratory.[29]

And Torula yeast was not limited to consumption by humans. One of the targets for Torula yeast was for hog feed. In the 1950s, hog feed consisted primarily of soy beans, which were predominantly imported at high cost, and sweet potatoes, which was also a human-consumed staple crop and a low-cost substitute for rice.[30] As sociologist Liu Chi-wei has argued, hog production and consumption of pork was vital to the commercialized, industrial food production in Taiwan emerging in the postwar era that created a dependency on foreign and US grain imports.[31] In a report from Taiwan Sugar Corporation president Yang Jizeng (楊繼曾, C. T. Yang) to J. G. White adviser Valerie de Beausset, Yang explained that one ton of dry yeast could provide the nutritional equivalent of three tons of soybeans, thus allowing a significant reduction in soy imports, which amounted to around a hundred thousand tons per year in 1956.[32] For the 2.8 million estimated hogs in 1956, this amounted to a significant potential market for Torula yeast. Yang argued that yeast was also a superior feed ingredient as well, producing less indigestion and diarrhea among pigs compared to the prior feed cakes that contained soybean oil as a significant source of nutrition.[33]

The largest issue faced by Taiwan planners, however, was that of cultural adaptation. As scholars such as Seung-joon Lee have shown, cultural preferences for foods hold significant sway over how humans consume their diets, even to the point of demonstrating pickiness during times of famine.[34] Unlike in Great Britain or the United States, in Taiwan, yeast was not usually consumed as a food but rather as a medicine for indigestion in the form of the imported Japanese drug Wakamoto (若元錠, Ruoyuanding). In its industrial production, Taiwan Sugar "had difficulty disposing" of yeast, despite it having value "from a nutritional point of view," implying the lack of demand stemmed from taste preferences.[35] In 1953, the Taiwan Sugar Corporation, in cooperation with the JCRR, the Taiwan Provincial Department of Education, and the Education Bureau of the Taipei Prefecture Government, conducted a food study of new yeast foods in primary school children. Dry yeast was distributed to every student across several schools in the Taipei vicinity, first in five-gallon tins, then redistributed to empty reused milk-powder cans, then provided to individual children in paper cones and supplemented with boiling water. Children were advised not to chew the yeast, "in order to avoid its sticking to gums and teeth," which many did not heed and that led to some minor gum irritation in some cases.[36] Overall, however, the report was upbeat and optimistic.

The study, prepared by nutrition specialist Yang Yueheng (楊月恆, Yang Yueh-heng) and Ralph N. Gleason, the American head of the Food and Fertilizer division of JCRR, and published in 1955 by the JCRR, suggested yeast supplements would be an important part of Taiwanese diets going forward.[37] In the tracked students, a 15 mg daily supplement of dry yeast to the average daily diet of 300 g of polished white rice provided increases to key vitamins as a percentage of daily recommended nutritional intake, from 30 percent to 40.83 percent of thiacin, 10 percent to 49.44 percent of riboflavin, and 37.5 percent to 90.25 percent of niacin.[38] The concluding recommendations called for creative combinations of yeast with other food pathways, such as enriching commonly used sweet potato and wheat flours with yeast to supplement vitamins, combining yeast with bone meal powder to also combat calcium deficiency in children, and introducing yeast into more food products instead of providing it merely as a nutritional supplement. Indeed, Yang and Gleason also understood that cultural affinities mattered—they recommended more attractive packaging than the plain tin containers and enhancing it with flavor additives so yeast could be added to soup, as was done with Torula in the United States at the time.[39]

Taiwan was keen to promote its yeast production activities as a sign of its progressive science-based food regime internationally. In the February 1960 issue of the US-based journal *Food Engineering*, Qian published a four-page article outlining the yeast production process at Xinying and its contribution to Taiwan's nutritional and economic needs. Qian began by contextualizing the problem in Taiwan, with a prolific agricultural economy centered on rice and sugar cane (representing 90 percent of its production) yet with poor nutritional sources of protein. As a result, Qian argued that "many people and their livestock will suffer severely from malnutrition. They will be starved for protein." Enter yeast. Qian argued that yeast was comparable in its amino acid content to milk casein and in its vitamin B content to liver. Most attractive about yeast aside from its nutritional content was its economy—fast and easy to grow, and efficient in terms of its land usage and input requirements.

Qian's article emphasized the technical aspects of yeast production in the Xinying plant, showcasing modern equipment, precision measurement, and factory-like efficiency. Qian pointed out the "rigid laboratory control in every stage," such as stainless steel equipment that allowed for careful control of pH levels and preventing the introduction of unwanted organisms and contaminants. There were "super-speed spray dryers" that allowed for "ultra-fine powders that directly form colloidal suspensions when stirred into water," in other words that rendered the yeast more dissolvable in water (and thereby preventing the sticking to the gums that plagued the Taiwanese schoolchildren in the JCRR study). Tests were implemented throughout the production process, including spectrophotometers to ensure vitamin content in the yeast product.[40]

Qian furthermore raised the possible applied food uses of Torula yeast. One was the aforementioned yeast autolysates, such as Marmite, that could be used to provide both the nutritional advantages of yeast and the glutamic acid that added an umami flavor. Other possibilities included adding a 2-percent yeast supplement to ground flour or including it in soy sauce fermentation, which would raise protein and vitamin B content.

In the end, however, Torula yeast did not become a mainstream food product, much for the same reasons it did not take off elsewhere: taste. As a direct supplement, the stickiness to gums and the unusual texture likely found few lovers among Taiwanese schoolchildren (see figure 36). Unsurprisingly, when food yeast did take root in Taiwan, it was not a yeast autolysate like Marmite or additives to canned meats or basic food commodities but something where the taste of food yeast was fundamentally altered—literally, sugarcoated. It was a yeast candy, *jiansutang* (健素糖, also known as *xiaosutang* 酵素糖).

Jiansutang stemmed in part from the conclusions of the 1955 JCRR report from Yang and Gleason that nutritional supplements were especially important for youth development. Whereas protein and vitamin B supplements could be added in other ways, candies appealed to children in a way that yeast autolysates like

FIGURE 36. Elementary school children in Taiwan consuming the Torula yeast provided by the JCRR. Yang and Gleason, *Yeast-Feeding Demonstration*, 5.

Marmite did not. Shaped like colorful flattened spheres that resembled Skittles candies sold today, *jiansutang* became a hit in Taiwan. Taiwan Sugar advertised *jiansutang* as a healthy food for adults and a tasty nutritional supplement for children, with fruit and cocoa flavors (see figure 37). In the decades since the creation and marketing of yeast candy in Taiwan in the late 1950s, *jiansutang* has become a standard fixture in Taiwanese youth consumption. One popular television report from major Taiwanese news channel TVBS in 2006 described it further: "Because of its colorful exterior and its slight sweetness, parents often purchased it for their children to supplement their nutrition. From the early resourceful packaging in a plastic bag, to the current sealed aluminum containers, *jiansutang* has never utilized advertising, but still has existed for 50 years" (though it seems that *jiansutang* was indeed advertised in the 1960s at least).[41]

For the Taiwanese planners behind Torula yeast, though nutrition was an important objective, the developmental needs of Taiwan were nonetheless the most important. Behind discussions of daily protein requirements was the idea that yeast was cost efficient and could yield industrial levels of production in the food realm. Indeed, nutrition was not seen in this context as an end in and of itself but rather as the means to a different end: a modern, capitalist, and industrial economy that applied the latest in food science and production technologies. By the late 1960s, when Taiwan had already achieved significant levels of improvement in nutrition from the 1950s, the instrumentalist and social nature

FIGURE 37. *Jiansutang*, yeast candy manufactured by Taiwan Sugar Corporation with Torula yeast, advertised as a nutritional supplement for children and adults in *United Daily News*. Taiwan Sugar Corporation, *United Daily News* (聯合報 , Lianhe bao), January 1, 1965.

of nutrition persisted. Then, in the 1970s, nutrition arose again in a scientific discourse on vegetables.

VEGETABLES

Although yeast did not become a widespread staple or supplementary food as some nutritional experts in the JCRR might have hoped, Taiwanese diets did shift from the "public diets" controlled by the GMD in the 1950s to increasingly diversified food sources over the decades that followed. This entailed decreased consumption of the primary cereals—rice and sweet potato—and an increase in consumption of pork, chicken, eggs, vegetables, and fruits (see table 1). For example, from 1960 to 1964, rice and sweet potatoes accounted for a total consumption of 188 kg per capita. By 1985–89, this had dropped to 77 kg per capita, approximately 41 percent of the 1960–64 amounts. Much of this was made up for with eggs, milk, vegetables, fruits, fish, and meat, which doubled, tripled, or even quadrupled in per capita consumption.[42]

TABLE 1   Taiwan's Agricultural Production, Consumption, And Trade

	1960–64	1965–69	1970–74	1975–79	1980–84	1985–89
Agricultural production as % of GDP	29.7	23.6	15.1	12.5	8.7	6.3
Production index (1986 = 100)	41.1	53.8	66.4	80.6	92.4	105.5
Production growth rate	4.5	4.8	4.2	5	1.7	2.4
Percentage of crop-livestock value:						
Crops	74.5	73.6	67.5	64.1	62.6	59.7
Rice	40.2	35.2	30.7	29.1	24.4	17.3
Sugar	6.6	4.8	4.5	5.7	4	3.9
Sweet potatoes	7.7	7.7	5.7	2.9	1.6	0.6
Fruits and vegetables	8.2	14.7	17	18	24.4	28
Others	11.8	11.2	9.6	8.4	8.2	9.9
Livestock and products	25.5	26.4	32.5	35.9	37.4	0.3
Hogs	17.7	17.2	20.7	20.5	20.3	24.9
Chickens and eggs	3.2	4.7	5.9	9.6	11.4	11.1
Others	4.6	4.5	5.9	5.8	5.7	4.3
Per capita consumption (kg)						
Rice	134.2	138.1	133.3	120.6	92.8	75.9
Sweet potatoes	53.8	38.9	15.5	7.1	2.7	1.1
Meats	16.8	23.8	27	34.1	46	57.4
Eggs	1.8	3	4.4	6.6	9.3	11.3
Fish	25.7	29	35	36.1	35.6	43
Milk	6.3	6	12.4	20.2	27.1	34.8
Vegetables	58.3	60.9	91.8	118.6	121.3	123.1
Fruits	20.4	34.5	49.1	59.1	73.1	94.7
Agricultural exports (per 1,000 tons)						
Rice	88.5	110.6	21.8	159.4	280.4	125.1
Sugar and products	712.9	758.6	509.1	455.1	275.2	85.6
Hogs and pork	3.1	2.3	16.3	18.4	30.2	102.9
Processed fruits and vegetables	95.8	211.6	363.5	505.8	517.4	391

Huang, "Structural Change in Taiwan's Agricultural Economy," 43.

The diversification of diets is unsurprising. As wages and economic conditions improved in Taiwan, so too did purchasing power, which led to the demand for more expensive and varied foods. Taiwanese farmers also increased production in non-cereal foods, which fetched higher prices and potentially higher profits. These also aligned with nutritional goals from government experts like Yang Yueheng, who recognized the importance of proteins, vitamins, and minerals for public health. But it also demonstrates that nutrition and public health are inseparable from political economy. Though the ROC state made efforts to increase nutritional uptake, such as introducing yeast into primary schools, ultimately it was rising incomes and decreased food costs that diversified the average diet among the Taiwanese.[43]

Further demonstrating the integrated nature of food and capitalism, Taiwan also focused on higher-margin foods that could be exported, especially vegetables, fruits, and processed foods. By 1963, Taiwan had become the world's leading exporter of pineapples.[44] During the 1970s, this grew to include canned pineapples, asparagus, and mushrooms.[45] During the 1975–79 period, processed fruits and vegetables overtook sugar and sugar products as the largest agricultural exports of Taiwan by volume, marking a shift from an agricultural commodity to higher-profit-margin and higher-value-added products (see table 1). In reaching this position, Taiwan developed special expertise in locating higher-margin products and markets. Sophia Wu Huang, an economist with the US Department of Agriculture's Economic Research Service, has argued that the shift in focus to processed foods stemmed from a need to earn foreign exchange, while taking advantage of Taiwan's ample labor supply in producing the labor-intensive canned products.[46] After the cessation of US development aid in 1965, Taiwan particularly focused on improving the marketing of Taiwanese processed foods abroad, which helped it secure its global market position.

These nutritional and profit-oriented changes played out as well in international development. In 1971, Taiwan founded its answer to IRRI that it hoped would put Taiwan in the global food map the way IR-8 did for the Philippines and CIMMYT did for Mexico: the Asian Vegetable Research and Development Center (AVRDC) (亞洲蔬菜研究發展中心, Yazhou Shucai Yanjiu Fazhan Zhongxin). An official history published by the AVRDC credited the initial idea to Frank Parker, an assistant director for research and technology at USAID. According to that history, the idea for a center specializing in vegetables emerged just soon after the founding of IRRI, in 1962.[47] Parker was an agronomist trained at the University of Wisconsin with significant international experience in India and with the UN Food and Agriculture Organization. He and others within USAID identified vegetables as the next frontier in agricultural science after cereal grains. In 1967, Eugene Black, former president of the World Bank and at the time special adviser to President Johnson, wrote to David Bell at the Ford Foundation describing the need for a vegetable research institute. With the cereal grains of the CIMMYT and the IRRI, wheat and rice, providing a raw caloric boost to the underdeveloped areas of the world, USAID saw "the need to augment and improve the high starch diet of the people in East Asia, and to increase rural income by upgrading the production, processing and marketing of vegetables."[48] Another document from the State

Department that chronicled the founding of the AVRDC reinforced this, framing the "research center" as one "to improve the diets of the Asian people by increasing the production of protein and protective vegetable foods."[49] This signaled a move beyond hunger and instead to a more holistic understanding of human livelihood and health based on nutrition, and especially household income as a means to germinate a household capital-led national growth.

Initial conversations among USAID and its development recipient nations identified three possible hosts in the Philippines, Thailand, and Taiwan.[50] Taiwan was particularly keen to see that the center be established in Taiwan.[51] Jiang Yanshi (蔣彥士, Y. S. Tsiang), a former commissioner of the JCRR who was Frank Parker's roommate while visiting a conference at MIT in 1964, introduced Parker to Taiwanese horticulturalist, Lu Zhilin (陸之琳, C. L. Luh). Lu was a graduate of Nanking University and then was the head of the Plant Industry Division of the JCRR, thus overseeing projects for improved varieties of fruits and vegetables in Taiwan. Lu would eventually serve as the associate director of the AVRDC. While in the JCRR, Lu pointed to the shift in Taiwan's development strategy after 1965 in a paper presented at a workshop on "Accelerating Agricultural Development" in Los Baños in 1976 that included "production of more nutritious food crops . . . containing more protein and vitamins and to the development of food processing industries."[52] This also complemented an increased focus on fisheries and animal husbandry in order to produce animal protein. Taiwanese bureaucrats and scientists thus also perceived the need to focus on nutrition instead of just calories.

The proposal eventually reached the desk of ROC minister of economic affairs Li Guoding and ROC premier Yan Jiagan (嚴家淦, C. K. Yen), who made the center a priority in discussions with USAID director David Bell. Though a formal proposal was drafted by Lu and submitted to the USAID by 1965, the center would not come to fruition until 1971 because USAID (in part driven by a desire within Congress for cost sharing from America's Asian allies) was unwilling to bear the full costs of the project alone. JCRR chairman at the time, Shen Zonghan, spent over half a decade pursuing funding from the Rockefeller Foundation, Ford Foundation, and Cornell University before finally securing the funding he needed. In 1972, the AVRDC finally opened its doors in Shanhua, located in southern Taiwan.

The ROC government granted 116 hectares of land to the AVRDC that was formerly a sugar cane plantation for the Taiwan Sugar Corporation.[53] The AVRDC hosted a research staff from a half dozen Asian nations—Taiwan, Vietnam, the Philippines, Japan, Korea, and Thailand.[54] It operated with a $1.5 million per annum budget in its first five years, 5 to 10 percent of which was contributed by most AVRDC member countries with the rest being covered by Taiwan, the United States, the Asian Development Bank, and the Ford and Rockefeller Foundations. Shen Zonghan, who at the time served as the chairman of the AVRDC Board of Supervisors, already had in mind Robert F. Chandler, who was due to

FIGURE 38. The Asian Vegetable Research and Development Center (now the World Vegetable Center) in Shanhua, Taiwan. Photo taken by author in 2013.

retire at the end of his term as director of IRRI. Chandler had been instrumental in establishing IRRI as its first director, and according to the official narrative, the board members who came from the Asian nations preferred an American as a director.[55] Chandler's background, having established and led the successful IRRI during its first decade, most probably appealed to Shen, who wanted the AVRDC to be Taiwan's IRRI.

The objective for the center was to serve the people of tropical and subtropical climates of East and Southeast Asia. The large variety of vegetables in Asia was daunting, so an initial focus was placed on six fruits and vegetables: tomato, soybean, mung bean, sweet potato, white potato, and Chinese cabbage. These vegetables were chosen based on their wide cultivation across multiple societies and climates. In the cases of the legumes and potatoes, they were also chosen because they provided a relatively large amount of calories. The AVRDC's mission of vegetable improvement included locating and storing different varieties from throughout the world, thus functioning as a seed bank, then selecting varieties that produced higher yields and higher-quality crops, as defined by resistance to disease, pests, and adverse climates.[56] Like TARI and other Taiwanese research and experiment institutions, the AVRDC collected cultivar samples, planted them comparatively in different experiment plots, and recorded results for analysis of factors such as response to fertilizer, resistance to disease, crop yield, and so forth. The difference was that the AVRDC's scope was far larger; in addition to collecting seeds globally, it sought to test its seeds for climates that would be applicable across Southeast and East Asia.

The AVRDC staffed and trained scientists in plant breeding, plant pathology, plant physiology, soil science, and chemistry, the typical sciences that constituted Green Revolution technologies of seeds, fertilizers, and pesticides.[57] As explained to Ford Foundation president David A. Bell by the AVRDC's training director, AVRDC training aimed to allow trained scientists, technicians, and extension agents to return to their home countries and "have the opportunity to make their own selections from the crosses they made while studying at AVRDC and to develop the production technology appropriate for their own local conditions [*sic*]."[58] This type of localization where trainees were given the expertise to make their own decisions based on their knowledge of local conditions showed the deference to local knowledge and a desire to make AVRDC seeds globally applicable.

Shen Zonghan, on the opening ceremony day, attributed the basic mission of the AVRDC to improving the "normal diet" of the average Asian citizen.[59] Shen proclaimed that vegetables weren't an "exotic crop" and would certainly be consumed widely in Asian society. Economic factors played a major role as well. Shen emphasized the greater profit potential from vegetables compared to cereal grains and their versatility for being grown in either home gardens or commercially for export.[60] These objectives underscored improving agricultural industries, agricultural productivity, and rural livelihood. Shen recognized that the introduction of foreign cultivars, typical of Green Revolution methods, was not a simple matter; local cultures were not always open to the taste of new foods. The improvement of local vegetables thus became a major objective of the AVRDC. Simultaneously, vegetables provided broader economic benefits, due to its higher profit margins and ability to be grown at both small and large scales, which had the benefit of improving mass agricultural industries as well as employment and revenues for individual farmers at rural and village levels. Finally, Shen indicated that vegetables could spawn dependent industries through postprocessing, such as canning for export.

Reflecting changes within international development, the AVRDC's focus on vegetables took aim at a rising concern: nutrition. With the increase in chemical inputs and the usage of high-yield varieties that responded well to fertilizers, many former Global South nations had fulfilled the basic caloric needs of their citizens. The development field turned its attention to making sure that diets provided healthy levels of minerals, vitamins, and other aspects of nutritional sufficiency. In making a case for why vegetables to the Technical Advisory Committee of the Consultative Group of International Agricultural Research (CGIAR), the AVRDC's first director, Robert F. Chandler, argued in 1972 that "looking at human nutrition alone, we should not forget that polished rice contains no vitamin C and no vitamin A, while many vegetable crops produce abundant amounts of these essential constituents for human nutrition."[61] Vegetables played well into this evolution past staple crops, and the addition of mustard green, cauliflower, snap pea, radish, and pepper in 1981 demonstrated that there was demand for vegetables beyond the staple crops such as legumes and potatoes that were the core of the AVRDC's efforts in the 1970s.[62]

As mentioned in Shen's opening-day speech, home gardens became an important avenue identified by AVRDC officials where vegetables could make a difference in both nutrition and economic livelihood. In explaining the rise of home garden research, the AVRDC explained that a small, four-by-four-meter garden could provide "enough vegetables to provide a family of five with a significant percentage of their recommended dietary allowance of protein, calcium, and iron, and complete requirements for vitamins A and C."[63] Yet the AVRDC's home garden project also identified economic uplift as an important goal alongside nutrition. Part of this is attributable to the integration of anthropologists into the AVRDC home garden program. Historian Leo Chu in particular identifies Berkeley-trained anthropologist Jack Gershon, who came to the AVRDC in 1980, as envisioning the AVRDC's home garden program, called "nutrition gardens," as filling in a void left by capitalist agriculture. Specifically, home gardens would target the small farmers who had "neither the large field for, nor the capital to invest in, fertilizers and pesticides."[64] The result was a training regimen focused on manual weeding and insect control, compost, and mulching.

Despite its idealistic outlook in an era where capitalist, industrial agriculture was still the norm, the home garden program encountered substantial issues. The AVRDC had integrated home gardening as part of its Thailand Outreach program. Yet the AVRDC's Thailand home garden program reflected a gender bias not uncommon in the development field during the 1980s. Home gardens were generally tended to by women, since women were "generally responsible for the family's food." Eighty percent of those involved in the AVRDC's home garden programs in the Philippines, Indonesia, and Thailand were female.[65] This gender disparity demonstrated how ideas influential in agricultural economics continued to allocate resources toward gendered divisions of household labor.[66] The designation of "family food" as a woman's responsibility indicated that women were still primarily seen as responsible for the health of the household, including the young and elderly. A later 1992 report evaluating the home garden program criticized how the home garden program disregarded gendered dynamics. Specifically, the AVRDC ignored that women were asked to take on large parts of household management, not just in terms of care but also managing the household as men in Thailand increasingly worked as migrant laborers in urban areas. The result was that few women had the resources or time to take on home gardening, and furthermore, decisions on home gardening, such as purchase of seeds and tools, still required the approval of men in the household.[67] In turn, this affected the AVRDC's mission focused on nutrition.

Home gardens and vegetables offered a promising venue for the AVRDC to pursue a goal of future relevance for itself and for Taiwan. Leveraging increased attention to nutrition and economic livelihood, the AVRDC pursued a path of scientific research and dissemination that it believed was missing in the larger field of international development.

FERTILIZER

Chemical fertilizers anchored industrialized agriculture in Taiwan. As chapter 3 explored, chemical fertilizers not only provided the necessary catalyst for Green Revolution agricultural productivity but in Taiwan also went hand in hand with authoritarian state power and top-down processes of rural control. The Food and Fertilizer Technology Center (FFTC) (糧食肥料技術中心, Liangshi Feiliao Jishu Zhongxin), established in 1970, directly drew on the importance of fertilizer for its mission. The FFTC was an idea first proposed as a "food and fertilizer bank" by the Taiwan government to the Asia-Pacific Council (ASPAC) (亞洲太平洋理事會, Yazhou Taipingyang Lishihui) in 1966.[68] Founded in 1965 and organized initially by South Korea (the Republic of Korea), the ASPAC was a short-lived organization of Asian states: Australia, the ROC, Japan, South Korea, Malaysia, New Zealand, the Philippines, the Republic of Vietnam, and Thailand, with Laos as an observer. At times called an "anti-Communist" and an "anti-Chinese" (PRC) league, and even suggested as the Northeast Asian equivalent of the Southeast Asia Treaty Organization (SEATO), the ASPAC consisted of non-Communist Asian states in a Cold War context. The function of the ASPAC was ambiguous and contested through its history, which in part contributed to its eventual dissolution in 1975. Members agreed to convene an annual forum of foreign ministers from member nations and to form multilateral institutions to serve member nations, such as the Registry of Scientific and Technical Services (based in Australia), a Social and Cultural Center (based in South Korea), an Economic Cooperation Center (in Thailand), and then the FFTC. The notable exclusion of the United States in the ASPAC proved to be a selling point for the organization, as several member nations wanted to maintain distance from Washington, but other members, including Taiwan, sought to militarize the ASPAC, which would effectively form an anti-Communist security organization. In this fashion, the ASPAC can be understood as a Cold War parallel to the US-centric network from which the AVRDC was born.[69] This latent anti-Communist orientation shaped its economic and scientific endeavors.

The FFTC was originally conceived of as a bank serving ASPAC members, not a research institution. The memorandum drafted in 1966 envisioned "an economic agency . . . to carry out mainly the activities concerning the operation of food and fertilizer warehouses and related financing work."[70] In furthering Green Revolution goals of industrialized agriculture, the focus on warehouses was meant to ensure that fertilizers would be able to reach rural villages as efficiently as possible. Much as the Industrial Revolution did not just entail changes within the factory floor but also through the vast armadas of ships, railroads, ferries, trucks, shipping boxes, and other vehicles and machines that crossed the globe, so too did the question of getting fertilizer from point A to point B become a key concern. As the memo further detailed, "Preferably the existing warehouses of the participating countries shall be utilized to store the food and fertilizer contributed by participating countries and to distribute them to other participating countries in need of these commodities."[71] The logistics of fertilizer supply, storage, and distribution, the physical infrastructure supporting those logistics, and the market mechanisms of supply and demand between centralized production areas and areas of consumption—that is, between rural and urban—remained salient issues for decades in Taiwan.

The goal of the Food and Fertilizer Bank was also framed in terms of multinational cooperation and the mutually beneficial goals of cooperative research. It aimed to "promote and increase the production and supply of food in the region through the interflow of food and fertilizer among the participating countries as well as the interchange of production technique and the stabilization of market supplies and prices with a view to solving the food problems now confronting most countries within the region."[72] It was believed that regional cooperation would be mutually beneficial and produce a greater overall good. The anti-Communist leanings of ASPAC members meant that these food problems were also linked to concerns over Communist spread.

Inherent in this regionalism was the assumption that the prime way to resolve food shortage was through market mechanisms, namely supply and production. Regional integration meant that the fickleness of the market could be overcome by linking supply markets, thus overcoming potential pains due to cycles of increased demand or decreased production. Shen Zonghan in 1967 wrote Xie Senzhong, his friend at the Asian Development Bank and former colleague at the JCRR, that "fertilizer is the most important" of production requisites and that the proposal for the bank would "promote the interflow of fertilizers among the countries through market development, exchange of technical information, credit arrangement and adjustment of demand and supply."[73] In other words, there was a faith in and a desire to expand upon a capitalist Green Revolution.

However, by 1968, the institution became reconceived as a "center" instead of a "bank," but the FFTC nonetheless retained its emphasis on the technical aspects of getting fertilizer to where it was needed. A JCRR document from that year emphasized "the increase of food production through increased application of chemical fertilizers" and "the need for increased use of fertilizers as a direct and speedy way of uplifting food production in the Asian-Pacific region," demonstrating once again the importance of chemical inputs for agricultural development.[74] What changed more was an emphasis on technology specifically, "an exchange of technical information and experiences" instead of a focus on infrastructure and regionalizing supply markets. Thus, like the AVRDC, an emphasis was placed on techniques, technologies, and knowledge in general. This shift in focus to technology also trimmed the FFTC's projected budgets, which was a concern to ASPAC members who were expected to contribute to FFTC operations. In the end, the idea of a center received a warm, but not ecstatic, reception in the ASPAC. It was referred to a subcommittee, and after 5 years it finally was completed in 1971 in Taipei with representation from Australia, the ROC, Japan, South Korea, Malaysia, New Zealand, the Philippines, the Republic of Vietnam, and Thailand.[75]

The 1970 annual report presented to the sixth meeting of the ASPAC showed results from its first year of operation. The results demonstrated a far more modest scope of activities than the initial discussions in the ASPAC might have implied. They included the following: (1) short-term training courses for extension workers from Thailand, Vietnam, and Malaysia; (2) seminars on "Crop Physiology and Fertilizer Application" bringing together experts from all the FFTC founding member nations except Australia; (3) writing and disseminating information bulletins, both of more technical nature for a scientific audience and of a general nature for extension workers; (4) a demonstration project (planned for the following year); and (5) feasibility and consultative trips.[76] The final aspect, feasibility trips, allowed the ASPAC to determine in its early years how best to aid the needs of its members.

The first year consisted of two feasibility trips, surveying Malaysia, Vietnam, the Philippines, Thailand, and Japan. The report of the feasibility trips remarked on a number of aspects. There were concerns over exchange rates in the Philippines making the purchase of fertilizer more expensive for farmers, which created concerns among Filipino policymakers that farmers would as a result use less fertilizers and drive down production. Observations included how credit for fertilizers was extended in Vietnam, as well as plans for the construction of a domestic fertilizer production plant, albeit with concerns about whether domestically produced fertilizer would in fact be cheaper than imported fertilizer. In Japan and Thailand, which both produced surpluses of rice and thus were net exporting countries, different problems were recorded. Thailand faced global decreases of rice prices, thus making exports less profitable. Japan, on the other hand, faced a shrinking agricultural labor market due to its rising industrial sector (a problem Taiwan would soon face).[77]

In synthesizing the findings of these feasibility surveys, FFTC staff wrote that there were common areas of interest for further research and demonstration: irrigation, fertilizer production and trade, fertilizer regulations and marketing, short-term consultants, and training courses.[78] These aspects once again reflected the ongoing changes in Taiwanese agricultural development and the growing hegemony of the Green Revolution. This was true in fertilizer especially, which combined the high modernism of Green Revolution soil science, plant breeding, and chemistry, as well as agricultural economics, development economics, and international trade. Though extension and farmers' associations were seen as crucial, they became more a means to an end than the end itself.

Over the years, the FFTC remained an organization limited in both scope and size. Its initial year of operation planned for only thirteen employees, two of whom were drivers.[79] Over time, its mission shrunk even further. On the back cover of a conference paper published by the FFTC from one of its sponsored 1981 conferences, the organization described its own mission as "to collect and disseminate agricultural information throughout the Asian Pacific region," which differed greatly from the mid-1960s conception of an economic agency designed to build and foster a logistical network to facilitate the shipment and usage of chemical fertilizers.[80] The FFTC's limitations were in part financial, as its initial nine founding member countries dwindled to six. When I visited the center in 2013, the office space and staff were both relatively small. Despite Taiwanese government efforts to co-opt fertilizers from the Green Revolution, the FFTC never reached the heights of more well-known research institutions like the IRRI or even the AVRDC.

GEOPOLITICS

As historians John Perkins and Nick Cullather have argued, the Green Revolution was inextricable from the global Cold War.[81] Green Revolution science was co-opted explicitly as a form of anti-Communism—replacing "red" revolutions with a "green" one. Taiwan's co-opting of its agricultural science was similarly done for political purposes. In 1971, the Republic of China had lost its seat in the UN to the PRC. This led to the paring back of Vanguard missions and reduction of efforts by the Ministry of Foreign Affairs to trade development diplomacy for UN votes (see chapter 5). Country-to-country development missions continued to the dwindling number of ROC allies that continued to maintain diplomatic relations after the ROC's departure from the United Nations.[82] Institutions like the AVRDC and the FFTC, however, attempted to counter those geopolitical currents through agricultural science.

Taiwanese state planners viewed the AVRDC and the FFTC as vehicles for building closer international relationships through global agricultural science. The USAID initially envisioned the AVRDC as becoming an internationally oriented research center like the IRRI that serviced Asia and the rest of the world, with US East and Southeast Asian allies both contributing funding and benefitting from the research. Both institutions enmeshed Taiwan within the American Cold War network. This was a natural extension of United States hegemony in the Pacific following the Korean War, when fears of a Communist domino effect gave rise to US intervention and support of authoritarian, anti-Communist regimes in East and Southeast Asia.[83] Establishing the AVRDC with the financial and political support of the United States allowed the Guomindang regime to forge closer international ties with other US allies after the loss of the ROC's seat in the United Nations to the PRC in 1971.

One of these allies, South Korea, expressed concerns over its financial contributions to a center specializing in subtropical vegetables. To address those concerns, the AVRDC early in its history established a "sub-center" in Suwon, South Korea, to provide vegetable experimentation in the more temperate Korean climate.[84] Founded in 1974, the Suwon sub-center was led by horticulturalist Chung-il Choi (최정일), an AVRDC board member and head of the Horticultural Experiment Station operated by the South Korean Office of Rural Development.[85] The first Suwon sub-center reflected both scientific (climate) and political (influence) concerns, but the latter would prove to be more problematic in years to come.

The AVRDC's first director, Robert F. Chandler, indeed fielded concerns in the opposite end, too, that Taiwan's relatively northern latitude in a subtropical zone would not produce vegetables well suited for more tropical climates.[86] A more southernly regional center was thus a major goal of the AVRDC. In 1981, the AVRDC established its first outreach program in the tropics (most of Taiwan is subtropical). The AVRDC Thailand Outreach program was sponsored by the Thai government and the Asian Development Bank.[87] It eventually grew to become one of three AVRDC regional centers focused on different areas of the world. The other two, in Tanzania and Costa Rica, covered Southern Africa and Latin American and the Caribbean, respectively.

As the AVRDC expanded, its regional centers focused more on cooperating with specific nations to localize seeds developed from Taiwan for local climates and soils. Regional centers were envisioned as operating hand in hand with national agricultural research systems, referring to the agricultural research and experiment stations of individual nation-states. The AVRDC was thus working with state partners, as opposed to directly to communities. This benefitted Taiwanese state objectives, too. Seeds developed from the AVRDC inevitably showcased Taiwan's central role in funding improved varieties for the purpose of increasing food production. Simultaneously, these seeds also offered a more visible platform for Taiwan's scientific capabilities, which in turn reinforced an image that the authoritarian Guomindang regime was eager to underscore abroad and at home.

The AVRDC was led by scientists such as Shen Zonghan and Ma Baozhi (who would later serve as the chairman of the board after Shen's retirement), who advocated for science leadership on a regional, and later, global, basis. As Yan Jiagan, premier of the ROC at the time, later becoming vice president and then president following Chiang Kai-shek's death, described in the tenth anniversary speech of the founding of AVRDC:

> I can say without reservation that the work of AVRDC has by association cast a most favorable reflection on the ROC. The Center in many ways serves as a window to the world, enabling those who might not otherwise see our island come and judge for themselves. And, by implication, AVRDC's successes are our successes: they are the successes of our people who work here, the success of the good neighbors who live in the vicinity of the Center, and they are the success of our national research programs that in many instances work side by side with AVRDC.[88]

Like the Vanguard missions, they also demonstrated Taiwanese expertise in modernist science to the rest of the world. These efforts continued along Cold War networks, relying on expertise and funding from US allies in Asia such as Japan, Korea, the Philippines, Thailand, and Indonesia. Yet whereas the Green Revolution might have found success in spreading a model of industrialized agriculture across the world, Taiwanese efforts to co-opt the Green Revolution met the headwinds of Taiwan's geopolitical pressures.

Specifically, efforts by the AVRDC to seek international integration met political obstacles in the wake of the ROC's ejection from the United Nations. This began almost immediately after founding. By the early 1970s, the success of the CIMMYT and the IRRI prompted international development organizations like the Rockefeller and Ford Foundations to band together and encourage the growth of other international agricultural science institutions to focus on what historian Tim Lorek has called "mega-environment" research.[89] This led to the Consultative Group of International Agricultural Research (CGIAR), which today counts among its members the premier international agricultural research institutes around the world.

The AVRDC was not a formal member of the CGIAR due to Taiwan's contested status as a nation, which made its funding a political liability. Initially, the USAID's investment in the AVRDC was meant to be a one-time expense, with continued annual support coming from its constituent member nation-states as well as international organizations like the CGIAR. However, a US report to Congress by the comptroller general revealed the unexpected geopolitical conditions that prevailed. It referenced a USAID memorandum stating "AVRDC is barred from inclusion in the CGIAR overall budget support program for political reasons. . . The most persistent problem which AVRDC will continue to face is caused by international political realities; diplomatic recognition of the People's Republic of China by an increasing number of countries and the related severing of formal diplomatic ties with the Republic of China." It ended with a blunt reality: "AID believed that a number of CGIAR donor members would be likely to support AVRDC if it were elsewhere than Taiwan."[90] The USAID's concerns reflected that Taiwan's international pariah status constituted an insurmountable barrier.

Moreover, CGIAR officials expressed concerns over the domestic political environment in Taiwan, an implicit reference to the authoritarian politics of the Guomindang state and its potential effects on the conduct of science. A 1972 correspondence between Robert Chandler and Lowell Hardin, an American agricultural economist and professor of agricultural economics at Purdue who was instrumental in the formation of the CGIAR, illustrated this clearly. In the letter, Hardin explains the position of John Crawford, an Australian agricultural economist and then chairman of the Technical Advisory Committee (TAC) of the CGIAR: "It may be necessary for the Center to change its charter in order to assure autonomy necessary for freedom of scientists to operate."[91] Chandler defended the work of the AVRDC, reiterating several years later in a 1974 letter directly to Crawford that "the government of the Republic of China, located on Taiwan, in no way enters into our financial and scientific affairs, other than to make financial contributions toward our efforts. All of our negotiations for support for both core budget and outreach programs are conducted directly with donor agencies, and the government here is not even consulted."[92] Yet these entreaties ultimately had no effect.

Compounding the issue of not having CGIAR funding, the AVRDC had difficulty independently seeking external funding from non-CGIAR affiliated donors without the CGIAR's blessing. As Chandler summarized for Crawford in 1974, "Our Center has never received the full endorsement of the Technical Advisory Committee (TAC) of the Consultative Group on International Agricultural Research." When the Japanese delegate to the CGIAR asked in September 1972 "why AVRDC was not a full member," CGIAR chairman Demuth "replied that because of the international political situation, the CG[IAR] was headed for internal disagreement if the discussion continued. . . . Therefore they decided to give AVRDC associate membership only. Then he added words to the effect that the TAC had not recommended that high priority be placed on support for AVRDC." The result was that the AVRDC encountered difficulty seeking grants directly from other nations. And this entailed an effective marginalization of the AVRDC. An initial hope among the AVRDC to focus on twelve vegetable crops was halved to six due to the budgetary constraints and lack of funding. Chandler continued to express his frustration, noting that TAC had since endorsed and funded proposals for studies of the same crops that the AVRDC proposed in 1971 with other CGIAR institutions such as the International Institute of Tropical Agriculture (IITA) in Ibadan, Nigeria, and International Center for Tropical Agriculture (CIAT) in Palmira, Colombia.[93]

In the same letter, Chandler expressed hope that the "two-China problem" might "await further political moves before it can be settled." Unfortunately, the political situation never changed. In 1975, a CGIAR mission sent to Southeast Asia included in its purview assessing the viability of greater CGIAR support for vegetables. The mission, led by TAC member Peter A. Oram, concluded that vegetables were indeed of utmost importance "deserving of international or regional action . . . because vegetables are such an important constituent of the general diet in Asia" and argued for further attention be paid to vegetables. Yet in the same report, he conveys the hope that "a new, fully internationally acceptable" research center would be proposed to replace the AVRDC, which would then be "phas[ed] out to become a national institution."[94] The report laid clear that the AVRDC's future was seen as untenable, with the politics of its location on Taiwan being the only mentioned concern.

The AVRDC was only able to be an associate CGIAR member, never achieving the full recognition and the benefits of the CGIAR. In CGIAR Technical Advisory Committee meetings where the AVRDC was discussed, representatives from the United Nations Development Programme needed to formally request "to be recorded as not participating in the discussion of" of AVRDC-related agenda items, showing how sensitive Taiwan was for UNDP representatives.[95] Though it maintained a scientific agenda that was global, its exclusion from international networks of funding spelled out its marginalized future. From 1971 to the 1980s, numerous founding member nations of the AVRDC and the Asian Development Bank withdrew their support, and in 1974, the Rockefeller Foundation, one of the key institutions behind the founding of the AVRDC, likewise withdrew its funding.[96] Other CGIAR institutions took up core objectives that the AVRDC had set out to accomplish in 1971, for example the International Board for Plant Genetic Resources and the aforementioned International Institute of Tropical Agriculture and International Center for Tropical Agriculture. As Chandler expressed to his friend Lowell Hardin, "I get the feeling (as you do too) that if it were not for the Geo-political factors, the going would not be quite so rough."[97]

The resulting isolation of the AVRDC frustrated the goals of its planners, which was to seek regional leadership through science and expertise. Yan Jiagan praised the efforts of the AVRDC despite its operating with what he bemoaned as "the smallest staff and the smallest budget of any of the international food crop improvement center."[98] Though its initial attempts were limited to East and Southeast Asian networks, it was in fact the lack of inclusion in the CGIAR, the withdrawal of its international networks, and the resulting limits on its budget that ultimately forced the AVRDC to the sidelines as the Green Revolution continued without it. The AVRDC continues today as the World Vegetable Center, but it never quite became the IRRI or the CIMMYT, which seemed at one point a real possibility.

Interestingly, despite its international isolation because of the PRC, the AVRDC served as a vehicle for cross-strait agricultural science. In 1970, the success of IR-8 as part of the Green Revolution in Asia reportedly prompted PRC officials to seek some of the seed. An article in the *Times of India* on February 19, 1970, claimed that the People's Republic of China had placed orders for IR-8 by proxy, via Nepal and Pakistan. The article also correlated these reports of IR-8 imports with increases in rice yields reported that year, though the report was wrong in stating that dwarf strains "have not been developed by Chinese geneticists, who, like their counterparts in Russia, still have a long way to go before they come abreast of the latest seed technology in the West," as Chinese scientists had been planting semi-dwarf varieties in the years before the development of IR-8.[99] The acquisition of IR-8 by the PRC caught the attention of development officials in Taiwan, including Shen Zonghan, whose own personal records of this included a handwritten note accompanying a report from Zheng Deci highlighting rumors of the PRC acquiring IR-8.[100]

Later, the establishment of the AVRDC Outreach Program in Thailand allowed for further engagement with the PRC. Thailand Outreach Program director Charles Y. Yang (楊又迪, Yang Youdi), visited the PRC along with AVRDC director Wilbur Selleck.[101] These visits continued in 1982 and again in 1984, when mung bean varieties collected throughout China were sent to the Thailand regional center for evaluation.[102] The Thailand center during this period began to accept training of PRC scientists and technicians where the AVRDC, headquartered in Taiwan, could not accept PRC visitors due to the political circumstances of the Cold War. One such program sent Chinese scientists to Kasetsart University in Thailand for an AVRDC training course on legumes. Another, funded by the Canadian International Development Center, sent over one hundred Chinese scientists to the Thailand center for training in mung bean evaluation and selection. By 1988, Chinese scientists constituted the largest national origin of trainees graduated from the Bangkok Regional Training Center.[103]

In 1984, the AVRDC had initiated projects in collaboration with China in a number of tropical vegetables: tomato, sweet potato, soybean, mung bean, and Chinese cabbage. The goals of these projects were in line with the standard mission of the AVRDC, which is "to improve yields and quality" of the vegetables, "strengthen the expertise of Chinese scientists," assess damage due to plant disease, and collect local varieties in China to bring back to the AVRDC.[104] Yang described encouraging officials within the Chinese Academy of Agricultural Sciences and the Ministry of Agriculture, Animal Husbandry, and Fisheries to increase Chinese scientists sent to training courses and conferences abroad, in Thailand and the Philippines, and to increase the number of international scientists visiting China.

In terms of seed, Yang dedicated much of the report to graphs and charts comparing the yields of AVRDC-selected varieties in mung bean (in Chengdu seeing an average increase of two tons per hectare) and in tomatoes (in one case in Nanjing, outperforming the highest yielding local variety by 522 percent) to local varieties grown throughout China. Yang concluded that AVRDC varieties showed a "very significant impact on the agriculture in the People's Republic of China is in the making" with "enthusiasm expressed by both the research scientists and the lay farmers in seeking for AVRDC's materials."[105] Not all varieties outperformed local varieties—soybeans planted in Xuzhou, for example, underperformed in both total yield and seed size—but nonetheless Yang indicated a silver lining in the possibility to breed in new genetic traits, specifically in resistant to soybean mosaic virus and in good branching character, at the Chinese Academy of Agricultural Science Oil-Seed Crop Research Institute in Wuhan.

Yang remarked that Chinese officials were highly receptive to efforts to work more closely with the AVRDC and indicated this was "facilitated by the trend in Chinese agricultural policy favoring an economic-oriented research and production approach."[106] In comparison to the socialist agricultural science and scientific farming in the PRC under Mao, the 1980s marked a turn away from science as revolution or mass participation, which was a hallmark of socialist scientific farming.[107] The shift to economic-centered and production-centered policies also meant looking outward and re-engaging global networks that were stronger during the pre-1949 era. As historian Sigrid Schmalzer had argued that the pre-reform era was a careful balancing of *tu* (土, meaning native and indigenous, implying the local knowledge of farmers and of mass participation) and *yang* (洋, meaning foreign, implying the elite knowledge of Western science and of ivory-tower research centers), the post-reform era returned to the embrace of *yang* science, through training courses and foreign selected high-yielding seeds. This convergence after decades of divergence mirrored the larger economic development histories of Taiwan and China, which saw a similar and much more well-known reconvergence via Taiwanese business investment and offshoring to the PRC.[108]

CONCLUSION

In a transition reflective of the agricultural development field as a whole, agricultural science, and specifically Green Revolution sciences that produced high-yielding seeds and chemical fertilizers, became emblematic of the Taiwan's international development in the 1970s. Seeds and fertilizers were complemented by concern for nutrition, as the basic food problem began to be conquered with increased self-sufficiency among staple crops of Global South countries. As a result, minerals, vitamins, and protein came to the foreground as desirable development goals, and vegetables represented a healthy diet as opposed to just a calorically sufficient one.

Taiwan attempted to capitalize on this shift toward nutrition and food. After its ouster from the UN, the Taiwanese government turned to the FFTC and the AVRDC as institutions to maintain international relevancy. Taiwanese planners imagined vegetables and fertilizers as the new frontier at which it could occupy the vanguard. They could secure Taiwan's international position as agrarian development missions to Southeast Asia and Africa did a decade earlier. Taiwanese bureaucrats and scientists hoped that the technical nature of agricultural science could transcend the geopolitics of international recognition that began to plague Taiwan. They were ultimately mistaken.

By the late 1970s, the Green Revolution had reached its apex, and practitioners began to move away from its associated methods. The 1962 publication of Rachel Carson's *Silent Spring*, which showcased the dangers of pesticides and agricultural chemicals, spurred an environmentalist movement that began to erode Green Revolution chemical dependence.[109] In 1979, Robert McNamara, president of the

World Bank, announced that World Bank loans would be made contingent on recipient nations adopting World Bank–imposed policy changes. This policy of structural adjustment lending, which often forced policies of open markets and austerity policies that negatively affected developing nations, was also shared by the International Monetary Fund and became the preponderant development philosophy of both Bretton Woods institutions in the 1980s.[110] Vegetables garnered less interest compared to structural adjustment lending. Even in the agricultural development field, vegetables were outshone by rice and wheat. The Taiwanese pushed for the importance of vegetables given the increasing attention on nutrition instead of calories as an emerging standard by the 1970s, but vegetables still lacked the allure of staple crops. After the Republic of China left the United Nations in 1971, its efforts to join international groups like the CGIAR were frustrated by its lack of official international status. Neither the FFTC nor the AVRDC ever received international funding that the CGIAR institutions had gained because of Taiwan's geopolitical status. Instead, the FFTC and the AVRDC remained small, underfunded, and by the 2000s, hollowed-out versions of their 1970s ambitions.

As Taiwan in the 1980s achieved increasing international attention for its tremendous export success from manufacturing shoes, bicycles, dolls, and later, electronics and semiconductors, few noticed the decline of agricultural science. Export processing zones, science and technology parks, industrial research, and contract manufacturing became the new scientific frontiers for Taiwan in the 1980s and 1990s. The heyday of Taiwanese vegetables, if there ever was one, was over. It was instead consumer goods and the nascent electronics industry that provided Taiwan with the international relevancy it had earlier sought in agriculture. In eclipsing agriculture, the rise of Taiwan's industrial strength marked the decline of international agrarian development.

Conclusion

Experiences with agrarian development began in a range of contexts in Republican-era China, from social reform and infrastructure engineering to agricultural science. The numerous debates and different approaches suggested a number of possibilities for agrarian development. In missionary communities, famine relief took priority, and eventually, many missionaries believed that relief was an insufficient approach in the long term. Reactive efforts transitioned to proactive prevention of famine, which in turn evolved into development. Institutions like the National Agricultural Research Bureau integrated several of these approaches, notably a network of agricultural research stations combined with agricultural extension. The United Nations Relief and Rehabilitation Administration and the Chinese National Relief and Rehabilitation Administration demonstrated some of the difficulties in attempting national-scale development in the face of political obstacles. Many of the approaches became integrated toward the end of the Republican-era within the Joint Commission on Rural Reconstruction.

The JCRR attained long-term gains in agricultural productivity and rural reform after its move to Taiwan in 1949. It oversaw land reform, tasked with turning the traditional landlord and tenant farmer classes into modern industrial and petty capitalists, respectively. Land reform was portrayed by the GMD government as simultaneously capitalist and for social welfare, utilizing the language of legal and financial modernity along with the GMD ideology of Minsheng zhuyi. The JCRR took over former Japanese colonial era research institutions, such as experiment stations and centers of agricultural research, continuing plant breeding and intensive cultivation methods associated with scientific and industrialized agriculture. It integrated the system of farmers' associations established under Japanese colonial rule into an agricultural extension system that allowed for rapid dissemination of practices and knowledge from research centers to rural villages, while also enabling the newly established state to exercise greater control and state capacity in the countryside. This included the use of print media such as *Harvest*, a periodical that utilized cultural forms, such as morality tales, to enact the modern and hygienic standards that the JCRR idealized. The JCRR implemented 4-H clubs, modeled after those in the United States, to organize village youth around principles of community involvement, democracy, and modern scientific practices. These pathways allowed the JCRR to push for a specific modern vision of development that entailed market-based capitalist approaches and community-organized middlemen while still exercising significant centralized control.

Elements of Taiwan's approach to modern science and technology, land reform, and social improvement were represented abroad as part of Taiwan's international development missions during the Cold War. First in Vietnam, Taiwanese technicians were recruited for their experience and knowledge in establishing farmers' associations. Then in Africa, the ROC Ministry of Foreign Affairs sent agricultural technical teams to over a dozen nations in agricultural extension, demonstration, and crop improvement. These missions represented Taiwanese agrarian experiences as particularly relevant for other developing nations like Taiwan. Taiwan occupied a similar tropical climate, possessed few natural resources or capital reserves, and most importantly, had been able to demonstrate sustained success operating under their model. Moreover, Taiwanese experts often drew parallels between the cultural characteristics of Taiwan and recipient nations of their missions—shared ethics of pragmatism, hard work, and rurality—to position Taiwan within the Global South. The purpose of these missions was driven by Cold War geopolitics. Taiwan leveraged its development expertise to seek diplomatic favors from other developing nations, especially African nations that could vote in the United Nations. These missions also served a more subtle purpose, to magnify the technical and political prowess of the Republic of China regime at home and abroad. Through international development, the GMD state was constructing a sociotechnical imaginary of Taiwan as leading a vanguard of the developing world.

Cold War development politics was especially evident in the dissemination of Taiwanese land reform. Sustained by a series of measures limiting tenant rents and capped with a forced land redistribution program, Taiwanese experts advertised Taiwanese land reform as a moderate, capitalist-friendly version of land reform that contrasted with the violence of Communist revolution. Joining with the foundation established by American philanthropic John C. Lincoln to proselytize the teachings of nineteenth-century economic thinker Henry George, the Taiwan-based Land Reform Training Institute hosted training sessions and conferences for dozens of developing nation bureaucrats interested in Taiwanese land reform model. Yet land reform was a highly selective aspect of the Taiwan model. It was proudly touted, but in practice, forced redistribution was rarely carried out due to its political infeasibility, a reality common in the history of development.

By the 1970s, Taiwanese international development emphasized its achievements in agricultural sciences as a result of the Green Revolution. Advances in vegetables, food production, and fertilizer attracted international attention. The Taiwanese attempted to capitalize on their scientific experience by establishing multinational scientific research institutes like the Asian Vegetable Research and Development Center. While the Green Revolution moment offered an opportunity for Taiwan's efforts to once again lead a vanguard of international scientific networks and institutes focused on global environments, it was thwarted by international geopolitics. The ouster of the ROC from the United Nations spelled disaster for Taiwan's hopes as the AVRDC and other Taiwan-based institutions were left out of the prestigious Consultative Group of International Agricultural Research (CGIAR) and funding from UN affiliated funding agencies. Other CGIAR institutions gained greater prominence, and Taiwan struggled to as its geopolitical isolation and the rise of neoliberalism led to a shift away from state-led development.

The rise and fall of Taiwanese development enable us to understand a broader history of development. Taiwanese development follows a familiar narrative in critical studies of development. Successes of development at home encouraged technocratic elites to aid others. Ostensibly superior foreign technologies, whether farmers' associations or high-yielding rice, were sometimes indeed more productive or more suitable than local practices. But they were flawed, difficult to scale and sustain, unsuited for local communities in unexpected ways, and came at costs to environments. Teams sent to Africa could bring higher-yielding rice that in demonstration farms outperformed native varieties, but the infrastructures of chemical and seed supplies and knowledge expertise did not persist after Taiwanese teams departed. Unforeseen by Taiwanese experts, Taiwanese rice did not necessarily sell well in African markets due to different taste preferences. Taiwanese farmers association experts, desired by the South Vietnam regime for counterinsurgency, could not "save" Vietnam from a nationalist revolution in the form of Communism. Development was a narrow, apolitical solution in a complex, political world.

Like American, Soviet, or PRC development in the Global South, this motivation was also political and not quite selfless or humanitarian. GMD state planners co-opted development to expand an anti-Communist alliance in Southeast Asi, and in Africa to prevent losing its valued position in the United Nations. Yet Taiwanese development was fundamentally shaped by postcolonial politics circulating within the Global South. Taiwanese technicians and scientists proudly modeled a pragmatic, learning-by-doing ethos. It was modern, but not because it flowed from a position of economic wealth. Taiwan touted its willingness to work hard under difficult conditions where capital was scarce. Though this was often performative and ironic given Taiwan's extractive and authoritarian policies at home, GMD planners placed value on farmer welfare in land reform and social improvement.

Finally, the Guomindang used agrarian development to construct a new sociotechnical imaginary centered on science, modernity, and economic success. Taiwan's technical capabilities in agriculture and international demand for that expertise allowed for the GMD regime to portray itself as leading a global vanguard of states. Development buttressed and in some cases surpassed GMD claims of legitimacy based on ethnic nationalism and anti-Communism. Since its arrival on Taiwan, the GMD staked its legitimacy on being the more "Chinese" regime of the two Chinese nation-sates. But by the 1960s and 70s, it was apparent that the GMD would not retake the mainland, and prior assertions of legitimacy seemed increasingly problematic. With development success, Taiwan pointed to wealth and modernity, especially in contrast to the PRC across the strait. Going abroad and teaching Taiwanese techniques to Africa, Southeast Asia, and the rest of the developing world demonstrated that the ROC was indeed the "superior" regime. These representations, reinforced through propaganda and in official discourse, allowed the GMD to continue its authoritarian grip and martial law on Taiwanese society.

Today, Taiwan continues its international development missions, known as overseas development assistance, in places like the Marshall Islands and Central America. Taiwanese methods have adapted to new changing circumstances of global development. Instead of focusing on rice or vegetables, Taiwanese now offer medical assistance in preventing the spread of diabetes among Pacific Island populations and infrastructure projects such as building bridges in Costa Rica.[1] Nonetheless, these missions continue to operate for political objectives. Taiwanese missions are provided to the few dozen nations that continue to recognize the Republic of China diplomatically over the People's Republic of China. And these nations dwindle in number as the PRC offers increasingly larger capital packages and investments than the ROC can.[2]

Ironically, it is the PRC today that has become the leading consumer of the Taiwan economic model.[3] The PRC's ongoing transformation from rural to urban economy poses some of the largest governance challenges for the Chinese Communist Party. Some of these include the strains that rural to urban migration have created on social services, real estate, and urban development amid rising inequality and concerns over environmental degradation.[4] Thus, PRC bureaucrats continue to look to how Taiwan managed its urban development. Land reform, previously an arena where the ROC vehemently objected to PRC methods, is now reimagined as land policy management, a field that attracted PRC local government officials to visit and undertake formal learning tours in Taipei in the 2010s when I was doing my fieldwork for this book.

As Taiwan's agricultural sector today represents just 1.8 percent of its GDP, this history might appear irrelevant. But most Taiwanese of a certain generation today will remember newspaper reports of Taiwan's *nongjituan* (農技團, agricultural technical teams) abroad. Few will proactively associate them with the Cold War, with a critical reexamination of the faith in science and technology, or with the Guomindang effort to consolidate its authoritarian regime. Even fewer outside that generation are aware of these missions unless they had a personal connection within their family or extended family to the development enterprise.

As a whole, development today remains a remarkably ahistorical discipline, in which many development economists have turned to increasingly quantitative and "scientific" means of analysis to accomplish their goals.[5] The turn to science is not new; it is only that scientific rigor is now used as a litmus test to determine whether a development initiative is considered productive. What seems to have been lost is the recognition that development is itself not a science in the sense that there is one objective truth that would unlock its secrets. It, too, is subject to the context in which it is constructed and practiced and is defined and ultimately restrained by the politics, culture, and society under which it is formed. Development is as much about the developer as it is about the developed. The Taiwanese, among most successful students of development in the past century, have learned this lesson well.

NOTES

INTRODUCTION

1. On how decolonization provided new opportunities for the developing world, see, for example, Walker, *States-in-Waiting*.

2. Growth, as represented by statistics or as a goal of economic management, is neither unique to Taiwan nor new in the 1960s, of course. For histories of growth dating as early as the nineteenth century, refer to Cook, *The Pricing of Progress*; and Macekura, *The Mismeasure of Progress*.

3. 中非農技合作討論會 [Sino-African Agricultural Technical Cooperation Conference], July 16, 1965, p. 1866, archive number 020000039124A, Ministry of Foreign Affairs Collection, Academia Historica.

4. Zanasi, *Saving the Nation*; Macekura, *The Mismeasure of Progress*.

5. Young, *Transforming Sudan*; Aerni-Flessner, "Development, Politics, and the Centralization of State Power in Lesotho"; Decker, *The Idea of Development in Africa*.

6. Gold, *State and Society in the Taiwan Miracle*; Wade, *Governing the Market*; Ash and Greene, *Taiwan in the 21st Century*; Greene, *The Origins of the Developmental State in Taiwan*; Hamilton and Kao, *Making Money*; Li, *Economic Transformation of Taiwan*; Amsden, "Taiwan's Economic History; Winckler and Greenhalgh, *Contending Approaches to the Political Economy of Taiwan*; Cumings, "The Origins and Development of the Northeast Asian Political Economy"; Ho, *Economic Development of Taiwan*; Looney, *Mobilizing for Development*.

7. Foucault, "Governmentality."

8. Escobar, *Encountering Development*.

9. Lin, *Island Fantasia*.

10. Jasanoff and Kim have utilized the term *sociotechnical imaginary* to refer to "collectively imagined forms of social life and social order reflected in the design and fulfillment of nation-specific scientific and/or technological projects" (Jasanoff and Kim, "Containing

207

the Atom," 120). In Moore's words, technology then becomes imbued with "ideological vision and meaning" (Moore, *Constructing East Asia*, 3).

11. Gupta, *Postcolonial Developments*; Anderson, "Introduction: Postcolonial Technoscience"; Thornton, *Revolution in Development*.

12. Immerwahr, *Thinking Small*; Ferguson, *The Anti-Politics Machine*.

13. Andrade, *How Taiwan Became Chinese*.

14. Huang, "Structural Change in Taiwan's Agricultural Economy."

15. Jacoby, *U.S. Aid to Taiwan: A Study of Foreign Aid, Self-Help, and Development*. Yager, *Transforming Agriculture in Taiwan*.

16. W. I. Myers to Shen Zonghan, March 15, 1963, archive number 034000000351A, folder "Myers, W. I." in "Shen Zonghan Letter Drafts" [沈宗瀚文件稿], Council of Agriculture, Executive Yuan Collection [行政院農委會], Academia Historica Archives 國史館, Taipei, Taiwan.

17. International Monetary Fund, "World Economic Outlook," April 2024. GDP ranking uses 2023 figures. National Statistics, Republic of China (Taiwan), "Unemployment Rate," July 2024. https://eng.stat.gov.tw/. Poverty and Inequality Platform, the World Bank, "Country Profile: Taiwan," 2021 (2017 PPP). The World Bank defines poverty as subsisting under $2.15 USD per day.

18. General Report, Issue 1 (1948/1950), Joint Commission on Rural Reconstruction. Taipei, Taiwan (ROC). "Statistics of External Trade for April 2022," Ministry of Finance, Taiwan, https://www.mof.gov.tw. Note that the 2022 figure includes prepared foods, vegetable and animal products, and beverages, but excludes fishery products.

19. Smith, "Taiwan's 228 Incident"; Louzon, "From Japanese Soldiers to Chinese Rebels."

20. Lin, *Taiwan, the United States, and the Hidden History of the Cold War in Asia*.

21. Masuda, *Cold War Crucible*.

22. Scholars of postcolonialism, or postcolonial theory, have argued that colonialism restructures societies around the world, even after the end of formal empire. These colonial continuities shape how peoples understand themselves and their relationships with their former colonizers into the present day; see Fanon, *The Wretched of the Earth*. Alternatively, postcolonialism is sometimes used to refer to the politics of nation-building within former colonies that emerged as independent nation-states after the end of formal empires, especially after the dissolution of the British, French, German, Dutch, and Japanese empires following World War II in Africa and Asia. In this definition, postcolonialism is temporally specific, referring to the era after formal empire. In the rhetoric of the post-1945 period, new leaders from formerly colonized peoples sought to consolidate power within new national entities that were formed out of formerly heterogeneous and hierarchical empires. On postcolonialism in Taiwan, see the classic work of Leo T. S. Ching, *Becoming Japanese*. For discussion of this based on Southeast Asian and African and Caribbean perspectives, see, respectively, Ewing, "The Colombo Powers"; and Getachew, *Worldmaking after Empire*.

23. Chen Kuan-hsing has used the term *subimperial* to describe Taiwan's 1990s Southbound Policy (南向政策, Nanxiang Zhengce), implemented under President Lee Teng-hui to shift Taiwan's economic gaze to Southeast Asia. Chen argues that the Southbound Policy was an imperial enterprise undertaken by the Taiwanese state and capitalist enterprises, which allowed Taiwan to resolve its capital overaccumulation from its economic growth to take advantage of developing markets in Southeast Asia; see Chen, *Asia as Method*. On

other approaches to Taiwan as part of a US-led Cold War Pacific ruling order, see Glassman, *Drums of War*.

24. Yang, *The Great Exodus from China*.

25. Winichakul, *Siam Mapped*.

26. Cowen and Shenton, *Doctrines of Development*; Rist, *The History of Development*.

27. Hart, "Development Critiques in the 1990s."

28. Jones argues that we should include in this category watershed moments in modern East Asian history, including the late Qing "search for wealth and power" exemplified by Yan Fu's translations of Adam Smith, Thomas Henry Huxley, and Herbert Spencer into Chinese. See Jones, *Developmental Fairy Tales*, 3–5.

29. Engerman, "Development Politics and the Cold War."

30. Immerwahr, *Thinking Small*.

31. Here I take modernity as a broad way of thinking what it meant to be modern, and not the modernization theory derived from the American academe in the 1950s and 60s. Some scholars have seen development as the manifestation of American modernization theory turned into practice. In this recounting, modernization theory, which arose in American academic circles of economists, political scientists, and sociologists, outlined a path for nations and societies to proceed to modernity. In most of these theories, modernity entailed something that resembled the postwar United States: urban, industrial, capitalist, wealthy, democratic, and so on. See Engerman et al., *Staging Growth*; Gilman, *Mandarins of the Future Modernization Theory in Cold War America*; and Latham, *The Right Kind of Revolution*. Other scholars have focused on the roles that modernization theorists, perhaps best exemplified by Walt W. Rostow, have played in foreign policy. See Pearce, *Rostow, Kennedy, and the Rhetoric of Foreign Aid*; and Latham, *Modernization as Ideology*. Although modernization theory's influence was significant among economist circles, it was less influential in other areas of development such as rural sociology and was never explicitly cited in fields such as plant science.

32. Scott, *Seeing Like a State*.

33. Immerwahr has argued that communitarianism and community countered a high modernist faith in science, technology, and rationality, instead espousing a "low modernism" or a desire to decentralize and focus on communities instead of the centralizing. Immerwahr, *Thinking Small*, 40, 44.

34. DeHart, *Transpacific Developments*.

35. Toner, "Imagining Taiwan."

36. Monson, *Africa's Freedom Railway*; Lee, *The Specter of Global China*.

37. Engerman and Unger, "Introduction." Also refer to Engerman, *The Price of Aid*.

38. Ferguson, *The Anti-Politics Machine*.

39. Oded, "Africa in Israeli Foreign Policy"; Douglass, "The Saemaul Undong in Historical Perspective."

40. Latour, *Science in Action*.

41. Schmalzer, *Red Revolution, Green Revolution*; Cullather, *The Hungry World*; Perkins, *Geopolitics and the Green Revolution*; Baranski, *The Globalization of Wheat*; Lorek, *Making the Green Revolution*.

42. Schwartz, *In Search of Wealth and Power*; Zanasi, *Saving the Nation*.

43. Ching, *Becoming Japanese*; Brown, *Is Taiwan Chinese?*; Phillips, *Between Assimilation and Independence*; Dawley, *Becoming Taiwanese*.

44. As historian Rebecca Karl has shown for the late Qing, the world became an important imagined and realized space in which intellectuals, elites, and ordinary citizens viewed their own identities and possible futures. I borrow this approach in showing how Taiwanese scientists and bureaucrats understood Taiwanese development in the 1960s and 70s. Karl, *Staging the World*.

1. FAMINE RELIEF TO PREVENTION: SCIENCE, MISSIONARIES, AND THE ORIGINS OF DEVELOPMENT, 1920–1948

Epigraph: Jiang Tingfu (蔣廷黻, Ting-fu Tsiang), "The Problems of China," speech before Naval War College, October 21, 1949, folder 1.0, general, box 1, Economic Cooperation Administration, Far East Program Division, China Subject Files, 1947–1950, Records of US Foreign Assistance Agencies, RG 469, National Archives at College Park, College Park, MD (hereafter cited as NACP). Jiang Tingfu, professor of history at Tsinghua University and director of the China National Relief and Rehabilitation Administration, had a long career as a diplomat and statesman, serving as ambassador to the Soviet Union, chairman of the Chinese delegation to the United Nations, and finally ambassador to the United States.

1. Buck, *The Good Earth*; Edgerton-Tarpley, *Tears from Iron*.

2. For example, state food management has been well documented in the imperial system in Will et al., *Nourish the People*; and Li, *Fighting Famine in North China*. At local levels, elites and religious organizations often functioned in distributing philanthropic aid after calamities (see Wong, "Benevolent and Charitable Activities"; and Fuller, *Famine Relief in Warlord China*).

3. Lavelle, *The Profits of Nature*.

4. For example, Cullather, *The Hungry World*; Ekbladh, *The Great American Mission*; Sayward, *The Birth of Development*. While the most prominent contemporary institutions associated with development—the World Bank, the Food and Agriculture Organization, the United Nations Development Program—indeed did not arise until the founding of the United Nations and the Bretton Woods conference near the end of WWII, the foundations for these institutions were laid well before the war. The United Nations had its predecessor in the League of Nations, which organized technical assistance missions, including those to China; see Osterhammel, "'Technical Co-operation' between the League of Nations and China." The Food and Agriculture Organization evolved from the International Institute of Agriculture in Rome, though its mission was largely one of collecting statistics rather than actively sending technical assistance missions.

5. For example, Perkins, *Geopolitics and the Green Revolution*; and Ekbladh, *The Great American Mission*.

6. Stross, *The Stubborn Earth*.

7. Merkel-Hess, *The Rural Modern*.

8. Though the faith in modernism and making society legible is shared among what James Scott might call high modernists, the modernists of early Republican China were not necessarily all believers in the need for authoritarian state power. See Scott, *Seeing Like a State*.

9. Letter from Houghton to Embree, May 19, 1921, box 45, folder 1040, series 1.2, RG 4 China Medical Board, Rockefeller Foundation, Rockefeller Archive Center (hereafter cited as RAC).

10. Hollinger, *Protestants Abroad*, 3.

11. Kumar, "'Modernization' and Agrarian Development in India, 1912–52." For more on the work North American missionaries in social uplift, see Fishburn, "The Social Gospel," 222.

12. Tyrrell, *Reforming the World*.

13. Letter from Houghton to Embree, May 19, 1921, box 45, folder 1040, series 1.2, RG 4 China Medical Board, RAC.

14. Bullock, *An American Transplant*.

15. Li, *Fighting Famine in North China*, 284.

16. "Starving Chinese Eat Baked Weeds: Thousands of Refugees, Migrating Afoot, Subsist on Cakes Resembling Clay," *Washington Post*, December 26, 1920, sec. Editorial and Society.

17. Memorandum, American Advisory Committee for Famine Relief, September 17, 1921, box 45, folder 1040, series 1.2, RG 4 China Medical Board, RAC.

18. Ibid.

19. Ibid.

20. This is discussed in more detail in Fuller, *Famine Relief in Warlord China.*

21. Letter to American Advisory Committee for Famine Relief in New York, October 1921, box 45, folder 1040, series 1.2, RG 4 China Medical Board, RAC.

22. Roger S. Greene to Vernon Munroe, January 25, 1922, box 45, folder 1041, series 1.2, RG 4 China Medical Board, RAC.

23. John K. Davis to Greene, April 19, 1922, box 45, folder 1041, series 1.2, RG 4 China Medical Board, RAC.

24. Sneddon, *Concrete Revolution*.

25. Nathan, *A History of the China International Famine Relief Commission*, 11.

26. Munroe to Greene, October 4, 1922, box 45, folder 1041, series 1.2, RG 4 China Medical Board, RAC.

27. Reisner to Greene, July 14, 1922, box 45, folder 1041, series 1.2, RG 4 China Medical Board, RAC.

28. Newspaper clipping, "Farm Expert to Aid China in Crop Boost," January 28, 1931, Agriculture, box 114, Narrative Reports 1904–1939, China; Records of the Foreign Agricultural Service, RG 166, NACP.

29. Love and Reisner, "The Nanking-Cornell Story."

30. February 23, 1929, letter from Case to Reisner, box 1, folder 2, Harry Love Papers, Division of Rare and Manuscript Collections, Cornell University Library (hereafter cited as CRML).

31. Case further continued to indicate that Reisner contrasted this to Korea and India, where "relatively a much larger amount of work had been done on research than on extension," and as a result, he believed that agricultural extension could be "utilized with great benefit" in Korea should their missionary population be leveraged for extension work.

32. Ralph A. Felton, memorandum, February 17, 1929, box 1, folder 2, Harry Love Papers, CRML.

33. Ralph A. Felton, memorandum, February 17, 1929, box 1, folder 2, Harry Love papers, CRML.

34. Thirteenth Annual Cornell School for Missionaries Brochure, February 14, 1942, box 4, folder 16, Harry Love Papers, CRML.

35. Thirteenth Annual Cornell School for Missionaries Biographical Sketches and Directory, February 14, 1942, box 4, folder 16, Harry Love Papers, CRML.

36. Fuller, *Famine Relief in Warlord China.*

37. For a biography of Yan, see Hayford, *To the People.*

38. Translation by Yan. Yan to Rockefeller, October 14, 1929, box 1, folder "Report Letters 1929 to 1940," International Institute of Rural Reconstruction Collection, Rare Books and Manuscripts Library, Columbia University (hereafter cited as IIRRC).

39. Yan to Auchincloss, October 1, 1930, box 1, folder "Report Letters 1929 to 1940," IIRRC.

40. C. C. Chen, Scientific Medicine as Applied to Tinghsien, 1933, box 1, "Health Program Reports 1933 to 1935," IIRRC.

41. Yan to Auchincloss, April 15, 1930, box 1, folder "Report Letters 1929 to 1940," IIRRC.

42. C. C. Chen, Scientific Medicine as Applied to Tinghsien, 1933, box 1, "Health Program Reports 1933 to 1935," IIRRC.

43. Merkel-Hess, *The Rural Modern.*

44. T. H. Shen, University of Nanking Report of Department of Agronomy, June 30, 1932, box 15, folder 8, Harry Love Papers, CRML.

45. James B. Grant to Selskar M. Gunn, October 13, 1936, box 9, folder 88, series 601, RG 1 Projects, RAC.

46. James B. Grant to Selskar M. Gunn, November 11, 1938, box 9, folder 89, series 601, RG 1 Projects, RAC.

47. K. S. Sie to Harry Love, September 26, 1934, box 1, folder 81, Harry Love Papers, CRML.

48. Annual report of insect control work to the Rockefeller Foundation conducted by the NARB, June 1939, box 9, folder 92, series 601, RG 1 Projects, RAC.

49. National Agricultural Research Bureau Ministry of Industry to Selskar Gunn, January 23, 1937, box 9, folder 89, series 601, RG 1 projects, RAC.

50. "Agricultural Research Organization in China," by T. H. Shen, October 9, 1946, Agriculture 1946, box 600, narrative reports 1946–49, China, records of the Foreign Agricultural Service, RG 166, NACP.

51. Grant 36154, April 15, 1936, box 9, folder 88, series 601, RG 1 projects, RAC.

52. Letter from Shen Zonghan to H. L. Richardson, August 16, 1952, archival number 入藏登錄號 034000000356A, folder "R," 沈宗翰文件稿 (4箱), Academia Historica Archives.

53. "Solution of Postwar Problems," editorial published by Chang Chung-fu, March 31, 1943, Postwar Planning, box 168, narrative reports 1942–45, China, records of the Foreign Agricultural Service, RG 166, NACP.

54. Ibid. On the importance of cotton and cotton improvement efforts, see Stewart, "A Community Crop."

55. J. Bartlett Richards, Memorandum of Conversation with Dr. Wong Wen-hao, May 24, 1943, postwar planning, box 168, narrative reports 1942–45, China, records of the Foreign Agricultural Service, RG 166, NACP.

56. Sayward, *The Birth of Development*; Borgwardt, *A New Deal for the World.*

57. Muscolino, *The Ecology of War in China.*

58. Newspaper clipping, "Farm Expert to Aid China in Crop Boost," January 28, 1931, agriculture, box 114, narrative reports 1904–39, China, records of the Foreign Agricultural Service, RG 166, NACP.

59. US Experts Assist China in Reconstruction, September 28, 1943, postwar planning, box 168, narrative reports 1942–45, China, records of the Foreign Agricultural Service, RG 166, NACP.

60. "Summary of Personal Data," "William John Green Retires," box 24, William John Green Papers, Hoover Institution Archives.

61. Mitter, "Imperialism, Transnationalism, and the Reconstruction of Post-War China."

62. Reinisch, "'Auntie UNRRA' at the Crossroads," 73.

63. However, historian Jessica Reinisch calls into question this nonpolitical stance in other countries, where the selection of recipients and scale of aid was clearly highly influenced by geopolitics. Reinisch, "'Auntie UNRRA' at the Crossroads," 73.

64. William John Green Diary, page 123, 151–52, "China, 1945–1948," box 9, William John Green Papers, Hoover Institution Archives.

65. United Nations Relief and Rehabilitation Administration First Session of the Council No. 12, November 11, 1943, reel DG14 Office of the Director General, United Nations Relief and Rehabilitation Administration Collection, Columbia University Library.

66. Summary of China Office Report for March 1946, Shanghai, April 25, 1946, reel DG15 Office of the Director General, United Nations Relief and Rehabilitation Administration Collection, Columbia University Library.

67. Muscolino, *The Ecology of War in China.*

68. Mitter, "Imperialism, Transnationalism, and the Reconstruction of Post-War China," 64.

69. Roger F. Evans China Diary, May 26, 1947, box 51, folder 430, series 601, RG 1, RAC.

70. William John Green Diary, page 123, 151–52, "China, 1945–1948," box 19, William John Green Papers, Hoover Institution Archives.

71. Increasing food production is explicitly mentioned in official correspondences as a recommendation of the Sino-American Agricultural Mission. Minister S.S. Tsao to Y.T. Miao, Mr. Koh, and C.W. Chang, May 22, 1948, page 4, 联合国粮农组织中国联络委员会第二三次年会资料（内有英文）UNFAO Chinese Delegation Second and Third Session Materials, folder 卷 2516, fond 全宗号 23, Ministry of Agriculture Collection, Number Two Archives, Nanjing, China.

72. "Editorial Comment on Exchange of Notes Providing for Establishment of Sino-American Commission on Rural Reconstruction in China," August 6, 1948, Agriculture 1948, box 600, narrative reports 1946–49, China, records of the Foreign Agricultural Service, RG 166, NACP.

73. Chiang, *Tides from the West,* 72.

74. Ibid., 73.

75. Original source: "杜威謂科學研究真理的方法，不外根據事實，以實驗求得其真理." "五年教學生涯," Shen Zonghan, *Gengyun Suiyue.*

76. Original source: "我現用心於中國農業改進的政策，即如何使科學改良的成果能普及於農民." "中年生活與家庭," Ibid.

77. "Bafang Zainan Fuxing Nongcun" [八方災難復興農村, Rural reconstruction in the midst of disasters], *Ta Kung Pao* [大公報], August 11, 1948.

78. "Editorial Comment on Exchange of Notes Providing for Establishment of Sino-American Commission on Rural Reconstruction in China," August 6, 1948, Agriculture 1948, box 600, narrative reports 1946–49, China, records of the Foreign Agricultural Service, RG 166, NACP.

79. Ibid.

80. Ibid.

81. Immerwahr, *Thinking Small*, 101-2.

82. Correspondences between Shen Zonghan and Yan Yangchu, three letters total, from March 8, 1950 to April 27, 1966, archive number 034000000367A, folder "Yen, James," in "Shen Zonghan Letter Drafts" [沈宗瀚文件稿], Council of Agriculture, Executive Yuan Collection [行政院農委會], Academia Historica Archives 國史館, Taipei, Taiwan.

83. See, for example, Immerwahr, *Thinking Small*; Cullather, "Damming Afghanistan"; and Cullather, *The Hungry World*.

2. EXECUTING CONTRACTS, NOT LANDLORDS: CAPITALISM THROUGH LAND REFORM, 1949–1968

Epigraph: Mellor, *Agriculture on the Road to Industrialization*, xiii.

1. Lee, "Intersectoral Capital Flows in the Economic Development of Taiwan."

2. "American Agricultural Economics Association: Reports and Minutes 1968–69."

3. As economist Talan İşcan explains, "A redistribution of ownership rights from land-lords to tenants changes the incentives, and cultivators respond by reallocating their effort. This within-sector resource reallocation improves farm productivity, and the higher the degree of initial land inequality, the stronger the effects of this channel on labor productivity." İşcan, "Redistributive Land Reform."

4. Studwell, *How Asia Works*. Land reform is also a factor credited by economist Dani Rodrik for economic successes in South Korea and Taiwan. Rodrik, "Getting Interventions Right."

5. Wang and Kim, "Land Reform in Taiwan, 1950–1961." Similarly, Chris Bramall argues that the creation of small, noncontiguous plots in land-to-the-tiller reform stymied economic growth in Taiwan. Bramall, "Chinese Land Reform," 135.

6. Chen, *Land Reform in Taiwan*.

7. Many of Chiang's associates and high-ranking GMD officials were similarly from military backgrounds, and some of them may have been capable field commanders but made for poor bureaucrats, notably Chen Yi (陳儀), whose actions during the February 28 Incident of 1947 likely exacerbated the mass killings that followed.

8. Chen, *Land Reform in Taiwan*, ix.

9. Strauss, *State Formation in China and Taiwan*.

10. Yang, "Soil and Scroll."

11. This follows the work of other scholars, such as Prasenjit Duara, who have sought to "rescue history from the nation," implying demythologizing historical narratives from political nationalist projects. See Duara, *Rescuing History from the Nation*. Paul Cohen has examined narratives of the Boxer Rebellion in a similar manner (what he calls "keys"), seeking to understand how the Boxer Rebellion came to be constructed in history and memory. See Cohen, *History in Three Keys*.

12. GMD policies were not new in this regard. Aaron Jakes has shown as early as the late nineteenth century how British colonial officials considered Egyptian peasants as "agrarian capitalists-in-waiting"; see Jakes, *Egypt's Occupation*. Juliet Lu has shown how the Lao state today continues to use a form of "turning land into capital" as a policy; see Lu, "Grounding Chinese Investment."

13. Levy, *Freaks of Fortune*; Rosenthal, *Accounting for Slaver*; Ott, *When Wall Street Met Main Street*; Cook, *The Pricing of Progres*.

14. Hsu, *Tudi zhengyi: cong tudi gaige dao tudi zhengshou*; Liao and Chu, "Weihe tudi gaige de yihan zhengyi duo?"; Liao and Chu, "Jiangu dizhu de tudi gaige."

15. Hsu and Hsiao, "The Impacts of Class Differentiation"; Hsu and Hsiao, "Taiwan tudi gaige zai shenshi."

16. Moore, "The Capitalocene."

17. Bergère, *Sun Yat-Sen*, 167.

18. Ibid., 169–70.

19. Taylor, *The Generalissimo*, 100.

20. Ibid., 107.

21. Averill, "The New Life in Action."

22. For an example of ROC struggles with local control, see Duara, *Culture, Power, and the State*.

23. Sands and Brandt, "Land Concentration and Income Distribution in Republican China," cited in Pitts, "From Revolution to Reform," 18.

24. Li, "War, Trade and Socialism," 94–97.

25. Rigger, *Politics in Taiwan*, 67, 77.

26. This includes Studwell, *How Asia Works*.

27. For a comprehensive history of American-led land reform as foreign policy, see Kapstein, *Seeds of Stability*. On the US and anticommunist efforts in Vietnam, see Conrad, "'Before It Is Too Late.'"

28. Though land reform largely fell off the radar by the late Cold War, this leftist critique of American foreign policy tending to support right-wing authoritarian regimes continued well after land reform exited center stage. See McCoy, "Land Reform as Counter-Revolution," 16.

29. Luo, "Redistributing Power," 10.

30. Olson, *U.S. Foreign Policy and the Third World Peasant.*

31. Huang, *Nongfuhui yu Taiwan jingyan*, 156.

32. Jacobs, *Democratizing Taiwan*, 61

33. Chen, *Land Reform in Taiwan*, 18–19.

34. Utilizing county-level archives from Sichuan, Wankun Li shows that rent reduction policies significantly reduced average rents by 22.9 percent (as a percentage of total annual production) in Bishan County and 30.8 percent in Ba County. Li, "War, Trade and Socialism," 117.

35. Ka, *Japanese Colonialism In Taiwan*, 154.

36. Hsu and Hsiao, "The Impacts of Class Differentiation," 20.

37. Ladejinsky, *Agrarian Reform as Unfinished Business*, 110–12.

38. Barclay, *Outcasts of Empire*, 25.

39. Ibid., 27.

40. Hsu and Hsiao, "The Impacts of Class Differentiation," 28.

41. Huang, *Nongfuhui yu Taiwan jingyan*.

42. Ibid.

43. Chen, *Land Reform in Taiwan*, 26–28.

44. Ibid., 315.

45. Ibid., 31.

46. Ibid., 29–40.

47. Ibid., 43–44.

48. Ibid., 49.

49. Ibid., 58.

50. Ibid., 55.

51. Chen, 69–81.

52. Chen, 84.

53. Hill, "Rice Supplies." This is also reinforced by findings in Wang and Kim, "Land Reform in Taiwan."

54. Chen, *Land Reform in Taiwan*, 76–77.

55. Ibid., 67.

56. Ibid., 68, 77.

57. Ibid., 67.

58. Hsu and Hsiao, "The Impacts of Class Differentiation," 2.

59. Yang, *Socio Economic Results of Land Reform in Taiwan*, 66.

60. Smith, *East Asian Agrarian Reform*.

61. Hsiung, *Living Rooms as Factories*.

62. Tang, *Land Reform in Free China*, 301.

3. THE TAIWAN MODEL: AGRICULTURAL SCIENCE, FARMERS' ASSOCIATIONS, AND CAPITALISM IN TAIWAN, 1949–1970

Epigraphs: Shen Zhongzhan, *Agriculture's Place in the Strategy of Development*, 1–2; Montgomery, Hughes, and Davis, *Rural Improvement and Political Development*, 1.

1. Gilman, *Mandarins of the Future Modernization Theory*.

2. Rostow, *The Stages of Economic Growth*.

3. For example, in US-Indonesian relations, as demonstrated by Simpson, *Economists with Gun*. This was true even outside of US-assisted regimes, including China. See Karl, *The Magic of Concepts*.

4. Memo, "Taiwan's Economic Development: Meeting at Dr. Rostow's Office," August 15, 1961, 893.00/7–761, box 2789, central decimal file, 1960–1963, China, internal, economic aid, records of the State Department, RG 59, National Archives at College Park, College Park, MD (hereafter cited as NACP).

5. Nominally, of course, Taiwan was a province of the Republic of China.

6. On Taiwan's rise as an Asian Tiger or Dragon, see Gold, *State and Society in the Taiwan Miracle*; Wade, *Governing the Market*; Vogel, *The Four Little Dragons*. On science and technology in industrial development, see Greene, *The Origins of the Developmental State in Taiwan*.

7. Historian Huang Chun-Chieh utilizes "Taiwan experience" (台灣經驗, *Taiwan jingyan*) to describe Taiwan's unique agricultural development. Huang, *Taiwan in Transformation 1895–2005*; Huang, *Nongfuhui yu Taiwan jingyan*. American observers sometimes also used *experience* or *relevance*; Yager, *Transforming Agriculture in Taiwan*; Christensen, *Taiwan's Agricultural Development*.

8. Practices were almost always represented as "Chinese" (or "our nation," 我國, in internal documents) to denote that the Republic of China regime was still fundamentally one that laid claim to all of China and was the true representative to the skills and values of the Chinese people.

9. Lee, *Intersectoral Capital Flows in the Economic Development of Taiwan*; Shen Zonghan, *Agricultural Development on Taiwan*; Shen Zonghan, *Agriculture's Place in the Strategy of Development*; Shen Zonghan, *The Sino-American Joint Commission on Rural Reconstruction*.

10. "Taiwan's Model of Agricultural Progress," S. C. Hsieh, page 11, August 28, 1969, box 15, folder "Phil. Academy of Sciences & Humanities Program—5th Lecture Pres F. E. Marcos Series on Chinese Culture and Civilization Manila 29 August 1969," Sam Hsieh Collection, Stanford East Asian Library.

11. Ibid., 12.

12. Scott, *Seeing Like a State*.

13. Ladejinsky, *Agrarian Reform as Unfinished Business*, 96.

14. Myers and Ching, "Agricultural Development in Taiwan."

15. Anderson, *Farmers' Associations in Taiwan*, 1.

16. Ibid.

17. Ka, *Japanese Colonialism In Taiwan*, 174.

18. Shen Zonghan, "Farmers' Associations in Taiwan," 2. Second International Seminar on Change in Agriculture, September 1974, Land Tenure Center Library, University of Wisconsin.

19. Shen Zonghan, *The Sino-American Joint Commission on Rural Reconstruction*, 72.

20. This wording was possibly the result of the secretary recording meeting minutes at the time, as the report by Zhang was produced originally in Chinese and translations to English were still in process. Zhou Xiuhuan 周琇環, ed., *Nongfuhui Shiliao* [農復會史料; Historical document collection on Joint Commission on Rural Reconstruction], vol. 2 (Taipei: Guoshiguan 國史館 [Academia Sinica], 1995), 438.

21. Jiang Menglin to W. I. Myers, May 23, 1951, archive number 034000000351A, folder "Myers, W. I." in "Shen Zonghan Letter Drafts" [沈宗瀚文件稿], Council of Agriculture, Executive Yuan Collection [行政院農委會], Academia Historica Archives 國史館, Taipei, Taiwan (hereafter COA/EYC)

22. Immerwahr, *Thinking Small*, 44–45.

23. Anderson, *Farmers' Associations in Taiwan*, 1.

24. Ibid., 3.

25. Shen Zonghan, *The Sino-American Joint Commission on Rural Reconstruction*, 74.

26. Anderson, *Farmers' Associations in Taiwan*, 16.

27. Hoffman, Postel-Vinay, and Rosenthal, *Priceless Markets*.

28. Guinnane, "Cooperatives as Information Machines."

29. Jiang Menglin to W. I. Myers, May 23, 1951, archive number 034000000351A, folder "Myers, W. I." in "Shen Zonghan Letter Drafts" [沈宗瀚文件稿], COA/EYC.

30. Ibid.

31. W. I. Myers, "Farm Credit," January 6, 1960, archive number 034000000351A, folder "Myers, W. I." in "Shen Zonghan Letter Drafts" [沈宗瀚文件稿], COA/EYC.

32. Ibid.

33. Li, *Economic Transformation of Taiwan*, 402.

34. End of Tour Report—Kenneth E. Boyden, credit advisor, November 1961 to June 1964, May 28, 1964, Agr—Economic Conditions, box 306, narrative reports 1962–1965, Taiwan, Records of the Foreign Agricultural Service, RG 166, NACP.

35. Shen Zonghan to W. I. Myers, undated (summer 1960?), archive number 034000000351A, folder "Myers, W. I." in "Shen Zonghan Letter Drafts" [沈宗瀚文件稿], COA/EYC.

36. Agriculture—Dr. W. I. Myers Report on Agriculture in Taiwan, April 9, 1962, Agr—Economic Conditions, box 306, narrative reports 1962–65, Taiwan, records of the Foreign Agricultural Service, RG 166, NACP.

37. End of Tour Report—Kenneth E. Boyden, credit advisor, November 1961 to June 1964, May 28, 1964, Agr—Economic Conditions, box 306, narrative reports 1962–65, Taiwan, records of the Foreign Agricultural Service, RG 166, NACP.

38. S. C. Hsieh to Gerald Huffman, August 30, 1965, archive number 034000000342A, folder "Hsieh, S. C." in "Shen Zonghan Letter Drafts" [沈宗瀚文件稿], COA/EYC.

39. Li, *Economic Transformation of Taiwan*, 285.

40. On quinine, see Yang, "Selling an Imperial Dream."

41. This was the subject of the popular 2014 Taiwanese film *Kano*.

42. H. J. Tong to Gil Levine, June 12, 1968, archive number 034000000346A, folder "L" in "Shen Zonghan Letter Drafts" [沈宗瀚文件稿], COA/EYC.

43. Professor Gil Levine, former JCRR consultant, interview by the author, October 19, 2013, Ithaca, NY.

44. USIS and JCRR Office of Information and Education to JCRR, "Rural Periodical Project, Operations and Budget," April 14, 1951, Robert Sheeks Personal Papers.

45. Conversation between Chiang Menglin and Willard Rappleye, "Rural Periodical Project," page 4, undated (1950?), Robert Sheeks Personal Papers. On the GMD policy of language decolonization and recolonization, refer to Chen, *The Sounds of Mandarin*.

46. Conversation between Chiang Menglin and Rappleye, "Rural Periodical Project," pages 5–6, undated (1950?), Robert Sheeks Personal Papers.

47. *Harvest* [Fengnian, 豐年] 1, no. 1 (July 15, 1951): 9.

48. Williams, "Cultivating Modern America," 8–9.

49. Rosenberg, *The 4-H Harvest*.

50. Date is according to USAID records; the video may have been produced earlier. "Lee Yu's 4-H Banner," February 1974, Records of USAID, RG 286.95, NACP.

51. Pomeranz, *The Great Divergence*.

52. "Plant Protection Center," Joint Commission on Rural Reconstruction in China (United States and China) Miscellaneous Records, box 9, Hoover Institution Archives.

53. "Studies on Post-harvest Physiology, Handling and Storage Techniques for Fresh Vegetables and Fruits," Joint Commission on Rural Reconstruction in China (United States and China) Miscellaneous Records, box 5, folder 2, Hoover Institution Archives.

54. Joint Commission on Rural Reconstruction in China (United States and China) Miscellaneous Records, box 9, folder 1, Hoover Institution Archives.

55. Bruce Billings, "Bruce Hadley Billings Mimeograph: A Study of the Role of Science and Technology in Taiwan," 24–25, Bruce Hadley Billings Papers, box 8, folder 8, Hoover Institution Archives.

56. Joint Commission on Rural Reconstruction in China (United States and China) Miscellaneous Records, box 2, folder 5, Hoover Institution Archives.

57. "Recommending Approval for CH Huang to Attend the Meeting on the Use of Seeds as Biological Monitors for Neutron Irradiations at Knoxville, Tennessee," Joint Commission on Rural Reconstruction in China (United States and China) Miscellaneous Records, box 4, folder 23, Hoover Institution Archives.

58. "Rural Youth in Agricultural and Rural Development," Joint Commission on Rural Reconstruction in China (United States and China) Miscellaneous Records, box 2, folder 5, Hoover Institution Archives.

59. Lee, "Intersectoral Capital Flows in the Economic Development of Taiwan."

60. Lee, *Intersectoral Capital Flows* , viii–ix.

61. For more on Lee's life, refer to Tsai, *Lee Teng-Hui and Taiwan's Quest for Identity*.

62. W. I. Myers to Shen Zonghan, March 15, 1963, archive number 034000000351A, folder "Myers, W. I." in "Shen Zonghan Letter Drafts" [沈宗瀚文件稿], COA/EYC.

63. Supervision over fertilizer distribution in Taiwan since 1949, United States, Economic Cooperation Administration miscellaneous records, XX679–10.V, Hoover Institution Archives.

64. "Report on Fertilizer Manufacturing by J. H. Stover, Fertilizer Adviser," November 28, 1946, file "Regional Agrehab Conference Nov 25–30 1946," series "Agricultural Rehabilitation" in United Nations Relief and Rehabilitation Administration China Mission funds, United Nations Archives.

65. Ibid.

66. "Food and Fertilizer Technology Center," Joint Commission on Rural Reconstruction in China (United States and China) Miscellaneous Records, box 2, folder 1, Hoover Institution Archives.

67. Zelin, *The Merchants of Zigong*.

68. Hsiao and Hsiao, *Economic Development of Taiwan*, 76.

69. Ibid.

70. Green, "End of Tour Report," 1, box 24, William John Green Papers, Hoover Institution Archives.

71. W. I. Myers to Shen Zonghan, March 15, 1963, archive number 034000000351A, folder "Myers, W. I." in "Shen Zonghan Letter Drafts" [沈宗瀚文件稿], COA/EYC.

72. Agriculture—Dr. W. I. Myers Report on Agriculture in Taiwan, April 9, 1962, Agr—Economic Conditions, box 306, narrative reports 1962–65, Taiwan, records of the Foreign Agricultural Service, RG 166, NACP.

73. W. I. Myers to Shen Zonghan, March 15, 1963, archive number 034000000351A, folder "Myers, W. I." in "Shen Zonghan Letter Drafts" [沈宗瀚文件稿], COA/EYC.

74. Shen Zonghan to W. I. Myers, October 22, 1962, archive number 034000000351A, folder "Myers, W. I." in "Shen Zonghan Letter Drafts" [沈宗瀚文件稿], COA/EYC.

75. Shen Zonghan to W. I. Myers, April 11, 1960, archive number 034000000351A, folder "Myers, W. I." in "Shen Zonghan Letter Drafts" [沈宗瀚文件稿], COA/EYC.

76. Shen Zonghan to W. I. Myers, "Farm Credit," July 16, 1960, archive number 0340000 00351A, folder "Myers, W. I." in "Shen Zonghan Letter Drafts" [沈宗瀚文件稿], COA/EYC.

77. Zhang Yanxian et al. 張炎憲等 , *Li Denghui xiansheng yu Taiwan minzhu hua* [李登輝先生與台灣民主化; Mr. Lee Teng-hui and Taiwan's democratization] (Taibei: Yushanshe 玉山社 , 2004), 44–45, 101. Quoted in Jacobs, *Democratizing Taiwan*.

78. *New York Times*, "Taiwan Economy Makes Wide Gains," January 13, 1964. https://www.nytimes.com.

79. "Fertilizer Industry," May 20, 1962, USAID/Taipei to AID/Washington, box 307. folder "Economic Conditions Quarterly-Foodstuffs," page 5, narrative reports 1962–65. RG 166 Foreign Agricultural Service, NACP.

80. "Fertilizer and Economic Development," March 14, 1963, USAID/Taipei to AID/Washington, box 307, folder "Economic Conditions Quarterly-Foodstuffs," page 1, Narrative Reports 1962–1965, RG 166 Foreign Agricultural Service, NACP.

81. Ibid.

82. "Fertilizer Industry," May 20, 1962, USAID/Taipei to AID/Washington, box 307, folder "Economic Conditions Quarterly-Foodstuffs," page 5, narrative reports 1962–65, RG 166 Foreign Agricultural Service, NACP.

83. Ibid.

84. Ibid. Ron, *Grassroots Leviathan*.

85. Bruce Billings, "Bruce Hadley Billings Mimeograph: A Study of the Role of Science and Technology in Taiwan," 2, Bruce Hadley Billings Papers, box 8, folder 8, Hoover Institution Archives.

4. MARTYRS OF DEVELOPMENT: TAIWANESE AGRARIAN DEVELOPMENT AND THE REPUBLIC OF VIETNAM, 1959–1975

Epigraph: Chiang Kai-shek, president of the Republic of China, in a telegram to Nguyễn Văn Thiệu, president of the Republic of Vietnam. Telegram to His Excellency Nguyen Van Thieu, 館藏號 archive number 020-011099-0045-0134a, 冊 folder "越南雜卷（二十三），" 全宗 Collection 外交部 (Ministry of Foreign Affairs), Academia Historica Archives 國史館, Taipei, Taiwan.

1. Telegram, November 14, 1963, 館藏號 archival collection number 020-011004-0101, 冊 folder "駐越農技團工作及協助華僑籌建紗廠及張篤生遇難等案"; 全宗 collection 外交部 (Ministry of Foreign Affairs), 中央研究院近代史研究所 Academia Sinica Modern History Institute Archives, Taiwan.

2. "Condolence to Tusun Chang," *Cheng Hsin Daily News*, Taipei, November 17, 1963. Translated document located in folder 842—Bản dịch các bài báo Taiwan liên quan đến cái chết của ông Tu-Sun-Chang, thành viên phái đoàn kĩ thuật canh nông Trung Hoa Dân Quốc đến Việt Nam năm 1963 [Translation of Taiwan newspapers concerned about the death of Tusun Chang], Nha Canh Nông (Directorate of Agriculture), Vietnam National Archives II, Ho Chi Minh City.

3. The ROC had several groups of military officials and advisors to the RVN following a 1960 meeting between Chiang Kai-shek and Ngô Đình Diệm. For more details, see Lin, *Taihai Lengzhan Jiemi Dang'an*, 288–91.

4. This was a sentiment relayed via the US embassy in Taipei and not a direct quote of Chiang's words. Telegram, "President Appreciation for Actions of Non-Communist Asian Peoples in Vietnam," July 27, 1965, #13, "China," box 238, country file, NSF, LBJ Library.

5. Garver, *The Sino-American Alliance*.

6. Lin, "Lengzhan shiqi Taiwan yu Yuenan de guanxi."

7. Toner, "Imagining Taiwan."

8. Ibid., 782.

9. Mizuno, Moore, and DiMoia, *Engineering Asia*.

10. Miller, *Misalliance*, 72.

11. Ibid., 79.

12. Jiang Menglin to W. I. Myers, May 23, 1951, archive number 034000000351A, folder "Myers, W. I." in "Shen Zonghan Letter Drafts" [沈宗瀚文件稿], Council of Agriculture, Executive Yuan Collection [行政院農委會], Academia Historica Archives 國史館, Taipei, Taiwan (hereafter COA/EYC).

13. William H. Fippin to Shen Zonghan, August 31, 1957, archive number 034000000337A, Shen Zonghan Document Drafts (four boxes) [沈宗翰文件稿 (4箱)], folder "Fippin, W. F.," COA/EYC.

14. Original source: "與美援署USOM之農業方面主持人菲平及越南農林部部長 Le Van Dong商談。目前USOM已備有三十餘萬美金可資聘請外籍農業專家二三十人前來指導協助." "Agricultural Technicians in Vietnam," April 4, 1959, "駐越農技團," archive number 入藏登錄號 020000030452A, Ministry of Foreign Affairs Collection, Academia Historica Archives.

15. Original source: "菲平因在台多年，與我國內額多農業界人士相處甚洽，極力主張向我方聘請。越南農林部長則有意聘法供人." "Agricultural Technicians in Vietnam," April 4, 1959, "駐越農技團," archive number 入藏登錄號 020000030452A, Ministry of Foreign Affairs Collection, Academia Historica Archives.

16. Original source: "À apporter des revenus à la population rurale . . . reconnaît aussi la valeur des programmes à longue portée de recherches et d'éducation." Programme de la Commission Mixte Pour la Reconstruction Rurale en Chine [Program of the joint commission on rural reconstruction in China], 1949, folder 02—Tài liệu về chương trình tái thiết nông thôn Trung Quốc năm 1948–1949 (Documents of the Rural Reconstruction Plan in China 1948–1949), Bộ Công Chánh và Giao Thông (Ministry of Public Works and Transportation), Trung Tâm Lưu Trữ Quốc Gia II [National Archives Center II], Ho Chi Minh City.

17. Original source: "Car l'expérience avait montré qu'en Asie, il était difficile, au moins au début, de depenser de grosses sommes rapidement et de façon raisonnable (sagement). Au contraire, c'est un programme vivant, dynamique, qui a commencé par chercher à trouver ce qui est nécessaire à une famille ordinaire d'agriculteurs." Programme de la Commission Mixte Pour la Reconstruction Rurale en Chine [Program of the Joint Commission on Rural Reconstruction in China], 1949, folder 02—Tài liệu về chương trình tái thiết nông thôn Trung Quốc năm 1948–1949 (Documents of the Rural Reconstruction Plan in China 1948–1949), Bộ Công Chánh và Giao Thông (Ministry of Public Works and Transportation), Trung Tâm Lưu Trữ Quốc Gia II [National Archives Center II], Ho Chi Minh City.

18. Stewart, "Hearts, Minds and Công Dân Vụ"; Miller, *Misalliance*, 233.

19. William H. Fippin to Shen Zonghan, August 31, 1957, archive number 034000000337A, Shen Zonghan Document Drafts (4 boxes) [沈宗翰文件稿 (4箱)], folder "Fippin, W. F.," COA/EYC.

20. Sneddon, *Concrete Revolution*; Moore, "Japanese Development Consultancies and Postcolonial Power in Southeast Asia."

21. William H. Fippin to Shen Zonghan, August 31, 1957, archive number 034000000337A, Shen Zonghan Document Drafts (4 boxes) [沈宗翰文件稿 (4箱)], folder "Fippin, W. F.," COA/EYC.

22. "對外宣傳彩色專刊—中日經濟簡訊、先鋒計畫第三國訓練," April 1975, folder "中華民國對外技術合作," volume 2, 館藏號 (Archival Collection Number) 36-01-006-025, Academia Sinica Modern History Institutes Archives, Taipei, Taiwan.

23. July 15, 1933, announcement of the Graduate School, official publication of Cornell University, 25:141, Cornell University Library; July 15, 1934, announcement of the Graduate School, official publication of Cornell University, 26:157, Cornell University Library.

24. September 26, 1964. "越南農村改進部官員來華考察肥料配銷," archival collection number 館藏號 020-011002-0087-0015a, Ministry of Foreign Affairs Collection, Academia Historica, Taiwan.

25. Tài liệu của phái bộ kĩ thuật Trung Hoa dân quốc ở Việt Nam về việc sản xuất lúa giống ở Việt Nam năm 1960 [Recommendations of the Chinese technical team in Vietnam on rice production 1960], February 1960, folder 1313, Nha Canh Nông (Directorate of Agriculture), Trung Tâm Lưu Trữ Quốc Gia II [National Archives Center II], Ho Chi Minh City.

26. Ibid., 21.

27. CATM was later changed to the Chinese Agricultural Technical Group (CATG).

28. Tran and Kajisa, "The Impact of Green Revolution on Rice Production in Vietnam."

29. Cullather, *The Hungry World*; Shiva, *The Violence of the Green Revolution*.

30. James P. Grant to Shen Zonghan, November 25, 1968, archive number 034000000339A, folder "G" in "Shen Zonghan Letter Drafts" [沈宗瀚文件稿], COA/EYC.

31. July 1, 1968. "駐越農技團第四年度工作報告," archival collection number 館藏號 020-011004-0102, Ministry of Foreign Affairs Collection, Academia Historica, Taiwan.

32. Biggs, "Americans in An Giang."

33. July 1, 1968. "駐越農技團第四年度工作報告," archival collection number 館藏號 020-011004-0102, Ministry of Foreign Affairs Collection, Academia Historica, Taiwan.

34. July 1, 1968. "駐越農技團第四年度工作報告," archival collection number 館藏號 020-011004-0102, Ministry of Foreign Affairs Collection, Academia Historica, Taiwan.

35. September 26, 1964. "越南農村改進部官員來華考察肥料配銷," archival collection number 館藏號 020-011002-0087-0015a, Ministry of Foreign Affairs Collection, Academia Historica, Taiwan.

36. Tài liệu của phái bộ kĩ thuật Trung Hoa dân quốc ở Việt Nam về việc sản xuất lúa giống ở Việt Nam năm 1960 [Recommendations of the Chinese technical team in Vietnam on rice production 1960], February 1960, page 21, folder 1313, Nha Canh Nông (Directorate of Agriculture), Trung Tâm Lưu Trữ Quốc Gia II [National Archives Center II], Ho Chi Minh City.

37. Original source: "越南之農業環境，耕作方法以及風俗習慣，大體與台灣相近，識者均認為發展農業必須以台灣為借鏡." 張廉駿 (Zhang Lianjun), "十二年在越南 (Shi'er Nian Zai Yuenan) [Twelve years in Vietnam]," 中國農村復興聯合委員會業刊 (Zhongguo Fuxing Nongcun Lianhe Weiyuanhui Yekan), June 1973.

38. Immerwahr, *Thinking Small*; Stewart, *Vietnam's Lost Revolution*.

39. "Agricultural Technicians in Vietnam," April 3, 1959, "駐越農技團," archive number 入藏登錄號 020000030452A, Ministry of Foreign Affairs Collection, Academia Historica Archives.

40. Tài liệu của văn phòng phó Tổng Thống, bộ Công Chánh và giao thông về chương trình hoạt động của chuyên viên Đài Loan về hiệp hội nông dân và giai đoạn thực hành các cấp hiệp hội nông dân liên hệ đến bộ Công Chánh năm 1959, October 27, 1959, folder 202, Bộ Công Chánh và Giao Thông (Ministry of Public Works and Transportation), Trung Tâm Lưu Trữ Quốc Gia II [National Archives Center II], Ho Chi Minh City.

41. Ibid.

42. Original source: "工作接觸階層甚廣，包括中央與地方，至最底層之鄉鎮農會," Memo from Ministry of Foreign Affairs to deputy minister of economic affairs, April 9, 1959, "駐越農技團," archive number 入藏登錄號 020000030452A, Ministry of Foreign Affairs Collection, Academia Historica Archives.

43. Ibid.

44. Original source: "以生產農貨." Memo from Ministry of Foreign Affairs to deputy minister of economic affairs, April 9, 1959, "駐越農技團," archive number 入藏登錄號 020000030452A, Ministry of Foreign Affairs Collection, Academia Historica Archives.

45. Original source: "工作人員無需高深學歷，然而需有長期在農會等有關機構服務卻有廣泛實際管理農會等有關機構之實際工作經驗." Memo from Ministry of Foreign Affairs to deputy minister of economic affairs, April 9, 1959, "駐越農技團," archive number 入藏登錄號 020000030452A, Ministry of Foreign Affairs Collection, Academia Historica Archives.

46. April 1965. "嚴家淦總統數位照片—臺灣農技團在越南工作成果," archival collection number 館藏號 006-030202-00011-001, Yan Jiagan Papers, Academia Historica, Taiwan.

47. Interview by author with Zhang Jiming, retired agricultural technician, Taichung, Taiwan, January 14, 2019.

48. Rosenberg, *The 4-H Harvest*.

49. Hsiung, *Living Rooms as Factories*.

50. Interview by author with Zhang Jiming, retired agricultural technician, Taichung, Taiwan, January 14, 2019.

51. Original source: "敬祝越南共和國農村繁榮農民康樂." January 27, 1973, "我緊急支援越南農作物種子及肥料," archival collection number 館藏號 020-011008-0007, Ministry of Foreign Affairs Collection, Academia Historica, Taiwan.

52. May 10, 1973. "我緊急支援越南農作物種子及肥料," archival collection number 館藏號 020-011008-0007, Ministry of Foreign Affairs Collection, Academia Historica, Taiwan.

53. "農夫會定期追悼張篤生," 聯合報 *United Daily News*, November 20, 1963.

54. Shen Zonghan to Austin B. Sanford, April 26, 1968, archive number 國藏號 034000000357A, folder "S" in 沈宗瀚文件稿, COA/EYC. Shen Zonghan to Willie Cook, April 26, 1968, archive number 034000000330A, folder "C" in 沈宗瀚文件稿, COA/EYC.

55. "News releases regarding death of JCRR technicians by Vietcong snipers," office memorandum, December 2, 1963, from the Chinese Technical Mission to Vietnam on crop improvement to Doan Minh Quan, chief, Rice Service, folder 842—Bản dịch các bài báo Taiwan liên quan đến cái chết của ông Tu-Sun-Chang, thành viên phái đoàn kĩ thuật canh nông Trung Hoa Dân Quốc đến Việt Nam năm 1963, Nha Canh Nông (Directorate of Agriculture), Vietnam National Archives II, Ho Chi Minh City.

56. "張篤生在越殉職," 聯合報 *United Daily News*, November 16, 1963.

57. "Condolence to Tusun Chang," *Cheng Hsin Daily News*, Taipei, November 17, 1963. Translated document located in folder 842—Bản dịch các bài báo Taiwan liên quan đến cái chết của ông Tu-Sun-Chang, thành viên phái đoàn kĩ thuật canh nông Trung Hoa Dân Quốc đến Việt Nam năm 1963 (Translation of Taiwan newspapers concerned about the death of Tusun Chang), Nha Canh Nông (Directorate of Agriculture), Vietnam National Archives II, Ho Chi Minh City.

58. Bergère, *Sun Yat-Sen*; Soon, "Science, Medicine, and Confucianism in the Making of China and Southeast Asia."

59. Kung, *Diasporic Cold Warriors*, 2.

60. Mok, "Negotiating Community and Nation in Chợ Lớn," 89.

61. Ibid., 92.

62. Ibid., 19.

63. July 14, 1960. "駐越農技團 (I)," archive collection number 館藏號 020000030452A. Ministry of Foreign Affairs Collection. Academia Historica, Taiwan.

64. July 14, 1960. "駐越農技團 (I)," archive collection number 館藏號 020000030452A. Ministry of Foreign Affairs Collection. Academia Historica, Taiwan.

65. Original source: "將來除供應本國飼料之需要外，並可擴展為出口作物," May 10, 1973, "我緊急支援越南農作物種子及肥料 ," archival collection number 館藏號 020-011008–0007, Ministry of Foreign Affairs Collection, Academia Historica, Taiwan.

66. While Diệm was well known as a devout Catholic, he was also exposed to Confucianism early on as a result of his friendship with a fellow nationalist activist and Confucian scholar, Phan Bội Châu. Confucianism was a common ground for many of the models considered by Diệm and other anticolonial activists who looked to Confucianism and to post-Meiji Japan as potential models for postcolonial Asian nationhood. Miller, *Misalliance*, 28.

67. Tran, "Contested Identities," 92.

68. "Asian Peoples' Anti-Communist Conference, Minutes of the Opening Session," June 15, 1954, History and Public Policy Program Digital Archive, B-387–039, documents related to the Asian Anti-Communist League Conference, papers related to treaty-making and international conferences, Syngman Rhee Institute, Yonsei University, http://digital archive.wilsoncenter.org/document/118328.

69. Tran, "Contested Identities," 92.

70. "Việt-Nam và Trung-Hoa là 2 dân-tộc cùng chung một nền văn-hoá, mà nền văn-hoá đó ngày nay đang đi Cộng-sản tàn phá," Hồ sơ về việc Tổng Thống Việt Nam CH viếng thăm Đài Loan năm 1960, undated (1960?), folder 1161, Bộ Công Chánh và Giao Thông (Ministry of Public Works and Transportation), Trung Tâm Lưu Trữ Quốc Gia II [National Archives Center II], Ho Chi Minh City.

71. Hồ sơ về việc Tổng Thống Việt Nam CH viếng thăm Đài Loan năm 1960, undated (1960?), folder 1161, Bộ Công Chánh và Giao Thông (Ministry of Public Works and Transportation), Trung Tâm Lưu Trữ Quốc Gia II [National Archives Center II], Ho Chi Minh City.

72. Hồ sơ về việc Tổng Thống Việt Nam CH viếng thăm Đài Loan năm 1960, undated (1960?), folder 1161, Bộ Công Chánh và Giao Thông (Ministry of Public Works and Transportation), Trung Tâm Lưu Trữ Quốc Gia II [National Archives Center II], Ho Chi Minh City.

73. Miller, *Misalliance*, 46.

74. Personalism also became the organizing principle for the Cao Lan organization that served to organize Diệm's grassroots political support. Chapman, *Cauldron of Resistance*, 71.

75. Tan, "Spiritual Fraternities"; Nguyen, "A Secular State for a Religious Nation."

76. Miller, *Misalliance*, 46.

77. Stewart, *Vietnam's Lost Revolution*, 99.

78. Ibid., 100.

79. Picard, "'Fertile Lands Await,'" 84–86.

80. Bergère, *Sun Yat-Sen*, 353.

81. Tan, "Spiritual Fraternities."

82. "Agricultural Technicians in Vietnam," April 3, 1959, "駐越農技團," archive number 入藏登錄號 020000030452A, Ministry of Foreign Affairs Collection, Academia Historica Archives.

83. Contract evaluation, May 3, 1972, folder 3832—hồ sơ kiểm soát ngân khoản hợp đồng với phái bộ hợp tác tái thiết nông thôn- Trung Quốc về yểm trợ tổng quát canh nông cho Việt Nam năm 1969–1973, Cơ quan phát triển quốc tế Hoa Kỳ, Trung Tâm Lưu Trữ Quốc Gia II [National Archives Center II], Ho Chi Minh City.

84. Auditing report of JCRR, November 14, 1970, folder 3832—hồ sơ kiểm soát ngân khoản hợp đồng với phái bộ hợp tác tái thiết nông thôn- Trung Quốc về yểm trợ tổng quát canh nông cho Việt Nam năm 1969–1973, Cơ quan phát triển quốc tế Hoa Kỳ, Trung Tâm Lưu Trữ Quốc Gia II [National Archives Center II], Ho Chi Minh City.

85. November 13, 1971. "駐越農技團," archival number 入藏登錄號 020000030454A. Ministry of Foreign Affairs Collection, Academia Historica Archives, Taipei, Taiwan.

5. "STRAW HAT DIPLOMATS": TAIWANESE AGRARIAN DEVELOPMENT AND AFRICA, 1961–1971

Epigraphs: Zhou Enlai (1898–1976), premier of the People's Republic of China, in a 1955 speech to the Bandung Conference, "Main Speech by Premier Zhou Enlai, Head of the Delegation of the People's Republic of China, Distributed at the Plenary Session of the Asian-African Conference," History and Public Policy Program Digital Archive, 1955, http://digitalarchive.wilsoncenter.org/document/121623. Shen Chang-huan, ROC minister of foreign affairs, to the 1309th Plenary Meeting of the UN General Assembly, December 21, 1964, "General Assembly, 19th Session: 1309th Plenary Meeting, Monday, 21 December 1964, New York," 1966, 8, https://digitallibrary.un.org/record/749200.

1. "ROC Flag-Raising Ceremony Held at Twin Oaks in D. C., First Time in 36 Years," Kuomintang News Network, accessed February 1, 2016, http://www1.kmt.org.tw1.

2. Eventually, these technical assistance missions abroad became institutionalized under a separate entity, the International Cooperation and Development Fund.

3. The most thorough analysis of the Vanguard missions comes from Philip Hsiao-pong Liu's (劉曉鵬) doctoral dissertation, a diplomatic history of the Vanguard missions to Africa; see Liu, "The Making of an Artificial Power." Liu also authored an article in the *China Quarterly* derived from his dissertation, "Planting Rice on the Roof of the UN Building." In the Chinese language literature, historian Wang Wen-lung (王文隆) has similarly written of the Vanguard missions to Africa; see Wang, *Waijiao Xiaxiang, Nongye Chuyang*. Development in Africa has been examined by scholars such as Deborah Brautigam, Jamie Monson, Ching Kwan Lee, and Gregg Brazinsky, but those are limited to the PRC. See Brautigam, *Chinese Aid and African Development*; Monson, *Africa's Freedom Railway*; Lee, *The Specter of Global China*; and Brazinsky, *Winning the Third World*. Geography scholars Kathleen Baker, Richard Edmonds, and Shiuh-Shen Chien have written about more contemporary Taiwanese overseas development assistance but have not discussed these from a historical perspective. See Baker and Edmonds, "Transfer of Taiwanese Ideas and Technology to the Gambia, West Africa"; and Chien, Yang, and Wu, "Taiwan's Foreign Aid and Technical Assistance in the Marshall Islands."

4. "United Nations Security Council Document S/1462; Letter Dated 21 February 1950 From the Representative of Yugoslavia to the Secretary-General," accessed February 8, 2016, http://digitallibrary.un.org/. See also Cohen and Chiu, *People's China and International Law*, 270–71; and Goodwin, Mahon, and Stauffer, *Foreign Relations of the United States 1950*, 267–68.

5. United Nations, "1668 (XVI). Representation of China in the United Nations," in *Official Records of the General Assembly, Sixteenth Session: Annexes*, 66, accessed February 7, 2016, http://digitallibrary.un.org/.

6. Memos Vol. 2, "US ROC Relations," 2/15/65, #73a, "China," NSF, box 238, country file, LBJ Presidential Library, Austin, Texas.

7. Memos Vol. 2, "US ROC Relations," 2/15/65, #73a, "China," NSF, box 238, country file, LBJ Presidential Library, Austin, Texas.

8. Chien, Yang, and Wu, "Taiwan's Foreign Aid and Technical Assistance."

9. Original source: "外交是外交，我們做的是實際的工作." Peng Ruiduan, retired Taiwanese agricultural technician, interview by author, January 12, 2019, Hualien, Taiwan.

10. Original source: "開墾工作：係將預定區城內的叢林，沼澤，荒野，和丘陵地予以開墾，使成為可作農耕之用的田地。試驗工作：根據當地氣候，水源，土環等自然環境，進行品種，植期，施肥量及栽培方法等之比較試驗，用以選擇優良品種，決定適當植期與妥善栽培方法，以供示範推廣只用。示範工作：將優良品種，用適當的栽培技術，新的農業器材作示範栽培，以顯示增產效果，耕觀摩會的舉行來引發當地農民的興趣並建立他們的信心。訓練工作：我駐非農耕隊採用「做中學習」的方法，在耕作現場上，用實際操作的方式，指導非洲農民使用農機具，熟悉我們的栽培技術。推廣工作：是把試驗示範和各階段所獲得的農業生產技術與經驗，鼓勵非洲農民實際採用以改善農民的生活和農業的發展." April 1975, "中華民國對外技術合作" folder "對外宣傳彩色專刊—中日經濟簡訊、先鋒計畫第三國訓練" volume 冊 2, archival collection number 館藏號 36-01-006-025, Academia Sinica Institute of Modern History Archives, Taipei, Taiwan.

11. Interview by author with Chen Shengyi, retired agricultural technician, Taichung, Taiwan, December 22, 2017. Interview by author with Shi Minnan, retired agricultural technician, Kaohsiung, Taiwan, December 21, 2017.

12. Xikun Yang, 楊西崑訪非歸來談話 [A discussion after Yang Xikun's return from Africa], Audio CD, 2011.

13. Original Chinese of quote in the text: "非洲工作非常艱苦的." Ibid.

14. Peng Ruiduan, retired Taiwanese agricultural technician, interview with author, January 12, 2019, Hualien, Taiwan.

15. Interview by author with Wu Lingde, retired agricultural technician, Kaohsiung, Taiwan, December 21, 2017. Interview by author with Chen Shengyi, retired agricultural technician, Taichung, Taiwan, December 22, 2017.

16. Chen Xindian, retired Taiwanese agricultural technician, interview with author, January 13, 2019, Hualien, Taiwan.

17. Peng Ruiduan, retired Taiwanese agricultural technician, interview with author, January 12, 2019, Hualien, Taiwan.

18. Ibid.

19. Saraiva, "California Cloning in French Algeria."

20. Wang, "Straw Hat Diplomats."

21. Ibid.

22. Compare this figure to 181,693 rice threshers counted in 1962. Joint Commission on Rural Reconstruction, Rural Economics Division, *Taiwan Agricultural Statistics, 1961–1975* (Taipei, Taiwan: Chinese-American Joint Commission on Rural Reconstruction, 1977), 174.

23. L. C. Chu, "Free China Receives a Farmer-President," *Free China Review*, April 1, 1962.

24. Ibid.

25. Ibid.

26. Though scholars like Gillian Hart have noted that Taiwanese immigrants in later decades were often capitalists seeking to relocate their factories to areas where lower wages prevailed. Hart, *Disabling Globalization*.

27. 劉治邦, "去薩哈拉沙漠種稻," 新聞天地 *Xinwen tiandi*, March 31, 1962.

28. Original source: "非洲地大物博，土壤肥沃，都具有發展農業的優良條件，也就是說具有建立富強國家的基本條件" 中非農技合作討論會 [Sino-African Agricultural Technical Cooperation Conference], July 16, 1965, page 1828, archive number 020000039124A, Ministry of Foreign Affairs Collection, Academia Historica.

29. Original source: "如果能在農業技術上加以研究改進，則非洲各友邦之前途實不可限量" 中非農技合作討論會 [Sino-African Agricultural Technical Cooperation Conference], July 16, 1965, page 1828, archive number 020000039124A, Ministry of Foreign Affairs Collection, Academia Historica.

30. Original source: "貢獻所有之農業知識，經驗及技術 ... 在一個共同願望及目標之下，協助非洲友邦充分運用自己的人力，智慧和資源，增加生產，改善環境，提高國民生活水準" 中非農技合作討論會 [Sino-African Agricultural Technical Cooperation Conference], July 16, 1965, page 1828, archive number 020000039124A, Ministry of Foreign Affairs Collection, Academia Historica.

31. 中非農技合作討論會 [Sino-African Agricultural Technical Cooperation Conference], July 16, 1965, page 1866, archive number 020000039124A, Ministry of Foreign Affairs Collection, Academia Historica.

32. For more on the Sino-US and Sino-Soviet competition for the Third World, see, respectively, Brazinsky, *Winning the Third World*; and Friedman, *Shadow Cold War*.

33. 中非農技合作討論會 [Sino-African Agricultural Technical Cooperation Conference], July 16, 1965, page 1866, archive number 020000039124A, Ministry of Foreign Affairs Collection, Academia Historica.

34. For a history of these ideas within PRC agricultural development, see Schmalzer, *Red Revolution*.

35. 中非農技合作討論會 [Sino-African Agricultural Technical Cooperation Conference], July 16, 1965, page 1868, archive number 020000039124A, Ministry of Foreign Affairs Collection, Academia Historica.

36. Ibid.

37. Ibid., 1872.

38. Ibid.

39. Ibid.

40. Ibid., 1873–74.

41. "Project Agreement between the Department of States, Agency for International Development, and the Ministry of Foreign Affairs, an Agency to the Government of the

Republic of China," November 25, 1969, archive number 055–431–3-0009, folder 中美資源交換計畫先鋒案部分, Taiwan National Archives Administration (國家發展委員會檔案管理局), Taipei, Taiwan.

42. "Yang, Hsi-kun (Yang, H. K.)," 1973, box 13, folder "Visits 1973," Bureau of East Asia and Pacific Affairs, Office of ROC Affairs, 1951–1978, Records of the State Department, RG 59, NACP. Yang was also a proponent of a "Chinese Republic of Taiwan" in the aftermath of UN Resolution 2758, an attempt to find a solution to Taiwan's loss of international status. Chen Yi-Shen, "戰後台灣「外省」菁英的台獨主張－從雷震到張忠棟的類型分析," 文史台灣學報, no. 12 (September 2018): 81–104.

43. Original source: "不僅為中國人民與非洲人民建立了史無前例 . . . 而且還糾正了由於毛匪侵略成性，滲透顛覆的劣跡在非洲所造成對中國人民的錯誤印象." Zhang Lixing 張力行, *Yang Xikun yu Feizhou* 楊西崑與非洲 [Yang Xikun and Africa]. Taipei: Zhonghua Wenwu Publishers [中華文物出版社], undated, 2.

44. Original source: "克勤克儉是我們中國人的傳統美德，也是創立任何事業的必要條件。我們在非洲工作，也必須牢記這一點。非洲國家，跟我們中國一樣，都是發展中的國家，我們一方面固然要【勤】，另一方面也必須要【儉】。。。我們在非洲為非洲友邦服務，隨時要把握我一個原則，那就是，花最少的錢以求收到最大的效果。只有這樣，我們能做的事，在我們一旦離開非洲以後，非洲友邦也能做，這是一點不錯的." Zhang Lixing 張力行. *Yang Xikun yu Feizhou* 楊西崑與非洲 [Yang Xikun and Africa]. Taipei: Zhonghua Wenwu Publishers [中華文物出版社], undated, page 8.

45. Original source: "我們也是一個開發中的國家，這幾年來，我們居然能夠參加其他開發中國家的經濟建設，特別在農業增產方面，能為非洲友邦人民服務，得到他們如此的信任，並獲得國內外如此熱烈的支持和讚譽，這應該是各位從事農業工作者在職業上所能希望得到的最高光榮." Zhang Lixing 張力行. Yang Xikun yu Feizhou 楊西崑與非洲 [Yang Xikun and Africa]. Taipei: Zhonghua Wenwu Publishers [中華文物出版社], undated, page 6.

46. Liu, "Planting Rice on the Roof of the UN Building," 391.

47. See, for example, Lee, *Gourmets in the Land of Famine.*

48. Liu, "Planting Rice on the Roof of the UN Building," 390.

49. Ibid., 392.

50. Memos, vol. 2, "US ROC Relations," February 15, 1965, #73a, box 238, "China" country file, NSF, LBJ Presidential Library, Austin, Texas.

51. "Meeting on October 14 with Dr. Caton," folder "Comments and Reports—Bruce Billings," Bruce Billings Personal Papers.

52. Ibid.

53. 中美資源交換計畫先鋒案部分 [Sino-American Resource Exchange Plan Vanguard Section], December 10, 1966, archive number 055–431–3-0009, Taiwan (ROC) National Archives 檔案管理局.

54. "Meeting on October 14 with Dr. Caton," folder "Comments and Reports—Bruce Billings," Bruce Billings Personal Papers.

55. Ferguson, *The Anti-Politics Machine.*

56. Cable, "Nationalist China's Position in the UN," April 16, 1964, #68, box 237, "China" country file, NSF, LBJ Presidential Library, Austin, Texas.

57. "The Taiwan Situation," April 15, 1965, Memo, #14, box 15, "China GRC 1964–1965–1966," Komer Files, NSF, LBJ Presidential Library, Austin, Texas.

6. CAPITALISM WITH SOCIALIST CHARACTERISTICS: THE LAND REFORM TRAINING INSTITUTE, 1968–1979

Epigraphs: Zedong Mao, *Selected Works of Mao Tsetung*, 1st ed., vol. 5 (Peking: Foreign Languages Press, 1977), 202. Dwight D. Eisenhower, address at a mass rally in Taipei, the American Presidency Project, https://www.presidency.ucsb.

1. S. K. Shen, Report to the Tenth Annual Meeting of the Board of Directors, October 20, 1978, Land Reform Training Institute, Land Reform Training Institute Library.

2. Based on my conversations with archivists at both the University of Hartford and the LRTI, I have been informed that I was the first to access both archival collections in their terms as employees of the institution. I borrow the term *rescue history* from Prasenjit Duara, who coined it in his historiographical book exploring the interpretation of history for nationalistic purposes. Duara, *Rescuing History from the Nation*.

3. Here, I borrow the term *keys* from Paul Cohen, whose innovative exploration of the Boxer Rebellion through three "keys" also explores the ways in which history is utilized and understood. Cohen, *History in Three Keys*.

4. Brown, "World Land Reform Conference."

5. Ibid., 92.

6. Ibid., 97.

7. Ibid., 109.

8. Immerwahr, *Thinking Small*, 4.

9. Brown, "World Land Reform Conference," 109–10.

10. Ibid., 120.

11. Chinese Delegation to the United Nations, "Land Reform in the Republic of China," 304.

12. Ibid., 304.

13. Ibid., 307.

14. Ibid., 319.

15. Scott, *Seeing Like a State*.

16. Chinese Delegation to the United Nations, "Land Reform in the Republic of China," 309–11.

17. Emmons, "Classic Cases Live on at HBS."

18. Ibid.

19. "The Lincoln Foundation," 1963, page 8, box 1, Lincoln Institute Collection, University of Hartford Archives.

20. Moley, *The American Century of John C. Lincoln*, 153.

21. Ibid., 163.

22. "The Lincoln Foundation," 1963, page 7, box 1, Lincoln Institute Collection, University of Hartford Archives.

23. Ibid., 8.

24. Bryson, *The Economics of Henry George*.

25. Quoted in Bryson, *The Economics of Henry George*, 6.

26. George, *Progress and Poverty*, 234.

27. Ibid., 240.

28. Ibid., 246–47.

29. Ibid., 288.

30. Ibid., 288–89.

31. Ibid., 320.

32. Ibid., 322.

33. Ibid., 320.

34. Kaila White, "The Lincoln Legacy," *Phoenix Magazine*, April 1, 2012, https://www.phoenixmag.com/2012/04/01/the-lincoln-legacy/.

35. Lincoln Institute of Land Policy, "About the Lincoln Institute of Land Policy," accessed May 13, 2015, https://www.lincolninst.edu/.

36. Ennis, "Dr. A. M. Woodruff, Economist."

37. Theodore Smith (land economist), in telephone interview with author, September 22, 2020.

38. Woodruff, "A Comparison between Henry George and Karl Marx," 1.

39. Ibid., 4.

40. Ibid., 13.

41. Ibid., 18.

42. Ibid. 9.

43. Ibid., 9.

44. Ibid., 9–10.

45. Ibid., 19.

46. Ibid., 21.

47. Ibid. 22.

48. James R. Brown's aforementioned report from the 1966 World Land Reform Conference was presented here at this Hartford Seminar, whose papers were later compiled and published in a volume by the University of Hartford.

49. Wei-ping Shen, in discussion with author, January 11, 2020, Taipei, Taiwan.

50. Theodore Smith (land economist), in telephone interview with author, September 22, 2020.

51. Wei-ping Shen, in discussion with author, January 11, 2020, Taipei, Taiwan.

52. Shen and Zhang, *Taiwan tudi gaige wenji.*

53. Woodruff et al., *International Seminar on Land Taxation*, 305–6.

54. Ibid., 305.

55. Ibid., 323–30.

56. "Comparison of Socio-Economic Structures in Taiwan and India, Effects of Land Reform," 1984, box 1, Lincoln Institute Collection, University of Hartford Archives.

57. Woodruff et al., *International Seminar on Land Taxation*, 351.

58. See, for example, the importance of the Japanese legacy in Shen and Zhang, *Taiwan tu di gai ge wen ji*, 18.

59. Woodruff et al., *International Seminar on Land Taxation*, 352.

60. Ibid., 352.

61. Ibid.

62. "俾使亦擬從事土地改革或已實施土地改革發生困難之國家，均可派員前來從事研究," April 8, 1968, report by Shen Shike to Huang Jie, chairman of the Taiwan Provincial Government, archive number 00502011309, Taiwan Provincial Government Committee Meeting Records, Taiwan Provincial Government Historical Records, Academia Historica, Digital Archives Taiwan. 典藏號:00502011309。臺灣省府委員會議等會議檔案, 國史館臺灣文獻館, 國史館, 典藏台灣。

63. Land Reform Training Institute Eighth Annual Meeting, October 15, 1976, Land Reform Training Institute Archives.

64. James C. Riddell, former Instructor with the Land Reform Training Institute and former Chief of the Land Tenure Service of the Food and Agriculture Organization, interview by author, May 13, 2013, Taoyuan, Taiwan.

65. "Second Annual Report," July 7, 1970, page 9, Land Reform Training Institute Archives.

66. "What Is the Land Reform Training Institute?," undated (1971?), page 11, Land Reform Training Institute Archives.

67. "Mary S. Wilson, 90," *Hartford Courant*, May 29, 1999, http://articles.courant.com.

68. Wilson, "Suggestions for LRTI" (draft manuscript), undated (1972), page 4, box 1, folder "Land Reform," Lincoln Institute Collection, University of Hartford Archives. Final draft in Alan S. Wilson, "A Report to the Board of Directors of the Land Reform Training Institute," undated (1972), Land Reform Training Institute Archives.

69. "What is the Land Reform Training Institute?," undated (1971?), page 17, Land Reform Training Institute Archives.

70. Shen Shike, "Third Annual Meeting," May 16, 1971, pages 15–16, Land Reform Training Institute Archives.

71. Ibid., 4.

72. "What Is the Land Reform Training Institute?," undated (1971?), pages 34–35, Land Reform Training Institute Archives.

73. Shen Shike, "Second Annual Meeting," June 25, 1970, page 28, Land Reform Training Institute Archives.

74. "What Is the Land Reform Training Institute?," undated (1971?), page 23, Land Reform Training Institute Archives. Shen Shike, "Second Annual Meeting," June 25, 1970, page 8, Land Reform Training Institute Archives.

75. "Phiếu trình Thủ Tướng Chánh Phủ về việc phái đoàn Việt Nam quan sát công cuộc Cải Cách Điền Địa tại Đài Loan và phái đoàn Đài Loan quan sát công cuộc Cải Cách Diền Địa tại Việt Nam" [Report to the prime minister regarding Vietnamese delegation's observation of land reform in Taiwan and Taiwanese delegation's observation of land reform in Vietnam], September 24, 1970, folder 27033, Phủ Thủ Tướng [Office of the prime minister], Trung Tâm Lưu Trữ Quốc Gia II [National Archives Center II], Ho Chi Minh City.

76. Shen Shike, "Second Annual Meeting," July 7, 1970, Land Reform Training Institute Archives.

77. Hunt, *Pacification*, 190.

78. Conrad, "'Before It Is Too Late,'" 57.

79. "Phiếu trình Thủ Tướng Chánh Phủ về việc phái đoàn Việt Nam quan sát công cuộc Cải Cách Điền Địa tại Đài Loan và phái đoàn Đài Loan quan sát công cuộc Cải Cách Diền Địa tại Việt Nam" [Report to the prime minister regarding Vietnamese delegation's observation of land reform in Taiwan and Taiwanese delegation's observation of land reform in Vietnam], September 24, 1970, folder 27033, Phủ Thủ Tướng [Office of the prime minister], Trung Tâm Lưu Trữ Quốc Gia II [National Archives Center II], Ho Chi Minh City.

80. Lindholm, and Lin, *Henry George and Sun Yat-sen*, 5.

81. Xiao Zheng authored a short paper on the use of Georgist taxation principles in the German concession of Qingdao, whose progressive taxation polices were "vitally

important" but "unfortunately abolished" after the transfer of Qingdao to Japan in 1915. Lindholm and Lin, *Henry George and Sun Yat-sen*, 124.

82. Ibid., 4.

83. Li, *Economic Transformation of Taiwan*, 409.

84. Ibid., 402.

85. Theodore Smith (land economist), telephone interview with author, September 22, 2020.

86. Smith, *East Asian Agrarian Reform*.

87. Ibid., 17.

88. Ibid., 90.

89. Ibid., 102.

90. Ibid., 103.

91. David Perry and Associates. "Broadcast TV Pioneer & KTSF Owner Lillian Lincoln Howell Dies." September 9, 2014. https://www.davidperry.com.

92. Lincoln Institute of Land Policy, "In Memoriam . . . Arlo Woolery," accessed July 7, 2015, https://www.lincolninst.edu.

93. Tim Metzger and Makoto Fujita, dir., *Taiwan's Transformation: Winds of Change* (Dateline Productions, Inc., 1987).

94. Ibid.

7. GREEN DEVOLUTION: TAIWANESE VEGETABLE SCIENCE, NUTRITION, AND THE DEVELOPING WORLD, 1969–1989

Epigraphs: Bruce Hadley Billings, final American commissioner in the Joint Commission on Rural Reconstruction, "Bruce Hadley Billings Mimeograph: A Study of the Role of Science and Technology in Taiwan," 1973, page 2, Bruce Hadley Billings papers, folder 8, box 8, Hoover Institution Archives. Robert F. Chandler, first director of the Asian Vegetable Research and Development Center, to Lowell S. Hardin, May 16, 1972, reel L-250 L67–435, Ford Foundation Archives, New York, NY.

1. The Green Revolution has been a well-researched topic among historians, with John Perkins and Nick Cullather producing important works examining its ties to the Cold War and the political contexts for its agricultural; see Perkins, *Geopolitics and the Green Revolution*; and Cullather, *The Hungry World*. Seeing the Green Revolution as embedded within the Cold War stems from a larger trend within the history of science and science and technology studies (STS). Scientific thought, practice, and technology are often socially constructed, meaning they are influenced by their social and political environment and interpreted and shaped by their practitioners. Bruno Latour's actor-network theory is a useful framework for studying scientific networks during the Cold War producing new paradigms in agricultural science, as is Sheila Jasanoff and Sang-Hyun Kim's sociotechnical imaginary for how these scientists and modernists saw the Green Revolution as the future of human society. See Latour, *Science in Action*; Jasanoff and Kim, *Dreamscapes of Modernity*.

2. Connelly, *Fatal Misconception*.

3. The Green Revolution has been deeply criticized, particularly from environmental studies, for its production of monocultures, pollution of natural environments resulting

from its increased utilization of harmful chemicals, and giving rise to corporations like Monsanto that have patented sterile, high-yielding crops, thus producing dependencies. The Green Revolution and its accompanying development regime have upended traditional means of agriculture, seen among Green Revolutionaries as backward, resulting in a derision and rejection of indigenous methods of agriculture that have in some cases produced negative consequences, including increased poverty and class stratification. See Gupta, *Postcolonial Developments*; Patel, "The Long Green Revolution"; and Shiva, *The Violence of the Green Revolution*. Taiwan was not immune to the negative effects of the Green Revolution. Anthropologists have examined, for example, the dependency of rice farming on fertilizers and the subsequent environmental damage caused by the increased utilization of chemicals. Lo and Chen, "Technological Momentum and the Hegemony of the Green Revolution."

4. Gaud, "The Green Revolution."

5. Perkins, *Geopolitics and the Green Revolutio*; Cullather, *The Hungry World*.

6. The other major trend emerging in the 1970s was from the World Bank's focus on fighting poverty. See Sharma, *Robert McNamara's Other War*.

7. Lavelle, "Agricultural Improvement at China's First Agricultural Experiment Stations."

8. H. J. Teng to S. C. Hsieh, September 19, 1969, archive number 034000000342A, folder "Hsieh, S. C." in "Shen Zonghan Letter Drafts" [沈宗瀚文件稿], Council of Agriculture, Executive Yuan Collection [行政院農委會], Academia Historica Archives 國史館, Taipei, Taiwan (hereafter COA/EYC).

9. Taiwan Agricultural Research Institute Rice Research, November 1958, box 2, folder 11, series 605D, RG 1.2 Projects, Rockefeller Foundation, RAC.

10. Cullather, *The Hungry World*.

11. For more on the history of IRRI, see Cullather, *The Hungry World*.

12. Mew and McClung, "Shu-Huang Ou, 1912 to 2001."

13. Even though the Green Revolution implied a sudden innovation through the focus on semi-dwarfing high-yielding varieties, it continued a longstanding, and slower, evolution in human agriculture toward an industrialized, capitalist enterprise. See for example Isett and Miller, *The Social History of Agriculture*; and Mau, *Mute Compulsion*, 261–66.

14. Hedden, "The Genes of the Green Revolution."

15. "Beachell, Chang, Jennings Receive Scott Award," August 1969, archive number 034000000330A; folder "C" in "Shen Zonghan Letter Drafts" [沈宗瀚文件稿], COA/EYC.

16. T. T. Chang to Shen Zonghan. November 20, 1969, archive number 034000000330A, folder "C" in "Shen Zonghan Letter Drafts" [沈宗瀚文件稿], COA/EYC.

17. Huff, "Corporeal Economies."

18. Fu, *The Other Milk*, 5.

19. Cullather, *The Hungry World*, 19.

20. Tseng, "The Wartime Regime and the Development of Public Diet in Taiwan."

21. Food and Agriculture Organization of the United Nations, *Nutrition Problems of Rice-Eating Countries in Asia*.

22. Yang and Gleason, *Yeast-Feeding Demonstration in Selected Primary Schools*, 1.

23. Torula yeast can refer to a number of species, including *Cyberlindnera jadinii*, *Candida utilis*, among others. Historical sources refer to *Torulopsis utilis*. Chien et al., "Torula

Yeast Manufacturing"; and "Food Yeast Production," *Nutrition Reviews* 13, no. 5 (May 1955): 145, https://doi.org/10.1111/j.1753–4887.1955.tb03447.x.

24. Forest Products Laboratory, "Food-Yeast Production from Wood-Processing by Products," *U.S. Forest Service Research Note*, no. FPL-065 (November 1964): 34; Bunker, "The Wartime Production of Food Yeast in Germany," 145.

25. Huang, "Structural Change in Taiwan's Agricultural Economy."

26. J. L. Brent to Chia-chin Shao, December 2, 1955, archive number 典藏號 040–010417–0058, Council for Economic Planning and Development, Executive Yuan Collection [行政院經濟建設委員會], Academia Historica Archives 國史館, Taipei, Taiwan.

27. Chien et al., "Torula Yeast Manufacturing," 249.

28. Cullather, "'Fuel for the Good Dragon.'"

29. John Godston to H. C. Chien, June 13, 1959, archive number 典藏號 040–010417–0015, Council for Economic Planning and Development, Executive Yuan Collection [行政院經濟建設委員會], Academia Historica Archives 國史館, Taipei, Taiwan.

30. Huang, "Structural Change in Taiwan's Agricultural Economy," 47. C. T. Yang to V. de Beausset, January 9, 1956, archive number 典藏號 040–010417–0015, Council for Economic Planning and Development, Executive Yuan Collection [行政院經濟建設委員會], Academia Historica Archives 國史館, Taipei, Taiwan.

31. Liu, "Hog Island."

32. For more on de Beausset, refer to Cullather, "Fuel for the Good Dragon."

33. C. T. Yang to V. de Beausset, January 9, 1956, archive number 典藏號 040–010417–0015, Council for Economic Planning and Development, Executive Yuan Collection [行政院經濟建設委員會], Academia Historica Archives 國史館, Taipei, Taiwan.

34. Lee, *Gourmets in the Land of Famine.*

35. Yang and Gleason, *Yeast-Feeding Demonstration*, 3–4.

36. Ibid., 5.

37. For more on Yang, refer to Liu, "Guoji nongliang tizhi yu Taiwan de liangshi yilai," 139.

38. Yang and Gleason, *Yeast-Feeding Demonstration*, 6–7.

39. Ibid., 15–16.

40. Chien, "Free China's Big Protein Project."

41. Original source: "因為彩色外型，又帶點甜味，家長常買給小孩吃補充營養，從早期很克難的塑膠袋包裝，到現在的密封金屬罐，健素糖沒有打過廣告，卻已經存在了50年." "走過50年健素糖　台糖今早急下架" (TVBS, June 15, 2006), https://news.tvbs.com.tw/entry/361379.

42. Huang, "Structural Change in Taiwan's Agricultural Economy," 45.

43. Chart taken from Huang, "Structural Change in Taiwan's Agricultural Economy," 45.

44. W. I. Myers to Shen Zonghan, March 15, 1963, archive number 034000000351A, folder "Myers, W. I." in "Shen Zonghan Letter Drafts" [沈宗瀚文件稿], COA/EYC.

45. Huang, "Structural Change in Taiwan's Agricultural Economy," 49.

46. Ibid., 62.

47. Fletcher, *The AVRDC Story*, 23.

48. Eugene Black to David Bell, July 6, 1967, reel L-250 L67–435, Ford Foundation Archives, New York, NY.

49. "Chronicle of the AVRDC Project," January 1971, Asian Vegetable Center 1972, box 11, Bureau of East Asia and Pacific Affairs, Office of ROC Affairs, 1951–1978, records of the State Department, RG 59, NACP.

50. "Chronicle of the AVRDC Project," January 1971, Asian Vegetable Center 1972, box 11, Bureau of East Asia and Pacific Affairs, Office of ROC Affairs, 1951–1978, records of the State Department, RG 59, NACP.

51. Fletcher, *The AVRDC Story*, 23.

52. Luh, "The Institutions and Programs Responsible for Agricultural Development in Taiwan."

53. Asian Vegetable Research and Development Center, *Annual Report for 1974*, xvi.

54. "Conclusions of the Conference on the Establishment of the Asian Vegetable Development Center," folder "Asian Vegetable Research and Development Center 亞洲蔬菜研究發展中心," page 166, file number 檔號 36–16–006–023, Ministry of Economic Affairs Collection, Modern History Institute Archives at Academia Sinica.

55. Fletcher, *The AVRDC Story*, 32.

56. Ibid., 48.

57. Ibid., 44.

58. Raymond William to David A. Bell, April 17, 1975, reel L-250 L67–435, Ford Foundation Archives, New York, NY.

59. "Address by Chairman T. H. Shen at the Opening Session of the Conference on the Establishment of the Asian Vegetable Development Center," August 16, 1968, folder "Asian Vegetable Research and Development Center 亞洲蔬菜研究發展中心," page 175, file number 檔號 36–16–006–023, Ministry of Economic Affairs Collection, Modern History Institute Archives at Academia Sinica.

60. Fletcher, *The AVRDC Story*, 24.

61. Robert F. Chandler to Peter Oram, May 30, 1972, report on the Asian Vegetable Research and Development Centre, CGIAR Technical Advisory Committee (TAC) reports, documents and meeting agendas, https://hdl.handle.net/10947/1199.

62. Fletcher, *The AVRDC Story*, 66.

63. Ibid., 70.

64. Chu, "With and against the Grain."

65. It is unclear if this percentage reflected actual gendered divisions in Southeast Asia or if AVRDC planners specifically sought women due to their preexisting biases. Fletcher, *The AVRDC Story*, 70.

66. Kabeer, *Reversed Realities*.

67. Chu, "With and against the Grain."

68. "Memorandum on Establishment of Asian-Pacific Food and Fertilizer Bank," November 15, 1966, archive number 034000000327A, folder "Black, Eugene" in "Shen Zonghan Letter Drafts" [沈宗瀚文件稿], COA/EYC.

69. C. W. Braddick, "Japan, Australia and ASPAC."

70. "Memorandum on Establishment of Asian-Pacific Food and Fertilizer Bank," November 15, 1966, archive number 034000000327A, folder "Black, Eugene" in "Shen Zonghan Letter Drafts" [沈宗瀚文件稿], COA/EYC.

71. "Memorandum on Establishment of Asian-Pacific Food and Fertilizer Bank," November 15, 1966, archive number 034000000327A, folder "Black, Eugene" in "Shen Zonghan Letter Drafts" [沈宗瀚文件稿], COA/EYC.

72. "Meeting the Diplomats from the Nine Countries," February 20, 1967, folder 020000030288A (入藏登錄號020000030288A), Ministry of Foreign Affairs Collection, Academia Historica Archives.

73. T. H. Shen, review of "Rice Production," archive number 034000000342A, folder "Hsieh, S. C." in "Shen Zonghan Letter Drafts" [沈宗瀚文件稿], COA/EYC.

74. "Food Fertilizer and Technology Center," December 18, 1968, page 2, box 2, folder 2–1, Joint Commission on Rural Reconstruction Papers, Hoover Institute Archives, Stanford, CA.

75. "Annual Report of the Food and Fertilizer Technology Center for the Asia and Pacific Region for the period ending in December, 1970," page 5, Executive Board of the Center to the Sixth Ministerial Meeting of the Asia and Pacific Council, July 14–16, 1971, Food and Fertilizer Technology Center, Taipei, Taiwan.

76. Ibid., 10–12.

77. Ibid., 23–29.

78. Ibid., 30–31.

79. "Organizational Chart," Work Group, Food and Fertilizer Technology Center, Asia and Pacific Council, Summary Record, Third Meeting, First Session, March 25, 1970, Food and Fertilizer Technology Center, Taipei, Taiwan.

80. Yi-Chung Kuo, "Structure of Employment and Income for Farm Households in Taiwan," November 1981, Extension Bulletin No. 168, Food and Fertilizer Technology Center, Land Tenure Center Library, University of Wisconsin, Madison.

81. Perkins, *Geopolitics and the Green Revolution*; Cullather, *The Hungry World*.

82. Chien, Yang, and Wu, "Taiwan's Foreign Aid and Technical Assistance."

83. Glassman, *Drums of War, Drums of Development*.

84. "Establishment of the Asian Vegetable Research and Development Center" [아시아 채소연구개발센터 설립문제], 1971, document 4085, Ministry of Foreign Affairs, Republic of Korea, http://opendata.mofa.go.kr/mofadocu/resource/Document/4085.

85. Asian Vegetable Research and Development Center, *Annual Report for 1974*, 138–39.

86. Lowell Hardin to Robert F. Chandler, September 1, 1972, Ford Foundation Archives, New York, NY.

87. Fletcher, *The AVRDC Story*, 64.

88. "卸任總統後：亞洲蔬菜研究發展中心" [Post-Presidency: AVRDC]. November 1983. archive number 006000000460A, Yan Jiagan Collection [嚴家淦], Academia Historica Archives 國史館, Taipei, Taiwan.

89. Lorek, *Making the Green Revolution*, 7.

90. "U.S. Participation in International Agricultural Research," report to Congress by the comptroller general of the United States, January 27, 1978, CGIAR—D-22—United States—documents 78/80–01, folder ID 1758784, ISAD(G), reference code WB IBRD/IDA CGIAR-4177S, records of the Consultative Group on International Agricultural Research (CGIAR), World Bank Group Archives, Washington, DC.

91. Lowell Hardin to Robert Chandler, September 1, 1972, Consultative Group on International Agricultural Research [CGIAR], H-2 Asian Vegetable Research Development Center [AVDRC], 1972/1974 correspondence, volume 1, folder ID 1762497, ISAD(G) reference code WB IBRD/IDA CGIAR-4177S, records of the Consultative Group on International Agricultural Research (CGIAR), World Bank Group Archives, Washington, DC.

92. Robert Chandler to John Crawford, February 25, 1974, Consultative Group on International Agricultural Research [CGIAR], H-2 Asian Vegetable Research Development Center [AVDRC], 1972/1974 correspondence, volume 1, folder ID 1762497, ISAD(G)

reference code WB IBRD/IDA CGIAR-4177S, records of the Consultative Group on International Agricultural Research (CGIAR), World Bank Group Archives, Washington, DC.

93. Ibid.

94. P. A. Oram, report of visit to Philippines, Thailand, Indonesia, Singapore, India, June 1975, Consultative Group on International Agricultural Research [CGIAR], F-1 Technical Advisory Committee [TAC], 1975/1977 correspondence, volume 3, folder ID 1759686, ISAD(G), reference code WB IBRD/IDA CGIAR-4177S, records of the Consultative Group on International Agricultural Research (CGIAR), World Bank Group Archives, Washington, DC.

95. CGIAR Third Meeting Summary of Proceedings, November 1–2, 1972, CGIAR: Copies of US AID Records Related to the Consultative Group on International Agricultural Research, correspondence 01, folder ID 1768263, ISAD(G), reference code WB IBRD/IDA CGIAR-07, records of the Consultative Group on International Agricultural Research (CGIAR), World Bank Group Archives, Washington, DC.

96. Fletcher, *The AVRDC Story*, 56.

97. Robert F. Chandler to Lowell S. Hardin, May 16, 1972, reel L-250 L67–435, Ford Foundation Archives, New York, NY.

98. "卸任總統後：亞洲蔬菜研究發展中心" [Post-Presidency: AVRDC], November 1983. archive number 006000000460A, Yan Jiagan Collection [嚴家淦], Academia Historica Archives 國史館, Taipei, Taiwan.

99. "Current Topics," *Times of India*, February 19, 1970. On China's semidwarf varieties, see Yuan, Li, and Xin, *Hybrid Rice Technology Development*, 26.

100. T. T. Chang to Shen Zonghan, November 20, 1969, archive number 034000000330A, Folder "C" in "Shen Zonghan Letter Drafts" [沈宗瀚文件稿], COA/EYC.

101. Fletcher, *The AVRDC Story*, 64.

102. Hughes, Shanmugasundaram, and Keatinge, *The Mungbean Transformation*, 10.

103. "Nationality Distribution of Trainees from AVRDC/TOP Regional Training Office, Bangkok, Thailand.," George Marlowe to David Hopper. September 6, 1988, page 170, AVRDC Library, Shanhua, Taiwan (ROC).

104. Charles Yang, "Progress Report on IDRC's Vegetable (China) Project," page 171. AVRDC Library, Shanhua, Taiwan (ROC).

105. Ibid., 177.

106. Ibid.

107. Schmalzer, *Red Revolution, Green Revolution*.

108. Rigger, *The Tiger Leading the Dragon*.

109. Carson, *Silent Spring*.

110. Sharma, *Robert McNamara's Other War*, 138.

CONCLUSION

1. Chien, Yang, and Wu, "Taiwan's Foreign Aid and Technical Assistance in the Marshall Islands"; DeHart, *Transpacific Developments*.

2. Rich, "Status for Sale"; Rich and Dahmer, "Should I Stay or Should I Go?"

3. Rigger, *The Tiger Leading the Dragon*.

4. Chan, *Urbanization with Chinese Characteristics*; Friedman, *The Urbanization of People*.

5. Randomized control trials (RCTs), for example, pioneered by economists Esther Duflo and Abhijit Banerjee, who shared the 2019 Nobel Prize in economic sciences. RCTs operate on a simple principle: one village is given development assistance, one village (the control) is not, and results are compared. Banerjee and Duflo, *Poor Economics*. Yet RCTs ignore a long field of development studies that seeks to understand broader contexts. For an in-depth critique, see Reddy, "Randomise This!"

BIBLIOGRAPHY

ARCHIVAL SOURCES

Taiwan

Academia Historica (國史館)
Council of Agriculture (Executive Yuan) Library
Digital Taiwan Archives (典藏台灣)
Food and Fertilizer Technology Center
Institute of Modern History Archives, Academia Sinica (中央研究院近代史研究所)
Land Reform Training Institute
National Archives Administration (國家發展委員會檔案管理局)
World Vegetable Center (世界蔬菜中心, formerly AVRDC)

Vietnam

National Archives II

China

Number Two National Archives

United States

Cornell University Library
East Asia Library, Stanford University
Ford Foundation Archives
Hoover Institution Archives
Land Tenure Center Papers, University of Wisconsin
Lyndon B. Johnson Presidential Library
Oberlin College Archives
Robert Sheeks Personal Papers

Rockefeller Archives Center
University of Hartford Library
US National Archives II at College Park
Wilson Center Digital Archive
World Bank Group Archives

WORKS CITED

Aerni-Flessner, John. "Development, Politics, and the Centralization of State Power in Lesotho, 1960–75." *The Journal of African History* 55, no. 3 (November 2014): 401–21. https://doi.org/10.1017/S0021853714000395.

"American Agricultural Economics Association: Reports and Minutes 1968–69." *American Journal of Agricultural Economics* 51, no. 5 (1969): 1645–99.

Amsden, Alice H. "Taiwan's Economic History: A Case of Etatisme and a Challenge to Dependency Theory." *Modern China* 5, no. 3 (July 1, 1979): 341–79. https://doi.org/10.1177/009770047900500304.

Anderson, Warwick. "Introduction: Postcolonial Technoscience." *Social Studies of Science* 32, no. 5/6 (October 1, 2002): 643–58.

Anderson, W. A. *Farmers' Associations in Taiwan: A Report to the Joint Commission on Rural Reconstruction Economic Cooperation Mission to China*. Taipei: Council of Agriculture Library, 1950.

Andrade, Tonio. *How Taiwan Became Chinese: Dutch, Spanish, and Han Colonization in the Seventeenth Century*. Gutenberg (e). New York: Columbia University Press, 2008.

Ash, Robert F., and J. Megan Greene, eds. *Taiwan in the 21st Century: Aspects and Limitations of a Development Model*. New York: Routledge, 2007.

Asian Vegetable Research and Development Center. *Annual Report for 1974*. Shanhua: 1975.

Averill, Stephen C. "The New Life in Action: The Nationalist Government in South Jiangxi, 1934–37." *China Quarterly*, no. 88 (December 1, 1981): 594–628.

Baker, Kathleen M, and Richard Louis Edmonds. "Transfer of Taiwanese Ideas and Technology to the Gambia, West Africa: A Viable Approach to Rural Development?" *Geographical Journal* 170, no. 3 (2004): 189–211. https://doi.org/10.1111/j.0016-7398.2004.00120.x.

Banerjee, Abhijit, and Esther Duflo. *Poor Economics: A Radical Rethinking of the Way to Fight Global Poverty*. Reprint ed. New York: PublicAffairs, 2012.

Baranski, Marci. *The Globalization of Wheat: A Critical History of the Green Revolution*. Pittsburgh, PA: University of Pittsburgh Press, 2022.

Barclay, Paul D. *Outcasts of Empire: Japan's Rule on Taiwan's "Savage Border," 1874–1945*. Berkeley: University of California Press, 2017.

Bergère, Marie-Claire. *Sun Yat-Sen*. Translated by Janet Lloyd. Stanford, CA: Stanford University Press, 1998.

Biggs, David. "Americans in An Giang: Nation Building and the Particularities of Place in the Mekong Delta, 1966–1973." *Journal of Vietnamese Studies* 4, no. 3 (October 1, 2009): 139–72. https://doi.org/10.1525/vs.2009.4.3.139.

Borgwardt, Elizabeth. *A New Deal for the World: America's Vision for Human Rights*. Cambridge, MA: Belknap Press of Harvard University Press, 2007.

Braddick, C. W. "Japan, Australia and ASPAC: The Rise and Fall of an Asia-Pacific Cooperative Security Framework." In *Japan, Australia and Asia-Pacific Security*, edited by Brad Williams and Andrew Newman, 30-46. New York: Routledge, 2006.

Bramall, Chris. "Chinese Land Reform in Long-Run Perspective and in the Wider East Asian Context." *Journal of Agrarian Change* 4, no. 1–2 (2004): 107–41. https://doi.org/10.1111/j.1471-0366.2004.00074.x.

Brautigam, Deborah. *Chinese Aid and African Development: Exporting Green Revolution.* New York: Macmillan, 1998.

Brazinsky, Gregg A. *Winning the Third World: Sino-American Rivalry during the Cold War.* Chapel Hill: University of North Carolina Press, 2017.

Brown, James R. "World Land Reform Conference." In *1966 International Seminar on Land Taxation, Land Tenure, and Land Reform in Developing Countries*, 87–126. Hartford, CT: University of Hartford, 1967.

Brown, Melissa J. *Is Taiwan Chinese?: The Impact of Culture, Power, and Migration on Changing Identities.* Berkeley: University of California Press, 2004.

Bryson, Phillip J. *The Economics of Henry George: History's Rehabilitation of America's Greatest Early Economist.* 1st ed. New York: Palgrave Macmillan, 2011.

Buck, Pearl S. *The Good Earth.* New York: Simon and Schuster, 2004.

Bullock, Mary Brown. *An American Transplant: The Rockefeller Foundation and Peking Union Medical College.* Berkeley: University of California Press, 1980.

Bunker, H. J. "The Wartime Production of Food Yeast in Germany." *Proceedings of the Society for Applied Bacteriology* 9, no. 1 (1946): 10–14. https://doi.org/10.1111/j.1365–2672.1946.tb04036.x.

Carson, Rachel. *Silent Spring.* 1st ed. New York: Houghton Mifflin, 1962.

Chan, Kam Wing. *Urbanization with Chinese Characteristics: The Hukou System and Migration.* London: Routledge, 2018. https://doi.org/10.4324/9781315159003.

Chapman, Jessica Miranda. *Cauldron of Resistance: Ngo Dinh Diem, the United States, and 1950s Southern Vietnam.* Ithaca, NY: Cornell University Press, 2013

Chen, Cheng. *Land Reform in Taiwan.* Taipei: China Publishing Company, 1961.

Chen, Janet Y. *The Sounds of Mandarin: Learning to Speak a National Language in China and Taiwan, 1913–1960.* New York: Columbia University Press, 2023.

Chen, Kuan-Hsing. *Asia as Method: Toward Deimperialization.* Durham, NC: Duke University Press Books, 2010.

Chen Yi-Shen (陳儀深). "Zhanhou Taiwan [waisheng] jingying de Taidu zhuzhang—Cong Lei Zhen dao Zhang Zhongdong de leixing fenxi" "戰後台灣「外省」菁英的台獨主張－從雷震到張忠棟的類型分析." *Wenshi Taiwan xuebao* 文史台灣學報, no. 12 (September 2018): 81–104.

Chien, H. C. "Free China's Big Protein Project." *Food Engineering* 32, no. 12 (1960): 92–95.

Chien, H. C., W. F. Tung, T. C. Chang, and S. K. Chu. "Torula Yeast Manufacturing in Food and Feed Factory of Taiwan Sugar Corporation [台灣糖業公司新營副產加工廠酵母之製造]." *Chemistry [Huaxue 化學]*, no. 4 (1959).

Chien, Shiuh-Shen, Tzu-Po Yang, and Yi-Chen Wu. "Taiwan's Foreign Aid and Technical Assistance in the Marshall Islands." *Asian Survey* 50, no. 6 (November 1, 2010): 1184–1204. https://doi.org/10.1525/as.2010.50.6.1184.

Chinese Delegation to the United Nations. "Land Reform in the Republic of China." In *Readings in Land Reform*, edited by Sein Lin, 303-334. Hartford, CT: University of Hartford, 1970.

Ching, Leo T. S. *Becoming Japanese: Colonial Taiwan and the Politics of Identity Formation.* Berkeley: University of California Press, 2001.

Christensen, Raymond P. *Taiwan's Agricultural Development: Its Relevance for Developing Countries Today.* Washington, DC: US Department of Agriculture, Economic Research Service, Foreign Development and Trade Division, 1968.

Chu, L. C. "Free China Receives a Farmer-President." *Free China Review*, April 1, 1962.

Chu, Leo. "With and against the Grain: The Asian Vegetable Research and Development Center and Modest Narratives of Green Revolution in Taiwan, 1963–2002." *Agricultural History* 97, no. 3 (August 1, 2023): 448–77. https://doi.org/10.1215/00021482-10474447.

Cohen, Jerome Alan, and Hungdah Chiu. *People's China and International Law.* Vol. 1, *A Documentary Study.* Princeton, NJ: Princeton University Press, 2017.

Cohen, Paul A. *History in Three Keys: The Boxers as Event, Experience, and Myth.* New York: Columbia University Press, 1998.

Connelly, Matthew James. *Fatal Misconception: The Struggle to Control World Population.* Cambridge, MA: Belknap Press of Harvard University Press, 2008.

Conrad, David A. "'Before It Is Too Late': Land Reform in South Vietnam, 1956–1968." *Journal of American-East Asian Relations* 21, no. 1 (March 2014): 34–57. https://doi.org/10.1163/18765610-02101002.

Cook, Eli. *The Pricing of Progress: Economic Indicators and the Capitalization of American Life.* Cambridge, MA: Harvard University Press, 2017.

Cowen, Michael, and Robert W. Shenton. *Doctrines of Development.* New York: Taylor & Francis, 1996.

Cullather, Nick. "Damming Afghanistan: Modernization in a Buffer State." *Journal of American History* 89, no. 2 (2002): 512–37. https://doi.org/10.2307/3092171.

———. "'Fuel for the Good Dragon': The United States and Industrial Policy in Taiwan, 1950–1965." *Diplomatic History* 20, no. 1 (1996): 1–26. https://doi.org/10.1111/j.1467-7709.1996.tb00250.x.

———. *The Hungry World: America's Cold War Battle Against Poverty in Asia.* Cambridge, MA: Harvard University Press, 2010.

Cumings, Bruce. "The Origins and Development of the Northeast Asian Political Economy: Industrial Sectors, Product Cycles, and Political Consequences." *International Organization* 38, no. 1 (1984): 1–40.

Dawley, Evan N. *Becoming Taiwanese: Ethnogenesis in a Colonial City, 1880s to 1950s.* Cambridge, MA: Harvard University Asia Center, 2019.

Decker, Corrie. *The Idea of Development in Africa: A History.* New Approaches to African History 16. Cambridge, UK; Cambridge University Press, 2021.

Douglass, Mike. "The Saemaul Undong in Historical Perspective and in the Contemporary World." In *Learning from the South Korean Developmental Success: Effective Developmental Cooperation and Synergistic Institutions and Policies*, edited by Ilcheong Yi and Thandika Mkandawire, 136–71. London: Palgrave Macmillan, 2014. https://doi.org/10.1057/9781137339485_7.

Duara, Prasenjit. *Culture, Power, and the State: Rural North China, 1900–1942.* Stanford, CA: Stanford University Press, 1988.

———. *Rescuing History from the Nation: Questioning Narratives of Modern China.* Chicago: University of Chicago Press, 1995.

Edgerton-Tarpley, Kathryn. *Tears from Iron: Cultural Responses to Famine in Nineteenth-Century China*. Berkeley: University of California Press, 2008.

Ekbladh, David. *The Great American Mission: Modernization and the Construction of an American World Order*. Princeton, NJ: Princeton University Press, 2009.

Emmons, Garry. "Classic Cases Live on at HBS—HBS Working Knowledge." *Working Knowledge* (blog), Harvard Business School, August 15, 2005. http://hbswk.hbs.edu/item/4949.html.

Engerman, David C. "Development Politics and the Cold War." *Diplomatic History* 41, no. 1 (January 1, 2017): 1–19. https://doi.org/10.1093/dh/dhw043.

———. *The Price of Aid: The Economic Cold War in India*. Cambridge, MA: Harvard University Press, 2018.

Engerman, David C., Nils Gilman, Mark H. Haefele, and Michael E. Latham, eds. *Staging Growth: Modernization, Development, and the Global Cold War*. Amherst: University of Massachusetts Press, 2003.

Engerman, David C., and Corinna Unger. "Introduction: Towards a Global History of Modernization." *Diplomatic History* 33, no. 3 (2009): 375–85.

Ennis, Thomas W. "Dr. A. M. Woodruff, Economist." *New York Times*, August 28, 1984, sec. Obituaries. http://www.nytimes.com.

Escobar, Arturo. *Encountering Development: The Making and Unmaking of The Third World*. Princeton, NJ: Princeton University Press, 1995.

Ewing, Cindy. "The Colombo Powers: Crafting Diplomacy in the Third World and Launching Afro-Asia at Bandung." *Cold War History* 19, no. 1 (February 2019): 1–19. https://doi.org/10.1080/14682745.2018.1500553.

Fanon, Frantz. *The Wretched of the Earth*. New York: Grove, 1966.

Fengnian [Harvest]. "Hao xiguan" [好習慣, Good habits], July 15, 1951.

———. "Yue Fei de chenggong" [岳飛的成功, Yue Fei's success], July 15, 1951.

Ferguson, James. *The Anti-Politics Machine: "Development," Depoliticization, and Bureaucratic Power in Lesotho*. Cambridge, UK: Cambridge University Press, 1990.

Fishburn, Janet. "The Social Gospel as 'a New View of Missions.'" In *North American Foreign Missions, 1810–1914: Theology, Theory, and Policy*, edited by Wilbert R. Shenk, 218–42. Grand Rapids, MI: William B. Eerdmans, 2004.

Fletcher, Alan Mark. *The AVRDC Story: Twenty Years of Service to Tropical Agriculture*. Publication No. 93–406. Taipei, Taiwan: Asian Vegetable Research and Development Center, 1993.

Food and Agriculture Organization of the United Nations. Nutrition Committee for South and East Asia. *Nutrition Problems of Rice-Eating Countries in Asia: Report of the Nutrition Committee, Baguio, Philippines, 23–28 February 1948*. Washington, DC: Food and Agriculture Organization of the United Nations, 1948.

Forest Products Laboratory. "Food-Yeast Production from Wood-Processing by Products." *U.S. Forest Service Research Note*, no. FPL-065 (November 1964): 34.

Foucault, Michel. "Governmentality." In *The Foucault Effect: Studies in Governmentality*, edited by Graham Burchell, Colin Gordon, and Peter Miller, 87–104. Chicago: University of Chicago Press, 1991.

Friedman, Eli. *The Urbanization of People: The Politics of Development, Labor Markets, and Schooling in the Chinese City*. New York: Columbia University Press, 2022.

Friedman, Jeremy. *Shadow Cold War: The Sino-Soviet Competition for the Third World*. Chapel Hill: University of North Carolina Press, 2015.

Fu, Jia-Chen. *The Other Milk: Reinventing Soy in Republican China*. Seattle: University of Washington Press, 2018.

Fuller, Pierre. *Famine Relief in Warlord China*. Harvard East Asian Monographs 423. Cambridge, MA: Harvard University Asia Center, 2019.

Garver, John W. *The Sino-American Alliance: Nationalist China and American Cold War Strategy in Asia*. Armonk, NY: M. E. Sharpe, 1997.

Gaud, William. "The Green Revolution: Accomplishments and Apprehensions." Lecture presented at the Society for International Development, Washington, DC, March 8, 1968.

George, Henry. *Progress and Poverty*. New York: Cosimo, 2005.

Getachew, Adom. *Worldmaking after Empire: The Rise and Fall of Self-Determination*. Princeton, NJ: Princeton University Press, 2019.

Gilman, Nils. *Mandarins of the Future Modernization Theory in Cold War America*. Baltimore, MD: Johns Hopkins University Press, 2003.

Glassman, Jim. *Drums of War, Drums of Development: The Formation of a Pacific Ruling Class and Industrial Transformation in East and Southeast Asia, 1945–1980*. Leiden: Brill, 2018.

Gold, Thomas B. *State and Society in the Taiwan Miracle*. New York: M. E. Sharpe, 1986.

Goodwin, Ralph R., David W. Mahon, David H. Stauffer, eds. *Foreign Relations of the United States 1950*. Vol. 2, *The United Nations: The Western Hemisphere*. Washington, DC: US Government Printing Office, 1976.

Greene, J. Megan. *The Origins of the Developmental State in Taiwan*. Cambridge, MA: Harvard University Press, 2008.

Guinnane, Timothy W. "Cooperatives as Information Machines: German Rural Credit Cooperatives, 1883–1914." *Journal of Economic History* 61, no. 2 (2001): 366–89.

Gupta, Akhil. *Postcolonial Developments: Agriculture in the Making of Modern India*. Durham, NC: Duke University Press, 1998.

Hamilton, Gary G., and Cheng-shu Kao. *Making Money: How Taiwanese Industrialists Embraced the Global Economy*. Stanford, CA: Stanford University Press, 2017.

Hargrove, Tom, and W. Bonnie Coffman. "Breeding History." *Rice Today*, December 2006.

Hart, Gillian. "Development Critiques in the 1990s: Culs De Sac and Promising Paths." *Progress in Human Geography* 25, no. 4 (December 1, 2001): 649–58. https://doi.org/10.1191/030913201682689002.

———. *Disabling Globalization: Places of Power in Post-Apartheid South Africa*. Berkeley: University of California Press, 2002.

He, Zhonghu, and Alain Bonjean, eds. *Cereals in China*. Veracruz: CIMMYT (International Maize and Wheat Improvement Center), 2070.

Hedden, Peter. "The Genes of the Green Revolution." *Trends in Genetics* 19, no. 1 (January 2003): 5–9. https://doi.org/10.1016/S0168-9525(02)00009-4.

Helleiner, Eric. *Forgotten Foundations of Bretton Woods*. Ithaca NY: Cornell University Press, 2016.

Hill, Emily. "Rice Supplies and the Chinese-American Partnership in Taiwan, 1950s." Unpublished manuscript, 2011.

Ho, Samuel P. S. *Economic Development of Taiwan, 1860–1970*. New Haven, CT: Yale University Press, 1978.

Hoffman, Philip T., Gilles Postel-Vinay, and Jean-Laurent Rosenthal. *Priceless Markets: The Political Economy of Credit in Paris, 1660–1870*. Chicago: University of Chicago Press, 2000.

Hollinger, David A. *Protestants Abroad: How Missionaries Tried to Change the World but Changed America*. Princeton, NJ: Princeton University Press, 2017.

Hsiao, Frank S. T., and Mei-chu Wang Hsiao. *Economic Development Of Taiwan: Early Experiences And The Pacific Trade Triangle*. Singapore: World Scientific, 2015.

Hsiung, Ping-Chun. *Living Rooms as Factories: Class, Gender, and the Satellite Factory System in Taiwan*. Philadelphia: Temple University Press, 1996.

Hsu Shih-Jung (徐世榮). *Tudi zhengyi: cong tudi gaige dao tudi zhengshou* 土地正義：從土地改革到土地徵收 [Land justice: From land reform to land expropriation]. 新北市 (New Taipei City): 遠足文化, 2016.

Hsu Shih-Jung and Hsin-Huang Michael Hsiao. "The Impacts of Class Differentiation and Cultural Construction on Post-War Land Reform in Taiwan." Academia Sinica, Taipei, Taiwan: Information Service for East Asian Research Program for Southeast Asian Area Studies, Academia Sinica, 1999.

———. "Taiwan tudi gaige zai shenshi—yi ge 'neiyinshuo' de changshi 台灣土地改革再審視－一個「內因說」的嘗試." *Taiwanshi Yanjiu* 台灣史研究 8, no. 1 (June 2001): 89–124.

Huang, Chun-chieh, ed. *Nongfuhui yu Taiwan jingyan* 農復會與台灣經驗 [The JCRR and Taiwan experience]. Taipei: Sanmin Books, 1991.

———. *Taiwan in Transformation 1895–2005: The Challenge of a New Democracy to an Old Civilization*. Piscataway, NJ: Transaction, 2011.

———. *Zhongguo Nongcun Fuxing Weiyuanhui: koushu lishi fangwen jilu* 中國農村復興聯合委員會：口述歷史訪問紀錄. Taipei: Academia Sinica Institute of Modern History中央研究院近代史研究所, 1992.

Huang, Sophia Wu. "Structural Change in Taiwan's Agricultural Economy." *Economic Development & Cultural Change* 42, no. 1 (October 1993): 43. https://doi.org/10.1086/452064.

Huff, Joyce L. "Corporeal Economies: Work and Waste in Nineteenth-Century Constructions of Alimentation." In *Cultures of the Abdomen: Diet, Digestion, and Fat in the Modern World*, edited by Christopher Forth and Ana Carden-Coyne, 31-49, New York: Palgrave Macmillan, 2005.

Hughes, Jacqueline d'Arros, Subramanyam Shanmugasundaram, and J. D. H. Keatinge. *The Mungbean Transformation Diversifying Crops, Defeating Malnutrition*. Washington, D.C.: International Food Policy Research Institute, 2009.

Hunt, Richard A. *Pacification: The American Struggle for Vietnam's Hearts and Minds*. Boulder, CO: Westview Press, 1995.

Immerwahr, Daniel. *Thinking Small: The United States and the Lure of Community Development*. Cambridge, MA: Harvard University Press, 2015.

International Monetary Fund. "World Economic Outlook," April 2024. https://www.imf.org/en/Publications/WEO/weo-database/2024/April/weo-report.

İşcan, Talan B. "Redistributive Land Reform and Structural Change in Japan, South Korea, and Taiwan." *American Journal of Agricultural Economics* 100, no. 3 (2018): 732–980.

Isett, Christopher, and Stephen Miller. *The Social History of Agriculture: From the Origins to the Current Crisis*. Lanham, Maryland: Rowman & Littlefield Publishers, 2016.

Jacobs, J. Bruce. *Democratizing Taiwan*. Leiden: Brill, 2012.

Jacoby, Neil H. *U.S. Aid to Taiwan: A Study of Foreign Aid, Self-Help, and Development*. New York: Praeger, 1967.

Jakes, Aaron G. *Egypt's Occupation: Colonial Economism and the Crises of Capitalism*. Stanford, CA: Stanford University Press, 2020.

Jasanoff, Sheila, and Sang-Hyun Kim. "Containing the Atom: Sociotechnical Imaginaries and Nuclear Power in the United States and South Korea." *Minerva* 47, no. 2 (June 1, 2009): 119–46. https://doi.org/10.1007/s11024-009-9124-4.

———, eds. *Dreamscapes of Modernity: Sociotechnical Imaginaries and the Fabrication of Power*. Chicago: University of Chicago Press, 2015.

Jin Yanggao (金陽鎬). "Zhongfei nongye jishu hezuo gaikuang" [中非農業技術合作概況, Sino-African agricultural technical cooperation summary]. Zhongguo Fuxing Nongcun Lianhe Weiyuanhui (中國農村復興聯合委員會), April 29, 1964.

Joint Commission on Rural Reconstruction. Rural Economics Division. *Taiwan Agricultural Statistics, 1961–1975*. Taipei: Chinese-American Joint Commission on Rural Reconstruction, 1977.

Jones, Andrew F. *Developmental Fairy Tales: Evolutionary Thinking and Modern Chinese Culture*. Cambridge, MA: Harvard University Press, 2011.

Ka, Chih-ming. *Japanese Colonialism In Taiwan: Land Tenure, Development, And Dependency*. Revised ed. Boulder, CO: Westview Press, 1998.

Kabeer, Naila. *Reversed Realities: Gender Hierarchies in Development Thought*. New York: Verso, 1994.

Kapstein, Ethan B. *Seeds of Stability: Land Reform and US Foreign Policy*. Cambridge, UK: Cambridge University Press, 2017.

Karl, Rebecca E. *The Magic of Concepts: History and the Economic in Twentieth-Century China*. Durham, NC: Duke University Press Books, 2017.

———. *Staging the World: Chinese Nationalism at the Turn of the Twentieth Century*. Durham, NC: Duke University Press Books, 2002.

Kumar, Prakash. "'Modernization' and Agrarian Development in India, 1912–52." *Journal of Asian Studies* 79, no. 3 (January 30, 2020): 1–26. https://doi.org/10.1017/S0021911819001219.

Kung, Chien-Wen. *Diasporic Cold Warriors: Nationalist China, Anticommunism, and the Philippine Chinese, 1930s–1970s*. Ithaca, NY: Cornell University Press, 2022.

Kuomintang News Network. "ROC Flag-Raising Ceremony Held at Twin Oaks in D.C., First Time in 36 Years." Accessed February 1, 2016. http://www1.kmt.org.

Ladejinsky, Wolf Isaac. *Agrarian Reform as Unfinished Business: The Selected Papers of Wolf Ladejinsky*. Edited by Louis Walinsky. Oxford: Oxford University Press, 1977.

Latham, Michael E. *Modernization as Ideology: American Social Science and "Nation Building" in the Kennedy Era*. Chapel Hill: University of North Carolina Press, 2000.

———. *The Right Kind of Revolution: Modernization, Development, and U.S. Foreign Policy from the Cold War to the Present*. Ithaca, NY: Cornell University Press, 2011.

Latour, Bruno. *Science in Action: How to Follow Scientists and Engineers Through Society*. Reprint ed. Cambridge, MA: Harvard University Press, 1988.

Lavelle, Peter. "Agricultural Improvement at China's First Agricultural Experiment Stations." In *New Perspectives on the History of Life Sciences and Agriculture*, edited by Denise Phillips and Sharon Kingsland, 323–44. Cham: Springer International, 2015.

———. *The Profits of Nature: Colonial Development and the Quest for Resources in Nineteenth-Century China*. New York: Columbia University Press, 2020.

Lee, Ching Kwan. *The Specter of Global China: Politics, Labor, and Foreign Investment in Africa*. Chicago: University of Chicago Press, 2018.

Lee, Seung-Joon. *Gourmets in the Land of Famine: The Culture and Politics of Rice in Modern Canton.* 1st ed. Stanford, CA: Stanford University Press, 2011.

Lee, Teng-hui. *Intersectoral Capital Flows in the Economic Development of Taiwan, 1895–1960.* Ithaca, NY: Cornell University Press, 1971.

Lee, Teng-hui, and Yueh-eh Chen. *Growth Rates of Taiwan Agriculture.* Economic Digest Series 21. Taipei, Taiwan: Joint Commission on Rural Reconstruction, 1975.

Levy, Jonathan. *Freaks of Fortune: The Emerging World of Capitalism and Risk in America.* Cambridge, MA: Harvard University Press, 2012.

Li, Kwoh-ting. *Economic Transformation of Taiwan, ROC.* London: Shepheard-Walwyn, 1988.

Li, Lillian M. *Fighting Famine in North China: State, Market, and Environmental Decline, 1690s–1990s.* Stanford, CA: Stanford University Press, 2010.

Li, Wankun. "War, Trade and Socialism: Grain Resource Control in Rural Chongqing, 1937–1953." PhD diss., University of Leeds, 2019.

Liao Yen-Hao (廖彥豪) and Chu Wan-Wen (瞿宛文). "Jiangu dizhu de tudi daige: Taiwan shishi gengzhe you qitian de lishi guocheng" "兼顧地主的土地改革：台灣實施耕者有其田的歷史過程 [A middle-of-the-road land reform: How Taiwan implemented the 'land-to-the-tillers' program]," *Taiwan shehui yanjiu jikan* 台灣社會研究季刊, no. 98 (March 1, 2015): 69–45.

———. "Weihe tudi gaige de yihan zhengyi duo?" "為何土地改革的意涵爭議多？ [The significance of Taiwan's postwar land reform]." *Taiwan shehui yanjiu jikan* 台灣社會研究季刊, no. 100 (September 2015): 257–60.

Lin, Hsiao-ting. "Lengzhan shiqi Taiwan yu Yuenan de guanxi" "冷战时期台湾与南越的关系." 南洋问题研究 *Southeast Asian Affairs,* no. 3 (2018): 15–30.

———. *Taihai Lengzhan Jiemi Dang'an* [台海冷戰解密檔案; The cold war between Taiwan and China: The declassified documents]. Hong Kong: Joint Publishing, 2015.

———. *Taiwan, the United States, and the Hidden History of the Cold War in Asia: Divided Allies.* New York: Routledge, 2022.

Lin, Wei-Ping. *Island Fantasia: Imagining Subjects on the Military Frontline between China and Taiwan.* Cambridge, UK: Cambridge University Press, 2021.

Lindholm, Richard, and Sein Lin, eds. *Henry George and Sun Yat-Sen: Application and Evolution of Their Land Use Doctrine.* Cambridge, MA: Lincoln Institute of Land Policy, 1977.

Liu, Chi-Wei. "Guoji nongliang tizhi yu Taiwan de liangshi yilai: zhanhou Taiwan yangzhu ye de lishi kaocha" "國際農糧體制與臺灣的糧食依賴 ： 戰後臺灣養豬業的歷史考察." *Taiwan shi yanjiu* [臺灣史研究, Taiwan historical research] 16, no. 2 (June 2009): 105–60.

———. "Hog Island: Agricultural Protectionism, Food Dependency, and Impact of the International Food Regime in Taiwan." PhD diss., State University of New York at Binghamton, 2008. http://search.proquest.com/docview/304324104/abstract/6ED8B51F8F0F4B75PQ/1.

Liu, Hsiaopong. "The Making of an Artificial Power: American Money and 'Chinese' Technicians on African Soil, 1961–1971." PhD diss., The University of Chicago, 2006.

Liu, Philip Hsiao-pong. "Planting Rice on the Roof of the UN Building: Analysing Taiwan's 'Chinese' Techniques in Africa, 1961–Present." *China Quarterly* 198 (2009): 381–400. https://doi.org/10.1017/S0305741009000368.

Liu, Zhibang (劉治邦). "Qu Sahala shamo zhongdao" "去薩哈拉沙漠種稻." 新聞天地 Xinwen tiandi, March 31, 1962.

Lo, Kuei-Mei, and Hsin-Hsing Chen. "Technological Momentum and the Hegemony of the Green Revolution: A Case Study of an Organic Rice Cooperative in Taiwan." *East Asian Science, Technology and Society* 5, no. 2 (June 1, 2011): 135–72.

Looney, Kristen E. *Mobilizing for Development: The Modernization of Rural East Asia.* Ithaca, NY: Cornell University Press, 2020.

Lorek, Timothy. *Making the Green Revolution: Agriculture & Conflict in Colombia.* Chapel Hill: University of North Carolina Press, 2023.

Louzon, Victor. "From Japanese Soldiers to Chinese Rebels: Colonial Hegemony, War Experience, and Spontaneous Remobilization during the 1947 Taiwanese Rebellion." *Journal of Asian Studies* 77, no. 1 (2018): 161–79.

Lu, Juliet. "Grounding Chinese Investment: Encounters between Chinese Capital and Local Land Politics in Laos." *Globalizations* 18, no. 3 (April 2021): 422–40. https://doi.org/10.1080/14747731.2020.1796159.

Luh, C. L. "The Institutions and Programs Responsible for Agricultural Development in Taiwan, Republic of China." Paper presented at the International Workshop for Accelerating Agricultural Development, April 26–30, 1976, hosted by the Southeast Asian Regional Center for Graduate Study and Research in Agriculture (SEARCA) in Los Baños, Philippines. Land Tenure Center Library, University of Wisconsin.

Luo, Kevin Wei. "Redistributing Power: Land Reform, Rural Cooptation, and Grassroots Regime Institutions in Authoritarian Taiwan." *Comparative Political Studies* (March 8, 2024): 1–34. https://doi.org/10.1177/00104140241237457.

Macekura, Stephen J. *The Mismeasure of Progress: Economic Growth and Its Critics.* Chicago: University of Chicago Press, 2020.

Mao, Zedong. *Selected Works of Mao Tsetung.* 1st ed. Vol. 5. Peking: Foreign Languages Press, 1977.

Masuda, Hajimu. *Cold War Crucible: The Korean Conflict and the Postwar World.* Cambridge, MA: Harvard University Press, 2015.

Mau, Søren Mads. *Mute Compulsion: A Marxist Theory of the Economic Power of Capital.* London: Verso, 2023.

McCoy, Alfred. "Land Reform as Counter-Revolution." *Bulletin of Concerned Asian Scholars* 3, no. 1 (1971): 14–49.

Mellor, John W. *Agriculture on the Road to Industrialization.* Baltimore, MD: International Food Policy Research Institute, Johns Hopkins University Press, 1995. https://ebrary.ifpri.org/digital/collection/p15738coll2/id/129333.

Merkel-Hess, Kate. *The Rural Modern: Reconstructing the Self and State in Republican China.* Chicago: University of Chicago Press, 2016.

Metzger, Tim, and Makoto Fujita, dir. *Taiwan's Transformation: Winds of Change.* Television documentary. Dateline Productions, 1987. https://vimeo.com/414022210.

Mew, T. W., and Colin McClung. "Shu-Huang Ou, 1912 to 2001." *Phytopathology* 92, no. 1 (January 2002): 32–32. https://doi.org/10.1094/PHYTO.2002.92.1.32.

Miller, Edward Garvey. *Misalliance: Ngo Dinh Diem, the United States, and the Fate of South Vietnam.* Cambridge, MA: Harvard University Press, 2013.

Mitter, Rana. "Imperialism, Transnationalism, and the Reconstruction of Post-War China: UNRRA in China, 1944–7." Supplement, *Past & Present* 218, S8 (January 1, 2013): 51–69. https://doi.org/10.1093/pastj/gts034.

Mizuno, Hiromi, Aaron Stephen Moore, and John Paul DiMoia, eds. *Engineering Asia: Technology, Colonial Development, and the Cold War Order*. New York: Bloomsbury Academic, 2018.

Mok, Mei Feng. "Negotiating Community and Nation in Chợ Lớn: Nation-Building, Community-Building and Transnationalism in Everyday Life during the Republic of Việt Nam, 1955–1975." PhD diss., University of Washington, 2016.

Moley, Raymond. *The American Century of John C. Lincoln*. New York: Duell, Sloan and Pearce, 1962.

Monica DeHart. *Transpacific Developments: The Politics of Multiple Chinas in Central America*. Ithaca, NY: Cornell University Press, 2021.

Monson, Jamie. *Africa's Freedom Railway: How a Chinese Development Project Changed Lives and Livelihoods in Tanzania*. Reprint ed. Bloomington: Indiana University Press, 2011.

Montgomery, John D., Rufus B. Hughes Jr., and Raymond Davis. *Rural Improvement and Political Development: The JCRR Model*. Washington, DC: Comparative Administrative Group, American Society for Public Administration, 1966. Prepared in 1964 for the US Agency for international Development.

Moore, Aaron Stephen. *Constructing East Asia: Technology, Ideology, and Empire in Japan's Wartime Era, 1931–1945*. Stanford, CA: Stanford University Press, 2013.

———. "Japanese Development Consultancies and Postcolonial Power in Southeast Asia: The Case of Burma's Balu Chaung Hydropower Project." *East Asian Science, Technology and Society* 8, no. 3 (September 1, 2014): 297–322. https://doi.org/10.1215/18752160-2416662.

Moore, Jason W. "The Capitalocene, Part I: On the Nature and Origins of Our Ecological Crisis." *Journal of Peasant Studies* 44, no. 3 (May 4, 2017): 594–630. https://doi.org/10.1080/03066150.2016.1235036.

Muscolino, Micah S. *The Ecology of War in China: Henan Province, the Yellow River, and Beyond, 1938–1950*. New York: Cambridge University Press, 2014.

Myers, Ramon H., and Adrienne Ching. "Agricultural Development in Taiwan under Japanese Colonial Rule." *Journal of Asian Studies* 23, no. 4 (1964): 555–70. https://doi.org/10.2307/2050238.

Nathan, Andrew J. *A History of the China International Famine Relief Commission*. East Asian Research Center, Harvard University, 1965.

Nguyen, Phi-Vân. "A Secular State for a Religious Nation: The Republic of Vietnam and Religious Nationalism, 1946–1963." *Journal of Asian Studies* 77, no. 3 (August 2018): 741–71. https://doi.org/10.1017/S0021911818000505.

Oded, Arye. "Africa in Israeli Foreign Policy—Expectations and Disenchantment: Historical and Diplomatic Aspects." *Israel Studies* 15, no. 3 (2010): 121–42.

Olson, Gary L. *U.S. Foreign Policy and the Third World Peasant: Land Reform in Asia and Latin America*. Praeger, 1974.

Osterhammel, Jürgen. "'Technical Co-operation' between the League of Nations and China." *Modern Asian Studies* 13, no. 4 (January 1, 1979): 661–80. https://doi.org/10.2307/312187.

Ott, Julia C. *When Wall Street Met Main Street: The Quest for an Investors' Democracy*. Cambridge, MA: Harvard University Press, 2011.

Patel, Raj. "The Long Green Revolution." *Journal of Peasant Studies* 40, no. 1 (January 1, 2013): 1–63. https://doi.org/10.1080/03066150.2012.719224.

Pearce, Kimber Charles. *Rostow, Kennedy, and the Rhetoric of Foreign Aid.* East Lansing: Michigan State University Press, 2001.

Perkins, John H. *Geopolitics and the Green Revolution: Wheat, Genes, and the Cold War.* Oxford University Press, 1997.

Phillips, Steven E. *Between Assimilation and Independence: The Taiwanese Encounter Nationalist China, 1945–1950.* Stanford, CA: Stanford University Press, 2003.

Picard, Jason A. "'Fertile Lands Await': The Promise and Pitfalls of Directed Resettlement, 1954–1958." *Journal of Vietnamese Studies* 11, no. 3–4 (November 1, 2016): 58–102. https://doi.org/10.1525/jvs.2016.11.3–4.58.

Pitts, Larissa. "From Revolution to Reform: Xiao Zheng and the Land Reform Movement of the GMD Right." Unpublished Research Paper. University of California, Berkeley, 2012.

Pomeranz, Kenneth. *The Great Divergence: Europe, China, and the Making of the Modern World Economy.* Princeton, NJ: Princeton University Press, 2000.

Reddy, Sanjay. "Randomise This! On Poor Economics." *Review of Agrarian Studies* 2, no. 2 (2012): 60–73.

Reinisch, Jessica. "'Auntie UNRRA' at the Crossroads." Supplement, *Past & Present* 218, S8 (January 1, 2013): 70–97. https://doi.org/10.1093/pastj/gts035.

Rich, Timothy. "Status for Sale: Taiwan and the Competition for Diplomatic Recognition." *Issues & Studies* 45 (December 1, 2009): 159–88.

Rich, Timothy S., and Andi Dahmer. "Should I Stay or Should I Go? Diplomatic Recognition of Taiwan, 1950–2016." *International Journal of Taiwan Studies* 5, no. 2 (June 20, 2022): 353–74. https://doi.org/10.1163/24688800-20221195.

Rigger, Shelley. *Politics in Taiwan: Voting for Democracy.* 1st ed. New York: Routledge, 1999.

———. *The Tiger Leading the Dragon: How Taiwan Propelled China's Economic Rise.* New York: Rowman & Littlefield, 2021.

Rist, Gilbert. *The History of Development: From Western Origins to Global Faith.* 4th ed. New York: Zed Books, 2014.

Rodrik, Dani. "Getting Interventions Right: How South Korea and Taiwan Grew Rich." *Economic Policy* 10, no. 20 (April 1, 1995): 53–107. https://doi.org/10.2307/1344538.

Ron, Ariel. *Grassroots Leviathan: Agricultural Reform and the Rural North in the Slaveholding Republic.* Baltimore, MD: Johns Hopkins University Press, 2020.

Rosenberg, Gabriel N. *The 4-H Harvest: Sexuality and the State in Rural America.* Philadelphia: University of Pennsylvania Press, 2015.

Rosenthal, Caitlin. *Accounting for Slavery: Masters and Management.* Cambridge, MA: Harvard University Press, 2018.

Rostow, W. W. *The Stages of Economic Growth: A Non-Communist Manifesto.* New York: Cambridge University Press, 1965.

Said, Edward W. *Orientalism.* New York: Vintage, 1979.

Sands, Barbara, and Loren Brandt. "Land Concentration and Income Distribution in Republican China." In *Chinese History in Economic Perspective,* edited by Thomas G. Rawski and Lillian M. Li, 179–207. Berkeley: University of California Press, 1992.

Saraiva, Tiago. "California Cloning in French Algeria: Rooting Pieds Noirs and Uprooting Fellahs in the Orange Groves of the Mitidja." In *How Knowledge Moves: Writing the Transnational History of Science and Technology,* edited by John Krige, 95–119. Chicago: University of Chicago Press, 2019.

Sayward, Amy L. *The Birth of Development: How the World Bank, Food and Agriculture Organization, and World Health Organization Changed the World, 1945–1965*. Kent, OH: Kent State University Press, 2006.

Schmalzer, Sigrid. *Red Revolution, Green Revolution: Scientific Farming in Socialist China*. Chicago: University of Chicago Press, 2016.

Schwartz, Benjamin I. *In Search of Wealth and Power: Yen Fu and the West*. Cambridge, MA: Belknap Press of Harvard University Press, 1964.

Scott, James. *Seeing Like a State: How Certain Schemes to Improve the Human Condition Have Failed*. New Haven, CT: Yale University Press, 1999.

Sharma, Patrick Allan. *Robert McNamara's Other War: The World Bank and International Development*. Philadelphia: University of Pennsylvania Press, 2017.

Shen Shike (沈時可) and Zhang Ligeng (張力耕), eds. *Taiwan tudi gaige wenji* [臺灣土地改革文集, Taiwan land reform collected works]. Taipei: Interior Ministry (內政部), 89.

Shen Zonghan. *Agricultural Development on Taiwan Since World War II*. Ithaca, NY: Comstock, 1964.

———, ed. *Agriculture's Place in the Strategy of Development: The Taiwan Experience*. Taipei: Joint Commission on Rural Reconstruction, 1974.

———. *Gengyun Suiyue: Shen Zonghan Xiansheng Zizhuan Ji Qita* [耕耘歲月:沈宗瀚先生自傳及其他]. Taipei: Zhengzhong shuju 正中書局, 1993.

———. *The Sino-American Joint Commission on Rural Reconstruction; Twenty Years of Cooperation for Agricultural Development*. Ithaca, NY: Cornell University Press, 1970.

Shiva, Vandana. *The Violence of the Green Revolution: Third World Agriculture, Ecology and Politics*. Lexington: University Press of Kentucky, 2016.

Simpson, Bradley R. *Economists with Guns: Authoritarian Development and U.S.-Indonesian Relations, 1960–1968*. Stanford, CA: Stanford University Press, 2008.

Smith, Craig A. "Taiwan's 228 Incident and the Politics of Placing Blame." *Past Imperfect* 14 (October 7, 2008). https://doi.org/10.21971/P7XK5F.

Smith, Theodore Reynolds. *East Asian Agrarian Reform: Japan, Republic of Korea, Taiwan and the Philippines*. Hartford, CT: John C. Lincoln Institute, 1970.

Sneddon, Christopher. *Concrete Revolution: Large Dams, Cold War Geopolitics, and the US Bureau of Reclamation*. Chicago: University of Chicago Press, 2015.

Soon, Wayne. "Science, Medicine, and Confucianism in the Making of China and Southeast Asia—Lim Boon Keng and the Overseas Chinese, 1897–1937." *Twentieth-Century China* 39, no. 1 (January 1, 2014): 24–43. https://doi.org/10.1179/1521538513Z.00000000033.

Stewart, Geoffrey C. "Hearts, Minds and Công Dân Vụ: The Special Commissariat for Civic Action and Nation-Building in Ngo Dinh Diem's Vietnam, 1955–1957." *Journal of Vietnamese Studies* 6, no. 3 (2011): 44–100. https://doi.org/10.1525/vs.2011.6.3.44.

———. *Vietnam's Lost Revolution: Ngô Đình Diệm's Failure to Build an Independent Nation, 1955–1963*. Cambridge, UK: Cambridge University Press, 2017.

Stewart, Spencer. "A Community Crop: Cotton, Science, and Extension in Interwar Shandong, 1918–1937." *Twentieth-Century China* 46, no. 2 (2021): 199–219.

Strauss, Julia C. *State Formation in China and Taiwan: Bureaucracy, Campaign, and Performance*. Cambridge, UK: Cambridge University Press, 2019.

Stross, Randall E. *The Stubborn Earth: American Agriculturalists on Chinese Soil, 1898–1937*. Berkeley: University of California Press, 1986.

Studwell, Joe. *How Asia Works*. New York: Grove, 2014.

Sun, Chen. "Land Reform and San Min Chu I." In *Henry George and Sun Yat-Sen: Application and Evolution of Their Land Use Doctrine*, edited by Richard Lindholm and Sein Lin, 40–54. Cambridge, MA: Lincoln Institute of Land Policy, 1977.

Ta Kung Pao [大公報]. "Bafang zainan fuxing nongcun" [八方災難復興農村, Rural reconstruction in the midst of disasters]. August 11, 1948.

Taiwan Sugar Corporation. *Lianhe Bao* [聯合報, United daily news]. January 1, 1965.

Taiwan Today. "Taipei Mission To Help Land Reform in Iran." September 10, 1967. http://www.taiwantoday.tw.

Tan, Mitchell. "Spiritual Fraternities: The Transnational Networks of Ngô Đình Diệm's Personalist Revolution and the Republic of Vietnam, 1955–1963." *Journal of Vietnamese Studies* 14, no. 2 (May 1, 2019): 1–67. https://doi.org/10.1525/vs.2019.14.2.1.

Tang, Hui-sun. *Land Reform in Free China*. Taipei: Joint Commission on Rural Reconstruction, 1954.

Taylor, Jay. *The Generalissimo: Chiang Kai-Shek and the Struggle for Modern China*. Cambridge, MA: Belknap Press of Harvard University Press, 2009.

Times of India. "Current Topics." February 19, 1970.

Thornton, Christy. *Revolution in Development: Mexico and the Governance of the Global Economy*. Oakland: University of California Press, 2021.

Toner, Simon. "Imagining Taiwan: The Nixon Administration, the Developmental States, and South Vietnam's Search for Economic Viability, 1969–1975." *Diplomatic History* 41, no. 4 (September 1, 2017): 772–98. https://doi.org/10.1093/dh/dhw057.

Tran, Nu-Anh. "Contested Identities: Nationalism in the Republic of Vietnam (1954–1963)." PhD diss., University of California, Berkeley, 2013.

Tran, Thi Ut, and Kei Kajisa. "The Impact of Green Revolution on Rice Production in Vietnam." *Developing Economies* 44, no. 2 (June 2006): 167–89. https://doi.org/10.1111/j.1746-1049.2006.00012.x.

Tsai, Shih-shan Henry. *Lee Teng-Hui and Taiwan's Quest for Identity*. New York: Palgrave Macmillan, 2005.

Tseng, Pin-Tsang. "The Wartime Regime and the Development of Public Diet in Taiwan (1947–1950s)." *Journal of Current Chinese Affairs* 47, no. 2 (August 1, 2018): 113–36. https://doi.org/10.1177/186810261804700205.

Tyrrell, Ian. *Reforming the World: The Creation of America's Moral Empire*. Princeton, NJ: Princeton University Press, 2010.

United Nations. "1668 (XVI). Representation of China in the United Nations." *Official Records of the General Assembly, Sixteenth Session: Annexes*, 66. Accessed February 7, 2016. http://digitallibrary.un.org/record/205650.

———. "General Assembly, 19th Session: 1309th Plenary Meeting, Monday, 21 December 1964, New York," 1966. https://digitallibrary.un.org/record/749200.

———. "United Nations Security Council Document S/1462; Letter Dated 21 February 1950 From the Representative of Yugoslavia to the Secretary-General." Accessed February 8, 2016. https://digitallibrary.un.org/record/475196.

Vogel, Ezra F. *The Four Little Dragons: The Spread of Industrialization in East Asia*. Cambridge, MA: Harvard University Press, 1991.

Wade, Robert. *Governing the Market*. Princeton, NJ: Princeton University Press, 1992.

Walker, Lydia. *States-in-Waiting: A Counternarrative of Global Decolonization.* Cambridge, UK: Cambridge University Press, 2024.

Wang, Chin-Hsing. "Straw Hat Diplomats." *Free China Review*, May 1, 1962.

Wang, Jen-Kuan, and Oliver Kim. "Land Reform in Taiwan, 1950-1961: Effects on Agriculture and Structural Change." SSRN Scholarly Paper. Rochester, NY, September 3, 2024. https://papers.ssrn.com/abstract=4951831.

Wang, Wen-lung. *Waijiao Xiaxiang, Nongye Chuyang: Zhonghua Minguo Nongji Yuanzhu Feizhou de Shishi he Yingxiang* [外交下鄉，農業出洋：中華民國農技援助非洲的實施和影響, Diplomacy goes to the countryside, agriculture goes abroad: The practice and influence of the Republic of China's agricultural assistance to Africa]. Taipei: National Cheng-chi University, 2004.

White, Kaila. "The Lincoln Legacy." *Phoenix Magazine*, April 1, 2012. https://www.phoenixmag.com/2012/04/01/the-lincoln-legacy/.

Will, Pierre-Étienne, R. Bin Wong, James Lee, Jean Oi, and Peter Perdue. *Nourish the People: The State Civilian Granary System in China, 1650–1850.* Ann Arbor: University of Michigan Press, 1991.

Williams, Amrys O. "Cultivating Modern America: 4-H Clubs and Rural Development in the Twentieth Century." PhD diss., University of Wisconsin, Madison, 2012. http://search.proquest.com/pqdtglobal/docview/1667768749/abstract/FDE9DAFBDE454566PQ/1.

Winckler, Edwin A., and Susan Greenhalgh. *Contending Approaches to the Political Economy of Taiwan.* Armonk, NY: M. E. Sharpe, 1988.

Winichakul, Thongchai. *Siam Mapped: A History of the Geo-Body of a Nation.* Honolulu: University of Hawai'i Press, 1997.

Wong, R. Bin. "Benevolent and Charitable Activities in the Ming and Qing Dynasties: Perspectives on State and Society in Late Imperial and Modern Times." *Revue Bibliographique de Sinologie* 18 (2000): 249–58.

Woodruff, A. M., James Robert Brown, Sein Lin, University of Hartford, and John C. Lincoln Institute, eds. *International Seminar on Land Taxation, Land Tenure, and Land Reform in Developing Countries.* West Hartford, CT: John C. Lincoln Institute, University of Hartford, 1967.

Woodruff, Archibald. "A Comparison between Henry George and Karl Marx in Their Approach to Land Reform." In *Readings in Land Reform*, edited by Sein Lin, 1–31. Hartford, CT: University of Hartford, 1970.

Yager, Joseph A. *Transforming Agriculture in Taiwan: The Experience of the Joint Commission on Rural Reconstruction.* Ithaca, NY: Cornell University Press, 1988.

Yang, Dominic Meng-Hsuan. *The Great Exodus from China: Trauma, Memory, and Identity in Modern Taiwan.* Cambridge, UK: Cambridge University Press, 2020.

Yang, Lawrence Zi-Qiao. "Soil and Scroll: The Agrarian Origin of a Cold War Documentary Avant Garde." *Modern Chinese Literature and Culture* 31, no. 2 (2019): 41–80.

Yang, Martin M. *Socio Economic Results of Land Reform in Taiwan.* Honolulu: University of Hawai'i Press, 1970.

Yang, Timothy. "Selling an Imperial Dream: Japanese Pharmaceuticals, National Power, and the Science of Quinine Self-Sufficiency." *East Asian Science, Technology and Society* 6, no. 1 (March 2012): 101–25.

Yang, Xikun. *Yang Xikun fang Fei guilai tanhua* 楊西崑訪非歸來談話 [A discussion after Yang Xikun's return from Africa]. Audio CD, 2011.

Yang, Yueh-heng, and Ralph N. Gleason. *Yeast-Feeding Demonstration in Selected Primary Schools Taipei Area Taiwan, 1953–54*. Taipei: Chinese-American Joint Commission on Rural Reconstruction, 1955.

Young, Alden. *Transforming Sudan: Decolonization, Economic Development, and State Formation*. African Studies 140. Cambridge, UK; Cambridge University Press, 2018.

Yuan, Longping, Jiming Li, and Yeyun Xin. *Hybrid Rice Technology Development: Ensuring China's Food Security*. Washington, DC: International Food Policy Research Institute, 2009.

Zanasi, Margherita. *Saving the Nation: Economic Modernity in Republican China*. Chicago: University of Chicago Press, 2006.

Zelin, Madeleine. *The Merchants of Zigong: Industrial Entrepreneurship in Early Modern China*. Columbia University Press, 2006.

Zhang Lianjun (張廉駿). "Shi'er Nian Zai Yuenan" [十二年在越南, Twelve years in Vietnam]. Zhongguo Fuxing Nongcun Lianhe Weiyuanhui Yekan (中國農村復興聯合委員會業刊), June 1973.

Zhou, Enlai. "Main Speech by Premier Zhou Enlai, Head of the Delegation of the People's Republic of China, Distributed at the Plenary Session of the Asian-African Conference," April 19, 1955. Translation from China and the Asian-African Conference (Documents) (Peking: Foreign Languages Press, 1955), 9–20. History and Public Policy Program Digital Archive. http://digitalarchive.wilsoncenter.org/document/121623.

Zhou Xiuhuan 周琇環, ed., Nongfuhui Shiliao [農復會史料 Historical document collection on Joint Commission on Rural Reconstruction], vol. 2 (Taipei: Guoshiguan 國史館 [Academia Sinica], 1995.

"Zouguo 50 nian jiansutang Taitang jinzao ji xiajia [走過50年健素糖台糖今早急下架]." TVBS, June 15, 2006. https://news.tvbs.com.tw/entry/361379.

4-H: and 4-T in Vietnam, 104–5, 107*fig.*22; community development and democracy, 12, 80–81, 91, 109; founding, 15, 80, 202; *Lee Yu's 4-H Banner*, 81–82; and Operation Vanguard, 126; public health, 12, 80; in US, 80–81, 109

AACFR (American Advisory Committee for Famine Relief) and AACB (American Advisory Committee in Beijing). *See* famine
Abt, Yitzchak, 159
Academia Sinica, 165
agricultural extension: ASPAC/FFTC report, 192–93; in AVRDC, 188; in Europe, 85; and farmers' associations, 70–73; and fertilizer, 88–89, 92; Guangxi Extension Station, 99; in LRTI, 163–64; as model for land reform surveys, 56, 58, 59*fig.*5; in Operation Vanguard, 126–30, 133, 136, 139, 202; overview of, 13, 15, 41, 175, 201–2; plant breeding, 19, 25–27, 38, 67, 94, 99–100, 173, 188, 193, 201; and Plant Protection Center, 174–75; in Republican era, 20, 23, 26–28, 31–34, 38, 126, 201; in Southeast Asia, 192; in Taiwan Model, 67–68, 70, 201–2; in US, 81; in Vietnam, 99, 100, 104, 107*fig.*23, 108–10, 117
agricultural science. *See* agronomy; science
agronomy: and famine prevention, 19; development of field in Taiwan, 1, 83, 108; Food Industry Research and Development Institute, 173–74; in Green Revolution, 172;

international agricultural research centers of the 1970s, 172–75; JCCR, 37, 134; Nanking-Cornell program and NARB, 31–32; plant breeding, 19, 25–27, 38, 67, 83, 94, 99–100, 171, 173, 188, 193, 201; Plant Protection Center, 83–84, 174–75; soil science, 67, 99, 173, 188, 193; and Taiwan Model, 67–68; UNNRA, 34; in Vietnam 108. *See also* AVRDC; fertilizer; sciences; seeds
Anderson, W.A., 72–73, 78
Andrade, Tonio, 6
anthropology, 189
anti-Communism: Asian People's Anti-Communist League, 114, 116; ASPAC, 190–91; and Georgism, 155–57, 169; and GMD, 93–94, 204; and Green Revolution, 172, 193; and land reform, 45, 161, 169; and Malagasy Republic, 133; propaganda, 78; and RVN, 108, 113–15, 118; and Three Principles of the People, 147
Asian Development Bank, 69, 186, 191, 194, 197
ASPAC (Asia-Pacific Council), 190–92
Australia: ASPAC member, 190, 192; as example of land reform, 156; participant in land reform seminars, 157; as source of crop varieties, 103
authoritarianism: control over media, 129, 133; extension into countryside, 16, 133; and farmers' associations, 77; and fertilizer system, 90–91; and land reform, 43–46, 48–49, 55, 148, 167, 169; as model for RVN, 95;

Inglorious, Illegal Bastards: Japan's Self-Defense Force During the Cold War, by Aaron Skabelund. Cornell University Press, 2022.

Madness in the Family: Women Care, and Illness in Japan, by H. Yumi Kim. Oxford University Press, 2022.

Uncertainty in the Empire of Routine: The Administrative Revolution of the Eighteenth-Century Qing State, by Maura Dykstra. Harvard University Press, 2022.

Outsourcing Repression: Everyday State Power in Contemporary China, by Lynette H. Ong. Oxford University Press, 2022.

Diasporic Cold Warriors: Nationalist China, Anticommunism, and the Philippine Chinese, 1930s–1970s, by Chien-Wen Kung. Cornell University Press, 2022.

Dream Super-Express: A Cultural History of the World's First Bullet Train, by Jessamyn Abel. Stanford University Press, 2022.

The Sound of Salvation: Voice, Gender, and the Sufi Mediascape in China, by Guangtian Ha. Columbia University Press, 2022.

Learning to Rule: Court Education and the Remaking of the Qing State, 1861–1912, by Daniel Barish. Columbia University Press, 2022.

Founded in 1893,
UNIVERSITY OF CALIFORNIA PRESS
publishes bold, progressive books and journals
on topics in the arts, humanities, social sciences,
and natural sciences—with a focus on social
justice issues—that inspire thought and action
among readers worldwide.

The UC PRESS FOUNDATION
raises funds to uphold the press's vital role
as an independent, nonprofit publisher, and
receives philanthropic support from a wide
range of individuals and institutions—and from
committed readers like you. To learn more, visit
ucpress.edu/supportus.

www.ingramcontent.com/pod-product-compliance
Ingram Content Group UK Ltd.
Pitfield, Milton Keynes, MK11 3LW, UK
UKHW022239260426
470381UK00004B/116